ILLUSTRATED
THEATRE PRODUCTION
GUIDE

ILLUSTRATED THEATRE PRODUCTION GUIDE

JOHN HOLLOWAY

Focal Press

An Imprint of Elsevier

Amsterdam London New York Oxford Paris Tokyo
Boston San Diego San Francisco Singapore Sydney

Focal Press is an imprint of Elsevier.

Permissions may be sought directly from Elsevier's Science & Technology
Rights Department in Oxford, UK: phone: (+44) 1865 843830, fax: (+44)
1865 853333, e-mail: permissions@elsevier.co.uk. You may also complete
your request on-line via the Elsevier Science homepage
(http://www.elsevier.com), by selecting 'Customer Support' and then
'Obtaining Permissions'.

This book is printed on acid-free paper.

Library of Congress Cataloging-in-Publication Data
Holloway, John, 1954-
   Illustrated theatre production guide/by John Holloway.
       p.   cm.
   Includes index.
   ISBN-13: 978-0-240-80493-4 ISBN-10: 0-240-80493-7 (alk. Paper)
   1.   Stage management. 2. Theatres-Stage-setting and scenery. I. Title.

   PN2085.H64 2002
   792'.0232—dc21

                                                    2001058495

ISBN-13: 978-0-240-80493-4
ISBN-10: 0-240-80493-7

British Library Cataloguing-in-Publication Data
A catalogue record for this book is available from the British Library.

The publisher offers special discounts on bulk orders of this book.
For information, please contact:
Manager of Special Sales
Elsevier
200 Wheeler Road
Burlington, MA 01803
Tel: 781-313-4700
Fax: 781-313-4802

For information on all Focal Press publications available, contact our World
Wide Web homepage at http://www.focalpress.com

10 9 8 7 6 5 4
Printed in the United States of America

TABLE OF CONTENTS

PREFACE

Working in the theatre is fun. Or at least it should be. Theatre people are bright, hardworking, and committed to an artistic pursuit. If not, they would never survive the long hours and hard work that a theatre career demands. It is not a job for wimps. I have always enjoyed the way that "show business" changes from day to day. It is not your normal 9-to-5 job, and you get to meet all sorts of interesting people and be involved in wonderfully zany situations. Once backstage at a production of *Nutcracker* I overheard the stage manager make this call to the dressing rooms: "Tiny mice and toy soldiers go to stage left. Tiny mice and toy soldiers go to stage left." Suddenly it occurred to me that there is no other occupation where you would hear someone say that. And best of all, there was soon a flood of small children in furry costumes.

Many times I have been privileged to see an audience greatly moved by a performance that I have helped to create. It is always so fulfilling to see that people's lives have been enriched by your own work.

This book started life as a journal. It was meant as a companion to a stagecraft class I often teach. Since then, it has grown into what you are holding in your hands. It is full of very specific information, and is intended for people who actually want to make things. It provides step-by-step instructions with lots of illustrations so that you can see visually what the narrative is talking about. Since it began as a journal, the drawings are mostly small thumbnails of the sort you would jot down as idea illustrations in a sketchbook. Much of it is written in the first or second person. That is, "I" talk about something that "YOU" can make happen yourself, and it is a direct result of teaching class and talking to students. My class tends to be very hands-on. We talk about things first, but later there is always a project to use that knowledge in a practical way. Learning by doing is an important philosophy. You can study music theory, but it would be hard to learn to play the piano without actually sitting down at the keys and practicing.

I WOULD LIKE TO THANK...

There have been so many people who have helped make this book a reality and deserve a word of thanks. First of course, would be the students in my classes over the years who have questioned me about practically everything since day one. That has really kept me on my toes, and made me want to learn more myself. Teachers often say that they learn so much from their students, and I am sure that to someone who has never taught that must be puzzling. But it is so true. You never understand something fully until you have to teach it to someone else.

I would like to thank the editors at Focal Press for having faith in the work: Marie Lee, and especially Diane Wurzel, for convincing their bosses to take a chance on this book, which is so different from the others.

My teaching colleagues Geri Maschio and Pat White for reading through some very tedious rough drafts, before there were so many diverting drawings, and Marilyn Hamann for suggesting them. Thanks to Marty Golia for double checking me on electrical theory. Thanks to Michael Lavin, Robert Jackson, Ricka White, Clay Watkins, and Bob Kinstle for being encouraging and making suggestions.

Many thanks to the members of IATSE local 346 for putting up with me talking about this for so long, and for allowing me to use their picture in the introduction.

A great debt is owed to Tom and Ann Barry for teaching me so much about the touring business. I was really green starting out, and they put up with me anyway. Special thanks to Ann for not firing me after the horrible incident in Minneapolis. (I swear to God, it looked like the right purchase line to me!) Thanks to Nanette Golia, Nick Rouse, and Mark Krauss, for teaching me how to behave on tour.

If you would like to contact me about this book, my email address is: jholl2@uky.edu

The poem on the next column is from the November 3, 1894 edition of the *New York Clipper.*, which was a newspaper of that time. It is funny how things have not really changed all that much over the years. Although wages have gone up somewhat from "five bones" a week (whatever that means!) since then. The IATSE was founded four years later in 1898. Perhaps that helped to boost salaries.

THE STAGE CARPENTER.

WRITTEN FOR THE NEW YORK CLIPPER.
BY MONROE H. ROSENFELD.

He wanders up, he wanders down,
   A phantom on the scene;
He talks to none, he does his work
   With countenance serene;
Although his purse is never fat,
   'Tis like his figure—lean.

What is there he cannot construct?
   An elephant to him
Is but a simple plight, or eke
   A dragon fierce and grim,
And golden goblets all begemmed,
   That never will grow dim.

He builds a ship, a paradise,
   Where angels music speak—
Bright angels with a salary
   Of just five bones a week;
And yet, in spite of genius,
   His actions are so meek.

Tanks are his special workmanship,
   And buzz saws meet his line;
And cottages and other things—
   At these he's very fine;
And he can make a thunder cloud,
   And moons that move and shine.

But who applauds his mystic art?
   The bass drum wouldn't nod
At him, while on his daily rounds
   The carpenter doth plod;
The manager? He knows him not—
   A stranger in the fold.

I wonder if he ever thinks
   Who cleverly will make
A little box for him, some day,
   That will not be a fake,
When Life's last scene on him shall close
   And Heaven's joy awake!

INTRODUCTION

PHILOSOPHY OF BUILDING SCENERY

One of the problems encountered in writing a book of this sort is deciding how much to put in it. It is not possible to include *everything* you might ever need to know about theatre production in one book. There just isn't enough space available. Instead, this book is limited to some specific ideas and techniques that are useful in and of themselves, but that also teach something about the process of working in the theatre. If you understand *process*, you can use that knowledge in new and creative ways. There are lots of ways to build scenery. The methods illustrated in this book are just that, methods. They are not intended to be the only, one true way to make the piece that is shown. Often there are alternate methods shown as well. The hope is that if you learn some basic methods of problem solving that have worked well in the past, you can use these ideas to help solve problems you will encounter in the future. That goal of learning about process is balanced with the need to learn some very specific skills used in working with wood, metal, plastics, and less physical things like electricity.

Certain topics recur a number of times. This is because they are very important cornerstones of scenery building philosophy. There are traditional methods of working in the theatre that are different from working in other building trades. Some of these basic ideas are:

Scenery is built in units.
They should be portable.
They should be lightweight.
They should be easy to assemble.

Building scenery is different from other types of general construction because scenery quite often needs to do more than just sit there. At times you must build scenery that flies in and out, rolls off stage, disappears, reappears, or sinks into the floor.

Building and painting scenery in a shop is a much better practice than building it in place on the stage. It sounds trite, but this actually does match the "real world" practice better than you might think. Of course shops in large cities must be able to move their product to a theatre or a TV studio. But even regional theatres must generally be able to transport what they build. In order for a resident theatre to remain solvent, it must have shows running all the time. The next production must be built while the present one is still in performance. Resident theatres most likely have only a week, or perhaps two, between shows to get the next one loaded in, teched, and open to the public. These are intense periods with lots of things to do, and you cannot afford to wait until you are in the theatre to start building the scenery. You may not need to worry about moving your show from town to town, but certainly it must at least travel from the shop to the stage. Learning to build scenery in units, or parts, that can be transported and easily assembled is very important. Even if you must use the stage space as a construction work area, you can still use these methods to make scenery easier to assemble.

The nature of scenery built in New York for a touring show and the type of scenery built for a university show are often quite different. Broadway shows have really big budgets that a university or regional theatre can never match. The tour versions of these shows sometimes use the original set, but more often, a special version is made that is more "tour friendly." Television studio work is vastly different from anything you might find in live entertainment. There are lots of different production styles in the entertainment business. I have tried to take the best of different worlds and bring them together into a way of producing plays that can work for most theatres.

DIFFERENT WORK ENVIRONMENTS

In talking to the editors at Focal Press, I became more aware of how my background has influenced the way I build scenery and my basic philosophy of how to approach the craft. My MFA is in scenery design, but most of my work experience has been as a technical director. I have been teaching college for over 20 years, but am also a longstanding member of Local 346 of IATSE (International Alliance of Theatrical Stage Employes). As a union stagehand, I have had the opportunity to travel with several different national touring companies, and have set up hundreds of tour shows and rock concerts.

The IA stagehand experiences have impressed me with the need to make sure that scenery is quick and easy to assemble, and that aspect of the craft leads to many clever inventions that are always fun to figure out. Being a teacher at a university has exposed me to many creative people and the enjoyment of being in on the development of artistic endeavors that most stagehands are never exposed to. It is very satisfying to find ways to make something actually happen that at first seem seemed completely impossible. My earliest work experiences were in regional theatres. I have also built scenery for television, mostly public TV, but also commercials and news programs. It is good to learn as much as you can about different work environments.

It has often interested me how different the two worlds of the union stagehand and the college theatre student are, and how little they sometimes seem to know about each other. In large cities, stagehands are mostly engaged in setting up shows and running them. Being a stagehand is often a family tradition, and you find many people with the same last names. The apprentice exam in my local is mostly about electrics, rigging chain motors, theatre fly systems, and followspot operation. These are the things that hands are most frequently asked to do. It is a craft that is learned by being an apprentice and then moving on to journeyman. Except for very specific union shops, most stagehand work occurs in theatres or convention centers. Most IA stagehands know a great deal about load-ins, load-outs, and running shows, but probably not so much about building scenery.

There are differences in terminology. In a union situation a "strike" requires you NOT to work. At a university, it is a very intense work period. A show that is in "production" is going through what schools call "tech." Production is a catchall term that means just about anything to do with a play that isn't related to acting, singing, or dancing.

A GROUP OF IA STAGEHANDS
WAITING BY THE STAGE DOOR

There are very specific departments set up to ensure that proper organization is achieved. They are: carpentry, electrics, sound, wardrobe, props, and hair. You almost never hear anyone use the words lighting or costumes in reference to the people who work in those departments. Instead, they are electricians and dressers. Workers tend to be specialists in a specific field and may not necessarily know that much about what happens in another department, unless it has a direct bearing on their own. They are often absolute masters of their particular craft. Schools like to give students a more well-rounded education in all phases of theatre, including things like history, playwrighting and acting. That is part of the mission of creating a person who thinks, questions, and reasons. Curiously, many of the people I have met who travel with commercial theatre tours are college theatre graduates as well as IA members. Perhaps the "lean how to think" aspect of college life makes it easier for them to adapt to new situations, and working their way up to being an IA journeyman gives them the specific work skills they need to do the job.

COLLEGE STUDENTS
IN A SCENE SHOP

THEATRE ORGANIZATIONS

Regardless of the type of theatre you work in, the actual process of mounting a show is more or less the same. Designers work with a director to invent a way of presenting the author's work to the audience. Shops go to work to build the scenery, lighting effects, and props that the designers have specified. The show is set up in a theatre, and the cueing process begins. Whether you call it tech or production, cue setting requires many hours of starting, stopping, and waiting around for things to begin again.

Commercial theatre (which has investors and must show a profit) is usually developed along the lines of the "long-run" concept of production, in which a show is put up with the intention that it will run until it stops making money and then close. That could mean at the end of ten years, or it could mean the end of Act I. If this were easy to predict we would all be producers. The scenery for such a show will most likely be trashed after the show closes, and rented equipment will be returned to the production company that supplied it. Scenery for a long-run show is built with only one specific use in mind, and there is no thought of reusing anything.

Universities, and most regional theatres, are organized around the concept of stock theatre. These theatre companies produce a number of plays in succession, and embrace the idea of having a "season" every year. They tend to save scenery, props, costumes, etc., in order to reuse them for another production. Some theatres save and reuse lots of things. Some theatres save very little. Things like platforms, escape stairs, curtains, and so forth are so generic that it only makes sense to reuse them in order to keep costs down.

This book often discusses the pros and cons of what should constitute stock items. My personal bias is that there is nothing more boring than last week's scenery. But the audience never sees 4x8 platforms or escape stairs. Actually, recycling scenery is mostly dependent on design factors. You can't reuse something that isn't asked for. Sometimes designers specifically request something from a previous show. That works well with things like doorframes that all look pretty much the same for a specific time period. Alas, there are relatively few shows that cry out for a sign advertising Mrs. Lovett's Meat Pies.

ORGANIZATION OF THE CHAPTERS

There are three distinct phases represented in the book. The first has to do with working in the theatre to mount a show, the second with tools and materials, and the last with the construction of scenery from designs presented by a designer. The first six chapters cover theatres and their equipment. They outline things like how to use rigging equipment, electrics, curtains, tying knots, and the spaces you find in different sorts of theatres.

It is important to have a strong appreciation of how to run a show in a theatre in order to better understand how to build scenery. Scenery must be built to accommodate stage equipment, and the sort of rigging used in theatres dictates often dictates how scenery must be built. The "construction phase" of lighting work occurs mostly in the theatre. Rather than actually building things, most of the electrician's work is involved in hanging and focusing lights. There are many ancillary projects like setting up dimmers and running cables. The inside-the-theatre chapters are presented first to help you to understand how a theatre building itself influences the construction of the scenery.

You can read the book in any order, for the most part, but there are some times when earlier chapters are mentioned. Sometimes ideas are repeated for subsequent sections. Rather than go into the full explanation every time, there is one instance (usually the first one) that has a more complete description.

There are a number of projects shown. You can build them directly from the plans in the book, but it would be even better to change them in some way to include something you actually need for a show. It is very important to be able to extrapolate from basic information, and to make it work in different situations. That is the real goal of learning, not just facts and figures, but the reasoning behind a process or method. That allows you to take information and use it in new and creative ways.

You may find that the same sorts of structures tend to repeat themselves over and over. In reality, most joinery, whether wood or steel, follows some pretty straightforward concepts that should be apparent by the time you finish with the book. Most construction is based on flat, two-dimensional structures that are grouped together to form more three-dimensional objects. If you learn the ideas behind making a cut list for one type of construction based on the way that the parts overlap one another, you can use the same ideas to plan a cut list for lots of other projects.

From time to time, there are small encouragements to be neat with your work. That comes under the heading of craftsmanship. Taking pride in your work is very important, especially if you want to go on to become a professional. The further you go in theatre, the more important it is to have a sense of craftsmanship. Many regional theatres are very well known for the excellent work they produce, and shows built for the Broadway market are incredibly well turned out. An audience will definitely appreciate quality, and you will too. Years ago, I worked for a carpenter who said, "The audience sees the front, but I have to look at the back. My view should be just as good as theirs." Finely crafted work is its own reward.

CHAPTER 1

THEATRE TYPES

An understanding of the development of the physical nature of theatres requires an understanding of history and its effect on the design of theatre buildings. Throughout history, the design of theatrical structures has been heavily influenced by the engineering and construction methods that were known to a particular culture. Styles of producing plays (and other types of entertainment) have also been a factor. The type of venue needed for a play is entirely different from one that can be used for a chariot race.

The Greeks did not arbitrarily select the amphitheater as a type of structure because they liked being outdoors, but rather used the construction methods available in their time period to create the most useful and efficient space possible, to be used in producing the type of entertainment that was popular in their time. Large indoor structures were simply not possible without modern engineering methods.

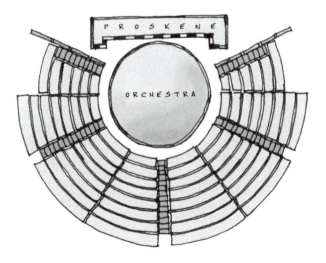

TYPICAL GREEK THEATRE

The Roman society spawned excellent civil engineers. They used their talents to create many civic improvements like roads, aqueducts and public buildings. Many of these achievements involved the use of arches. An arch is formed when the forces created by one stone curve cancel out the forces created by one or more adjacent structures. This concept allowed the Romans to use a series of arches to build the Colosseum, a freestanding oval structure best suited to the games, races, and physical contests that were the most popular types of entertainment in that period. The Colosseum was an architectural marvel of its day, not only because of its size, but also because of its clever high-tech features like stage elevators and trap doors that allowed performers to enter the space unexpectedly.

In a Greek style amphitheater, with a round performance area or Orchestra, it was necessary to curve the seating rows around the shape of the orchestra in order to ensure that audience members would be as close as possible to the action of the drama. Having the audience and performers in close proximity to one another is almost always good for the relationship between actor and audience. When the Greek choral form of entertainment began to give way to individual actors speaking lines of dialogue, a raised platform area was provided to give them prominence, or focus. This area was called the skene by the Greeks, and is the root of our word proscenium.

RAKED SEATING IMPROVES SIGHTLINES

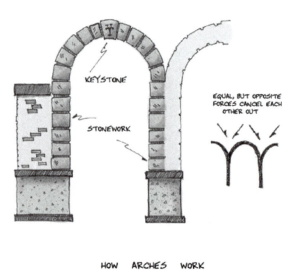

KEYSTONE

STONEWORK

EQUAL, BUT OPPOSITE FORCES CANCEL EACH OTHER OUT

HOW ARCHES WORK

Roman theatres were constructed in much the same manner as the Greek ones were, with the major differences being that the elevated stage area was greatly enlarged and elaborated upon, and the circular choral area was cut in half to form a semicircle. As with the Colosseum, the Romans were able to build freestanding banks of tiered seats for their theatres rather than depending entirely upon the geography of hillsides. These theatres generally were somewhat smaller in scope than their Greek counterparts.

The earliest Greek theatres took advantage of existing hillsides to form a sloping audience area that curved around a circular performance area. Pre-Industrial-Revolution technology did not provide their culture with heavy earth-moving equipment to form the slopes from scratch, and oftentimes large amphitheaters were asymmetrical as a result of following the existing terrain. Greek theatres are an excellent early example of the science of sightlines as used in designing a performance space. The study of sightlines is a notion whereby the ability of the audience to see the performance area can be enhanced by the proper arrangement of the seating area. This term can also be used to indicate which portions of a stage space are visible from the audience. Obviously, another person sitting directly in front of you will impede your ability to properly view the stage. By banking (also known as raking) the seating rows up and away from the front of the stage, sightlines are vastly improved.

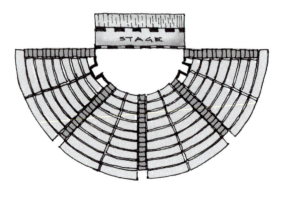

STAGE

TYPICAL ROMAN THEATRE

The Romans were also innovative in the introduction of a front curtain that could be used to mask the stage from the view of the audience. As these early theatres were open-air, daytime-use structures, there was no way to hang a curtain from above; the Romans used instead a series of poles coming out of the stage floor to hold up the drape. When these poles were lowered, the stage and its occupants were revealed. This seems at best a cumbersome arrangement, but lacking the technology to construct large open spans inside a building, it was the best method available at the time. It is mentioned here as a contrast to the ease with which curtains may be hung in a modern proscenium theatre using a counterweight system. The ability to construct the type of structure needed to house today's modern rigging systems did not appear until much more recent times.

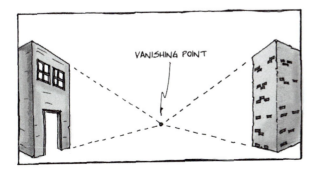

DISAPPEARING ROMAN CURTAIN

The next period to greatly influence the progress of theatrical design was the Italian Renaissance. The development of theories pertaining to illusionist painting and perspective rendering created the need for much more advanced production methods. The type of scenery utilized during the Renaissance period was often based on the methods used in one-point perspective drawing, where a single vanishing point is located somewhere near the bottom center of the viewing plane.

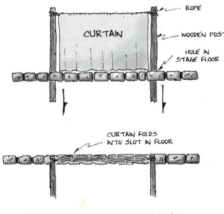

Objects in the foreground are shown in a larger scale than those objects in the distance. This technique creates an illusion of depth and three-dimensionality. This effect was further realized by using a series of viewing planes spaced at intervals, moving away from the audience. Objects farther upstage were rendered in a smaller size. For a city scene, this would require a number of building images painted on flat panels, with each successive building being rendered in a scale somewhat smaller than the one preceding it. This style of design is known generically as "Wing and Drop" scenery. In order to assure that the carefully created illusion of depth was not shattered, all action was required to occur in front of the first plane. Naturally, an actor who ventured too near the rear of the stage would appear grotesquely large in proportion to the scale of the scenery. This latter technique can be seen in modern-day amusement parks, and movie special effects.

The concepts embraced by Wing and Drop scenery are still very much present in the 21st century. Scenery designed for proscenium theatres today has many parallels to this earlier style of design.

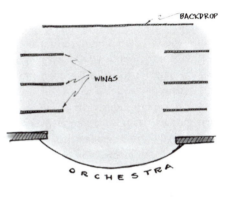

WING AND DROP SCENERY

Because the vanishing point in this "forced perspective" style of design must be elevated from the stage floor in order for the lines to appear realistic, the stage floor behind the acting area was raked upward, away from the audience to achieve the desired effect. This was, of course, the origination of the terms upstage and downstage. In later periods when permanent theatres were larger and grander, the immense size of the settings negated somewhat the requirement that actors remain at a distance from the painted scenery. Hence an actor who traveled toward the back wall would literally be walking "upstage," and on the return trip would be treading "downstage."

The question arises of how to easily change the appearance of the stage setting while a show is in progress. Some 15th- and 16th-century theatres used the "chariot and pole" system of shifting scenery. This consisted of a series of slots cut into the stage floor running left to right, and a number of symmetrically arranged poles that rose up through them. These upright poles were mounted on carts in a basement area that allowed the poles to roll easily (a relative term) back and forth. Using an intricate system of ropes, pulleys, and other linkages, groups of these devices could be operated in a more or less synchronized fashion. When one set of wings was moved off stage, a second set was revealed, telling the audience that the action of the play had shifted to a new location. This method of crude animatronics seems many times more complicated and clumsy than Roman efforts to elevate a simple front drape by using poles in the floor. However, when viewed in the context of the period, the chariot and pole system was an elegant engineering solution in a time that offered only limited facilities for suspending scenery from above.

The Renaissance period saw the development of the proscenium theatre as we know it today. The farthermost downstage set of flats (also known as wings) became a permanent architectural feature of the building. When supplemented by an overhead masking piece, this feature became recognizable as the proscenium arch so common in our own era. The proscenium not only serves as a frame for the setting, but also separates the audience from the stage, allowing for the use of intricate mechanical devices that are completely hidden from patrons in the auditorium. By the late 19th century it became possible to construct an overhead fly house of the sort in use today. The advent of realism and "box sets" in the early 20th century eventually did away with the practice of raking the stage for forced perspective settings.

The most common type of theatre in use in North America is the proscenium house. Its advantages are most obvious when spectacle is an important element of the production. Professional touring companies of Broadway shows are restricted to proscenium theatres because of their large audience capacity and also because of the similarity of stage equipment available in all proscenium houses. Although the lobbies and auditoriums of various road houses throughout the country are vastly different in style and size, equipment available upstage of the plaster line is more or less standard. An in-depth discussion of the proscenium theatre can be found in Chapter 2.

Thrust theatres began a surge in popularity in the 1960s and 70s in an effort to break through to a more "actor friendly" type of space. It is interesting to note that this type of theatre was also popular in Elizabethan times, and the reasons for its success now and then are largely the same. Thrust theatres are best suited to the production of more intimate dramas. Plays that depend on the accurate understanding of words and/or the transmission of intimate emotional moments are well served by the close proximity of audience and actor found in thrust theatres.

Generally, the audience seating wraps around three fourths of the stage area, giving the stage the appearance of "thrusting out" into the spectators. Since more stage area is abutting the audience, a large number of seats can be fitted into a small number of rows. A smaller number of rows results in audience members being closer to the stage.

The thrust theatre is not without its drawbacks, however, as the layout of the stage leads to some rather difficult sightline problems. In a proscenium house, the audience view of the stage is more or less constant throughout the theatre. Although some seats on the extreme sides have a somewhat skewed view of the action, the stage retains a kind of movie-screen quality. In a thrust theatre, the audience view from the far left is completely the opposite of that from the far right. Patrons seated at the downstage edge of the stage see the action from straight ahead. This may lead to some serious design and/or performance issues.

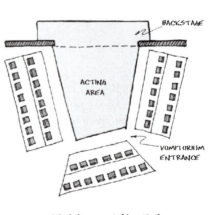

THRUST THEATRE

Most thrust theatres have either a modified proscenium opening, or some type of architectural staging at the upstage end of the playing area. This facade is in the center of vision for those seated downstage, but may not be visible at all for audience members in the far left and right sections of the house. Designers must be careful not to place too much emphasis on scenic units that may be barely visible to a large portion of the audience. Likewise, care must be taken not to use visual elements downstage that might block the view of

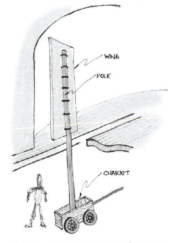

CHARIOT AND POLE SYSTEM

persons sitting in that area. Anything such as a wall, or a refrigerator, or a large wingback chair is certain to annoy anyone who cannot see past it to the action of the play.

Seats in a thrust theatre are generally quite steeply raked to help alleviate this issue, and as a result the stage floor assumes a much greater focus than is usually found in a proscenium theatre. Low platforms and other intricate floor treatments are popular choices in a thrust theatre. Low-mass scenic elements like lampposts, bentwood chairs, and small props are also often used in downstage areas. Lighting becomes an extremely crucial element to change the stage picture in the absence of solid physical items.

Theatre in the round is another popular modern form. As the name suggests, the audience seating wraps entirely around the stage, eliminating the upstage opening found in many thrust theatres. Other than the loss of the upstage facade, the sightline rules are primarily the same for theatres in the round as they are for thrust theatres.

At this point you might well wonder how actors will be able to enter the acting space, as there is apparently no backstage area to enter from. A vomitorium entrance can be used to solve this dilemma. A vomitorium is a passageway under the audience seating from the backstage space to the stage itself. They are also popular in thrust theatres, where they provide a more direct route to the downstage area. "Voms" are also used to provide entrance to audience seating in stadiums, arenas, and very large proscenium houses.

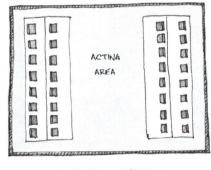

STADIUM SEATING

The black box style of theatre is especially popular with off-off-Broadway types of theatre groups because of its low cost, extreme intimacy, and its ability to conform to more experimental genres of performance. The seating may be set up to resemble virtually any style of theatre: proscenium, thrust, in the round, as well as more offbeat arrangements such as stadium (in which the performance area is flanked on two sides by seating, as in a football stadium). Or it may be truly flexible, allowing the performance area to flow in and around the seating (or standing) area. Audience members in this latter concept may move from place to place during the performance, blurring the dividing line into performance art. Scenic elements become less important in black box theatres, although lighting, props, and sound retain a great deal of influence.

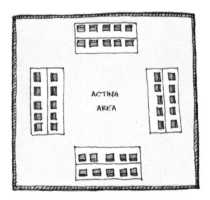

THEATRE IN THE ROUND

Another form of theatre space is the black box or flexible seating theatre. Either of these names is actually quite descriptive. This type of theatre is generally housed in a large, black, rectilinear room. Audience seating chairs may be moved around and set up in whatever configuration is desired. Risers are often used to facilitate better sightlines. Some theatres actually have bleacher seats that can be moved around the space.

CHAPTER 2

PROPERTIES OF THE PROSCENIUM THEATRE

This chapter goes into greater detail about the spaces and devices that are generally found in a proscenium theatre. This type of theatre is given special prominence, since it is the most commonly found and since it is the type of venue that allows for the greatest amount of spectacle and use of scenery. If you are producing a ballet, opera, or Broadway musical, this is the theatre for you.

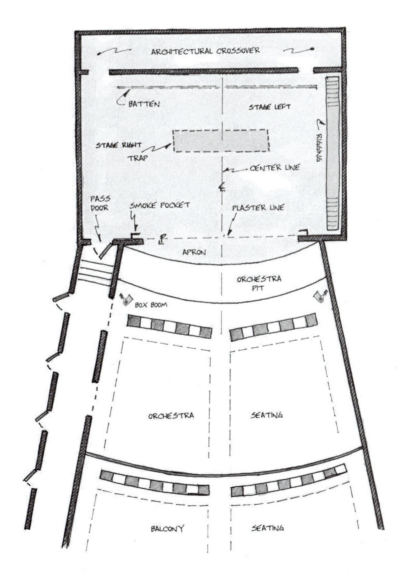

PLAN VIEW OF A PROSCENIUM THEATRE

As may be seen in the plan view, the central part of the proscenium theatre is the stage itself. As previously discussed, downstage is down toward the audience, and upstage is up toward the back wall. Stage left is to your left if you are facing the audience, and stage right is to your right. Audience left and right are just the opposite. The proscenium frames the stage for the audience.

Space to the side of the stage and past the edge of the proscenium opening is called a wing. Some theatres have very little wing space, and some have a great deal.

Wings are quite important for the movement of scenery that must be carried or rolled offstage. It is common to have less space on the side of the stage that is occupied by the rigging or flying equipment. Many times there is a hallway directly behind the stage that may be used to travel from one side of the stage to the other, and this passageway is know as a crossover. A less useful type of crossover runs under the stage and is accessed by a set of stairs on either side. Naturally the latter is the most common type, especially in older theatres in urban settings. Since travel back and forth out of sight of the audience is generally a necessity, and quick movements are often required of actors, a temporary crossover is often created by hanging drapes across the upstage part of the stage. A space is left between the drapes and the back wall.

There is often a door on the back of the proscenium wall, down left or right, that leads to the front-of-house areas. This passage is often referred to as the "pass door."

An imaginary line that runs across the stage from one side to the other directly upstage of the proscenium opening is known as the plaster line and is used as a point of reference for locating scenery on the stage. The stage area downstage of the plaster line is referred to as the apron. Downstage center on the apron is a most popular spot for actors, but not very useful for scenery as there is no practical way to move anything to that location. Static pieces that wind up there cannot be hidden by the main drape which is usually located just upstage of the proscenium opening. Off the front edge of the stage, and sometimes partially underneath, is the orchestra pit. (What was that round area in front of a Greek or Roman stage?) Superior planning by the architect will have provided an entrance door to the pit from an area under the stage. Unfortunately, many times the pit entrance may be from the house instead.

Seats on the lower level of the auditorium are known as orchestra seats, and in some houses additional seating is provided through the use of balconies. If there are multiple balconies, the lowest one may be called the mezzanine. Balconies are usually placed over a portion of the orchestra seats in order to reduce the average distance from any one seat to the front of the stage. Many modern theatres have technical positions for lighting and sound in the rear of the auditorium. A position for followspots, or frontlights, is essential. It is interesting to note that many sound booths are enclosed in glass to provide a sound barrier from the auditorium. That is sometimes OK for sound playback, but it is an awful place to hear the mix of a show that requires sound reinforcement through the use of microphones. Mixers are usually set up in an area cleared of seats in the rear of the auditorium. Some newer theatres have a permanent house mix position, and that is by far the best option.

Overhead lighting pipes located in the auditorium of a theatre are known as front-of-house or FOH positions. These positions may be laid out in many various ways, depending mostly on the uses of the theatre and the architectural features found in it. FOH pipes may be concealed in soffits, rigged on trusses lowered by chain motors, or may simply be exposed pipes reachable only by a ladder. Front-of-house positions are numbered in relation to their proximity to the stage. The pipe that is closest to the stage is the first FOH. The next closest will be the second, and so forth.

Another popular lighting position in the house of a theatre is the box boom position. A boom is any vertical pipe used to hang lights. Box booms are located in the place where theatre box seats were traditionally placed, on the side of the auditorium and close to the front of the stage. This is an excellent lighting angle for side lights across the front of the stage and is a favorite with lighting designers.

There are as many different arrangements of FOH positions as there are theatres that house them. Touring companies that travel with a lighting package usually designate two front-of-house locations, box boom and balcony rail. Once in a particular theatre, the design is modified somewhat to accommodate the existing road house positions. Sometimes there is an actual balcony rail, which is a pipe that has been secured to the front edge of the first balcony. Or there may be a more traditional FOH placement, such as a catwalk or a pipe hanging from the ceiling.

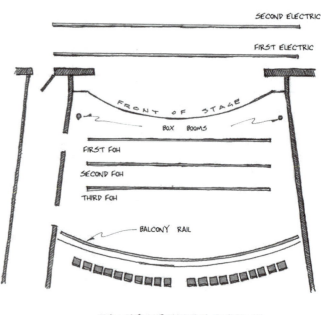

PLAN VIEW OF LIGHTING POSITIONS

Pipes used to hang lights over the stage are called electrics. Electrics are also numbered from the front of the stage, and hence the numbers run backward from those used for the FOH positions. The electric that is farthermost downstage is the first electric, and the next one upstage is the second.

Some theatres have permanent lighting electrics, which is to say that the same battens are always used for that purpose. Consequently these pipes have a permanently attached plugging strip running along the batten to provide power to the lighting instruments.

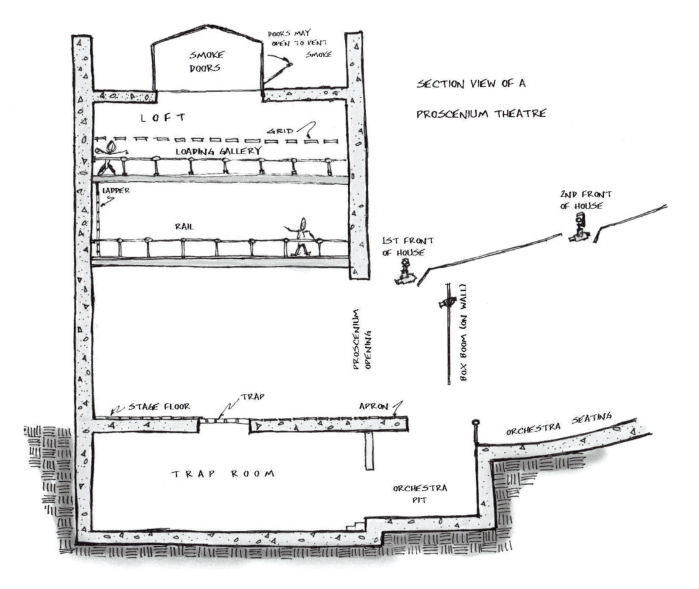

SECTION VIEW OF A

PROSCENIUM THEATRE

Other theatres use a system of drop boxes that may be moved from one batten to another in order to make any pipe available into an electric. Drop boxes consist of a large diameter multicable containing a number of conductors that feed a junction box with several connectors in it. Many lighting cables may be plugged into one box. Drop boxes may be lowered from above and clamped to any batten being used as an electric. This second type of powering system is much more flexible than the dedicated electric type but also requires more effort to set up and use.

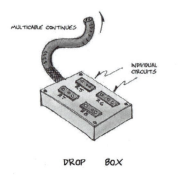

DROP   BOX

Quite often you will find that the third or fourth lineset upstage of the plasterline is dedicated strictly for use as an electric even if movable drop boxes are used for all the other electrics. This position is the traditional location of the first electric, which is required for virtually all lighting designs. Often this batten is rigged for use with some kind of motorized winch system. This avoids the necessity of loading and unloading what is oftentimes a large number of weights that are needed to counterbalance the very heavy load created by hanging a large number of lights. Electrics are typically the heaviest pipes in any show, and the first electric is usually the weightiest of them all.

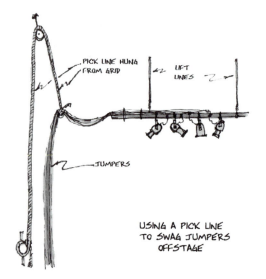

USING A PICK LINE
TO SWAG JUMPERS
OFFSTAGE

Tours of Broadway shows carry their own lighting packages of dimmers, cables, lights, and control equipment. Electrics are formed by running multicable from the lights, off whichever side of the electric the dimmers are located, and down to the floor. It is necessary to swag the cables offstage and out of the way of the fly system, actors, scenery, and other such stuff. This can be accomplished by using a cable pick-up line, or pick. The cable pick is tied to the cable with a clove hitch, and the bundle is raised into the air. Then the pick line is tied off at some convenient spot off stage. Some theatres have a specific area know as a jump that is used for this purpose, or pick lines can be hung from the pin rail, if the rail is an elevated one and on the proper side of the stage.

Many theatres have holes in the stage floor equipped with removable covers. These passages are known as traps. Traps are useful for productions that require that actors or props be able   to disappear into the floor. If a theatre does not possess a trapped floor, and the effect is required, decking will need to be installed to raise the floor level of the setting in order to "invent" the required space. This can obviously become a problematic process. In years past it was common for chariot and pole type theatres to have a large number of traps since the space was already set up along similar lines. Traditions die hard, so many modern facilities are constructed with large basements under the stage. This area is often used as a dressing room, green room, and/or passageway to the orchestra pit. Perhaps the traditional availability of traps has caused playwrights to continue writing them into their work, such as in the fairly recent play, *The Foreigner*.

The major architectural element of any proscenium theatre is the fly house, or tower. Theatre buildings are quite often easy to spot on a college campus because they are large, square, unattractive buildings with no windows. Older urban theatres were quite often built with a row of in-house offices over the lobby, and were covered on at least one side by another structure. They are not so easy to spot. On the interior, a fly tower is a large open space, very tall, with a loft space above. The floor of the loft is a series of beams with spaces in between and is known as a grid. The loft space is used for the installation of rigging equipment. In some theatres the rigging is under-hung from beams in the ceiling in order to save on cost, but this can lead to some serious problems in reaching the equipment when servicing is required. A good rule of thumb for determining the most desirable height for this type of structure is to triple the height of the proscenium opening, or at least 65 feet. Actual heights vary widely and may easily range from 45 to 110 feet.

There are very stringent fire code restrictions placed on theatres because of the large crowds involved, and also due to the many catastrophic accidents which occurred in the days before electric lighting came into vogue. The use of open flame candles, and later gaslights, spawned some spectacular and deadly fires. Code requirements vary from city to city and state to state, but theatres are generally required to be equipped with smoke detectors, heat detectors, automatic alarms, sprinkler systems, and emergency lighting systems. Many municipalities require that scenery be flameproofed and prohibit the use of open flames onstage. Large draperies and wooden scenery can provide ample fuel for voracious fires.

The term "flameproofing" has a specific meaning. Technically, the definition is that the treated material will not support flames, but will merely smolder and go out if ignited. "Fireproof" is a misleading term as it indicates an inability to burn at all, and virtually anything will burn if heated to a high enough temperature. Flameproofing is intended to prevent a large, self-sustaining blaze from becoming established. Once that has happened, only a well-trained fire company will be able to extinguish the flames.

It has been demonstrated that most people who die in fires are in fact killed from smoke inhalation. This is especially true when modern petrochemical materials such as those used for carpeting and seating are considered. For this reason, theatres are generally required to have equipment designed specifically to remove smoke from the building and to separate the audience from any smoke and/or fire which may emanate from the stage. The most easily visible of these is the fire curtain.

but they are not permitted in all jurisdictions. As an alternative to the asbestos curtain, some theatres are equipped with a very large steel door that slides down into place when a fire is detected. Other theatres are equipped with a deluge system that dumps an incredible amount of water. (Just imagine that going off by accident!) Whatever method is used, the purpose of the curtain is to seal off the auditorium from the stage house.

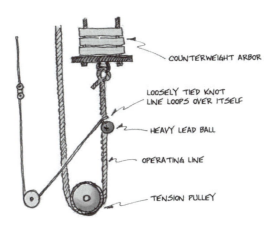

RETAINING LINE — COUNTERWEIGHT ARBOR
LOOSELY TIED KNOT LINE LOOPS OVER ITSELF
HEAVY LEAD BALL
OPERATING LINE
TENSION PULLEY

Fire curtains are hung directly upstage of the proscenium wall and are rigged to fall automatically in case of an emergency. Ropes and pulleys connect the curtain to a balancing counterweight that weighs slightly less than the curtain itself. When a restraining line is released, the fire curtain will drop into place by virtue of its own weight. The curtain can be released in one of several ways, all of which depend on the use of a lightweight rope that is stretched from one side of the proscenium opening to the other. This line restrains the fire curtain from falling. When slack appears in the line, a special knot tied to the counterweight operating line releases the weight, and the curtain falls.

There are several ways of cutting the line. Many theatres have a knife fastened to the back of the proscenium. (An oft-sighted article: "In case of fire, cut rope.")

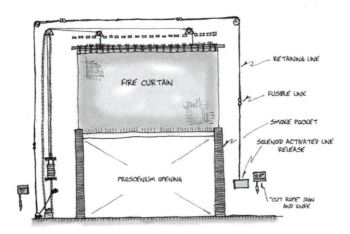

RETAINING LINE
FIRE CURTAIN
FUSIBLE LINK
SMOKE POCKET
SOLENOID ACTIVATED LINE RELEASE
PROSCENIUM OPENING
"CUT ROPE" SIGN AND KNIFE

Fire curtains are traditionally made of asbestos, a fibrous mineral that can be stranded and woven into a fabric. Being a mineral (or rock), it is highly resistant to fire. However, unless you have been in a coma for the past twenty years, you should be aware that asbestos is a very dangerous substance. Even so, it is still in use in many theatres. Sealers are applied to lessen the possibility that flaking of the material into the air will occur. When small, airborne fibers get into a person's lungs, damage is done to the tissues. Curtains of this type should be used with care and be left alone as much as possible. There are some substitute materials for fire curtains,

Another method of releasing the line is through the use of fusible links. These are two small pieces of metal that have been soldered together with a material that will melt at a temperature of 160 degrees. The high temperature of a fire will cause the link to pull apart, severing the line and dropping the fire curtain.

A final method of operating the fire curtain is through the use of electronic fire detection devices such as heat detectors, smoke detectors, and sprinkler water pressure detectors. These electronic devices can be used to trigger a solenoid that releases the line from its extreme end. Some combination of these various methods is almost certain to bring the curtain in as planned, but if all other methods fail, a good hard yank on the restraining line will break apart one of the fusible links and release the system. Fire curtains are sealed at the edges by heavy steel flanges that wrap around the curtain and help to prevent smoke from entering the auditorium. These flanges are called smoke pockets.

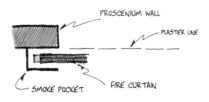

PLAN VIEW OF CURTAIN AND SMOKE POCKET

It is important to keep the fire curtain and all other safety equipment in good working order. Any problems should be taken care of as soon as they arise. If you have tied off the fire curtain counterweights to circumvent a problem with the system, the curtain will not work in the event of an emergency.

A fire curtain does a great job of protecting the audience from fire and smoke, but will also seal everyone upstage of the plasterline into a burning inferno! To avoid this, the stage itself is protected in two ways: a sprinkler system to douse the flames, and smoke removal equipment on the roof to draw air and smoke upward and away from the floor. Sprinkler heads are activated automatically at high temperatures and spray water over an area several feet in diameter. They are used in multiples to cover the entire stage area and should not be obstructed. Sprinkler pipes are traditionally painted red so that they are easily spotted. Do not use them to hang up curtains, lighting cable, or anything else.

Exhaust fans are located on the roof of the fly tower to draw smoke from a fire upward. In older buildings, smoke doors are used in place of the fans. Smoke doors are a passive system based on the same principle as a chimney. A shed type structure that is entirely surrounded by doors is constructed on the roof. The doors are hinged at the bottom so that they will open down and out by force of gravity alone. The same type of fusible links that are used to rig a fire curtain hold them in place. In the heat of a fire, the links melt, fall apart, and release the doors, which then flop open on their own.

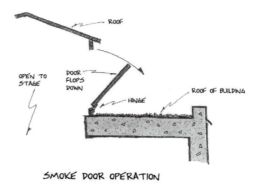

SMOKE DOOR OPERATION

Most fire marshals will agree that the best thing for you to do in a serious fire is to get yourself and others out of the theatre as quickly as possible.

CHAPTER 3

THEATRICAL RIGGING

"Rigging" is an entertainment business term with a variety of uses. A definition using the widest possible latitude might say that rigging means to put something into a workable state. A shirt may be "rigged" with Velcro when a change happens too fast for buttons. Flats may be "rigged" with stiffeners when they are too floppy to stand on their own. Rigging for a rock show in an arena has its own specific meaning, which is using wire rope and shackles to hang chain motors. As dealt with in this section, the term rigging pertains to equipment used in hanging scenery and lighting over the stage. Ropes, pulleys, arbors, and pipes are all a part of this equipment.

CHAIN MOTORS HAVE BEEN USED EXTENSIVELY
IN ARENA RIGGING FOR DECADES. THEY HAVE BECOME
INCREASINGLY IMPORTANT IN THEATRES IN RECENT YEARS.

There are two main types of rigging systems. The first and oldest type is known as the hemp system, and a second, newer type is known as a counterweight system. The word "system" is used to denote that there are many parts to each type and that these parts work together in concert to form a method of flying scenery. There are also theatre buildings that use various types of electric and/or hydraulic winches to fly scenery. The problem with that is that precise control of automated equipment can be difficult to achieve. These machines have no ability to "feel" when something is going wrong. A good flyman can slip a batten past a crowd of others in a graceful way that a machine cannot possibly mimic. This is an example of how the art of theatre meets the science of technology.

Chain motors have become very popular in recent years as scenery has become heavier and more complex. Most of the time motors are used for items that are dead hung, and consequently do not move during the normal course of a performance. Chain motors are very noisy to operate. They are often used without a problem in the concert business where performances are very loud, but they are problematic in a quiet theatre.

HEMP SYSTEM

The hemp system was developed in the mid nineteenth century by stagehands who were recruited from the ranks of the merchant marine. As sailors, these stagehands were familiar with methods of using hemp lines to hoist heavy objects. As a result, many stagehand terms are derived from nautical sources. They will no doubt become obvious during this discussion of hemp rigging.

In studying the hemp system it is helpful to imagine a practical rigging problem. For the purposes of the following example, imagine that a curtain needs to be hung across the stage parallel with the plasterline, and that at some point in the evening's entertainment this curtain will need to be flown up out of sight.

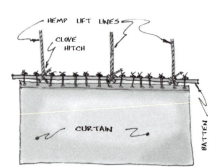

BATTEN SUSPENDED WITH
HEMP LIFT LINES

If the curtain is laid out on the deck (stage floor), it becomes immediately apparent that the first thing required for this rigging job is a batten, or horizontal pipe to which the drapes may be tied. Also we will need some method of hoisting this batten up into the air and leaving it suspended. This can be accomplished by attaching hemp lines (ropes) to the batten and pulling the lines upward toward the grid. At one time, battens were made from wood, but modern battens are made of steel pipe.

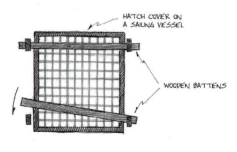

HOW BATTENS ARE USED ON A SAILING SHIP

Notice that three stagehands will be required to haul the piece into position, and tie it off at its designated trim. The word "trim" is used to indicate proper positioning of a flown piece. "Setting a trim" means to adjust a piece to its proper location and then mark that spot so that it can easily be found again. These stagehands have little choice but to tie off their lines and have them remain in one place.

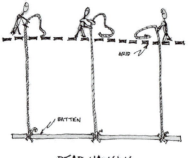

DEAD HANGING

A curtain that has been tied off in one position like this and just hangs there is said to be "dead hung." In general practice, dead hanging is a last resort situation because it is a difficult and time-consuming procedure. As stated from the outset, this drape will need to move on cue, so dead hanging would not be an appropriate solution to this rigging problem because it would be too cumbersome.

There are other difficulties that need to be addressed. First, it would be more efficient to use only one stagehand to run the curtain up and down rather than three. This would save on labor and also make sure that all lines are synchronized to move at the same time and speed. Second, it would be wise to find a method of balancing some of the weight of our load, or to get beefier stagehands. A large curtain may weigh several hundred pounds, far too much for one flyman to handle without assistance in balancing the load. These concerns can be addressed by employing a system of pulleys and weights.

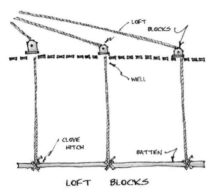

LOFT BLOCKS

Actually, the word pulley is somewhat of a misnomer as it has been used here. Generally, a device with a sheave (the rotating part of a pulley) used to change the direction of rope travel is referred to as a pulley if it is free to swivel or travel, and as a block if it is stationary. A device that has been bolted to the wood or steel of the grid where it is not allowed to move in any direction is therefore a block. Those particular blocks are known as loft blocks because they are in the loft area of the flyhouse. Loft blocks change the direction of rope travel from vertical to horizontal, that is to say from an upward motion leading from batten to grid, to a cross stage inclination from the loft block to the side of the stage. When they reach the side of the stage, the three hemp lines are together in one group, and are able to be handled by one person. But we still have not addressed our second concern about balancing the weight of the piece.

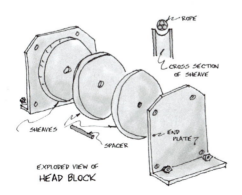

EXPLODED VIEW OF
HEAD BLOCK

Here you can count on gravity as an aid, but before that can happen the direction of rope travel must change again. If the three lines head downward at the side of the stage they will be much easier to work with. This second change in direction is accomplished with what is called the head block. Again, this pulley is referred to as a block because it remains stationary. In our example, the head block has three sheaves because there are three lines used to lift the batten. The block is constructed so that the three sheaves are side by side in the same housing.

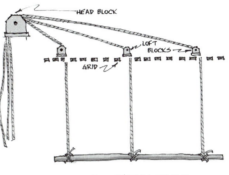

HEMP SYSTEM RIGGING

Our hemp lines are now hanging downward in the direction of the pin rail. Better leverage is gained because it is physically much easier to pull down on a rope than it is to pull sideways. It is important to note at this point that when the ropes are pulled down, the batten will move upward. Conversely, when tension is released, gravity will cause the batten to move in a downward direction.

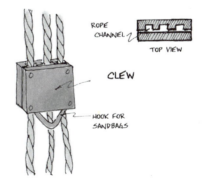

CLEW

You can now turn your attention to the problem of balancing the weight on the batten by adding weight to the downward hanging lift lines. In a hemp house, sandbags are used for this purpose. The easiest and most effective means of attaching sandbags to ropes is to use a clew that has been fastened to the lift lines themselves. (Some flymen use a special rope and knot known as a sunday.) A clew is little more than a clamp with individual channels in it for the various ropes.

A clew makes it possible to effect small adjustments in the lengths of the different lift lines, and thus to adjust the trim of the batten so that it will hang level and parallel to the stage floor. If a proper trim is not reached, the pipe will be bowed or slanted, and the curtain will not hang straight. There is a hook at the bottom of the clew that is used to attach sandbags. Be aware that it is necessary for the weight of the bags to be slightly less than the weight of the load on the batten. This condition is referred to as batten heavy. If the lineset is batten heavy, its own weight will cause it to fly in (down) when tension is released from the ropes. If the loads are perfectly balanced, it will be necessary to push up on the rope to get the batten to fly in. (This is a method reserved exclusively for Indian fakirs.)

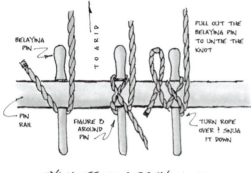

TYING OFF TO A BELAYING PIN

The final step in operating a hemp system is to secure the group of lines to the pin rail when the batten is not in use. The rail itself is a horizontal pipe, which runs up and down stage. There are holes drilled through the rail from top to bottom that are used in conjunction with belaying pins. (Belay means to stop, or hold fast.) The hemp lift lines are figure-eighted around the cleat into a special knot that will come completely untied whenever the belaying pin is removed from the rail. This method of tying off makes it easier to deal with several ropes at once, and to move a lineset in a hurry.

There are a number of shortcomings associated with the hemp system of rigging. The largest of these is the difficulty of attaching sandbags to the line sets. This is at best a cumbersome task, and when the weight to be added is over two or three hundred pounds, the sheer size of the bags is a test of anyone's strength and endurance. The largest bags used for electrics at the Lyric Theatre in Baltimore weigh 1,500 pounds! Also, since there are many such linesets arranged side by side, it becomes quite a trial to maneuver the bags past one another as several linesets are being simultaneously worked. On occasion it is physically impossible when there are several heavy loads in close proximity to one another. In addition, there is the problem of the hemp lines stretching. Hemp rope tends to stretch when there is a load placed on it, and also when there is a change in humidity. There are sev-

eral different types of synthetic line available. They are not affected by humidity, but they do have their own stretching/contracting quirks. Some become shorter and fatter over time, just the opposite of hemp.

The various ropes that make up a lineset are of differing lengths, since the opposite side of the stage is farther away. As the proportional amount of stretch is a function of the length of the rope, the far side of the batten will tend to droop as that line stretches excessively, and the problem will need to be adjusted by using the clew. This can be a time-consuming chore, and it requires a great deal of skill to be done properly. It is also difficult to deal with tying off the individual hemp lines at the rail, and to keep the massive amount of line that ends up on the floor neat. Several years of apprenticeship is required to develop the necessary skills. As you will see, the invention of the counterweight system was a giant step forward.

COUNTERWEIGHT SYSTEM

The counterweight system of rigging works on the same basic principles as the hemp system, but with a number of important refinements. Aircraft cable, a very high-strength stranded steel cable, is used in the place of hemp for the lift lines. This product was originally developed for use in linking the control surfaces of early airplanes, hence the odd name.

Most installations are equipped with a 1/4" size cable generally rated at around 7,000 pounds. This far exceeds the strength of any reasonably sized hemp rope. Another advantage of aircraft cable is that the stretching factor is negligible, and steel is not affected in the least by changes in humidity. However, the very stiff cable is not at all suitable for tying off to a pinrail.

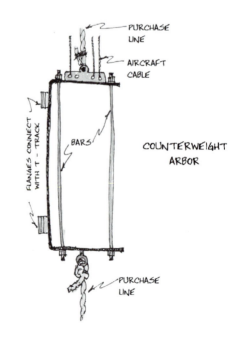

Instead, the counterweight system uses an arbor that holds steel or lead weights rather than sandbags. The metal used in manufacturing counterweights is dense, and hence these weights take up much less space than bags do. Aircraft cable lift lines are attached to the batten, run upward through the loft blocks, across the grid to the head block, and down to the top of the arbor. Either at the batten or arbor (or perhaps both) you will find a trim chain or turnbuckle that may be used to adjust the exact length of the cable. Counterweights are added to the arbor to exactly balance out the weight of the batten and its load.

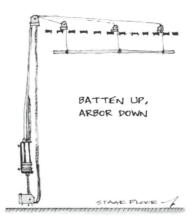

BATTEN UP, ARBOR DOWN

COUNTERWEIGHT RAIL

It is not necessary to leave the lineset batten heavy because there is a positive way to haul the arbor both up and down. This motion is accomplished by the use of a large diameter hemp line known as the purchase or operating line. A 3/4" line is standard, and the large size is easy to grip. Although the term "hemp" is still commonly used, modern practice dictates the use of a synthetic line with a braided casing exterior. Although there is still lots of hemp in use, it may eventually become a thing of the past.

The purchase line is attached to the top of the arbor, passes over the head block, down to a tension pulley and back up to the bottom of the arbor where it is again secured. Pulling down on the rope will cause the arbor to move upward. As the arbor travels up, the batten travels down. Hence pulling down on the purchase line will cause the batten to also go down, and in reverse, pulling up will move the batten upward.

As the purchase line is composed of either hemp or a synthetic such as nylon, it will tend to change length over a period of time. A bottom tension pulley (remember pulleys move) serves to keep the line taut at all times. It is set into special guides known as T-tracks that allow it to move downward by force of gravity, but cause it to jam rather than slide back up. The rear side of the arbor is guided by the same T-tracks that prevent the arbor from swaying from side to side as it travels up and down. Older systems use a cable-guiding device that is not nearly as effective.

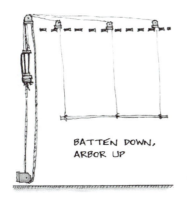

BATTEN DOWN, ARBOR UP

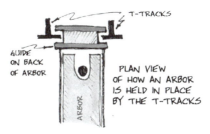

T-TRACKS

GUIDE ON BACK OF ARBOR

ARBOR

PLAN VIEW OF HOW AN ARBOR IS HELD IN PLACE BY THE T-TRACKS

In some theatres, there is a need to leave the floor space under the rail free, so that scenery and actors may pass back and forth. This is made possible with a 2 to 1, or double purchase counterweight system. In this case, the rail is located approximately halfway between the deck and the grid. With that ratio, if the same type of cable system were used as in the 1 to 1 model just discussed, then the battens would only come down halfway to the floor. That would be as low as the cable length would allow. In the 2 to 1 system, cable length is increased by tying off the lift lines at the grid (rather than the top of the arbor), passing them around a pulley on top of the arbor, and then on their regular route over the head block and out to the loft blocks.

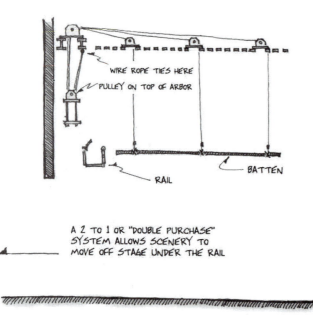

WIRE ROPE TIES HERE

PULLEY ON TOP OF ARBOR

RAIL

BATTEN

A 2 TO 1 OR "DOUBLE PURCHASE" SYSTEM ALLOWS SCENERY TO MOVE OFF STAGE UNDER THE RAIL

What this means is that for every foot the arbor rises, two feet of lift line will pass over the head block, and as a consequence, the batten will drop two feet. You can clearly see how the name "2 to 1" originated. One drawback of this system is that it also requires twice the amount of weight to be loaded into the arbor. If your scenery weighs 150 pounds, then 300 pounds must be loaded onto the arbor. When hanging a heavy load, these arbors will tend to fill up in a hurry. Theatres with a 2 to 1 system may find it best to use lead weights rather than the standard steel ones, since a same-size lead weight is about twice as heavy as a steel one.

At this point it seems prudent to offer a word of caution. Flying scenery is dangerous. It involves lifting heavy objects over the heads of actors and stagehands. Accidents can and will result in serious injury. You should be very familiar with any type of rigging system you use and should never exceed the limits of your abilities. If you are unsure of what you are about to do, stop and seek advice from someone with more experience.

Before discussing the operating procedures of a counterweight rigging system, it is wise to review the relationship between battens and arbors. Remember that when a batten has been flown all the way in (down) as far as it will go, its

arbor will be all the way up. Actually, the arbor will stop when it reaches its barrier at the top of the T-track. When the batten is flown out, the arbor will be stopped by a similar barrier at the bottom of its travel, preventing it from colliding with the tension pulley. This barrier is usually a piece of angle iron with a rubber or wooden cushion bolted to it. This assembly is bolted at a 90-degree angle across all of the T-tracks. When an arbor is snug against the top barrier, it is physically unable to move any higher. If the arbor cannot move any higher, the batten cannot sink any lower, at least until the weight limit of the various component parts is reached. This limit should be several thousand pounds at least, depending upon the quality and construction of the system, but in any case more than the largest amount of weight the arbor could hold. When the batten is flown all the way in and the arbor is all the way out and snug against its barrier, it is safe to load any practical amount of scenery or lighting equipment onto the batten without fear of it falling to the floor. Of course this presupposes that you securely fasten that load to the batten and that your rigging system is in proper working order.

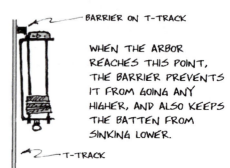

BARRIER ON T-TRACK

WHEN THE ARBOR REACHES THIS POINT, THE BARRIER PREVENTS IT FROM GOING ANY HIGHER, AND ALSO KEEPS THE BATTEN FROM SINKING LOWER.

T-TRACK

Let us suppose for a moment, that the load on the batten is 400 pounds. With no weights in the arbor of a 1 to 1 system you would need to pull down on the purchase line with a force of 400 pounds in order to haul the batten into the air. Clearly it would be terribly unsafe to do this, if it were even possible. You would need to weigh at least 401 pounds yourself, or as a group. Then the batten would have a potential to fall, with the inertia gained from the distance involved and its 400 pounds of mass. That would be illogical, however, because the whole point of using a counterweight system is to allow the weights in the arbor to balance a load placed on the batten.

Counterweights are generally stored on the loading gallery. The loading gallery is positioned near the grid where it is possible to reach the arbors when they are at their highest point of travel. Weights, which are often referred to as bricks because of their shape, may be loaded into the arbor to match the amount of load which has been placed on the batten, in our case 400 pounds. Bricks most commonly have rounded indentations at either end that are intended to fit around the upright bars found on an arbor. Bricks are tilted at an angle for placement into the arbor and then laid flat. It is impossible for one of these weights to fall out of the arbor when it has been properly placed between the bars. (Is anything really impossible?)

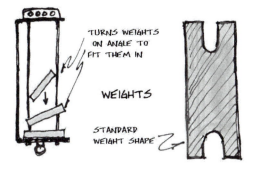

Most arbors have one or more flat pieces of metal connecting the two upright bars. These "spreader plates" can slide up and down on the rods, and they are intended to prevent the bars from warping out of shape from the weight of the bricks. Spreader plates should be distributed more or less evenly throughout the stack of weights in the arbor.

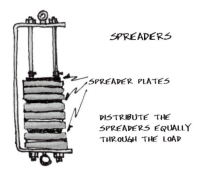

Counterweights are manufactured in a variety of different poundages, but the 20-or 25-pound weights seemto be the most popular. Theatres often have a small number of half-sized bricks so that a more exact balance can be reached than is possible with the standard types. Sometimes lead is used in place of steel in manufacturing the weights, with the advantage being that the same size brick weighs approximately twice as much. This can be very useful in theatres that have unusually short arbors that cannot hold very many weights, and especially in a 2 to 1 system.

Remember to load the batten first and the arbor second.

This prevents creating a potential for the heavy arbor to fall. If the arbor were to be loaded first, the only thing holding it up would be the rope lock on the rail. That is a completely unsafe procedure, as the rope lock can only be expected to hold back a few pounds at best, and not nearly the 400 that were mentioned earlier. Remember that the batten is always loaded first because it has nowhere else to go. It has no potential for movement. Conversely, when removing objects from a batten, the arbor should always be unloaded first to avoid the same unsafe situation from occurring in reverse. If a batten is unloaded before its corresponding arbor, the system will be very far out of balance, and a dangerous situation will exist. Again, the weight of the arbor will be held in check from falling only by the pressure of the rope lock on the purchase line.

The proper chain of events should be as follows: first load the batten taking care to make certain that the load is properly secured. Second, load the proper amount of stage weights into the arbor, and third, fly the lineset out to its proper trim. When unloading: fly the batten in to its extreme bottom position, unload the arbor, and then remove the load from the batten. There are a number of complexities that will be discussed in the next section.

Usually, the weight of the pipe itself will need to be balanced out by one or two weights in the arbor that need never be removed. This is often referred to as "pipe weight." It is helpful to strap these weights down, or to paint them a safety color, or otherwise mark them in some way so that they are not accidentally removed. It is customary that when the loaders, as they are called, are finished unloading an arbor they will yell down "pipe weight" so that the flyman will know that it is safe to unload the pipe, and can announce this to the stagehand on the deck.

Unless you are touring and have hung the same show a number of times, it is often difficult to know exactly how much weight any one batten will require. There is a danger of greatly overloading the arbor so that it is vastly heavier than the batten and thus creating a safety hazard. When an exact weight total is not known, it is best to load the arbor with the purchase line unlocked, slowly and until repeated testing shows that a proper balance has been achieved. If the same scenery or lights are to be hung again at some future date, make a note of the precise weight involved so that this time-consuming procedure can be eliminated. But when you are unsure of the weight, load the arbor the safe way. It is very important not to greatly overload the arbor.

Unfortunately, it is often the case that scenery or drapes hung on a batten may be too large to hang without at least some portion of the load resting on the floor. This will obviously affect your ability to judge the weight of the load by the process just described. In this event it will be necessary to determine the weight by some other means (such as an educated guess) to within a hundred pounds or so of the actual amount. After the load has been secured to the batten, a "bull line" is used to safely get the piece into the air.

A bull line is a stout length of rope that is comfortably large enough to bear the weight of the load you are hanging.

The larger the diameter of the line, the easier it will be for the hands to grip. It should be doubled over the batten and long enough so that both ends will reach the floor even after the pipe has been flown out far enough for the entire weight of the load to be resting on the batten. Do not tie it to the batten, but do tie both of the ends together so that the line will not accidentally slip off the pipe. If you tie the bull line to the batten you will be subsequently unable to remove it without a ladder or a Genie lift. Stagehands can take the place of the eventual load by keeping tension on the bull line as the batten is flown out. Make absolutely certain that the bull line rope is able to handle the strain and the load is not too much for the stagehands to easily handle. If the load is not more than a hundred pounds or so out of weight, you should be able to manhandle it all the way out, causing the arbor to come in far enough to be fine-tuned from the rail. It is very important that a knowledgeable flyman be on hand when using a bull line.

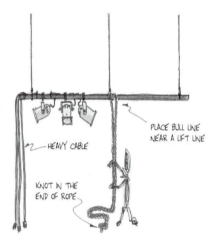

USING A BULL LINE

On occasion, and especially with a double purchase system, a need arises to hang a piece that is heavier than the amount of counterweight that can be fitted into one arbor. When this happens, it is possible to use a second lineset as a helper.

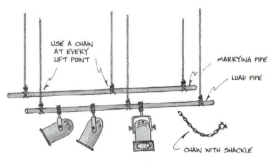

MARRYING PIPES TOGETHER

This is known as "marrying" the two pipes. It is good to keep on hand a number of short chains and shackles that may be used for this procedure. Make sure that the chains in question have a capacity rating high enough to hold the weight involved, plus a safety factor of at least four.

How can you know this? Suitable hardware has a rating. Shackles are the best connectors because they generally have a known working load limit, or WLL. Snap hooks and quick links generally do not.

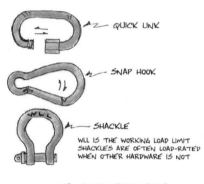

HANGING HARDWARE

Use one marrying chain for each of the lift lines in your particular system. Fly in a pipe that is either just upstage or downstage from the one which is being loaded, and wrap the chains around the two pipes so that they are tightly bound together. It is best to put the chains next to the lift lines. This will ensure that they are evenly spread out along the length of the pipe.

It really doesn't matter how the weight is distributed between the two arbors, but as a practical consequence, it is easier to load and unload if a majority of the weight is in the primary arbor. This also places less of a load on the marrying hardware. If the piece is to work (move during the show), then both linesets must be unlocked and moved together. It takes more physical strength to overcome the inertia of a heavy weight, but it is still possible for one person to fly the piece. When one purchase line is pulled, the other will automatically follow as a slave.

The aircraft cable itself has a certain weight. This weight can really add up in a large system. If the arbor and batten are visualized as opposite ends of a set of balance scales, the passage of the aircraft cable from one side of the scales to the other can make a measurable difference in the balance of the system. Therefore, when the batten is very far in, the lineset will seem a bit batten heavy, and when it is all the way out it may seem quite arbor heavy. This is a natural occurrence and there is not much that can be done about it. In extremely tall and wide houses, a heavy cable running the opposite direction through the head block is sometimes used to account for the difference in the in/out weights.

There are times (such as those calling for a bull line) when loading and unloading weights will require that the system be very arbor heavy for a short while. When this situation occurs there are special steps that can be taken to insure that the lineset does not become a "runaway," meaning that the arbor is falling and out of control.

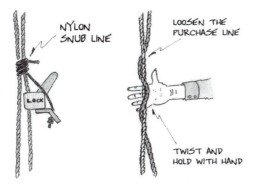

THREE WAYS TO SAFETY A LINESET

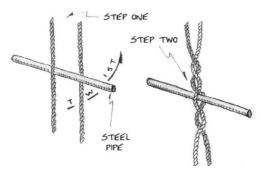

One method is to tie a line from the stationary part of the rail to the purchase line and secure it with a timber hitch or other suitable choking knot. The friction between the two ropes lashed together will keep them from slipping.

Another is to take a short length of pipe and twist the front and back portions of the purchase line together several times until there is enough friction created to prevent the line from slipping. If you wish to leave the lineset unattended for a moment, it is possible to jam one end of the pipe in-between two of the T-track rails so that it will stay put. (Just make sure that it does.) The last method is to create slack in the purchase line by pushing down on the front of the tension pulley. Not all systems work this way. If yours does, the pulley will become unjammed and jump up several inches, creating slack in the line. You can then twist the front and rear portions of the purchase line around one another and hold them together tightly with a gloved hand. This last method

has the added advantage of allowing the flyman to slowly let the two lines slide through his or her hands while flying the piece out. For loads that are not too greatly out of balance, this technique can take the place of a bull line, but be careful, as it takes a great deal of experience to know the difference. Do not exceed your limitations, and as they say, better safe than sorry.

RUNNING THE SHOW

Running a show from the rail involves the marking of trims (the limits a purchase line should move), the clear labeling of all linesets in use, the making of a cuesheet, and the establishing of some means of communication from the stage manager. Flymen should exercise a great deal of caution when flying scenery. The inertia of a heavily laden batten can cause severe damage to scenery or props on the deck, as well as to humans. If it is not possible to see the stage while running a cue, it is best to have someone else watch for you. During work calls, a flyman should always announce a batten moving in or out. The most common way is to call "Pipe number so and so, coming in. Heads up!" Remember to speak loudly, from the diaphragm.

Although the term fly*man* is used here in an effort to respect tradition, the rail is by no means an exclusively male domain. There are many fine women flymen, and the term is in no way intended to exclude them.

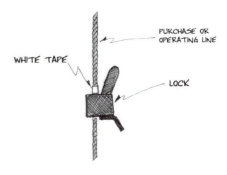

MARKING THE IN TRIM

Trims may be marked in one of two basic ways, either with colored tape wrapped around the purchase line, or with small pieces of yarn or ribbon that are worked between the strands of the same line. The ribbon is easier to see, and less likely to become dislodged from the purchase line, but it is somewhat more difficult to install, and unkind to the rope. The yarn method will not work at all with a newer braided line such as Stage Set X. Whichever method is used, the basic concept is to take the batten to its desired trim, and mark the purchase line where it lines up with a stationary point on the rail. In this way the pieces to be flown in can be stopped at a precise, predetermined point without hesitation.

It is the best practice to mark the "in" trim with white tape or ribbon so that the mark is even with the top of the rope lock when the low trim is reached. If the purchase line is white, use a dark color.

As the scenery is flying in, the front part of the purchase line will be moving down. When you see the trim mark come into view, cover the mark with your hand and gently stop the momentum of the lineset as the mark reaches the top of the rope lock. It is important not to run past the mark, as the scenery may well hit the deck with some force and make an unpleasant noise. Running a soft piece past its trim and piling it up on the deck is known as overhauling. The error is particularly heinous if it extends to a point where the batten shows to the audience.

After the scenery or drop has had its moment in the footlights, it must be flown up or "out" of view of the audience. It is best not to mark the out trim so that it matches up with the top of the rope lock because you may confuse it with the in trim. Also, since the front section of the purchase line is moving upward when the piece flies out, a mark in that position would be coming from the wrong direction to be easily seen. The tape would be invisible until it suddenly popped up past the lock and had already passed its stopping point.

It is far better to mark the high trims on the rear part of the rope. It will be passing downward as the scenery flies up. In this way you can see the mark approach and more easily stop at the proper trim. With this method both trim marks will be coming down toward you. Usually there is some horizontal framing member that is a part of the T-track system that can be used as a visual reference for the stopping point. If not, one can easily be established using marker or paint to create a line across the tracks themselves. Out trims are most often marked with red tape or ribbon, but the color does not really matter so much as long as you are consistent with it. Avoid using the same tape as is used for the in trim mark.

On occasion, there will be a need to mark an intermediate trim. That is a point for scenery to stop somewhere between the high and low trims. You should mark this trim as you would the low trim, but find some means of differentiating the two either by color or size of the trim mark.

All linesets should be clearly marked by name. Often there is a card holder or marker board on which to write. I personally prefer to use white gaff tape and a medium black marker. The tape is unlikely to fall off at some crucial time. Marking in the clearest possible manner can prevent some fairly embarrassing, though perhaps memorable moments in the theatre. Clearly marking every thing backstage that must be found in the dark is always a good idea. In some theatres working pieces (linesets that will move during the show) are marked with red tape above the name card so that they are easier for the flymen to spot. Some rails will go so far as to lash together the front and rear purchase lines of all the non-working linesets so that they will not be grabbed by mistake.

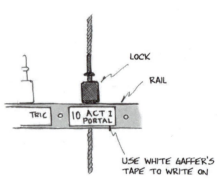

MARKING THE NAME OF A LINESET

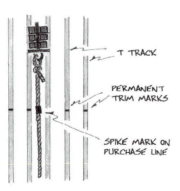

MARKING THE OUT TRIM

Do whatever is required to prevent an accidental pull on the wrong line. Bear in mind when you set up your show that stagehands do not necessarily think about their work at all times. Extremism in the pursuit of clarity is no vice.

Flyrail cuesheets should be made in a large enough format that several people can look at them at the same time. It is not at all unusual for three or four lines to move at the same time, meaning that the same number of flymen will need to review their cues all at once. Most often, each flyman is given a number to use as a reference when reading the cue sheet. Sometimes there is a change in personnel, and rather than changing the cue sheet, simply tell the new person their number.

The sheet should list the number of the rail cue, the numbers of the flymen involved, the name of the piece each will be pulling, its speed and direction, and the color of cue light on which the "pull" is to occur. Cue lights are double sets of small colored bulbs controlled by the stage manager.

When the cue light comes on, it is a warning to get ready for the cue. When the light goes out, the cue should be taken immediately. This method allows any number of flymen to see the command at one time, and synchronizes their moves. Trying to run a headset to each person would involve far too many pesky wires and would unnecessarily burden the stage manager with too many verbal commands. Two bulbs are used on each circuit to guard against the inevitable burnout. When there are a series of cues going in a close time period, it is best to use a different color of light for each section of the cue to reduce confusion. Switches at the stage manager's desk are used to control the cue lights, which are often used on the deck as well as the fly floor.

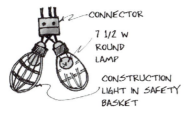

CONNECTOR

7 1/2 W ROUND LAMP

CONSTRUCTION LIGHT IN SAFETY BASKET

CUE LIGHT

It is a good practice to use a red clothespin or some other small clamp to mark your place on the cue sheet. After a cue is taken, the pin is moved down to the next reference. When the cue light comes on, and the hands gather to check their next pull, the red pin marks the appropriate spot.

RAIL CUE SHEET				
SOUND OF MUSIC ACT I				
CUE #	MAN	PIECE	DIRECTION	LIGHT
1	1	MAIN	↑	RED
1A	2	SCRIM	↑	BLUE
2	1	PORTAL	↓	RED
3	1	LEGS	↑	BLUE
	2	BORDER	↑	BLUE
4	2	SCRIM	↓	RED

USE THE CLOTHESPIN TO MARK WHICH CUE IS NEXT

Running a fly cue involves knowing which lineset you are to use, the direction of travel (in or out), the speed, and the color of cue light. If a line is to be pulled down so that the scenery is to fly into the view of the audience, you should unlock the lineset when the cue light comes on and stand ready. Watch the light carefully until it goes out. On that command, pull down on the rope until the trim mark is seen. Cover the mark with your hand, slow down the line as the trim mark approaches the lock, and stop it gently in the right spot. Remove your hand, and after checking to see that you are indeed correct, replace the lock and ring. If you have flown in a large piece with a ridged structure like a flat or a hard framed portal, you will notice that there is a tendency for the piece to sway back and forth unless it is firmly snuggled into the deck. Once the piece has been flown to its low trim, give it just a slight bit of extra pressure to ensure a good fit. This is called "touching in."

In some theatres the rail crew has a tradition of creating decorative rings made from string or tie line and festooned with fancy knots and personal items. Each flyman has his/her own particular, easily recognized style. This ring is placed over the lock handle of the lineset the flyman will be pulling next as a means of marking their place.

Sometimes when the exact positioning of a piece is critical, and/or the flymen have proven themselves to be unreliable, a "knuckle buster" may be used. This is essentially a small clamp, which may be attached to the purchase line at the low trim mark. It is too large to fit through the lock and is a certain means of assuring that the line cannot travel through the lock any farther than is intended. Even limited experience with a knuckle buster will well acquaint a novice flyman with the origins of its colorful name. They are really a last resort and should be avoided in most situations.

KNUCKLE BUSTER

Flying a piece out to its high trim is essentially the same as flying one in, but there are several important differences. Some pieces of scenery are quite heavy, and as a result, the amount of inertia that must be overcome in order to begin moving the lineset can be rather large and difficult to handle. Bear in mind that it is much easier to pull down on a rope than to pull up. Notice that when a lineset is going out, the front portion of the purchase line (the one nearest you) is also going out, but the back line is going down. Hence, by grabbing the rear line and pulling down, the piece will actually fly out. This is the line you should pull, at least until the pipe is up to speed. As the trim mark comes down into view, you can stop by using downward force on the front line at the appropriate point.

Another difference encountered in flying out lies in the position of the scenery just before the cue is taken. By definition, if a piece is to be flown out, then it must be in view of the audience. Often when a lock is pulled open the lines will tend to creep a bit, and this might be seen by the audience, or worse yet, by the stage manager. To avoid this occurrence, you can grasp both the front and back lines together before the lock is undone, and hold them together until the cue is taken. This will prevent the scenery from moving visibly.

There are many small nuances that make a really experienced flyman an expert in the field. There are other methods of working that are just as good, but I have found the practices outlined here to be the most easily understood and universally practiced. Perhaps the best advice is to simply watch carefully at all times and pay attention to what is happening around you. There will be many occasions when lines will foul, wrong lines will be pulled, or pieces will move in the wrong direction. If you are watchful, these mistakes can be caught when they are still relatively minor and corrected.

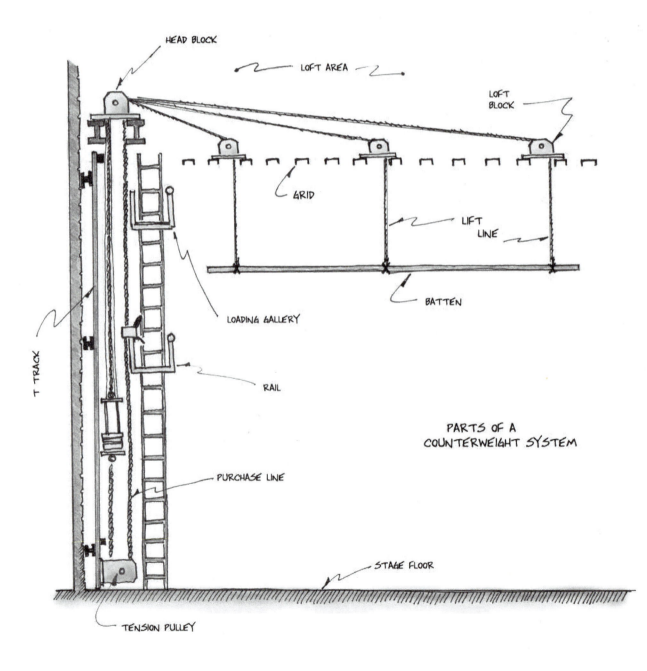

PARTS OF A
COUNTERWEIGHT SYSTEM

CHAPTER 4

ROPES AND KNOT TYING

It is not surprising that the proper handling of ropes is very important in stagehand work, considering that sailors were the originators of our craft. Rope handling and the quick, accurate tying of knots are skills you should learn early on in your training. Poorly executed knots can lead to serious injury for anyone unfortunate enough to be underneath a falling piece of scenery or lighting equipment. Rope lines should be selected with an understanding of the capabilities of the line itself and the use to which it will be put. Knots should be tied with the same understanding. There are literally hundreds of different kinds of knots. It is best to begin with a few of the most common, so that they can be appropriately mastered.

THIS IS A TWO-COLOR NYLON ROPE THAT HAS A BRAIDED EXTERIOR LAID OVER INTERIOR STRANDS. THE END HAS BEEN MELTED TO KEEP IT FROM FRAYING.

A TRADITIONAL HEMP ROPE MADE BY TWISTING FIBERS TOGETHER. THE END HAS BEEN FRAYED OPEN TO EXPOSE THE INDIVIDUAL YARNS.

A good knot should be easy to tie, hold well, be easy to untie, and should not place undue stress on the line. Some types of knots, especially if misused, may dangerously reduce the load limit of a rope. When overstressed, ropes almost always break at the point where a knot has been tied or some other kink has disturbed the straight passage of the line.

A SIMPLE OVERHAND KNOT CAN DERATE THE BREAKING STRENGTH OF A LINE BY AS MUCH AS 50%

There are two basic types of cordage used in the theatre, those made by stranding fibers into twisted yarns, and those manufactured with a braiding process. Stranded ropes are made from fibers that are spun into loose strands known as yarns, which are then twisted together to form the line. The size and weight rating of the rope depends upon the number and size of the yarns, as well as the material used in making the rope. Yarns are usually twisted together in a right-handed orientation (clockwise as you look toward the end), making it easiest to coil ropes in a clockwise direction. Rope fibers of this type may consist of sisal, Manila hemp, or a synthetic like polypropylene.

Braided lines are formed by braiding together many very small yarns to form a cover, or sheath, that fits over an interior group of strands. Since they are not twisted together, these ropes are easier to work with and less likely to become kinked. Nylon rigging ropes are made in this way, and so are cotton sash cord and tie line. Sash cord gets its name from its

original and intended use as a line meant to connect counter-balancing weights used in old-style windows. The sash is the part of a window that moves up and down when it opens and closes. The same properties that make sash cord bend well around a small diameter window pulley also make it an excellent choice for tying knots. It is very supple and is often used where great strength in a line is not required, but tie line is not enough.

Number 4 black or white tie line is really just a smaller version of sash cord and is the most popular choice for tying cable to an electric, or for the ties on top of a curtain. Jute tie line is also used, but it is so loosely put together that it does not last very long and is not at all suitable for use on drapes or other goods that must be frequently tied and untied.

Manila is a variety of the hemp plant and is the best choice for a hemp line used to carry weight over the stage. The grade-one type is easily spotted by the blue fiber that runs through it. Polypropylene and/or nylon ropes have become much more common in recent years. These synthetics are more easily manufactured into rope, and are somewhat stronger and rot resistant in most situations. Hemp is rapidly loosing favor for rigging applications.

There are some basic terms used in tying knots that you should learn in order to understand the descriptions in this chapter.

The free end of a line is called the tail. It is the part that you actually manipulate to tie the knot. The standing part is the long length of a rope that may be formed into a coil, or be tied to the grid, or laid out in some other fashion. It is important to visualize which is which, especially if you are using a short length of cord to learn how to tie the knots in this chapter. Anything used for tying can be called a line, but rope indicates something large enough to rig with. Most knots begin with a loop of some sort.

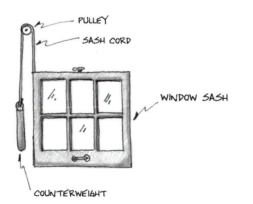

PULLEY

SASH CORD

WINDOW SASH

COUNTERWEIGHT

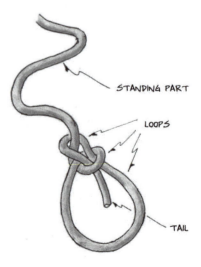

STANDING PART

LOOPS

TAIL

THE BOW KNOT

OK, so you already know how to tie your shoe. But if we start off with an easy one, it will build confidence for the harder knots ahead. The bow is actually the most often used knot in theatre because it is used to hang drops and curtains. Drapes are traditionally manufactured with a tie every twelve inches, so a forty-foot long border has forty-one knots to tie. Multiply this number by however many curtains are being hung and the importance of the bow knot becomes clear. The bow contains the same basic building blocks that are used in all knots. It is essentially a square knot in which the two tails are doubled over before making the final half hitch. Pulling on the very end of the tails slides the two loops back through the knot and the bow is untied. If you can visualize that process, it will make it much easier for you to understand more complex knots.

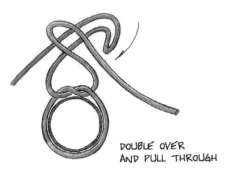

DOUBLE OVER
AND PULL THROUGH

THE CHOKE

This is a very simple knot that is quite useful for attaching a piece of tie line to a pipe or lighting cable so that it grips with holding force and will not slide down. It is one of a family of knots that use a double wrap around a pipe for extra gripping power. It is also the most common manner of attaching a sling. Slings, or spansets, are endless nylon bands often used in rigging.

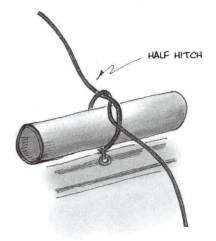

HALF HITCH

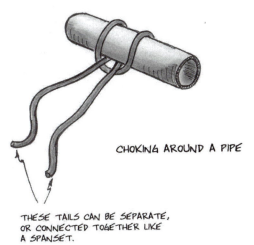

CHOKING AROUND A PIPE

THESE TAILS CAN BE SEPARATE,
OR CONNECTED TOGETHER LIKE
A SPANSET.

The bow knot requires two tails, or ends. The first part of the knot involves tying a half hitch, which is simply wrapping the two tails around one another, and tightening. The friction of the two lines rubbing against one another tends to make them stay tightly together. But a half hitch will not stay tied on its own; the friction is not great enough. Double over the two tails so that they are about half of their original length. Now tie a second half hitch using the doubled over tails. This completes the knot. It is easy to tie, and it is very easy to untie, by pulling on one of the tails. When untying curtains from a batten, if you pull one tail all the way straight up, it will untie the entire knot in one easy motion.

As an example, a choke works well if you want to tie up some lighting cable onto a boom so that it is up off the deck. Apply the choke so that it is about chest high off the floor. Then coil the cable and secure it with a bow knot.

The greater the force exerted on the choke, the tighter its grip will become, preventing it from sliding down the pipe and lowering the coil to the deck. This method also works for tying cable (or any other reasonable object) to a truss, handrail, rope, or other tubular item.

THE SLIP KNOT

The slip knot can be used to make a loop in the end of a line that will tighten when force is exerted. It has many useful applications for attaching tie line when speed is essential. The slip knot is also used in tying another knot, the trucker's hitch. For anyone who is a knitter, you may recognize it as the same knot that is used to start yarn onto a knitting needle.

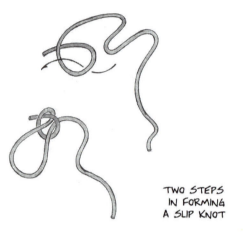

TWO STEPS
IN FORMING
A SLIP KNOT

Make a small loop in the tail near its end. Double the standing part and draw it through the loop. (The standing part is the long end.) Hold the doubled over loop and pull on the tail to secure the knot. If the knot has been properly tied, pulling on the standing part makes the loop smaller, while pulling on the loop itself makes it larger. If you tug on the loop and the tail pulls through and the knot is lost, you have tied the knot backward and it will not work properly. An easy way to avoid this problem is to make sure that your first loop is formed very close to the end of the tail. Then there will not be enough of the tail sticking out to make the mistake of pulling it rather than the standing part through the loop.

THE CLOVE HITCH

The clove hitch is used to fasten a line around a pipe, handrail, or other rounded object. It is an important theatrical knot that every stagehand should know and be able to tie without thinking. Like the choke we looked at earlier, this knot grips more tightly when force is applied. Unlike the choke, the clove is meant for use with a long line, and especially one that is under load while the knot is tied. One example of this might be while dead hanging a drape or a piece of scenery. There is weight on the line as you haul it up into the air, and a clove hitch is easy to tie under these circumstances because you can take a wrap around the pipe to safety the line while you tie the knot.

The actual tying of a clove hitch is a very simple procedure. The line is draped over the pipe, then wrapped around the right side of itself. Next you pass the line around the left side and slip it under the first wrap that was taken. That's all there is to the clove hitch. However, a common practice is to add an extra half hitch around the standing part to ensure that the line will not accidentally untie itself under stress, especially when the load is repeatedly shifted.

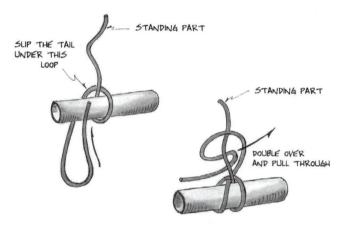

TYING THE CLOVE HITCH

There is often a great deal of excess rope on the floor after hauling something into the air for a dead hang. When this happens, the clove hitch can be tied by doubling over a few feet of the line and using this doubled over part as though it were the end. That will avoid pulling many feet of excess line through the knot. It is a common practice with many different kinds of knots and is similar to what happens when tying a bow.

THE BOWLINE

This knot is pronounced "bolyn" and not "bow line." If you mispronounce it, you run the risk of becoming an object of ridicule by your fellow stagehands and/or climbing enthusiasts. The bowline is used to create a fixed loop in the end of a rope. It is another of the quintessential stagehand knots that everyone must know. It is the basic knot used by rock and roll riggers to hang chain motors. The bowline's popularity stems from the fact that it is easy to tie, it is very safe, and it is also easy to untie, which are all essential elements of a good knot.

It will be much easier to tie the bowline if you keep these two ideas in mind: Make the first loop small. Make the second loop (the one you want to keep) large.

There is a story that goes with the tying of this knot that may make it easier to remember the steps. "There is a hole in the ground (the small loop). A rabbit (the tail) comes up out of the hole and runs behind a tree (the standing part). The rabbit circles the tree and runs back down into the hole." This is a silly story, but I didn't make it up, and it is the traditional method of teaching the bowline. Feel free to adapt it to any animals and/or objects you feel are appropriate.

The left-handed approach is really just a mirror image of the instructions that were just given for a regular bowline. Notice that in either version, the tail should wind up to the inside of the large loop rather than to the outside. If you are a left-handed person, you are already aware that lefties are generally shafted by tool manufacturers, so enjoy something that works just as well left-handed.

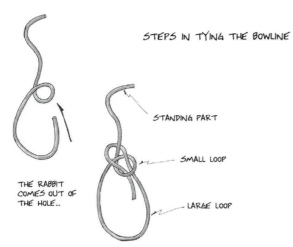

STEPS IN TYING THE BOWLINE

STANDING PART

SMALL LOOP

LARGE LOOP

THE RABBIT COMES OUT OF THE HOLE...

The following method of tying a bowline is probably the easiest, although there are others. These instructions are intended for a right-handed person. If you are left-handed it is probably best to try the right-handed method first, and then adapt it to your own style later. Basically, the left-handed approach is a mirror image of the right and will work just as well.

Hold the line across your left palm so that the long, standing part is lying away from you and the tail is several feet long. The length of the rope used for the tail dictates the size of the loop in the bowline. For some rigging jobs, the size of the loop is critical.

Coil the rope counterclockwise so that there is one small loop in your hand. Pass the tail through the loop from back to front, then around the back of the standing part and then through the small loop passing back against itself. Tighten the knot by pulling on the tail in opposition to the standing part.

THE SQUARE KNOT

The square knot is another very basic knot used in a variety of different situations such as tying two lines together, tying a bundle, or in combination with other knots.

Tying the square knot requires two tails. Holding one tail in either hand, lay the right tail over the left and twist it around to make a half hitch. Then take the left tail and pass it over the right making another half hitch. Right over left, left over right, as the saying goes. Tighten this up and you will have a square knot. Right over left twice, or left over right twice will make a granny knot that is harder to untie and is prone to slipping. A true square knot appears as two loops choked over one another and is easily recognizable.

THE SQUARE KNOT

A LEFT-HANDED BOWLINE

A GRANNY KNOT

THE TRUCKER'S HITCH
OR SNUB AND LOOP

The most complicated has been saved for last. The trucker's hitch is a popular knot to use when you need to put a great deal of tension on a line. It is often used to tie down loads for trucking, hence its name. Of course in a modern trailer used for touring, straps and load bars are the preferred method, but there are still plenty of other uses for the trucker's hitch. This knot is excellent for stretching cycs, holding scenery tight to a wall, and for making small changes in the trim of a dead hung piece. There are methods of tying the trucker's hitch with either one piece of rope or with two, depending on the situation at hand.

It is easiest to learn the two-rope method first. A practical illustration may make it easier to understand how the trucker's hitch is used. Visualize a cyclorama that needs to be stretched to remove its wrinkles. First clamps must be fastened to the edges of the cyc so that lines can be tied between the clamps and the offstage wall of the theatre. By applying tension to the lines, you can stretch the wrinkles out of the fabric.

BOWLINE

DOUBLE OVER AND PULL THROUGH

USING TWO LINES FOR A TRUCKER'S HITCH

First attach a piece of tie line to the clamp with a bowline. At a convenient distance from the clamp, tie another bowline in the other end of the line. Tie the second piece of tie line to whatever point is available on the wall of the theatre. Bring the two lines together and pass the tail of the second line through the loop of the first. If you then pull this tail back in the direction of the wall, tension will be placed on the line, and the friction of the tie line doubling back through the loop will keep it from slipping as long as tension is kept on the tail you are holding.

Finish the knot by tying off to the loop. Hold the doubled back line with two fingers where it is kinked through the bowline loop. The friction of the two lines and the pressure from just your two fingers should be plenty to keep the line from slipping. If you try to hold it with more than that, your hand will be in the way of tying the rest of the knot. Double a small portion of the tail and wrap it through just as you would if tying a bow. It will take some practice to get this to work without losing tension on the line.

Untie the knot by pulling on the tail. The doubled-over section will pull through just as it does when untying a bow knot.

To tie the one-line trucker's hitch, fasten the line at one end with a suitable knot and then tie a slip knot in the middle of the line an easy distance away from the second tie-off point. The slip knot should be tied so that the loop size is dependent on the tail rather than the standing part. If you do this backward, the loop will shrink to nothing when tension is applied, and it will be obvious that something is wrong. The line should be able to pass easily around the second tie-off point without jamming, or the one-line method won't work.

ONE-LINE METHOD OF TYING
THE TRUCKER'S HITCH

It is possible to make the first small loop by doubling over the line and making a half hitch rather than using a slip knot, but it is very hard to remove this alternate knot later on down the road.

Pass the line around the second tie-off point and run it back through the loop, making it fast in the same manner as used in method one. Using the trucker's hitch to tension the line provides a two-to-one mechanical advantage and will allow you to pull the line really tight. This is to say that for every pound of force on the tail, the standing part will be two pounds tighter. But it also doubles the load on the line and increases the possibility that it will break.

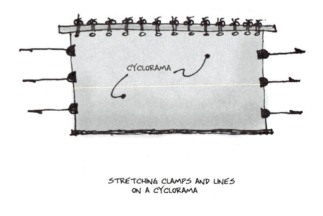

CYCLORAMA

STRETCHING CLAMPS AND LINES
ON A CYCLORAMA

CHAPTER 5

DRAPERIES AND DROPS

Any stagehand should have a good working knowledge of stage draperies. Curtains are used for just about any show that you can think of, and without them the audience could see all of the magic happening backstage. There are different types of curtains intended for use in specific situations. This chapter is a discussion of those different types, as well as construction methods, and the working practices used to hang stage curtains and other fabric scenery.

Drapes and drops are different things. Drapes are usually made from some kind of opulent fabric. They tend to have a generic quality and can be used in many different ways, whereas drops are backgrounds designed for a specific purpose. Drops are most often rendered on scenic muslin and are essentially large paintings. They are flat with no folds or pleats. Drops may cover the entire stage picture, or they may be cut in order to cover only the outside edges, as in a portal. They may have some other unusual shape, and/or have textural materials stuck to them.

Drapes, on the other hand, are generally unpainted and are most often used as masking. Drapes are often constructed of a heavier fabric, like velour, that has a thick sound and light absorbing pile. Duvetyn is a less expensive substitute. Duvetyn has a nappy, textural surface but no actual pile. This nappy surface helps to trap light, making the drapes non-reflective and less obtrusive. Black is the most popular color for all stage drapes, because that color is the most light absorbing. Drapes that belong to a certain theatre are often called the house "rags."

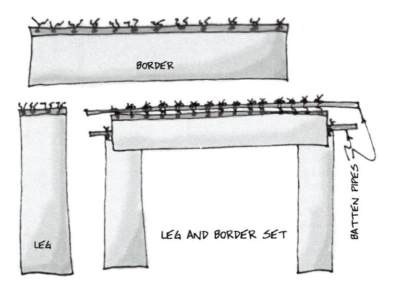

Curtains that mask the overhead space of a stage are called borders. Borders are wide but not very tall. Ideally, they should be the same width as the battens that they are hung on, so that they run all the way from one side of the space to the other. Legs mask the off stage space or wings. Legs are tall, but usually not very wide. They should be at least several feet taller than the proscenium opening, but not so tall that the bottoms do not clear sightlines when they are flown all the way out. In a stage house that is very short this may not be possible, and some sort of happy medium should be reached.

There is a standard method for using legs and borders to mask the stage. It is customary to hang one border in front of a set of two legs in order to create a frame for the stage picture. These leg and border sets are used from downstage to upstage in repetition. The legs should be wide enough and close enough together so that the audience cannot see around them to the wings. Sometimes this is not possible if there is very little offstage space, and/or if the auditorium is especially wide.

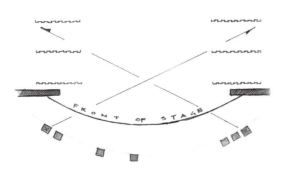

SIGHTLINES

Again there will often need to be some sort of compromise between the two objectives. The spaces between these border and leg sets are often referred to as the in one, in two, in three, etc. This terminology refers to the spaces between the legs and is often used to indicate the place where an

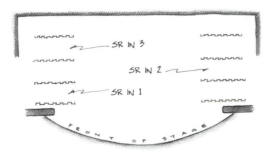

THE "IN BETWEENS"

actor or a piece of scenery should enter. "Enter through the stage left in one with the chair and place it on the red spike marks downstage." Leg and border sets are a direct descendent of the wing and drop scenery used in early proscenium theatres.

There is often a need for a large black drape that covers the entire width of the stage, either at the rear of the stage or about halfway back. This curtain may be used as a dark background that covers the back wall and forms a crossover, or as a covering device for shifting scenery upstage while a scene is being played downstage. This type of curtain is commonly known as a blackout. It is most often constructed as two solid panels that are hung side by side. You can also put together a blackout from multiple sets of legs that are overlapped to create the same effect. Be sure to overlap the edges by at least one foot (also equal to one tie) to prevent a split from showing. Blackouts are often hung on a traveler track.

Some theatres are equipped with a batten that curves around the entire stage area rather than merely from side to side. This type of batten is known as a cyclorama or "cyc" pipe. The two arms of the cyc are run up-and-down stage rather than from side to side. If the cyc is meant to be lighted in order to create a sky effect, it is known as a sky cyc.

As you could well imagine, it is almost impossible to arrange for entrances and exits if the sides of the stage have been closed off by using a wraparound cyc. A sky cyc can also be used on an ordinary straight batten. It is still called a cyc even though it only goes from side to side. This method is so prevalent that most stage workers will assume this is what you mean when a cyc is mentioned. Cycloramas are used extensively in television studios, where they are almost always the wraparound version. Different colors of fabric are used for special effects.

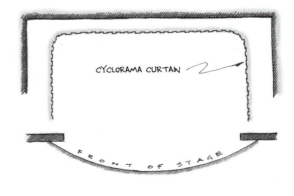

AN OLD-STYLE CYCLORAMA

Sharkstooth scrim is one of a family of net-type fabrics that are used in the theatre. The name of "sharkstooth" is derived from a loose weave structure made up of tiny triangular shapes, which, if you squint and cock your head to the side, may resemble a tooth. Scrims are used in a variety of ways. They can be painted in the same manner as a regular opaque fabric or can be used as a toner for cycs or other drops. Sometimes scrim may be used as a low-tech (but quite effective) method of materializing a person or object, such as the ghost of Hamlet's father.

Scrims have a common operating principle however they are used. Variations in light intensity are used to create variations in the opacity of the scrim fabric. An analogy can be found in observing the way window screens reflect light. You may have noticed that a window screen restricts your ability to see into a house from the outside when there is bright sunshine lighting it, yet at night when the only light source is inside the room, a person outside may quite easily see through the screen to the room inside. When light strikes the surface of the screen, the screen itself reflects this light and appears as a solid object. At night when no light reflects off the screen it tends to disappear, and anything that is lit behind the screen becomes visible. Theatrical scrim curtains work in exactly the same manner.

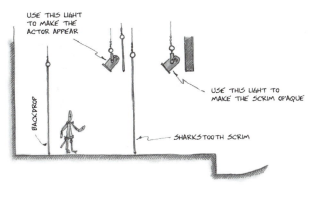

HOW A SCRIM WORKS

This principle is put to good use in a process known as a "bleed-through." A bleed-through is used to change from one scene to another by means of a lighting effect. A painted backdrop scrim is lit from the front so that the painting on it is visible, as well as the actors who are standing in front of it. The bleed-through effect is created by fading light down on the front of the scrim while simultaneously fading light up on the scene behind it. One picture fades out as the other fades in, much the same way that movie editing fades from one scene to another. As the lighting change is completed, the scrim is flown out for an unobscured view. It can be problematic to plan on playing a lengthy, full-stage scene behind a scrim, because the hazy quality that it creates can become distracting after a minute or so. But the dreamy quality of bleeding from one scene to another is quite stunning. Black scrims are often used in front of a sky cyc to

create darker, more vivid colors. As an added bonus, the scrim leaves a black background when the cyc lights fade all the way down. This is much like a bleed through in reverse. More information about scrims and other theatrical fabrics can be found in the chapter on Shop Supplies.

"Grand drape" or "main" refers to the curtain that is hung in front of the stage to separate it from the auditorium. It is often a decorative, very plush curtain, since it may be all the audience has to look at while waiting for the show to begin. A matching decorative valance is often used to finish off the top of the main rag. Grand drapes are almost always sewn with a large amount of fullness to give them a more opulent appearance. Fullness is the technique of gathering the fabric at the top to form folds or pleats in the curtain. The greater the amount of pleating, the richer and heavier the curtain appears to be. Achieving 100% fullness requires a velour panel 80 feet wide to produce a drape 40 feet wide. After a backing is added, the curtain will be quite heavy.

On occasion, scenic designers opt to paint a special drop that is used in place of a front curtain. It is almost always related stylistically to the design of the production, and may indeed include a logo or the name of the play being presented. This practice is principally used for musicals. A drop of this sort is generally referred to as a "show drop."

A grand drape may be rigged to operate with a traveler when there is no room for it to fly in and out. There are several ways of coping with a lack of overhead space, which is unfortunately a common occurrence in small venues. Small auditoriums and some older movie theatres may be rigged with one of several types of systems that require only limited overhead space.

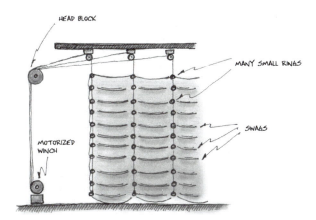

AUSTRIAN CURTAIN

One system is the Austrian curtain. This type of drape has a series of small nylon lift lines evenly spaced across the back of the curtain. Each lift line feeds through a number of small rings that are sewn to the back of the Austrian. As the lift lines are pulled upward, the drape gathers itself up from the bottom creating small swags as it rises. An Austrian curtain is sewn with many small horizontal pleats to enhance the effect.

Another method of dealing with a low overhead is to use an oleo curtain, which was quite popular in the days of vaudeville. An oleo is actually a painted drop like a show curtain. There is a large round tube attached to the bottom. Ropes at either side of the tube are used to pull it up and roll it at the same time.

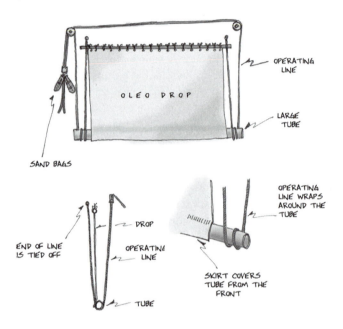

The drop rolls up on the tube as it rotates. A full stage oleo requires a very large diameter bottom tube for two reasons. First, because of the distance, the tube must span without sagging, and also because the large diameter of the tube makes it possible for the drop to roll easily even if it is relatively stiff from being repainted several times. A large oleo is difficult and expensive to construct, although this type of curtain may easily be shop built in smaller versions and put to good use for window treatments and other smaller openings.

TRAVELER TRACKS

Travelers are the most popular type of low overhead curtain-moving device. Stage travelers are similar to ones that you might see in a house, but they are much larger and able to hold more weight. A traveler consists of a metal channel and some rollers that fit into it. The curtain is tied to chains that extend downward from the rollers. A pull rope is used to drag the rollers, and thus the curtain, from side to side. Travelers can be rigged to part in the middle, or to extend all the way from one side of the stage to the other.

Rigging a traveler is one of those jobs that looks very complicated because a large number of parts is involved, but in reality the process is fairly straightforward and quite logical once you get the hang of it. The shape of the metal channel that the rollers or "carriers" fit into is such that the wheels of the carriers fit into grooves in the bottom that act as guides, allowing the wheels to roll freely back and forth. Each carrier has a rounded opening just below the wheels for the operating line to fit through. Below this opening is a chain used to attach the curtain to the carrier.

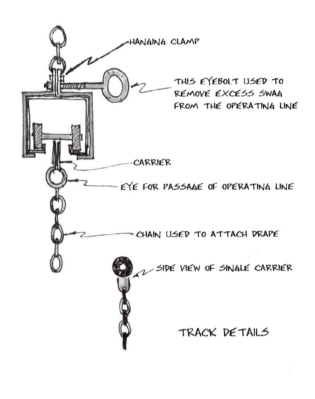

The traveler channel is hung on a batten using a series of hanging clamps. They come in two parts and bolt together around the outside of the channel, and then chain is used to secure the entire rig to a batten or some other secure position. Chain is used because altering the links of the chain is an excellent way of adjusting the trim so that the traveler can be made level to the stage floor, even if the batten is not. When properly used, chain is also very secure. Make sure that the chain you use is large enough to hold at least four times the weight that will be placed on it, and remember to include the weight of the draperies that will be hung on the traveler. The clamps come in two pieces so that they can be bolted on around the sides only. It is very important not to obstruct the bottom of the traveler track, because that would prevent the carriers from rolling back and forth.

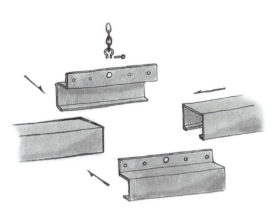

JOINING TRACKS WITH A SPLICE CLAMP

The direction you would like the curtain to move dictates how the traveler should be hung. If the curtain is intended to go all the way side to side across the entire width of the stage, then you need only one continuous channel. If the sections of channel are not long enough, then a splicing clamp may be used. A splicing clamp works in much the same way as a hanging clamp, but the splice is somewhat longer.

The onstage leading edge of the curtain is attached to a master carrier that has four wheels rather than two and is substantially larger than the single carrier. The master carrier has a clamp on the side so that the operating line can be securely connected to it. Here is how the line is rigged to make the curtain travel all the way across the stage from one side to another.

grommet gets fastened to the off stage end of the channel. The most common spacing for grommets is on 12" centers with one grommet in the corner at either end, so the rule of thumb for the number of carriers is to take the total width of the curtain in feet and subtract one. For a drape 40 feet wide, 39 single carriers and one master carrier would be required.

After passing through the individual carriers, snake the line over one of the sheaves of the live end pulley at the operating end of the track. The live end pulley has two sheaves on it, one to change the direction of the rope when it goes down to the floor, and one when it passes back up to the track.

The operating line connects with a tension pulley when it gets to the stage floor. As the name implies this pulley helps to keep the line taut and prevents it from becoming twisted and tangled. If the traveler track stays in one position, it may be possible to permanently attach the tension pulley to the deck. If it is occasionally necessary to fly the traveler out, then it is best to use a temporary method of securing the pulley, and there are several different ones employed by different manufacturers. A commonly used shop-built method is to secure the pulley to a small section of plywood that can be weighted with counterweights when the traveler is in its down position.

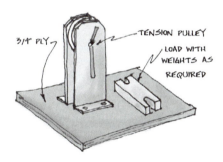

SHOP-BUILT TENSION PULLEY BASE

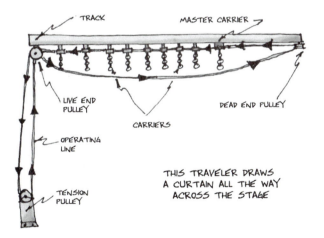

THIS TRAVELER DRAWS
A CURTAIN ALL THE WAY
ACROSS THE STAGE

Clamp the operating line to the side of the master carrier, and pass it through the center of each of the single carriers. There should be enough single carriers so that there is one for each grommet on the drape, except for the first and last ones. The first is attached to the master carrier. The last

When the operating line passes back over the second sheave in the live end pulley, it shoots straight down to the dead end pulley at the opposite end of the track. Here the line reverses direction back to the master carrier where it is held fast by the clamp. There are two clamps side by side, and the ends of the ropes will just touch each other. If the track is very wide, it may be necessary to provide some support to the operating line as it crosses the stage from the live end pulley to the dead end pulley. Unless the line is exceptionally taut, it will tend to sag in the middle and may become visible to the audience. An eyebolt attached to the side of one of the hanging clamps can be used to avoid that. Run the line through one or more of the eyes as required by the width of the stage. Sometimes idler pulleys are used for the same purpose.

When hanging the traveler curtain, make sure one side is attached to the master carrier. All but one of the remaining grommets are secured to successive single carriers, and then the last grommet is tied to an end stop at the offstage edge of the track. The endstop is used to keep the carriers from running off the end of the track, and it is a handy place to secure the offstage edge of the curtain. It must be held fast, or the curtain will roll too far onstage, creating a gap. You can use either end of the track as the place where the curtain bunches up. Just place the single carriers on that side of the master carrier. The "bunching up" side does not necessarily have to be the same as the operator side, although it most often is.

If the traveler is required to part in the center and move toward both sides, it must be rigged a bit differently, but the basic concept remains the same. Hang the track in two sections connected by a lap splice so that they overlap one another a foot or more. Of course, the curtain must be in two sections in order to split. The two halves of the traveler operate exactly the same way as the side-to-side type, but one half is the slave of the other.

its full onstage position. Slide the slave carrier along the track to its full onstage position and tighten the clamp to secure it in place. The two master carriers now move symmetrically with one another. Hang drapes on either side to complete the rigging job. Follow the same rules as before to connect the on-and-offstage edges of the two curtains.

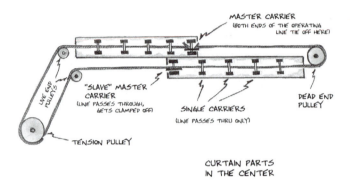

CURTAIN PARTS
IN THE CENTER

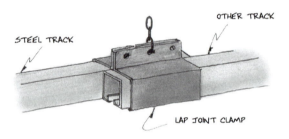

OVERLAPPING TWO SECTIONS OF TRACK

Sometimes cueing requires that a traveler open a preset amount that is less than the maximum distance. It is easy to mark a trim on the operating line so that it is possible to do this with a great deal of accuracy. Open the traveler the desired amount. Use tape to mark both sides of the rope with spikes that are right together at a comfortable height for the operator to see. The exact distance from the floor does not affect how the marks work. When the operator opens the traveler they should stop pulling on the rope when the two spike marks line up with one another. Use different colors of tape to spike multiple positions.

Attach the operating line to the master carrier on the side of the stage where you would like the tension pulley to be. Feed it through the single carriers, and then pass it through one sheave of the live end pulley. The line should go down to the floor, through the tension pulley and then back up through the live end pulley. So far this process is exactly the same as the one previously described where there is only one curtain in use, but now the method differs. The line passes through the clamp on the second master carrier, the one that is in the channel of the track which services the opposite side of the stage. The line passes through the clamp on this second master carrier without being cut.

The operating line continues through the opposite side single carriers and around the dead end pulley. Then it passes back to the first master carrier and is clamped off there. To operate properly, the placement of the "slave" master carrier must be calibrated with its master. Take the slack out of the operating line and pull on it until the first master carrier in

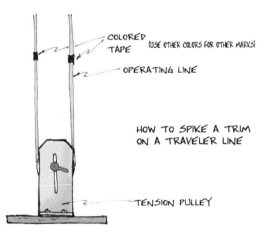

HOW TO SPIKE A TRIM
ON A TRAVELER LINE

There are occasions when it is useful to install tab curtains on the sides of the stage so that the audience cannot see into the wings. This is especially common in theatres where the architecture of the building itself creates problematic sightlines. Many touring shows use side tabs because the quality of sightlines in the various theatres they visit cannot be predicted or assured. The name "tab" is used for several different types of curtains, but in this case it refers to a short traveler that runs up and down stage between two leg and border sets. Tabs are most commonly used across the "in one" position, because this is the place where sightlines are usually at their worst. It is possible to rig this type of traveler so that it is self-closing, and hence cannot be accidentally left open to offend the modesty of actors quick changing in the wings.

A self-closing tab curtain of this type is hung with the traveler track at an angle, so that gravity causes the curtain to close on its own. The track itself is probably no more than 6 to 8 feet long, because the distance between the first set of legs and the second is only about that far.

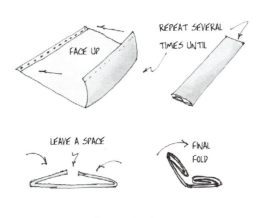

FOLDING A DROP

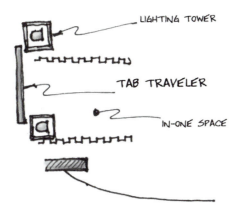

The track should hang at about a five-degree angle, but that is somewhat dependent on the type of curtain, its height and weight, how well the carriers roll, etc., and some experimentation will be required. You will most likely have to dead hang the track from the grid or some other structure, because it runs up- and-downstage rather than across the stage like a regular batten.

Touring shows often use towers for side lighting because the lights can travel inside the truss, and also because towers keep the lights from being hit and becoming unfocused during the show. Towers are an excellent place to hang the side tabs, especially if the use of tabs is taken into consideration when the placement of the towers is planned. Tie pulleys to the tower tops before they are raised to make it easy to hoist the track into position with ropes. Pulleys also make it easy to adjust the trim of the track's angle to give the proper amount of closing force.

The tab can be rigged so that it opens either from down to up or from up to down. There may be some reason peculiar to the production you are working on to make the tab operate one way or the other, but mechanically it makes no difference. The actual rigging of the track is quite simple. You need a master carrier for the leading edge of the curtain, and single carriers for the balance of the grommets except for the last one, which should be secured to the live end pulley. There is no need for a dead end pulley, because the pull rope does not need to return. It is secured to the master carrier, passes through each of the single carriers, over the live end pulley (only one sheave is used), and down to a comfortable height for operation. A figure eight tied in the end of the rope is a nice finishing touch. If you are a whiz-bang knot tier with time on your hands, a monkey's fist is even better.

Pulling on the rope causes the tab to open, and gravity closes it for you when the rope is released. If the curtain does not close well, try a slightly greater angle to the traveler track. This will cause the curtain to hang somewhat askew, but considering its position and use, that is not generally a concern. If the curtain is very light, fasten a small weight of some sort to the top of the curtain where it attaches to the master carrier. The added mass should help the rig to overcome the friction of the carrier wheels inside the traveler track.

STORING DROPS AND CURTAINS

Folding curtains and drops is one of the oldest stagehand skills. (It seems like there are a lot of those!) It is essential to understand the methodology if you are to consider yourself a stagehand. You can just imagine how early stagehands may have equated drop folding with sail folding.

There are a few basic techniques to follow in folding any type of hanging goods. One of these is to remember to leave the webbing and ties in an accessible position. This makes it possible to see whatever markings are written on the webbing and also makes it easier to see how to lay the goods out for retying to a batten. Proper folding will also reduce the amount of wrinkling that occurs, and generally keep the goods in better condition. It is not really possible to clean or iron most drops and curtains. Since they are quite expensive, great care is taken to ensure that they are well kept. In stage-hand lingo, any type of drop or drape may be referred to as soft goods, or simply "goods."

Begin any type of folding with the goods laid out flat on the floor with the front side up. It is customary that the back side be touching the floor to save the front from damage. Put a stagehand at each of the four corners to pull the goods out and stretch them. Try to get the goods as flat and smooth as possible. Flopping the corners up and down while pulling makes the job easier, because a small amount of air under-neath allows the fabric to float around with less drag.

Legs and scrims are different, but for a full drop the two hands at the bottom two corners should lift their corners, pull against one another to keep tension on the drop, and then quickly move up to the top two corners. The two hands at the top of the drop grab the corners and match them with their own. Again, a bit of air captured in the curtain makes it easier to float the bottom to the top. Too much will cause you to overshoot. The same two stagehands who carried the bottom to the top the first time return to the middle of the drop, which has now become the bottom by virtue of the folding. Straighten everything out, let the air escape from the inside, and repeat the procedure as many times as neces-sary until a two- or three-foot wide strip has been created.

Bring both ends to the center. Leave a space about one foot wide so that there will be enough slack for the final fold. Repeat bringing the ends to the middle until a two- or three-foot bundle is left on either side. Fold one side over the other, and folding is completed.

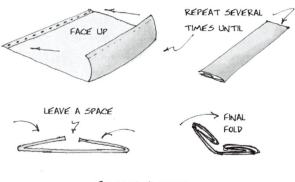

FOLDING A DROP

Soft goods are traditionally stored in large laundry ham-pers. If you have carefully folded an expensive drop, it only makes sense that you should exercise the same amount of care when easing it into the hamper. On occasion you may

encounter a piece that is so large and heavy it is impractical to consider lifting it up and into a hamper. When this happens it is best to roll the drop. Once the bottom of the drop has been folded to the top and the sides are to the middle one time, begin rolling the drop from one end to the other. Place a hamper on its side at the far end and simply roll the goods into the hamper. Since this is a technique for very large pieces, the one curtain will most likely fill it completely.

Legs and other goods that are taller than they are wide are folded side to side first. Repeat this until a workable size is reached. Do your final folding by bringing the bottom to the top, rather than both sides to the middle like a full stage drop. This will leave the webbing exposed. The bottom part tends to curl up a bit with every fold, so you will need to straighten it out each time. Repeat the process until a happy size is reached.

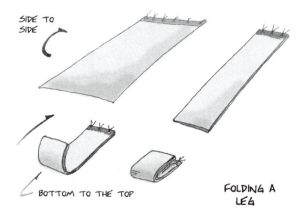

FOLDING A LEG

Curtains that are sewn with fullness are a real bear to fold. In all honesty there is no really good method, and you must do the best you can. Sometimes legs are simply low-ered into a hamper when the lineset is brought in, and there is no attempt at all made to fold them. If the drapes are velour, and will be taken back out relatively soon, then this is a fine solution. Velour tends not to wrinkle badly, but I wouldn't try this with a finely woven fabric with no pile or nap. The problem in folding goods with fullness is of course that the webbing is so much smaller than the body of the curtain, and when stretched out the curtain makes a fan shape. Do your best using the same process as above, but stop and straighten everything at each step as you go along.

Scrims and other very lightweight drops are sometimes west-coasted. In this procedure, many stagehands are positioned under the drop as it is flown into the deck. The hands should position themselves with arms extended so that the scrim furls up on their arms, creating a bundle rather than hitting the floor. Untie about every fifth tie from the batten and retie it around the bundled scrim so that a kind of tube is created with the goods. Untie the remaining ties from the batten and feed the bundle into its hamper.

Curtains sewn with fullness often have a chain sewn into the hem, which adds a bit of weight to the bottom and encourages the goods to hang straight. A better solution when possible is to use a bottom pipe. A bottom pipe works well on any drop or curtain that is sewn flat. When a pipe is used, the weight in the bottom is greater and tends to do a better job of straightening out any horizontal wrinkles. Also, the goods can be stretched along the length of the pipe, thus removing a great many of the vertical wrinkles along the bottom. Drops must be sewn with a pipe pocket installed in order to use a bottom pipe.

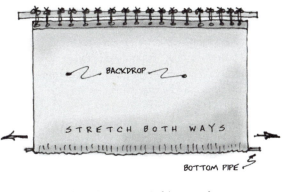

REMOVING WRINKLES WITH A
BOTTOM PIPE

Hanging drops and curtains on a batten involves tying hundreds of bow knots. Like any task in the theatre (or elsewhere, I would imagine), there are a few tricks that make the job a bit easier. After you have determined which lineset to use, you will need to know where to locate the curtain on the batten. If you are hanging legs, the designer's groundplan can be consulted to find the distance of the onstage side of the leg from the centerline of the stage. In most theatres the center of the battens is marked with red tape or paint. If not, there is generally some architectural feature which will give you a clue. Measure along the batten from the center to the appropriate point and make a mark. Oftentimes there is enough dust on the top of the pipe to make an excellent mark, but if the theatre is exceedingly clean a piece of chalk

is a valuable tool. Always measure distances from the center of the batten, never from the end. Plans are notoriously inaccurate about the length of battens. If you are moving from theatre to theatre, there is no way to draw a plan that is accurate for all of them, but the center of the stage is always an easily defined starting point.

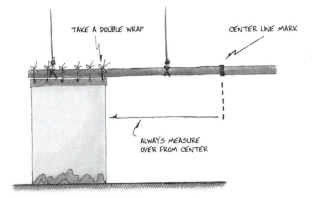

Tie on the leg beginning from the place you measured, working your way toward the offstage end of the pipe. It is helpful to begin the first tie with a double wrap around the pipe and then the regular bow knot so that the tie line is choked onto the pipe. This keeps the onstage edge from creeping offstage along the batten as you stretch the goods out tight. Oftentimes the leg will be too wide for the batten and will need to be tied back by folding it to the rear and continuing to tie it to the pipe, but back toward the center of the stage. Reverse and repeat. The other choice is to accordion pleat the goods at the end of the batten. This can sometimes be a better choice when a bottom pipe is involved.

Most drops are hung with the center of the drop aligned with the center of the batten, so there will be no need to measure anything. The drop should have a centerline marked on the webbing and/or have a different colored tie that marks the center. It may not be immediately apparent which way to lay out the goods before tying them to the batten. Quite often there is a lot of confusion with ten stagehands arguing about which way the thing should go, but I have found that this method always works. If the drop has been folded in the normal way, and you lay it out on the floor with the webbing pointing upstage, the goods will be in the proper position to face toward the audience.

Begin by double wrapping the center tie. If the drop is heavy, it is often best to skip along and tie every fifth or sixth tie, stretching the goods each time. This way you will not have to pick up the full weight of the top of the drop with every tie. If there is a group working, be sure to reach over the pipe each time or your arm will be in the way of the others. It is easy to come back and fill in the missing ties when the goods are secured. Again, it may be necessary to tie back the offstage ends of the drop.

If you are using bottom pipe, it should be installed after the drop has been flown out, with the bottom of the drop about waist high off the floor. The pipe itself is usually in sections that are screwed or taped together. One stagehand holds the pocket open while two others slide in the length of pipe, and then attach the second section to the first. Repeat until the pocket is full, but don't leave too much bare pipe sticking out the end as a hazard. It is often helpful for one or more stagehands to hold up the end of the pipe as it works its way through the pocket and across the stage. Sometimes lightly bouncing the pipe will help it pass. Special care should be exercised when the pocket is old and torn, which unfortunately is a common occurrence. When the pipe is in place, the bottom of the goods can be stretched by gently but firmly pulling on the extreme sides.

I was recently watching the Tony Awards on television and could not help but notice that someone had forgotten to stretch the bottom of a drop used in one of the production numbers. It looked awful in the sidelight that highlighted every wrinkle. No matter how many things you do right, the one wrong thing is what everyone notices.

If you are touring, or if you have occasion to rent painted backdrops, you may well have a problem fitting drops into a theatre that is too small for them. If the drop is too wide or the stage is too narrow, then the drops can be folded back on the batten as described earlier. If the drop is too tall, and cannot be flown out far enough to clear the sightlines, then some other remedy is required. There are two possible solutions: tripping the bottom and rolling the top.

Tripping involves using a second batten to fly out the bottom of the drop. On rare occasions a drop will be sewn with a special pipe pocket halfway down that is intended from the get-go to be used for tripping. This is done when the design of the show calls for a drop that is extraordinarily tall and unlikely to fit anywhere. More commonly, a second method is employed when it suddenly becomes apparent that the drop "just won't fit."

A batten directly upstage of the drop is used to pick up the bottom pipe. The easiest way to attach the second batten is to connect a number of small lines that run from the bottom pipe of the drop to the upstage pipe. These "tail down" lines are required because the tripping batten cannot fly in all the way to the deck to meet the bottom pipe when that bottom pipe is on the floor. A variety of different small line types are workable, but make sure that whatever you use will indeed bear the weight of the drop and bottom pipe safely. Use a number of lines, one every six to eight feet, and not just one on either end. This means, of course, that you will need to poke several holes in the pipe pocket in order to pass the line around the bottom pipe. (This is just one of the reasons that the pocket gets so torn up.) Make sure that all of the tail downs are the same length so that the pipe will be picked up evenly.

This method works by flying out the tripping pipe just a few feet ahead of the regular pipe. This will pick up the bottom and make the out height of the bottom twice as high as it was when you began. When coming in, it generally looks best if the tripping pipe precedes the regular pipe by several feet. Obviously the two flymen must work well together in a coordinated effort. These linesets will not be weighted properly at all times, and this technique will only work if the drop is relatively light.

A second method of shortening a drop is by rolling. Rolling the top of the goods reduces the height of the drop but also temporarily takes away part of it. If the top cannot be seen anyway, then this is no great loss. Sometimes there is no extra batten to make tripping possible, and rolling is the only solution. Whether tripping or rolling is appropriate must be decided on a case-by-case basis.

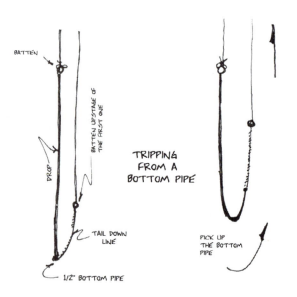

TRIPPING FROM A BOTTOM PIPE

BATTEN

BATTEN UPSTAGE OF THE FIRST ONE

DROP

TAIL DOWN LINE

1/2" BOTTOM PIPE

PICK UP THE BOTTOM PIPE

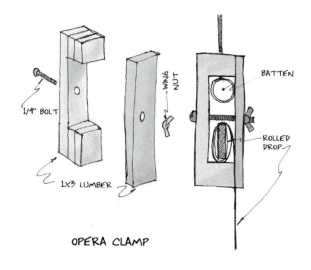

OPERA CLAMP

1/4" BOLT

WING NUT

1X3 LUMBER

BATTEN

ROLLED DROP

Rolling occurs before the drop is hung and requires some special equipment that must be secured beforehand. You will need some 1x4 lumber and a number of roll drop clamps as described in the accompanying diagram. After the supplies are gathered, lay the drop out on the floor face up and as straight and square as possible. Perhaps the top can be lined up with a long straight joint on the stage floor. Take several very straight 1x4s and lay them out even with the top of the goods. These boards should go all the way from side to side. It will take a number of people to hold the boards, and to rotate them, rolling the fabric onto the boards. It is important to roll together, and to keep everything nice and neat.

Continue to roll until the desired height is reached. Use the same horde of stagehands to pick up the rolled top and secure it to the batten with the roll drop clamps. Attach the roll drop clamps by rotating the flat part, and make use of the u-shaped part by hanging one end on the pipe and using the other to hold onto the rolled part of the drop. Rotate the flat part to seal in the pipe and drop, and then tighten the wing nut to secure it. If the drop does not hang straight, try again and be more precise. It may be possible to straighten the drop by adjusting the batten trim chains, if there are any.

CONSTRUCTION TECHNIQUES

I have found that the construction of stage draperies is quite a difficult chore, and is best left to professionals who have a shop devoted to that work. It is not easy to get curtains to hang straight, especially large ones. Undoubtedly there is a vast body of technique that takes great practice to acquire. On the other hand, sewing drops is not nearly such a problem. The fabric is much lighter, it comes in wider widths, and methods of laying out the drop, sizing, and preparing for painting give you a bit of latitude. This margin for error is not found in sewing drapes that must hang straight from the outset.

A good fabric choice for drop construction is 120" wide, heavyweight, non-flameproofed muslin. Muslin is chosen because the 100% cotton type has a good "tooth" for painting, and it sizes well. Heavyweight muslin is strong enough to hold up over a period of time, but is not as expensive and difficult to work with as canvas is. Flameproofing is very important and is required by most local fire officials, but it is less expensive to buy untreated fabric and then treat it yourself with an after-market product. This is especially true if you have lots of wooden pieces to treat as well. Spray everything down at once.

Most smaller theatres have a proscenium opening height of around 20 feet. Even if the opening is taller than that, a valance is often used to close down the space a bit. Borders used over the stage trim at around the same height. Drops need to be a few feet taller than the bottom of the borders in order to mask well.

To make this description of constructing a drop easier to understand, imagine that the stage being used trims out around 18 feet in height. So a height of 20 feet is sufficient for the drop you have to sew. (Of course, in reality the designer dictates the size of the goods, but this gives you an idea of how the process works.) If 120-inch wide muslin is used, only two strips of fabric must be sewn together to get a drop 20-feet tall. If some other odd size is required, it may make sense to buy some other width of muslin. If a drop is to be painted on duvetyn or scrim, I would suggest having a drapery house put that together.

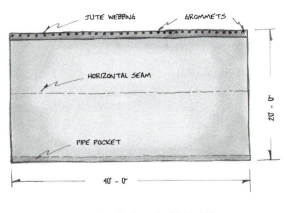

PARTS OF A MUSLIN DROP

It is helpful when sewing drops to have a large open space to lay out the pieces. I often find a time when the movement studio is not in use and lay out my pieces in that space for cutting. The scene shop is not generally a good choice since it is so dirty with sawdust and old spattered paint.

Not much equipment is required; a sewing machine that can make a straight stitch through fairly heavy goods, a large tape measure (like a construction tape, not a sewing tape), some scissors, thread, pins, and grommeting equipment. If you are really good with a sewing machine you may not need the pins. An industrial-type sewing machine works really well, and remember that you only need a straight stitch.

Scenic muslin is usually sold by the bolt, roll, or bale. The pieces are fifty to sixty yards long, uncut, from the factory. If you buy less than a full bolt, the price is substantially higher. Since muslin is a mainstay of any scene shop, it makes sense to buy it in quantity. Jute webbing is 3 1/2" wide and comes on a roll that is 72 yards long and is quite cheap. The standard size of grommet to use is the #2. It is easy to ruin grommets, especially when you are new to the process of installation, so it is best to buy plenty of extras. You will need a #2 grommet hole cutter and setter for the purpose. Plain old #4 tie line is used for the ties. Some professional shops use a twill fabric tape that looks like thick bias tape for their ties.

Unless you are working on some really odd shape, the seams in a drop should run horizontally. The jute webbing is sewn to the top of the drop so that there is a stable and sturdy strip for the grommets. A pipe pocket is made for the bottom of the drop so that it can be properly weighted and stretched.

Consider that there is a request for a drop that is twenty feet tall and forty feet wide. If 120" wide muslin is used, and the seams are horizontal, it will take only two strips of the muslin to make up the drop. The pipe pocket at the bottom of the drop will add several inches to the finished height. A few inches will be taken away by seams, so the finished product will most likely be an inch or two larger than the ideal. There is no need to be any more precise than that. The 120" measurement for the width of the muslin is somewhat nominal anyway, and the actual size is often an inch or so smaller. Unless there are very unusual circumstances, drop sizes are not that critical. The fabric tends to stretch out and draw up over time. Of course it would probably NOT be OK if the drop is a foot short.

Lay out the bundle of muslin on the floor and measure off a couple of inches more than forty feet in length. Use scissors to cut through the thick selvage edge, and then rip the muslin straight across the warp. Ripping actually makes a much straighter cut than the scissors can, because the rip follows one thread straight across the fabric. It is also much faster than trying to establish a right angle to use as a guide. Do this a second time for the second piece, and set the muslin off to the side for a few minutes.

It is easiest to begin construction by making the pipe pocket. If the drop is to receive heavy use, it is best to beef up this pocket by making it in two layers, the inside being a heavier canvas, and the outside the same muslin as is used for the body of the drop. If the drop is to be used for only one in-house show, then you may feel that a simple pocket made from one layer of heavyweight muslin will do. It is important that the outside of the pipe pocket be made of the same material as the rest of the drop to avoid a difference in texture.

Rip some 12" wide strips of cloth from scrap, and sew enough of them together end to end to form a strip that is at least as long as the width of the drop, in our case 40'-0". You don't need to be terribly precise, it won't hurt if this strip is a bit longer because it will get trimmed off later. Fold the strip in half lengthwise and sew it together creating a tube 6" wide. Make sure that any seams previously made by sewing together the smaller strips go to the inside where they will not be seen. If you are using an inner sleeve of canvas, the joining seams of that strip should go to the outside, so that the interior of the sleeve is not obstructed. This allows the pipe to slide through easily. Sometimes a very slick and tough nylon fabric is used for the inner sleeve. At any rate, you should wind up with a tube more than 40' long, with no seam allowances showing except for the one at the top.

There is no need to turn the tube inside out; the top seam will wind up on the back of the drop and will not show. Sew the completed pocket to the bottom piece of muslin. Make sure that your seam allowance is large enough to include the entire selvage, which on scenic muslin is sometimes quite large. Usually about a 1" allowance is enough.

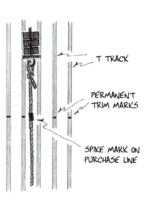

MARKING THE OUT TRIM

The second stage is to secure the jute webbing to the top section of the muslin. Lay out the muslin on the floor so that it is flat and one edge is in a reasonably straight line. Turn down the straight edge of the muslin 3 1/2", which is the width of the jute. There is no need to iron it; just crease it with your hand, as you would a piece of thick paper. Muslin typically has a stiff quality from all of the sizing that is in it. Use a small piece of the webbing to measure the distance.

Cut a section of webbing that is 40'-6" long. Turn under three inches at one end and mash it down so that a crease is formed. Pin the webbing to the muslin so that the turned-under section of the jute is down and the edge of the webbing is flush with the edge of the muslin. I find it helpful to use a pin at least every foot or so to make it easier to get the drop through the sewing machine. Fold over and pin down the last three inches of the webbing just like you did the first three inches. It is very likely that the ends of the jute and the muslin will not match up very well. Excess muslin can be trimmed off later, but in any case don't run the webbing off the end. Extra material folded over at the top and ends creates a greater thickness and more strength in these areas, especially at the corners, which get the most intense use.

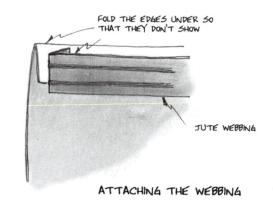

ATTACHING THE WEBBING

Sew down the webbing with a straight stitch $1/4$" from each edge, and also down the middle. A setting of 8 or 10 stitches per inch is good. An industrial machine is by far the best to use, because of the thickness of the jute and the extreme length of the seams. Do not run a seam down the colored threads that make two stripes on the jute. The top one will be used to locate the placement of the grommets. The resulting holes would cut through the seam and weaken it.

Now is the time to connect the top and bottom sections of the drop together. Obviously, care should be taken to ensure that the middle seam, jute webbing, and pipe pocket seam all fall on what will become the upstage side of the drop. It is best to begin sewing on the side where there was the most accurate alignment of the webbing with the side of the drop. This will force all of your error to occur on the side that is easiest to trim. Saving the joining of the big parts until the very last means that you only have to deal with the weight of the whole drop once.

When the drop is stretched out and stapled to the floor for painting, the edges should be arranged so that a true rectangle is achieved. Snap lines on the floor to delineate a 20'-0" by 40'-0" area. You may need to make a slight adjustment in size after double checking the true dimensions of the finished drop.

Rather than letting the sewn material define the shape of the drop, the edges of the muslin should be brought in line with the layout marks on the paint floor. If the sewing process left excess fabric on the edges of the drop, trim it off before stapling the drop to the floor. The muslin will shrink, loose its wrinkles, and conform to the shape and size defined by the staples on its perimeter, and it is not necessary to do any stretching. A proper layout is of paramount importance in order to avoid a misshapen product. The drop can be a few inches too wide or too short without much notice being taken, but if it hangs crookedly, everyone will see that.

Grommeting can be done either before or after painting, as time permits. Turn the drop so that the back side of the webbing is visible. Lay down a tape and make marks across the back at one-foot intervals from either side. Make sure that the center mark is dead in the middle of the drop, because that will make it easier to properly tie the drop onto the batten when it gets to the theatre. It is best to use a permanent marker and to center the marks on the top red or blue stripe. The center of the top stripe is used to measure proper spacing of the grommet holes from the top of the drop. Use the hole cutter to punch holes on the marks in the webbing. It is best to place the drop on top of a block of wood and/or some thick scrap leather when punching the holes to prevent damage to your floor and tool. The leather (perhaps an old belt) seems to help keep the punch from dulling so quickly. Arbitrarily move the corner holes in a comfortable distance from the edge so that they are on the sturdiest part of the fabric.

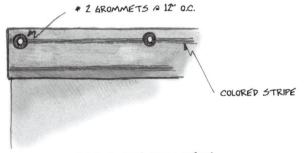

PLACING THE GROMMETS

Follow the instructions that come with your grommet setter to attach the #2 brass grommets. Basically, this involves threading the male side through the hole, placing it on the base, slipping the female side over the male, and then using the setter to curl the male side flange down so that it secures the female side. The instructions will most likely say something about not trying to do the job with one hard blow, but rather with many small taps. That is good advice.

Grommeting is one of those processes that sounds really easy but takes considerable practice to master well. Expect to ruin a few grommets in learning how.

Cut some tie line to a length of 30" and then tie one to each grommet using a square knot. It is traditional to use a contrasting color of tie to mark the center of the drop. Use a Sharpie to mark a centerline on the back of the webbing.

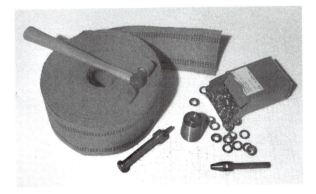

GROMMETING SUPPLIES AND TOOLS

CHAPTER 6

ELECTRICITY AND
LIGHTING EQUIPMENT

Lighting designers create light plots, but the implementation of a design is the work of stagehands. A light plot is a sheet of drafting that shows an electrician the different types of lights to be used, their varying locations on the stage, patterns and colors, and sometimes how the lights are to be circuited. A well-executed plot is drawn to scale using USITT standard graphic symbols to indicate instrument type and size. Units are shown graphically in the space they will occupy on an electric, boom, tower, or front-of-house position. There should be a Legend on the plot that explains how symbols are used. It should also explain the numbering system for gel colors, channels, and instrument numbers. Paperwork is very important in lighting design because there are so many numbers to keep track of. CAD programs do an excellent job with paperwork.

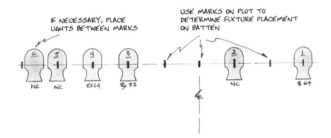

USING REGISTRATION MARKS TO AVOID MEASURING

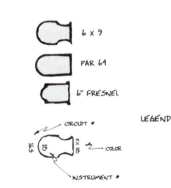

The duties of the head electrician differ from one situation to another, but generally include the following: studying the plot to determine what equipment is needed, locating that equipment (perhaps from a rental house), hanging the lights in their proper locations, cabling, recording circuit numbers, completing the hook-up, cutting color and putting it into frames, troubleshooting, and focusing. This is also more or less the order in which the work is done. In some theatres it will also be necessary to tie in dimmer power and/or run feeder cables to the dimmers. The head electrician has a management function as well. This person usually supervises the crew that helps do all of the actual labor. Learning to effectively oversee the work of others and to make their work more efficient is a subject for a book in and of itself.

It is not the job of the electrician to write cues, pick colors, talk to the director, or handle any of the "artistic" chores associated with a lighting design. An electrician should pay close attention to all of these things and should jump in when necessary and attempt to aid the designer, but should never offer unsolicited advice about artistic matters. A good electrician (or any other stagehand) should strive to anticipate the next step and plan ahead.

Being an effective electrician requires a good working knowledge of the equipment used in theatres. Since the field of lighting is inextricably linked to the use of electrical power (at least since Thomas Edison in 1879), it is important to begin with at least some understanding of the principles of electricity.

E**LECTRICAL** T**HEORY**

As you may recall from practically any beginning science class, all matter is composed of atoms. The neutrons, protons, and electrons that make up an atom determine what element the matter is. Electrons are the parts of atoms that are shared between them to create a chemical reaction. Electrons can also be shared between adjacent atoms of certain elements, known commonly as metals, without a chemical reaction occurring. Electricity is created when electrons flow between atoms, and most often between metallic atoms.

A conductor is a material that allows current to flow through it, and in practical situations is usually a copper wire. An insulator, such as plastic or rubber blocks the flow of electrons. You can relate this to the rubber or plastic insulation that coats most wires. Wires have copper in the center for electricity to flow through, and plastic or rubber on the outside to keep the current from escaping. Without insulators, electricity would flow chaotically in all directions. Insulation focuses the movement of electricity into a useful direction. The pathway that wires and other conductors create is called a circuit. A wiring circuit must be continuous and unbroken in order for electron movement to occur. If a wire comes loose, the circuit is broken open, and no current flows.

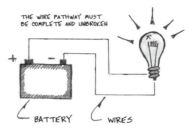

A COMPLETED CIRCUIT

There are two basic kinds of circuits, series and parallel. Series circuits are not often used in lighting, other than in control equipment such as a light board. In a series circuit, loads are connected together so that current must flow through each load in order to get to the next one. A load is a device that does work; for example a light bulb, or a toaster.

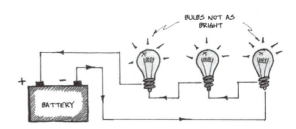

A SERIES CIRCUIT

There are some major drawbacks to a series circuit. First of all, if one of the loads is removed (such as a light bulb burning out), the circuit will be broken, and no more current will flow through it. In the olden days when I was a lad, it was common practice to wire Christmas tree lights together in a series circuit in order to lessen the amount of copper wire used. But it was so annoying to try and find one burned out bulb among so many that manufacturers gave up on the idea years ago. Another problem with the series circuit is that the amount of voltage present to any one load is decreased each time an additional load is placed on the line.

Electricity is formed by pushing electrons through a conductor. Voltage is a way of expressing how much pressure is being used to push the electrons forward. Lamps in a series circuit will never reach their full output unless they have been specially engineered to work on a lowered voltage. One type of specialty lamp fitting this description (other than those Christmas tree lights) is the aircraft landing light, or ACL.

In the entertainment business they are used to emit a thin shaft of light on stage, but are really manufactured to use on airplanes. ACL's are designed to operate at 28 volts, which is apparently a standard aircraft voltage. To use them with a normal earth-bound voltage of 110v, it is necessary to gang four of these lamps into a series circuit so that the voltage reaching each one is only one fourth of the available 110v, or 27.5v. The concept of voltage is not terribly precise, and the difference of one half of one volt is not very important. Voltage must pass through all four loads in order to form a completed circuit.

This "sharing" of voltage in a series circuit can be better understood if you take some voltage measurements. In the llustration with four loads in series, the voltage flowing through all four loads is equal to the rounded-off supply voltage of 100v. The voltage potential across one load is one-fourth of the supply voltage, or 25 volts. Across two loads is 50 volts, and across three is 75 volts. If the voltage supplied to a light bulb is less than the lamp was designed for, the bulb will be dimmer than normal, so unless you have low voltage lamps, bulbs in series usually emit a reddish glow. Dimmers use this same principle when they reduce voltage to a light causing the bulb to be less bright.

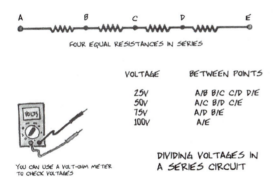

FOUR EQUAL RESISTANCES IN SERIES

VOLTAGE	BETWEEN POINTS
25V	A/B B/C C/D D/E
50V	A/C B/D C/E
75V	A/D B/E
100V	A/E

DIVIDING VOLTAGES IN A SERIES CIRCUIT

YOU CAN USE A VOLT-OHM METER TO CHECK VOLTAGES

Electricity arriving from outside lines often fluctuates by several volts, depending on local conditions. The stated voltage of 110v is nominal, meaning that it is just an amount used as a name. Many times voltage is listed as 117V, and if you check voltage with a meter at a wall outlet you will find that it is very often in the 120- to-125 volt range.

Parallel circuits are much more commonly found in stage lighting than series circuits are. In this arrangement, power flows directly from its source to each load. The wiring used as delivery system may carry power to several lamps along the same two wires, but in no case will electricity flow through one load to get to another one. Hence the on/off status of any one particular lamp will not affect the status of the others, and since each lamp has its own direct source of power, the amount of voltage reaching each lamp will remain constant without regard to any of the other lamps.

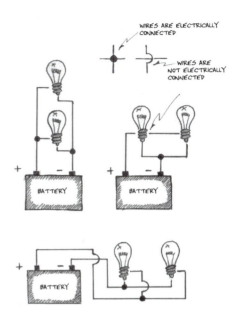

WIRES ARE ELECTRICALLY CONNECTED

WIRES ARE NOT ELECTRICALLY CONNECTED

VARIATIONS ON PARALLEL CIRCUITS

There are two basic types of electric current, direct (DC) and alternating (AC). These two types are defined by the way each one causes electrons to move through a conductor. In direct current (DC) electrons move in one direction only, from a source of surplus electrons known as the negative terminal (-), toward a collection point known as the positive terminal (+). A terminal is an ending point for a circuit. You can find the plus and minus signs on any battery next to its terminals.

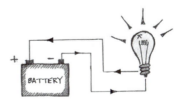

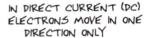

IN DIRECT CURRENT (DC) ELECTRONS MOVE IN ONE DIRECTION ONLY

A power source like a battery provides a potential for electrons to move. Batteries use a chemical reaction to force electrons to move through the circuit. A car battery uses lead and hydrochloric acid to do that. It is very toxic and messy. Dry cell batteries use solids like carbon and zinc, which are much more stable and user friendly. Once the chemicals in a battery have been exhausted, it produces no more electrical charge. It is very common for electronic devices to use a power supply to convert AC power from a wall plug into DC power. That lowers your dependence on expensive batteries for appliances like jam boxes.

Direct current is not often used for lighting purposes except for very special arc-type lamps that require DC to operate. These are found mostly on followspots or large movie lights, most notably xenon or HMI lamps.

Any type of ordinary filament bulb will operate with either direct or alternating current with no problem, but electric motors are wired for one or the other. The speed of DC motors can be adjusted by varying the voltage supplied to them, much like varying the voltage will cause a light to vary in brightness. DC motors are used for equipment like gobo rotators and color changers because their speed is so easily controlled. Alternating current motors will burn out if you try reducing their voltage. That is why you should never connect an AC motor to a dimmer. AC motor speed can be controlled by altering the frequency of the current, but that is a much different process.

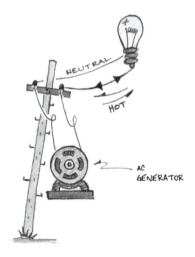

ALTERNATING CURRENT

AC HAS A HOT AND A NEUTRAL
RATHER THAN A PLUS AND MINUS
LIKE IN DIRECT CURRENT

Alternating current is much more commonly available because it was long ago adopted as the standard method. It is easier to transmit and requires smaller and less expensive wires. It is the type of current that is supplied to most homes and businesses.

AC differs from DC in that its electrons move through the conducting wire in two opposite directions following a regularly scheduled pattern. There is a constant ebb and flow from the source of power, with electrons first being forced down the wire and then being allowed to lapse back toward the source. The speed at which this change of direction occurs is given in cycles or Hertz (Hz). Sixty cycles per second is standard in North America. The inscription 110VAC 60Hz on an electrical appliance indicates that it requires 110 volts of alternating current operating at 60 cycles per second. If you look, you will find this value on most of your household appliances, at least the ones that get plugged into the wall. Other countries use different values, and equipment is not usually interchangeable. A television set made for the European market will not work in the States without a special adapter, and vice versa.

Rather than having a positive and a negative terminal like a direct current battery, AC is said to have a hot and a neutral. The "hot" is the wire that is used to push electrons through the circuit. The word hot is indicative of the fact that this conductor is energized. The neutral is the wire that provides a resting place for electrons to go when they are not being used. Even though the neutral does not carry any usable electrons, it must be in place for the circuit to operate. When wiring electrical devices, it is important to make sure that the hot and neutral wires are attached to the proper terminals.

Alternating current is produced at a power station where some other form of energy, such as heat from fossil fuels or the inertia of falling water, is used to turn a generator. Rotating magnetic fields inside the generator induce electron flow that is cyclical in nature. As the generator rotates, wire coils pass in and out of magnetic fields. When a coil of wire moves through a magnetic field an electric current is induced in the wire. The speed and direction that the coil of wire takes in its passage through a magnetic field causes the current to become stronger and/or weaker.

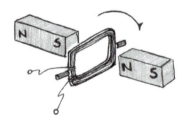

AS THE COIL OF WIRE ROTATES BETWEEN
TWO MAGNETS, A VOLTAGE IS INDUCED.
ELECTRONS FLOW FIRST IN ONE DIRECTION,
AND THEN IN THE OTHER

When the wire is passing at a right angle to the lines of magnetic force, the greatest current is induced. When passing parallel to the lines of magnetic force, no current is induced. When the coil of wire rotates halfway around the generator its polarity is reversed, and the current flows in the opposite direction. As a result, the current produced by an AC generator follows a pattern of strength and polarity demonstrated graphically by a sine wave. Over a period of time, the strength of the current becomes stronger to a certain point, then weaker down to zero. It reverses direction, becoming stronger in a negative direction to a certain point, and then returns to a zero point. One complete sine wave represents one complete cycle or Hertz.

current is used, either the coil of wire or the magnet must be moving in order to induce that current flow. But if an Alternating Current is used, the magnetic field from the primary coil of wire is constantly expanding and contracting in time with the voltage changes that are occurring. This movement of the field itself is enough to induce a current in the secondary coil of wire. The proportion of the voltage in the primary coil to the voltage in the secondary coil is mostly a function of the number of turns of wire in each of the coils.

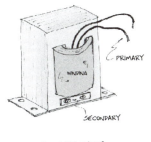

LOW VOLTAGE
POWER TRANSFORMER

ONE CYCLE OF ALTERNATING CURRENT

THE USEFUL VOLTAGE THAT IS APPLIED TO THE LOAD IS THE **AVERAGE** VOLTAGE. THE RMS AVERAGE VOLTAGE IS INDICATED BY THE SHADED-IN AREA. THE ACTUAL PEAK VOLTAGE IS MUCH HIGHER.

VOLTAGE TRAVELS ONE DIRECTION WHEN THE CURVE IS IN THE POSITIVE QUADRANT, AND THE OPPOSITE DIRCTION WHEN THE CURVE IS IN THE NEGATIVE QUADRANT

Power transformers are used to "step up" and "step down" voltages. A higher voltage is more dangerous than a low voltage. Electric current can jump across an open-air gap a distance of about one inch for every ten thousand volts. It is possible to be killed by a high voltage source without ever having touched any of the conducting surfaces. Lightning contains billions of volts, allowing its spark to jump across vast distances. Water, or more correctly the ions in it, make it much easier for electrons to flow. This is why you should be especially careful around electricity in wet areas.

Power coming into a large facility runs at a very high voltage because that is the most effective method of transmission. Electricity at a very high voltage can pass through wires more efficiently. A transformer is used to transform, reduce, or "step down," the high voltage to a more user-friendly voltage, which is generally 110 volts. Transformers for residential use are the large gray round things that are seen at the tops of telephone poles. They are much bigger than they look from the ground. Most commercial transformers are large square metal boxes with "Danger High Voltage" written on the side. Please trust the manufacturer that there are no user serviceable parts inside and stay away. Small transformers are used inside all sorts of things to provide a low voltage power supply. Six to 12 volt transformers that are used for doorbells are quite easily found at any hardware store. If you want to experiment with transformers, this is the type to use.

Basic transformers use two coils of wire to a change voltage. When electricity passes through a coil of wire it produces a magnetic field. Also, as discussed earlier, a magnetic field can be used to induce an electric current in a coil of wire. When a DC

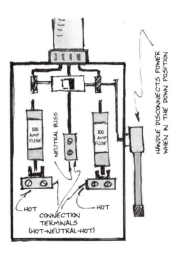

DISCONNECT BOX

You may often find alternating current that uses more than one hot conductor. In a theatre situation each of the hot wires carries its own separate 110v supply of power. A distribution panel that houses two hots and one neutral will therefore have a capacity of 220v when both of the hot "legs" are taken into consideration. This is the type of installation that is found in most homes. Some electrical devices, such as stoves, air conditioners, and clothes dryers, are designed to operate using both of the hot legs and are said to require a 220-volt line. Hence they have three conductors, two hots and a neutral. Smaller dimming systems are also commonly wired to use 220 volts. For stage use, it is not intended that any one lamp will be fed the entire 220v but rather that some of the lamps will be fed by one of the 110v legs, and others will be powered by the second one. The power will have been split up by the dimming system. In any case, there is no single potential that equals 220 volts.

When more electricity is required, three-phase power may be used. Three-phase has three separate hots and one common neutral. The name is derived from the timing sequence that is used for the various hot legs. For each hot in a three-phase hookup, the 60-cycle ebb and flow of electrons occurs at a slightly different timing schedule, and hence there are three distinct and separate phases. This is done in order to more effectively create and transmit the electricity. Some large motors are specifically wired to operate on three-phase because it is more efficient for them to do so. In reality, the timing of the phases will have little or no effect on lighting equipment.

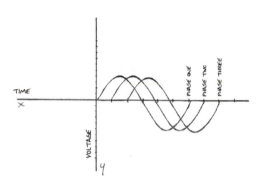

THE AC GENERATOR CONTAINS A NUMBER OF COILS OF WIRE. IT USES THEM TO CREATE THREE SEPARATE CURRENTS. EACH CURRENT FLOWS AT A SLIGHTLY DIFFERENT TIME, OR PHASE. ALL THREE HOT PHASES CAN USE THE SAME NEUTRAL.

Lightbulbs have a small wire or filament inside them that is heated to create light. At a certain temperature, the filament becomes "incandescent," and energy that was in the form of electricity is transformed into light energy. The wire filament becomes hot because it is too small for so many electrons to pass through easily. When there is too much electricity flowing through a wire, the conductor itself obstructs the passage of electrons. The extent of that obstruction is known as the resistance of the conductor. Resistance is one of the values used in the mathematical assessment of electronic circuits. It is present in any practical device used to conduct electricity, and any conductor will heat up when there is too much current running through it.

DISCONNECT FOR 3-PHASE POWER

NOTE THE 3 HOT LEGS WITH FUSES
WHITE TAPE ON NEUTRAL BUSS AT LEFT
GROUND CONNECTION AT THE BOTTOM

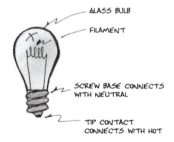

PARTS OF A LIGHTBULB

Resistance occurs in both AC circuits and in DC circuits. Since incandescent lightbulbs operate purely on the principle of resistance, it makes no difference at all whether the power supplied is AC or DC.

Any difference in the change or direction of the electron flow happens so quickly that it is not possible to see its affects. Even though electrons stop moving for the briefest of moments when the change in direction occurs, the lamp filament does not cool fast enough to record it. Sometimes though, the alternation of the current will cause the filament of a lightbulb to vibrate or rattle and this vibration can be heard as a buzzing noise. It is sometimes referred to as a "60 cycle hum." Hum is more noticeable in a lamp with a large filament. You can easily hear it coming from many streetlights.

Sixty-cycle hum can be a serious problem for sound equipment. Low voltage lines such as microphone cables should be kept as far as possible from lighting cables, especially those carrying a large amount of current. Care should be taken in coiling the wire used to feed dimmer racks. Feeder cable typically carries a very high current, and coiling it in a circle can cause a large amount of induction such as is found in a transformer. This induction can cause a variety of problems for other electrical circuits backstage, and can even influence the power delivered to the dimmer rack itself. It is a better practice to "figure 8" the cable instead. This will prevent harmful induction from occurring.

STRAIGHT COIL CREATES
INDUCTANCE

FIGURE 8 FEEDER CABLE TO
AVOID EXCESSIVE INDUCTANCE

A color coding system is used to differentiate between the various conductors that are used for hot, neutral, and ground wires. The neutral is always white, colored with either paint, tape, or by the insulating rubber itself. If there is only one hot it will be black. If there are two hot legs the second will be red, and in three-phase the third will be blue. This practice is standard in North America. Ground wires are always green. Grounding an electrical device is a matter of safety and should not be taken lightly. Serious electrical shocks can cause severe burns, and if the electron flow passes through vital organs, death can easily result.

Electricity follows along a path of least resistance. Ground wires are used to provide a safe and easy pathway for electrons that have been misdirected due to some mechanical malfunction. Without a ground, your body may in effect become the path of least resistance should you inadvertently come into contact with a hot wire or some piece of metal that has come into contact with that wire. A copper ground wire is a better conductor than the human body, and the current will take that route if it is available.

A mishap with sparks and misdirected current is generally referred to as a short circuit, or short, meaning that the circuit pathway being taken by the electricity has been shortened. The current takes a new pathway and the device will malfunction. Most likely a fuse or circuit breaker will blow.

A related, but altogether different wiring problem, is that of a loose connection leading to an open circuit. Here the circuit path is broken, but no new pathway is found. This can often occur when a wire has come loose inside a connector or lighting instrument, or when a wire has been bent one too many times and breaks. If this happens inside the wire's insulation it may not be apparent from a visual inspection. Generally, the device will just not switch on. Sometimes a loose connection will result in the electricity arcing, in that electrons will jump over a small air gap in order to reach their normal pathway, much like the spark plug in a car. This may cause a light to flicker on and off. Arcing can create tremendous heat and can easily lead to a fire. It can be diagnosed by noting melted plastic, black scorch marks, or pitting of metal surfaces. The methods of troubleshooting short circuits and/or loose connections are different, and it helps to be able to distinguish between the two problems. Most commonly, a loose connection is known for failing so that the device does not work at all, or is intermittent. A short circuit will almost always trigger the circuit protection.

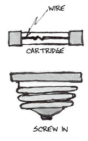

WIRE

CARTRIDGE

SCREW IN

SMALL FUSE TYPES

Fuses and/or circuit breakers are intended to protect an electrical system against a flow of electrons which is too much for it to handle. This can happen when a short allows all available electricity to flow through a system like a dam bursting. Overloading is a slower and more problematic cause. Virtually all electrical devices are rated at a certain number of amps. The ampere rating is an indication of the amount of electricity that can safely flow through the device. Sometimes too great a load may be placed on a wiring or dimming system. This is known as an overload. Many times it is the result of too many lights being plugged into one circuit or dimmer. When too great an electron flow passes through a conductor, resistance to this flow will cause the conductor to heat up. Too much heat can cause insulation to melt, and fires to occur.

Resistance can be put to a good use in circuit protection devices. Fuses contain a strip of metal that has been carefully chosen to be of just the right size to heat up, melt, and break the circuit when a predetermined load limit has been reached. Fuses can provide this protection only one time, because after the metal strip has been melted, it cannot be repaired. Fuses should be discarded after they have blown. Jumping across a fuseholder with wire or any other piece of metal creates an extremely hazardous situation because it removes the protective action and can allow wires to overheat to the melting point.

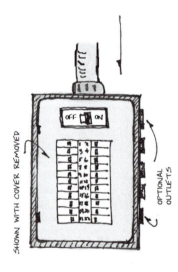

BREAKER PANEL

Another type of circuit protection is the circuit breaker. Breakers use either electromagnets or bimetal strips to stop electron flow. In either type of breaker, an excess of current causes a spring-loaded switch to trip within the breaker, and current is stopped. This switch should be reset only after the cause of the overload has been found and corrected.

TYPICAL
CIRCUIT BREAKER

MEASURING ELECTRICITY

The three basic units for measuring electricity are volts, watts, and amps. It is important to understand the theoretical relationship between them in order to understand how electricity can be used safely. Oftentimes mentioning these three words in the same breath can cause a student's eyes to glaze over, but this need not necessarily be the case. A practical understanding of these three concepts is easily reached when they are viewed in a logical manner.

As shown earlier, a change in voltage causes a change in the brightness of a lightbulb. This is how dimmers work, by varying the amount of voltage supplied to a lamp. Although dimmers may alter voltage in one of several ways, it is a reduction in the voltage pressure that causes the light to dim. Voltage is a measurement of the pressure of the current that is passing through a wire. It is often compared with water pressure, and there are many similarities between the two. Imagine that you need to water the lawn. You lay out a hose that is a conductor for the water just like a wire is a conductor for electricity. A sprinkler can be likened to a lightbulb, or any other electrical device that does work. When you crack open the faucet a small amount, the sprinkler will have a bit of water spurt out, but it will not go far, and if the sprinkler is a type that rotates, it will barely turn. Notice that as you turn the handle and increase the water pressure that the sprinkler rotates faster and faster. This is much the same as increasing the voltage to a light bulb and having it get brighter and brighter.

Wattage is a measurement of how much power is actually consumed by an electrical load when it is performing its work. A lightbulb that puts out more light also consumes more power. A 100-watt bulb puts out more light than a 25-watt bulb, but it also uses more power. A larger sprinkler will spray water over a larger area, but it will use more water in the process.

It could be said that the wattage of any particular load is an indication of how much electricity is being transformed by that device into some other form of energy. Blow dryers create heat and moving air. Lamps create light and heat. A washing machine converts electricity into motion. If you look on the back of an electrical device, you will likely find a record of its power requirements. Anything with a plug should list 110VAC 60Hz, and also some indication of the power it will consume. Lightbulbs have a wattage rating and so do blow dryers and microwave ovens. Some devices have an amperage rating instead.

Amperage is a unit that describes how much current is flowing in a circuit, but it can also be used to express how much power is available to be used. We have all had the experience of plugging one too many things into an outlet and having the breaker that protects it trip and cut the power. If you were to look into the breaker panel at your home, you might see that the main breaker is rated at 200 amps. This means that there are 200 amps of electricity available to power all of the devices in your home.

If you were to turn on everything in the house, all the lights, stoves, dryers, open the refrigerator, and then go next door to borrow all of their reading lamps and blow dryers, bring them back, and plug them in too, you would most likely trip that main breaker. Of course you would have to divide the loads evenly among the individual breakers to prevent tripping them before the main breaker. As you will recall, circuit breakers are there to protect the wiring from overheating. The amperage rating of different appliances is a reflection of how much electricity will pass through them when they are in operation. The amperage rating of a breaker tells how much current can pass through it before it trips.

So what is the relationship between watts, volts, and amps? George Simon Ohm discovered that there is a mathematical relationship between power in watts, current flow in amperes, electric potential in volts, and resistance in ohms. All of these units are named for scientists who made important discoveries.

Ohm's law states that *power* (watts) is equal to *current* (amps) times *voltage* (volts), and further, that *voltage* is equal to the *current* times the *resistance* (Ohms). The letters used to represent these measurements are:

P = power in watts
I = current in amps
E = voltage in volts
Ω = resistance in ohms

The Greek letter omega is the symbol for ohms.

The relationship between power, current, and voltage is often called the "pie" formula and it is written as P = IE. That makes it easy to remember. The second formula involving resistance is I R = E. The pie formula is much more commonly used in stage work.

P = IE

Power Formula

A very practical application of the P=IE formula can be found in calculating how many lights of a certain wattage can be used on a circuit with a breaker of a known capacity, when that capacity is expressed as an amperage rating. In practical applications, voltage is usually assumed to be a constant 120 volts. Although you already know that is not really the case, and especially not when dimmers are used to vary the voltage. It must be assumed for safety reasons however, that any dimmer will at some point reach a value of 100% and develop its entire 120-volt output.

If you wish to connect two 500-watt lamps to one dimmer, the amperage required to power them with 120 volts can be calculated mathematically. First add the total number of watts, 2 x 500 watts = 1,000 watts, so that is the total wattage on the circuit. The voltage value is a constant at 120 volts. These numbers may now be plugged into the P=IE formula, and expressed as 1,000 = I x 120. The unknown is I, the number of amps required. The problem can be transposed to I = 1,000/120. Dividing 1,000 by 120 results in a figure of approximately 8.3, to the nearest tenth, which is certainly close enough in lighting work. The most common amperage rating for small dimmers is 20 amps. As 8.3 is smaller than 20, it is easy to see that the two 500 watt lamps will easily fit into this dimmer. Of course you should inspect the actual dimmer system you are using to discover the exact amperage rating of the dimmers in it.

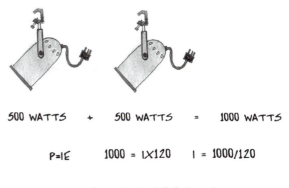

500 WATTS   +   500 WATTS   =   1000 WATTS

P=IE   1000 = IX120   I = 1000/120

CURRENT EQUALS 8.3 AMPS

There are a couple of shortcuts that may prove useful. Using the PIE formula, you can also describe a 20 amp dimmer as being a 2,400 watt dimmer, and 30 amps will provide a 3,600 watt power supply. By using this method it is only necessary to add the wattages of the various loads and compare this total to the capacity of the dimmer itself. For example 750 +750+ 750 = 2,250, which is less than 2,400 watts or 20 amps. 575+575+575+575= 2300.

You may have noticed a discrepancy where many devices use a voltage rating of 110 or 117 volts, while most dimmers consistently have a nameplate rating of 2.4kW. This is because theatrical lighting engineers use a nominal voltage figure of 120 volts to do the calculations. This amount is actually a much more practical figure. As previously discussed the voltage present in practical circuits is somewhat variable.

A second shortcut uses 100 volts as a constant when computing the number of amps required. This will do two things. Since 100 is smaller than 120, using it as the divisor will cause the answer you get for the number of amps to be a bit larger than the answer the 120 divisor would give you. This provides for a safety factor; 1,000 watts translates to 10 amps, and 1,500 to 15 amps. As should be apparent, this also permits the arithmetic to be simplified so that all that is really necessary is to move the decimal point two places to the left. In this way 1,000 becomes 10, 1,500 becomes 15, 2,000 becomes 20, and so forth. This is a good method for making rough estimates in your head. Of course it is not as accurate as the longer method.

Always keep in mind that although electricity has been a great boon to mankind, it can also be quite dangerous. When working with large amounts of current, do not go beyond your knowledge of the subject. Do not touch anything electrical (except the Energizer Bunny) unless you are absolutely certain of the hazards involved.

HOW DIMMERS WORK

There are three basic kinds of dimmers: resistance, auto-transformer, and SCR. They each work in very different ways, but the end result is that each one reduces voltage to a given circuit as a means of dimming lighting. Auto-transformers and SCRs are used almost exclusively in lighting circuits. Many years ago, resistance dimmers were used for lighting, but it would be difficult to find one still in use at the present time. Even so, resistance dimmers are often used as volume controls on radios and other sound devices. They are also used on manual boards like a two-scene preset. In these applications they are only controlling a very small voltage that in turn controls something else. On a lighting board the "sliders" typically manipulate a 0- to 10-volt signal to operate a dimmer that actually controls current to the lights themselves.

A resistance dimmer is placed in series with the load. The resistance of the "potentiometer," as they are often called, is variable according to the position of the knob or slider. When the resistance is high, most of the voltage in the circuit is expended across the "pot." When the resistance is low, more voltage is applied across the intended load. The main drawback to resistance voltage control is that current is being consumed at all times, and this can be very wasteful at higher voltages. It is not so problematic at low voltages. Old resistance dimmers got very hot, because they converted all of the unneeded electrical energy into heat energy.

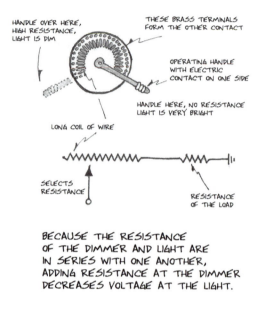

BECAUSE THE RESISTANCE OF THE DIMMER AND LIGHT ARE IN SERIES WITH ONE ANOTHER, ADDING RESISTANCE AT THE DIMMER DECREASES VOLTAGE AT THE LIGHT.

Auto-transformer dimmers use a variable transformer to alter voltage, and could more properly be called a variable transformer. (Some are.) Transformers use coils of wire to "transform" a voltage from high to low or vice versa. The length of the wire in the coil, and the proximity of the coils to one another determine the various voltages. In a standard power transformer, the coils have set values. In an auto-transformer the two coils can be rotated into and out of, proximity to one another. Moving the coils back and forth varies the amount of voltage that is induced from one to the other. Dimmers of this type tend to be very heavy and difficult to operate physically because they contain huge coils of very heavy wire. They can only be controlled by mechanical power, such as a human arm or a motor. This makes them problematic for use with a computer light board, so auto-transformers now have a limited use in stage lighting. They are still used architecturally in some specific ways, and are a good example of how transformers work.

SCR and other types of electronic dimmers are very common in stage lighting. They can be controlled by a digital signal from a computer, and this opens the door for much more complicated lighting design schemes for the designer. An SCR or Silicon Controlled Rectifier is a type of semiconductor transistor that can turn a circuit on and off. Electronic dimmers are actually very fast switching devices. They switch power on and off at a very fast rate, so fast that it is not apparent to the human eye. They are used to "chop" up the alternating sine curve of AC power into small chunks that can be either on or off. AC voltage is commonly expressed as an average amount since it is constantly changing anyway. The Root Mean Square (RMS) method is used to take this average.

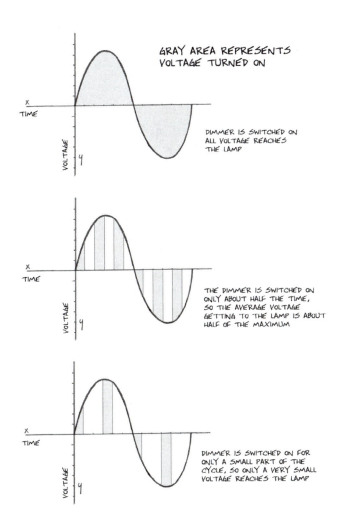

LIGHTING INSTRUMENTS

There are many different types of theatrical lights, but the few discussed here are by far the most commonly used. The largest manufacturers, such as Altman, Strand Century, ETC, and Major, have somewhat different engineering approaches to the manufacture of lighting equipment, but the actual workings of the lights themselves are more or less the same. The most often used theatrical lights are the ellipsoidal, Fresnel, PAR light, and strip or border light. In recent years moving fixture lights have become much more available and widely used, especially in the concert industry.

Virtually all theatres use some form of c-clamp to attach lights to a pipe such as a boom or an electric. This is a specialized clamp that is able to grasp a round pipe easily. At the bottom of the c-clamp is a $1/2$" bolt that connects the clamp to the yoke. It also allows the light to move from side to side. Most of the time the yoke is a piece of flat steel that is bent into a U shape. It curves around the sides of the body of the light and is attached on either side with bolts or handles. They allow the light to move up and down.

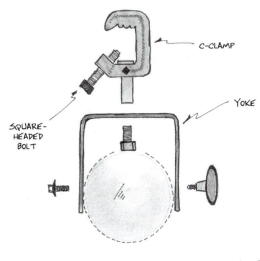

MOUNTING HARDWARE

The actual peak voltage of an alternating current sine wave is much higher than the average voltage. If the sine curve is chopped up so that voltage is present inside parts of the curve, but absent from other parts, then the resulting average will be lower still. When the voltage output is tested with a suitable meter, the RMS average voltage is a function of how much of the sine curve has been removed by switching the circuit on and off. The voltage can be so low as to keep the light bulb filament from incandescing, and no light will come out of it. Or the switching rate can be adjusted so that all of the voltage coming into the dimmer is applied to the light.

If the light is to be secured to a truss or tower, then the yoke is usually bolted straight to that frame with no clamp. Some tour lights are bolted on to six or eight-foot sections of unistrut so that they are hung as a group in order to speed up hanging. The unistrut is fitted with two clamps, one at either end. Clancy clamps are used instead of normal c-clamps. Clancy manufactures a quick attachment clamp that is spring loaded with a retaining nut that can be closed very quickly by hand and requires no wrench. Strip lights have a half yoke and a c-clamp at either end.

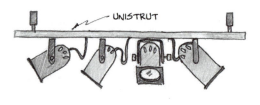

PAR CANS HUNG ON UNISTRUT

On the front of a light is a slot where gel frames may be fitted. On the back is a power cord, or pigtail, that is used to plug the light into a circuit. Most lights have either handles or bolts (or both) on the side, which are used to secure the light from tilting up and down.

FRESNEL

The Fresnel is perhaps the oldest kind of still existing lighting instrument and has been around longer than any of the others listed here. It was named for the man who invented the type of lens they use. August Fresnel knew that light passing through a dense medium such as glass is slowed, and the trajectory of the beam is altered.

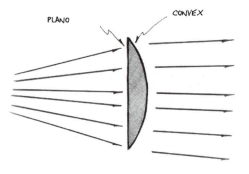

LIGHT REFRACTION
THRU A PLANO-CONVEX LENS

Glass lenses that are thicker in the middle tend to concentrate light passing through them into a more coherent beam. This type of lens is known as a plano-convex lens when it is flat on one side and curved outward on the other. The problem that Fresnel faced was that these lenses were very thick and often cracked from the heat of the light source.

Monsieur Fresnel discovered that the curvature of the convex side could be stepped back as long as the curvature on the surface remained constant. This resulted in a much thinner lens, which is helpful in preventing cracking due to heat expansion and contraction. In reality, the stepped concept doesn't work all that great because of all the inaccuracies

that creep in during the manufacturing process, but the optics in a Fresnel don't need to be too terribly precise. In fact, most of the lenses are "pebbled" with a rough texture on the back so that the light emitted is more diffuse. This helps to cover up any irregularities in the beam of light. Fresnel was actually working on lighthouse fixtures that are much larger and more powerful than your typical theatrical unit. Hence the heat build-up factor was much more important.

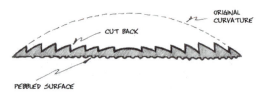

FRESNEL LENS

Fresnels use a reflector that is shaped like a segment of a sphere to bounce light vaguely back in the direction of the lens. Both the lamp and the reflector are fastened to a "sled" that can be moved back and forth, toward or away from the lens. The closer the sled is to the lens, the more spread out the beam pattern will be. This position is referred to as flood. (Just remember, forward = flood.) When the sled is moved away from the lens, the beam output is sharpened into a position known as spot. There are an infinite number of stops in between the two extremes.

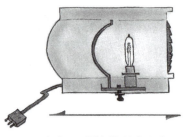

SLED MOVES BACK AND FORTH

Regardless of the number of degrees of beam spread, the light output of a Fresnel is always somewhat diffuse, with a bright or "hot" spot in the center, and a gradual lessening of intensity toward the edge of the beam. A common accessory used in limiting the beam spread of a Fresnel is a set of "barn doors." Essentially, barn doors are hinged metal flaps on a mounting plate that can be fitted into the gel frame at the front of the light. They are especially popular in a television studio. By adjusting the angle of the flaps it is possible to mask the leakage of unwanted ambient light that tends to angle obliquely outward from the imperfect Fresnel lens. A "top hat" is a rounded masking device based on the same principle.

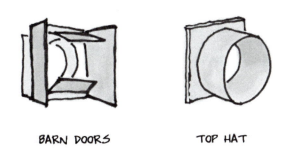

BARN DOORS   TOP HAT

The most common sizes of Fresnels are those that are six or eight-inches in diameter. Larger Fresnels are common in television and film. On occasion, Fresnels are called by their lamp wattages, such as a 2 or 5K (2,000watt or 5,000watt).

It is interesting to note that ETC does not currently offer a Fresnel lighting instrument in its family of theatre lights. Apparently ETC feels that the Source Four "Parnel" style lamp can provide the same functions as a Fresnel without the complexity involved in offering another line of fixtures. The trusty old Fresnel may be on its way out as a theatre light.

ELLIPSOIDAL REFLECTOR SPOTLIGHT

Sometimes ellipsoidals are called Lekos, because they were developed by two people named Lee and Cook. (That was in the 50s, hence the "Krazy K".) Their company used that as a trade name. Ellipsoidals are the workhorse units of the theatre and account for a majority of the fixtures used. Their main advantage lies in the type of optics used and consequently their ability to shape the light beam they produce. An ellipsoidal can be used in more subtle ways than other kinds of lights because it can be more finely controlled. They are used extensively in theatre because theatre lighting is a more subtle art form than TV or concert lighting. TV lighting tends to center around high wattage Fresnels, and concerts (where the PAR once was king) now use moving fixture lights almost exclusively.

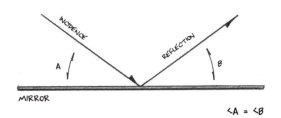

LIGHT RAY IS REFLECTED AT THE SAME ANGLE IT STRIKES THE MIRROR

As the longer name implies, a Leko utilizes an elliptically shaped reflector. A well known axiom about the reflection of light states that the angle of incidence is equal to the angle of reflection, meaning that a light ray will be reflected at the same but opposite angle at which it hit the reflector.

An elliptically shaped reflector puts this principle to good use. By definition, an ellipse has two focal points. If you extend a straight line from one focal point to the ellipse, and then back to the other focal point, the angle on either side of the two lines will be the same. If a lamp is placed at the first focal point, the reflector will send all the light rays emanating from it back to the second focal point. This means that most of the light from the lamp is concentrated at the second focal point. Of course there are some light rays that never hit the reflector at all, because the system has imperfections. Light that is uncoordinated is call ambient light, and it tends to spill out in the most unwelcome places.

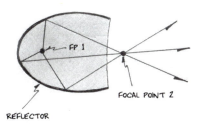

HOW THE ELLIPTICAL REFLECTOR WORKS

Still, this method of coordinating light rays is very efficient. Once the light has been concentrated at the second focal point, the rays cross over themselves and are then further concentrated by a pair of plano-convex lenses. Plano-convex lenses focus light into a tighter pattern as described earlier.

This system results in a very coherent light beam that is quite uniform in intensity from one side to the other. A modern ellipsoidal uses a double set of thinner plano-convex lens rather than one thick one. By varying the placement of the lenses, the output may be brought into a sharp focus. These qualities of high intensity, a coherent beam, and adjustable focus account for the most useful feature of an ellipsoidal, its ability to shape the light beam.

It is possible to mask part of the light beam when it is in the space between the two focal points and then to project the resulting shape onto the stage itself. The area of an ellipsoidal where shaping of the beam occurs is known as the gate. The shaping operation occurs before the light rays have merged and crossed over themselves at the second focal point. Consequently, any masking that takes place will appear as reversed when the beam reaches the stage. The optics in an ellipsoidal are quite similar to those in a slide projector.

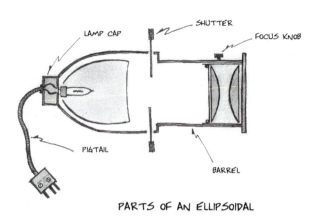

PARTS OF AN ELLIPSOIDAL

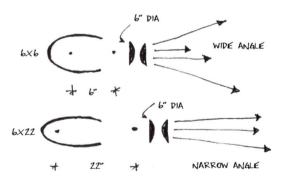

GOBO HOLDER WITH A BREAK-UP PATTERN IN IT

Two different approaches may be taken to masking the beam. The most common is to use shutters, four thin pieces of metal that slide in and out of the gate and are a permanent part of the instrument. Shutters can make the beam of light into a semicircle, or a square, or, by angling the shutters, a triangle. Shutters are quite useful in shaping the light to fit a specific object such as a window or a door.

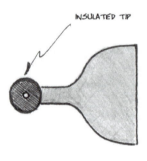

INSULATED TIP

SHUTTER

The second type of masking creates actual patterns of light with very thin stainless steel sheets that have been chemically etched into complex shapes such as leaf patterns, clouds, starbursts, or windowpanes. Hundreds of different types are available. These patterns are also known as gobos or templates. Patterns of this type are put into holders and inserted into a slot next to the shutters.

In order to project properly, patterns must be inserted upside down and backward, similar to slides in a slide projector. Shutters work in the same way, so that the left shutter affects the right side of the beam, the bottom the top of the beam, and so forth. It is not possible to shape the output with barn doors, top hats, or any other equipment that is fitted into the gel frame holder, although these are sometimes used to mask away ambient light created by imperfections in the instrument.

The light coming out of an ellipsoidal increases at a given angle, and the farther away the light is from the stage the more spread out its pool of light will be. Theatres have specific lighting positions that are at different distances away from the "target." It is important to have lights with different angles of beam spread so that the various distances can be accommodated. Otherwise, a great deal of efficiency would be lost from shuttering away too much of the light pool on some occasions, while at other times the shaft of light from the ellipsoidal might be too small to cover the intended part of the stage.

6" DIA

6x6

WIDE ANGLE

6"

6" DIA

6x22

NARROW ANGLE

22"

FOCAL LENGTH AND BEAM ANGLE

Traditionally, ellipsoidals were named and rated according to two factors, the diameter of the lens and the distance between the two focal points. A newer system gives a degree angle spread for a specific light. It is the designer's responsibility to determine which angles are appropriate, but it is important to know how the choices are made so that you can understand the logic behind them.

There are several ways to describe the size and use of ellipsoidals. The most popular lens diameter is six inches, but other sizes are available. Generally speaking, larger diameter lenses enable a bigger fixture that can hold a higher wattage lamp. Of course, the larger the lighting instrument is, the more difficult it is to hang and focus. Six-inch diameter lights have proven to be a comfortable size.

The distance between the focal points in a light determines the amount of spread that occurs in the beam angle. The farther apart the two focal points are, the narrower the angle will be. Focal lengths for traditional lights in the six-inch-diameter size range from six inches to twenty-two inches. The beam spread of a 6×6 is much wider than the beam output of a 6×22, and as a result, the pool of light emitted by the 6×6 (at the same distance) will cover more area on the stage than the 22 will. Generally, a 6×6 is intended to be used from a hanging position that is very close to the lighting area, whereas 6×22s are usually hung from a far distance. As you can see, the lens diameter is always written first, and the focal point spread second. The most common sizes are 6×6, 6×9, 6×12, and 6×22.

There is a newer system that uses a different approach in describing and creating the beam angle spread. Some manufacturers' fixtures are designed so that they all use the same housing, and different lens arrangements are used to produce the different beam angle spreads. These range from a very narrow angle of 5 degrees to a wide angle of 50 degrees. It is possible to purchase extra lenses so that one body can produce different angles by switching lens tubes. It is also possible to rotate the shutter section, making it easier to angle the shutters to an odd position.

PARABOLIC ALUMINIZED REFLECTOR SPOT

PAR cans are essentially round car headlights that have been manufactured to operate at 110 volts, rather than at the standard automobile voltage of 12v. The fixtures themselves are very simple, lightweight, and inexpensive because all of the optics have been built into the lamp itself. As a consequence, PAR lamps tend to be somewhat expensive. It is the nature of a parabolic reflector that it reflects straight outward whatever light rays strike it. So the lens is really meant to slightly blur the light beam into a more homogenous pool.

PAR cans were the standard rock-and-roll light for many years because they are so lightweight and durable, and because rock shows do not require a great deal of precision in focusing. The beam that comes from a "can" is similar to that generated by a Fresnel, except that it is oval in shape and the

instrument does not allow for changing from spot to flood. Instead, a variety of lamps may be used. They range in angle from wide to medium to narrow to very narrow. Even narrower ACL lamps may be used, but these require a different voltage as described earlier. The obvious disadvantage to this system is that the entire lamp must be changed rather than simply cranking from spot to flood.

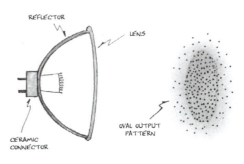

PAR LAMP

It is possible to rotate the lamp within its housing in order to change the orientation of the oval beam shape from vertical through horizontal, in accordance with how the light can best cover its intended area.

PAR cans come in either black steel or shiny aluminum versions. The gel frame holder has a spring-loaded clip at the top to prevent the frame from sliding out during transport. Cans come in two main sizes, the 64 and the 56, with a few oddballs in the 38 category. PAR 64s are far and away the most common. The peculiar sizes refer to the diameter of the lamp given in one-eighths of an inch. (64=8")

A newer type of PAR is very different from the traditional light. It has a standard reflector and lamp, and the lens is changed to alter the beam angle of the light. A ring known as the "bottle" is rotated to change the direction of the oval, and that oval is much less pronounced than in a regular PAR. These fixtures are much more expensive than a regular PAR can, but they have the advantage of using a much cheaper lamp that just happens to be the same lamp as is used in many other lights. A cheaper lamp really starts to make sense the longer you use the fixture.

STRIP LIGHTS

Strip lights are also known as border lights and on occasion are referred to as x-rays by a few elderly stagehands. As the name implies, they are lamps that are manufactured in strips, where a number of lamps are ganged together in a parallel circuit. The typical unit has two or four lamps in each circuit, depending mostly on the size and/or wattage of the lamps. Mini Strips have a large number of very small lamps placed in groups of two. The standard hookup uses a staggered approach so that the lamps are lit in this fashion: ABCDABCDABCD. The alternation provides for a more even spread of light from each of the groups.

By plugging several strip light units together end to end, it is possible to create a swath of light across the entire stage, and/or as they are most commonly used, across a sky cyclorama. Strip lights allow you to have several different groups of evenly spaced lights that are independent of one another. By using different colors in each circuit, colors on the cyc can be mixed together. If red, green, and blue are used (the primary colors for lighting) a theoretically infinite color range may be achieved.

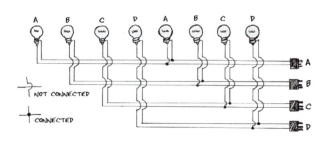

PARALLEL CIRCUITS IN A STRIP LIGHT

It is generally best to use one set of strip lights from above, and another one on the stage floor to achieve an equal distribution on the cyc. A scenic ground row is often used to mask the bottom strips. Confusingly, the bottom strips themselves are also referred to as a ground row, and that term can be used to describe either the lights or the scenery. Many theatres use strip lights as work lights for the stage. This is very common in older theatres as well as public school theatres. Lamp sizes and styles are quite varied, and strip lights are often described by their length, such as a six-foot or eight-foot strip. The standard old-style border lights use ordinary PS or A-shaped medium screw base lightbulbs, but newer types use high wattage quartz lamps. Round glass color filters, known as roundels, are often used on the older lights.

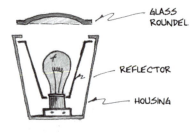

OLD-STYLE STRIPLIGHT

Strip light circuits are easy to overload because of the large number of individual lamps that are used. Care should be taken to determine the individual lamp wattage and multiply it by the total number of lamps in use. Compare this wattage rating with the dimmer capacity, or use the P=IE formula to convert to amps. One development in strip light technology is the Mini Strip, which uses tiny 12-volt lamps wired in series of ten (accounting for 120 volts). A three-circuit strip has thirty of these lamps in it. They are worth mentioning just to get one more insight into how a series circuit changes voltage. The advantage to this fixture is that it is very slim and will fit into tight spaces. Also, the sheer number of tiny lamps ensures a more even wash on a cyc. However, they can be a real pain when one of the lamps blows, and it is necessary to locate the offending bulb by the trial-and-error method.

Coming out with a new kind of lamp is a very expensive proposition for a lighting manufacturer. It would not be cost-effective to invent an entirely new lamp just to use in the Mini-Strip. It makes much more sense to design the fixture around very small low-voltage lamps developed for use in homes and businesses.

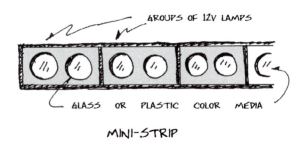

MINI-STRIP

MOVING FIXTURE LIGHTS

This heading covers a lot of territory, because there are many new types of moving fixture lights. This corner of the market is just beginning to really blossom as their cost has fallen. The generic name "moving fixture light" reflects the notion that the light itself can move under its own power. These lights can pan and tilt all on their own, but even more than that, most are able to change colors, change beam angle, and many can change and rotate gobos. Color changing is accomplished using a dichroic filter, a prismatic device that changes white light to different colors by tilting the angle of the filter to a pre-determined setting used for that color. Prismatic action selects the desired hue.

There are two main categories of moving fixture lights that are based on how they produce the motion. In the earliest fixture designs, the entire light was made to move. There is a large motorized yoke that allows the center part of the fixture to tilt up and down, while the yoke itself pans from side to side. Most cannot spin an entire 360 turn, but must stop and go back if necessary.

The other basic type are lights that use a mirror to move the light beam. All of the mechanics of the fixture are stationary except for a mirror that is angled to reflect the light beam in different directions. This type saves on the complexity of large moving parts. Curiously, these lights tend to be somewhat larger that the original type. Both varieties are still in full production.

The moving fixture concept was made viable because of the development of a complex control mechanism. Originally, it was necessary to use a computerized lighting control board designed specifically for these lights. They operate from a DMX (Digital MultipleXing) signal but require many different channels to control the various light functions of panning, tilting, color changing, etc. That was problematic to program on a standard lighting console. Newer theatre control boards accommodate the increased demands of moving fixture lights, although a board designed specifically for them has more options.

The concert lighting industry has been completely changed by the technological revolution of these new systems. How far they will go in legitimate theatres remains to be seen. It is hard to imagine how moving fixture lights could be used to improve a production of *Uncle Vanya*, but it is easy to see their value for *Jesus Christ Superstar*.

LIGHT PLOTS

The designer should provide a light plot. It should be a scale representation of the theatre and its lighting positions, showing the lighting equipment types in their proper locations. Computer-Aided-Design (CAD) plots are often used. CAD programs come into their own in lighting design because they are really good at keeping track of all the numbers used for dimmers, channels, circuits, gel colors, and the like. It is also much easier to add and delete lights on the computer and then print out a new plot than it is to start over from scratch the old way. However, it should be noted that there were many very artistically satisfying lighting designs created in advance of CAD technology. The computer just makes the paperwork a lot easier.

The aesthetic quality of individual light plots tends to vary greatly, but there is a general consensus about the information that should be on the plot. If your designer shows up with some scribbles on the back of a paper bag, you have my permission to laugh and say "No way!" Of course, then you have to hang it anyhow.

The plot should include a legend, which is a guide to the meanings of various symbols for different types of lights and to the numbering system for gel color, circuit numbers, dimmer channel numbers, and instrument numbers. This is just like the legend used on a road map to indicate types of roads, hospitals, airports, etc. Front-of-house positions should be labeled, as well as the battens being used as electrics. Electrics should have an indication of their trim height.

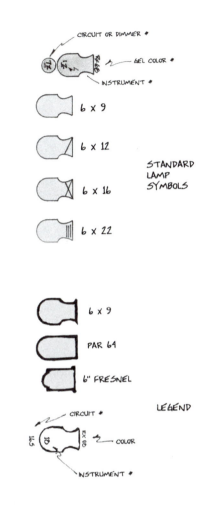

Some plots have marks on the battens at 18-inch centers. This is the most common spacing alternative for hanging instruments. Maintaining this spacing ensures adequate room to properly focus the lights. Using corresponding marks on the battens can make a light hang go really fast. If the design calls for lights to be too close together, focusing will become problematic somewhere down the road.

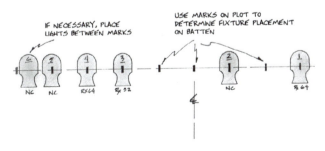

USING REGISTRATION MARKS TO AVOID MEASURING

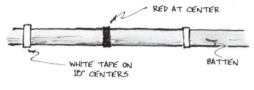

LIGHTING MARKS ON A BATTEN

If no marks are shown, it is necessary to "scale off" the placement of lights using a scale rule. Half-inch scale is standard for theatrical drawings of all types, but $1/4$" is also quite common. Generally, if you can get the measurements correct to within a few inches this will be close enough. An ordinary tape measure can work well if the plot is in $1/2$" scale. For that scale, one inch is two feet, an inch and one half is three feet, and so forth. Experienced designers tend to use a standard spacing, rather than making each space a different size. This speeds up the hang and leaves more time for focusing.

Hanging lights can be done very quickly if you organize the event before starting. Proper management is the key to success.

Research the plot to find gel colors, also the number and size that you will need of each one. Cut the gels and load them into the proper frames. Any sort of resident or university theatre will most likely have a filing cabinet with previously used gels stored in file folders. They are sorted according to the number each is assigned by the manufacturer. The colors have names too, but most everyone uses the numbers to specify. It is helpful to mark the color numbers with a china marker or a white lead pencil of some type. Do this right in the center of the gel, large enough to be easily read in the dark. The output of light and the quality of the color will not be noticeably affected, and readable labeling will make focusing much easier. Some purists will disagree with that, but the reduction in light output has never been apparent to me, so being a very practical and organized person, I always tend to want clear labels.

Holes are provided so that brass office brads may be used to secure the gel in the holder. Some people use tape instead, but over a period of time the intense heat generated by the light will cause the tape either to fall off, or to become permanently bonded to the frame, depending on the type of tape used. Tape can also be a fire hazard. The manufacturers clearly intend for brads to be used.

This is also a good time to prepare any patterns or gobos that may be required, as well as to find barn doors and other accessories.

HANGING THE LIGHTS

Electrics are the most straightforward hanging positions because they are generally the same in all theatres. Front-of-house positions vary greatly from space to space. These instructions are meant for an electric but can be adapted somewhat for FOH positions.

Fly in the batten to be used as the first electric. In a perfect world, it is best to hang your electrics before loading in any scenery that would be in the way. Select the lighting equipment needed for this electric, and place the lights in their approximate positions on the floor beneath the batten. If both the plan and the batten are marked with 18" centers it is an easy matter to count the number of marks to determine the exact placement of an instrument. If you do not have this luxury, it will be necessary to measure as previously described. In any case, you should always begin from the center and work toward the two sides because designers may be somewhat lax about drawing battens to their proper scale length. Starting at the end often causes the lights to be hung off center. The center of the batten is a well defined location.

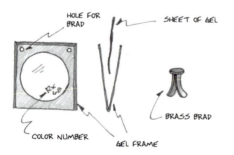

GEL FRAME HOLDER

ALWAYS MEASURE FROM THE CENTER OF THE PIPE

If you must measure the placement of lights with a tape, it is helpful to determine all of the measurements on the plot first, and then mark all of the places on the batten at one time, using a piece of chalk to mark the hanging locations. Have someone hold the end of the measuring tape at center while you do this. The crew can hang the lights on your marks and finger tighten the C-clamp bolts. After all the lamps are hung, it is a good idea to double-check placement with the plot, as this is the last time when it will be easy to move a light. C-clamps are constructed so that they will not come off unless the bolt is very, very loose. Finger tightening will prevent the lamps from falling during the short time that you are hanging and double-checking. When it is time to tighten the clamps with a crescent wrench, it is only necessary to tighten the bolts enough so that they are tight enough to not vibrate loose. Over-tightening with a giant wrench will damage both the clamp and the batten. Having one person go along and tighten all of the bolts in order at one time is an efficient way of ensuring that none of them are left loose accidentally. If you are not sure, it is always best to go through and double check.

Rotate the lights so that they are pointed vaguely in the direction shown on the plot. Most lights have a "this side up" issue that becomes obvious when you look at the gel frame holder. Check to see that all the handles and bolts used in focusing are snug, but not overly tight. Make sure that all shutters are pulled out on all of the Lekos. Shutters are often completely closed when the fixture is in storage. In that position, they don't allow any light to escape and will turn a 1,000 watt ellipsoidal into a 1,000 watt heater. The shutters will soon warp out of shape to a point where they will need to be replaced.

Safety cables should be attached so that they go around the yoke of the light and also around the batten. This will keep the light from falling should someone have forgotten to tighten the C-clamp. You are now be ready to cable and circuit the electric.

If your theatre is equipped with plugging strips that are permanently attached to dedicated electric battens, this process is very easy. Simply plug the lights into the nearest circuit and record the number on the plot. Recording circuit numbers is essential so that a patching hook-up can be generated later on. A soft-patch in the dimmer board is used when the theatre has a dimmer-per-circuit system. If there is a patch panel to connect dimmers and circuits, the patch will be made there. In either case, you will need to know which dimmer or circuit is being used for which light.

The only concern with dedicated electrics is the fact that it limits the number of possible hanging positions. Drop boxes are much more difficult to work with, but they provide a high degree of flexibility. A drop box typically consists of a long piece of multicable (a large cable with many conductors) that ends with a box that contains a number of panel-mounted female connectors. The multicable extends downward from the grid, allowing the drop box to be moved around the stage. When lowering a drop box it is important to let the cable in directly over the batten so that the cable does not foul any of the surrounding battens. They will be needed for other work. Sometimes drop boxes are hung off to the side of the rigging system and are maneuvered with a pick line as shown in the chapter on theatres.

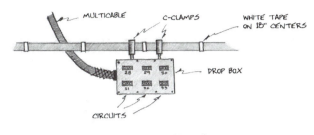

DROP BOX ON A BATTEN

A good method of attaching drop boxes to an electric is to use a C-clamp that has been bolted to the metal housing of the box. If this is not possible, be sure to use a stout line and a secure knot, because the box and cable are often surprisingly heavy.

You can determine the number of circuits needed, and hence the number of drop boxes, by counting the number of lights on the batten as described by the light plot. Sometimes the designer will know in advance that two or more lights will be ganged together into one dimmer and will show that on the plot. In this case it will not be necessary to provide an entirely different circuit for each one of these fixtures. The designer indicates ganged-together lights by drawing a line on the plot from one light to another, which is the normal way of indicating "two-fering" (two for one). A special twofer cable having one male plug connected with two female plugs is used for this purpose. Although it is the designer's responsibility to have determined in advance the proper power requirements dictated by connecting lamps together in this fashion, it is a good practice to double-check how much power will be required by the total number of lamps linked together by two-fering. This is especially true if two-fering becomes three-fering, or perhaps four-fering. Use the P=IE formula to do that. Some theatres use the branch-off, a device that allows three or even four lights to fit into one circuit.

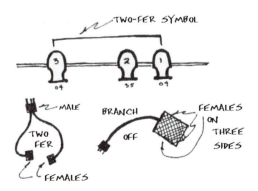

Extension cords used to connect the pigtail of a lighting instrument with a drop box circuit are referred to as jumpers, because they "jump" power from one location to another. Jumpers consist of a single circuit with a male plug at one end and a female at the other. Hopefully it is not necessary to describe which plug is which sex. It should be noted that male plugs are never "live," meaning that no electricity is supplied from them, but rather only to them. If this were not the case, electric shocks from the exposed prongs of the male plug would happen constantly. Female plugs are generally designed so that the conducting material is recessed back into the insulating material of the plug housing, and thus humans are shielded from the electricity. Only female connectors are a source of power.

Using jumpers to connect lights and circuits can be either very straightforward or a nightmare depending on how organized an approach you employ. Here is the method I have used to avoid cable snarls and mispatching.

Jumpers of varying lengths are needed to cover the distance from the fixture pigtails to circuit boxes. It is helpful to color code the different jumper lengths with vinyl electrical tape so that you can easily tell them apart. Then it is possible to tell at a glance which jumper is the proper one for the job. All cables should be fastened to the batten with tie line. Do not use tape or wrap the cable itself round the batten repeatedly. These two inferior methods are quite difficult to remove after the show is over, and the entertainment business is all about changing from one show to another.

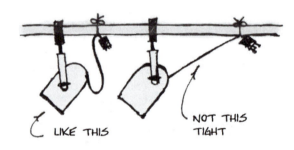

Jumpers usually have a piece of tie line attached to keep them together when coiled and not in use. If you tie this piece of line a few inches from the female end, using a clove hitch so that it is permanently attached, it can also serve as the first tie used to secure the jumper to the batten. There are also some great little Velcro strips made for this purpose. Tie the female end near the C-clamp of the light to be connected. Tie it close enough so that there is enough slack in the pigtail for the instrument to pivot easily during focusing. Run the jumper along the floor and plug it into a circuit or dimmer. Record this number next to the light as it appears on the plot. Repeat this procedure until all of the lights have been plugged.

This is a good time to test the lights to make sure that all of the elements are in proper working condition (lights, jumpers, and drop box circuits). Patch each circuit into a load test, or run each dimmer to full one at a time. The exact method differs from system to system. Check each circuit one at a time and troubleshoot any problems as you go along. If there are individual circuits involved, it is best not to torture a dimmer by having it pop on at full repeatedly. Use a load test circuit or non-dim to do the testing. Non-dims are switches that operate through the lighting system to connect things like work lights and electric motors that will not function properly on less than 110 volts of electricity. With a dimmer per circuit system, you can just bring up the dimmers one at a time.

It is important to test your hang while it is on the ground and still relatively easy to troubleshoot. It is much easier to trade out or repair any faulty equipment before the batten is way up in the air. Make sure all of the shutters are pulled out and that safety cables are in place. Some designers like for the color to be put in now before the focus, and some like to do it after.

Once troubleshooting is over, and all the lamps are working, it is time to tie up the cables to the batten. Start at the end that is farthest from the drop boxes and use tie line to secure the cable. Put on a tie every four feet or so, and pick up the additional jumpers as you go along, tying them all at once using a bow knot. Thirty inches is a good length for tie lines because it will usually allow the line to be double wrapped around the cable. The two turns around the pipe makes it easier to get a tight bundle. If #4 black tie line is used, the ties can be recycled several times. When you reach the end where the drop box is, squish the excess cable against the batten and tie it on as neatly as possible. A bit of tidiness now will pay off when you focus, and will also help keep other flown pieces from snagging on the electric. Try to keep the rubber insulation of the jumpers away from the instrument housings, which get very hot during the show. The pigtail wires are usually OK, as they are manufactured with this in mind.

When the electric is ready to be flown out to its trim, use a small piece of gaffer's tape to secure the end of a 50- or 100-foot tape measure to the pipe before it goes up. Use the tape measure to determine when the batten has reached the proper trim height. Reel off the tape so that you can hold the exact length on the floor with your foot. When the slack is out of the tape you are at trim. Once the trim is set the tape measure can be yanked down. (Don't use too much gaff tape!)

Front-of-house positions are so varied that it is impractical to discuss how they may be hung or circuited, but the basic principles just covered should still apply.

When all of the lights have been plugged into various circuits, and a number identifies each of the circuits or dimmers, connections need to be made. In systems with a patch panel, circuits must be plugged into dimmers. Dimmer-per-circuit systems need to be soft patched. The default setting causes the dimmer numbers to equal the channel numbers. Assigning dimmers to specific channels makes it possible to have a rational order to the numbering system rather than the random order produced by hanging. Keep in mind that a dimmer is an actual piece of hardware. Channels are a method of renumbering dimmers so that they are easier to catagorize.

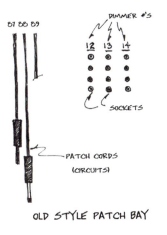

OLD STYLE PATCH BAY

The most common patch bay is the old plug or switchboard type. Male plugs at the ends of flexible cords hang down in front of a panel with sockets in it, much like an old-style telephone system (now only seen in old movies). There should be a list of numbers on the panel, which represent the dimmers that are available. Each dimmer number normally has several sockets next to it, so that you can plug more than one circuit into the same dimmer. Use the P=IE formula to determine that you are not asking too much of any one dimmer, and insert the male plugs into the sockets as required.

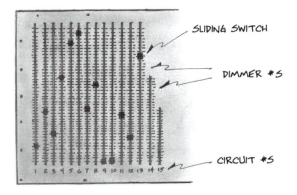

SLIDING CONTACT PATCH PANEL

Another method of patching is to use a system of sliders. In this type, each of the circuits is represented by a sliding contact switch that moves through a slot and connects with various contacts in the back, which represent the various dimmers and non-dims. You slide the knob along until it makes contact with the proper location. It is best to set up this type of panel with the power turned off to prevent unnecessary sparking and arcing. The concept of matching circuits and dimmers is the same as for the plug type.

These systems are for permanent installations. Sometimes individual cables are run to the dimmers themselves when the dimmers are near the stage and readily accessible, especially when dimmer "packs" of some sort are in use. The dimmer pack units themselves should have outlets on them that will make this possible. This is the sort of thing that you find in a touring situation. Tour packages are set up to operate using multicable and breakouts instead of individual jumpers, so that load in time is reduced.

The trend in lighting system design is definitely in the direction of the dimmer-per-circuit concept, but there are still plenty of all different types in use.

CABLES AND CONNECTORS

Wiring used in the theatre is different from the ordinary Romex that is used in a house. Theatrical wiring is by nature very temporary, and the National Electric Code takes note of this in the rules it lays down for theatres. Permanent wiring is most often done with solid core wire that is not meant to be moved after it has been installed. Repeatedly bending solid core copper wire will eventually cause it to break from metal fatigue, just like the steel wire in a clothes hanger will break if you bend it back and forth a number of times.

Portable cable is made from many small strands of copper wire that have been twisted together like a rope. Stranded wire is much more flexible and durable than the solid wire, and the same size is rated to carry more amperage. As a matter of physics, alternating current tends to pass along the surface of a conductor. Stranded cable has a lot more surface area than solid cable does.

The insulation used on these portable cables is different also. It must be capable of withstanding much more abuse than the insulation on wiring that spends its entire life protected inside a wall or metal conduit. A theatrical jumper requires a thick flexible coating of rubber, and the cable should be manufactured in such a way that the finished product is round like a rope rather than oval or flat, as this will make it much easier to coil. The American National Standards Institute sets the standards and nomenclature for all sorts of hardware and equipment. They (and the National Electric Code) describe the type of portable wire that may be used in a theatre as either type SO or the slightly smaller type SJ. The conductors inside are twisted together in a right-handed way, just like a rope.

ANSI and the NEC have also set up specifications as to the size of wire that may be used to carry a certain amount of electrical current. This is expressed as a gauge number. Twelve-gauge wire can be used to carry a 20-amp load, and this is the standard size used in theatres for a jumper. Since the circuit must be grounded, the wire will have three conductors and is usually described as 12/3 SO.

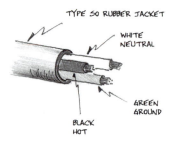

12/3 SO CABLE FOR JUMPERS

The 20-amp, 12-gauge wire is used because it matches up with the amperage rating of commonly used dimmers and connectors. All parts of an electrical delivery system should have the same amperage rating, or the chain will fail at its weakest link.

The most commonly used lighting connector is the pin connector. These have been around for many years, and in modern form consist of three metal pins that extend from a plastic housing. The pin in the center is for the ground wire. The pin closest to it is the neutral, and the remaining pin is used to connect the hot. Usually, the neutral terminal of any wiring device will have a nickel-plated set screw while the hot is the natural brass color, but this is a fairly recent standard which is not always seen on pin connectors. Although there are a few 60-amp pin connectors in use, the vast majority are rated at 20-amps. That is a good fit with the 20-amp SO cable and the 2400-watt dimmers.

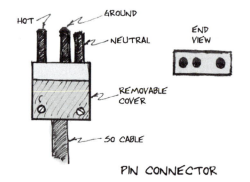

PIN CONNECTOR

Twist lock connectors have become quite popular in the past two decades. Notice that the blades have a slight L shape to them. When you press two connectors together and give a slight turn to the right, they lock together and will not come apart. (Sometimes it is necessary to tie pin connectors together.) Each of the blades is shaped a bit differently so that the connector will fit together only one way. This ensures that hots will not be accidentally be joined with neutrals or grounds. The only drawback is that the prongs or blades are much thinner and more delicate than those on a pin connector. They often require straightening. Pin connector pins are about the diameter of a pencil and are almost indestructible.

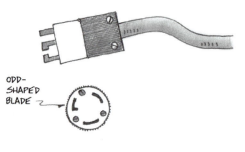

TWIST-LOCK CONNECTOR

There are dozens of different types of twist lock connectors that are intended for a variety of uses, and for many areas besides lighting. They are often used for chain motor power, and also to hook up sound PAs. When using twist locks for lighting purposes, you should make sure that you ask for a three-pin, 20-amp twist lock. Check the manufacturer's numbering system if you are matching existing plugs.

Solid wire can be bent into a hook, a shape that a terminal screw can easily grasp and hold down. This will not work with stranded wire because individual strands fray and warp out of shape, preventing the connection from carrying its full electrical load. SO cable should have terminals attached to the ends of the wires so that a firm connection is made when using pin and some other types of connectors. This kind of terminal is a small metal device that can be crimped onto the wire.

ELECTRICAL TERMINALS

Ring terminals have a closed loop and are available in either a straight or "flag" version. The flag type attaches at a right angle to the wire and is required for some kinds of pin connectors. You can tell which kind you need by looking at the inside of the connector. Terminal ends usually come with the device, but they can be purchased from an electrical supply house for repair work. Flag ring terminals will most likely have to come from a theatrical supplier, because it is an unusual item for most electrical supply houses. It is generally not necessary to use terminals for twist lock plugs because of the way their connections are made.

Touring shows and concert lighting companies use a number of different connector types for special purposes. Cam locks are used to connect heavy feeder cables. Cam locks are more commonly used for welding cable. Large multicable connectors may have up to forty, 20-amp pins. Some people refer to these simply as "military connectors." There is a similar type known as the Socapex that is smaller and designed for fewer conductors. When a multicable is prepared with many individual connectors at the end of its run, it is called a break out, or a fan out. This is done so that the cable can then be used to connect with individual lights.

CAM LOCK CONNECTORS ARE USED
ON SINGLE CONDUCTOR FEEDER CABLES

IF THE PICTURE WERE IN COLOR
YOU COULD SEE THE TAPE MARKS
THE DIFFERENT HOTS AND THE NEUTRAL

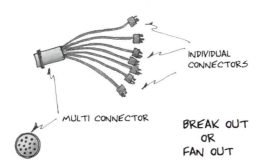

INDIVIDUAL
CONNECTORS

MULTI CONNECTOR

BREAK OUT
OR
FAN OUT

In the past few years, it has become increasingly common to use data cable to operate digital equipment like color changers and computer control boards. This digital information operates at an extremely low voltage, and very small conductors are sufficient. Four pin XLRs are used for DMX information. These look like the XLRs that are used for mic cables, but mic cables have only three pins. That standard three pin version is used to control many moving fixture lights.

Any extra time spent in carefully installing connectors will pay you back several fold in the long run. Make sure to use the correct terminals, and to properly connect the strain relief. The strain relief is a kind of clamp that keeps the wires from pulling out of the connector. Sometimes extra insulation is cut and placed in the strain relief to ensure a tight fit.

TROUBLESHOOTING

It is important to keep lighting equipment in proper working order because of the safety concerns that arise anytime 110 volt lines are used. Any piece of equipment that has been damaged or that is known to be faulty should be set aside for repair. It is quite common to see a wire pulled out, or a connector smashed by some heavy object. Sometimes it is difficult to tell just what part of a system is at fault. There are some easy ways to isolate the source of an electrical difficulty.

If a light fails to come on when you patch it into its circuit, unplug it and replug an adjoining light that is known to work into the suspect circuit. If the second light comes on, then power must be getting to the end of the jumper, and the problem is in the light itself. It is most likely a lamp failure. Most of the time a blown lamp is obvious, but if it is difficult to tell by eye, then use a continuity tester on the lamp's contacts. If the filament is intact you should find continuity through the bulb using a Volt-Ohm-Meter.

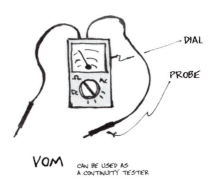

DIAL

PROBE

VOM CAN BE USED AS
A CONTINUITY TESTER

Quite often the lamp may not be seated properly in the socket, and you can try wiggling it back and forth, with the power off, of course. Bad contact with the socket is a very common problem. Especially with bi-pin lamps like the EHG or the HPL. Heat expansion and contraction often cause lamps to work themselves loose. Resetting the lamp in the socket may well be only a temporary fix, and quite often the socket must be replaced if it has become corroded.

If the lamp is good, then the problem might be in the lamp cap and/or the connector. It is fairly common for a wire to get pulled out of either one of these. Try the connector first because it is the easiest to check.

Going back to the beginning, if the second light did not come on when you plugged it into the suspect circuit, then no power was present at the plug. Try plugging a test lamp into the drop box, or whatever location the circuit came from. If there is power at the drop box, then the jumper is at fault. If there is no power at the drop box, double check to see that you have patched correctly and the dimmer is good. If all of these things are in order, call a licensed electrician to find out what is wrong with the building circuitry. This is almost never the case, but it does happen. Double-check all of your own work first.

You can see why it is easier to troubleshoot your electrics while they are still on the ground. Many times an electrician may make up a special test light with a theatrical connector and a small bulb to use in testing circuits. It can be carried in a pocket, ready for use. A cue light or a dance spotting light will work just as well.

SPECIAL EQUIPMENT

There are a few pieces of equipment that do not fit easily into any of the previous categories. You might not use them on every show, but they do come up often enough.

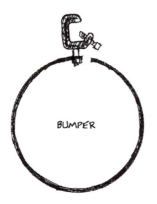

BUMPER

Bumpers are used on electrics whenever there is a working piece on the next batten that might get fouled in an instrument or knock one out of focus. A bumper is a section of flat iron bar that has been bent into a circle about 18 or 20 inches in diameter. A C-clamp is used to fasten the bumper to an electric at a convenient location along the pipe. You will most likely need three or four for each electric.

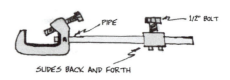

SIDE ARM

A side arm is used to attach lighting equipment that will not fit on the pipe in the normal way. It is really just a long extension of the yoke and C-clamp. Side arms can be used for other purposes. One of these is to prevent a batten from rolling. Lights are usually hung with the yoke pointing straight down, but sometimes there is a reason to yoke them out to the side, or even to hang them standing up on the top of the pipe. Sometimes this is to get a better angle with the light, and sometimes it is just a matter of getting more units into less space. At any rate, hanging lights to the side makes the pipe want to roll downward, and if you let this happen it will change the focus of the lights. To keep the pipe from rolling, fasten a side arm to the batten near one of the lift lines and then attach the pipe part to the aircraft cable with some tie line.

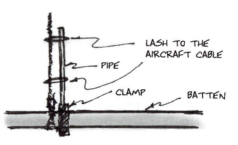

USE A SIDE ARM TO KEEP A BATTEN FIXED

A side arm can also work as a makeshift pipe wrench when the actual tool is not available. It can be used to tighten pipes into flanges or boom bases.

Booms are vertical pipes used to hang lights. Sometimes they are attached to the wall or some other architectural feature, and sometimes they are freestanding on a base. Boom bases are very heavy cast metal pieces that keep the pipe from falling over.

There are practical limits to how high you can take a boom before it is unsafe, and you must determine what that limit is for your particular situation. Sometimes it is possible to tie up the top of the boom as a safety. It is best to hang lights on a boom so that the load is balanced rather than to hang all of the fixtures on one side. A lighting tower is a much safer alternative when there is a large number of fixtures to hang and/or they must be very far off the floor. More information on towers can be found in the "How Do You Make..." chapter.

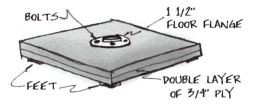

SHOP-BUILT BOOM BASE

You can quite easily make shop-built bases from some 3/4" plywood and a pipe flange. Use two layers of plywood for the base, and be sure to securely bolt the flange to the wood (this is very important!). Use 1 1/2" black steel pipe and the appropriate type of screw-on floor flange. Use a number of stage weights on top of the plywood to hold the base in place, or lag bolt it to the floor. These shop-built bases are excellent in a reduced size for small, one fixture floor mounts, especially if these lights are "rovers" (lights that get moved around during the show). If there is only one light on a floor mount, remove the clamp from the light and bolt the yoke directly to the wood.

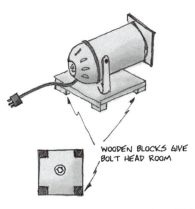

MAKE A SMALL BASE
FOR "ROVER" LIGHTS

FOCUSING

Focusing lights is like dancing a tango. You need to observe what your partner is doing, and be ready to respond. The lighting designer leads, and if the technician follows well, the job can be done very quickly. Sometimes on tour where the designer is not available, focusing is done with the stage manager instead.

Use a six- or eight-inch crescent wrench to focus lights. Some people use a safety line on the wrench, to prevent it from falling. The lights get hot in a hurry, so you might consider a pair of gloves, but they will definitely get in your way. If you are quick, the lights will not heat up enough to make the gloves necessary. Either a lift or a ladder is required to focus lights that are up in the air, which means almost all of those on an electric. It is best to have one person on the board to bring up the proper channels, two moving the lift, and one who actually focuses.

It is common for the designer to begin at one end of an electric and work her way down to the other end rather than to hop around from place to place. It is much faster not to have to move the lift any more than necessary. Most designers understand this. They will ask for the correct channel number to be brought up and then go to the proper spot to focus the light and just stand there and wait. The general idea is to focus the center or "hot spot" of the light on the chest or back of the designer, and then lock off the bolts that hold the light in place. Some designers will direct you by staring at the filament to see when it is brightest. (Yikes! But they really do this.) Some stand with their backs to you and watch where their shadow falls within the light. If a relationship of mutual respect is developed, the designer may simply trust that the electrician has the hot spot in the proper location.

Whatever method is used, the designer gives directions on moving the light. Up and down movement is called tilting. Side-to-side motion is known a pan. The designer might say pan left, and tilt up a bit. This usually means your left, but not always. Some designers just point: up, down, left, right, especially if there is a lot of noise. A clinched fist means "Stop, you've got it." If you are exceptionally in tune with your focusing partner, you will most likely be able to hit them just right without so much talking, and they will just say "Lock it" when you've got it right. Locking means to tighten the bolts that hold the light in place. Tighten them enough to make it hold, but don't make it your life's work. The light won't be there that long.

If the light is an ellipsoidal, you will most likely need to make some shutter cuts. You may need to sharpen or loosen the focus of the light first by moving the barrel back and forth, just like focusing a slide projector. There is a knob on the top near the front that can be loosened to allow the barrel with the lenses in it to move back and forth to adjust the sharpness. Push in on the top shutter to mask the bottom of the light beam. Push in on the left shutter to change the right side. Very often, the shutters are hard to move and you will find that it is easier if you jiggle the handle back and forth a bit to get it started. Try not to change the direction the lamp is pointing, or you will have to start over. Shutters do not just travel straight in and straight out. It is quite possible to tilt them to a severe angle, but not always as far as the designer would like. The barrel on some fixtures can rotate when necessary, but don't plan on doing that for every light unless you are being paid by the hour.

If the designer is uncertain which light is casting which shadow, she may ask you to "flag" the light. This means to pass your hand or foot or some other convenient body part in front of the light. This will make the beam flash on and off, making it easy to spot.

Patterns or gobos must be inserted into a special holder before they are lowered into a slot next to where the shutters operate. It probably won't matter for a break-up pattern, but in order to read properly, patterns should be put in upside down and backward. Running the barrel for a sharp focus can make a world of difference with a gobo. On occasion, a donut is used to sharpen the focus even more. A donut of this sort is a black metal sheet that fits into the gel holder slot. It has a hole in the center about two inches in diameter. This device cuts down on ambient light and has a dramatic effect on how pronounced the projection appears. A larger hole will emit more light. A small one will sharpen the focus more. If you would like a quick peek at what effect the donut will have, make a circle with your hands and hold them in front of the light.

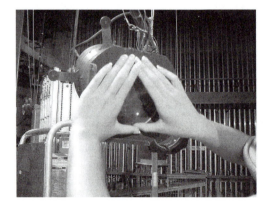

USE YOUR HANDS LIKE THIS
FOR A QUICK IDEA OF HOW
A DONUT WILL AFFECT THE LIGHT

If you are focusing a PAR can, it might be necessary to change the direction of the lamp in order to adjust the direction of the oval. There is a ceramic socket in the back of the light that can be used for this purpose. There is a limit to how far it will turn in one direction, so it may be necessary to try both ways. Some PAR fixtures use a ring around the outside to "spin the bottle" of the reflector.

If you are focusing a Fresnel, you may need to change from spot to flood. Some fixtures have a crank on the back or side, but most have a knob on the bottom. Loosen it and move it in the right direction. Flood forward, spot back.

When the light has been set, put the gel frame in and move to the next light. If you are on a lift, you can most likely reach several lights before moving. When you are ready to go, tell the fellows on the deck. If you say, "Moving stage left," they will know exactly what to do. If you say, "OK", or "Go", or make some other nebulous statement they may not. Remember that moving onstage means toward the center, and moving offstage means toward the wing of the side you are closest to.

Be sure to employ any and all of the safety devices that come with the lift you are using. Follow the instructions given in the instruction booklet. If you do this there is very little chance of the lift being knocked over. The same cannot be said if you choose to ignore the safety rules. Never set up a lift on a raked stage for any reason. It is a good practice to always have two stagehands move the lift, and to stand by while work is being done.

If there is ever a hold-up of some sort, be sure to announce what it is and that you are working on the problem so that people on the ground have some idea of what is happening. As a result they will be less frustrated and impatient.

OPERATING A FOLLOWSPOT

Followspots are used in many productions. In some areas of the country they are known as a frontlight, or perhaps simply as a spotlight, or spot. As the name implies, a followspot is a lighting instrument used to follow the action of a play. They are the original moving fixture lights. The basic idea of a followspot is for the operator to "open up" on an actor and then stay with them until the scene is over, no matter where they may move on the stage. This ensures that the audience's attention will remain focused on that particular actor. A spot may also be used as a special to highlight an inanimate object, and other times, it may be used as effects lighting. Spots can range in size from tiny club instruments of about 1000 watts to giant behemoths used in sports arenas. IATSE stagehands and others are often called upon to run a spot for concerts, ice shows, wrestling bouts, and other entertainments, as well as for theatre shows. Information about those techniques is included here in order to better understand the full range of followspot operation.

THIS SPOT IS USED IN A LARGE SPORTS ARENA

Traditionally, a followspot in the theatre was used to create a hard-edged circle of light that said, "Look at me, I'm singing now." This approach is unmistakably presentational, and still works well for 1950s musicals and other shows of that nature. In recent years that style has often given way to a more subtle method that uses diffusion gel in the spot. It creates a softer beam of light that can be used to simply highlight an actor and give them focus, without the unnatural look of the hard-edged circle. Spots aren't just for musicals anymore.

In earlier times, followspots used a DC arc between two carbon rods to create an incredibly bright and white beam of light. A large rectifier unit was used to supply the necessary DC current. A pair of copper clad carbon rods was clamped into two terminals in front of a parabolic reflector that had a hole in the center for the rods to pass through. A motor and gear system was used to slowly move the two rods together as they were consumed by the heat of the arcing electricity. It was necessary to maintain a precise gap between the two rods in order to ensure maximum light output. The gap itself had to be positioned in just the right place with respect to the reflector in order to work efficiently. New rods had to be inserted and "trimmed" several times during a single performance. Keeping the spot running was a difficult process that required almost constant attention and a very experienced operator.

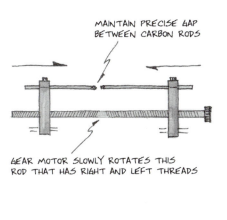

MAINTAIN PRECISE GAP
BETWEEN CARBON RODS

GEAR MOTOR SLOWLY ROTATES THIS
ROD THAT HAS RIGHT AND LEFT THREADS

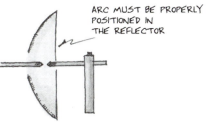

ARC MUST BE PROPERLY
POSITIONED IN
THE REFLECTOR

Carbon-arc lights had one other really problematic aspect in that the burning rods gave off toxic fumes, which in more recent years required some sort of exhaust system. Modern spots use a sealed-beam arc lamp like the Xenon or HMI and don't have the same problem. These lamps still require a rectifier unit to provide the necessary DC current, but the arc terminals in the lamp itself aren't consumed by the arcing process (at least not during any one performance). This means that the lamp can be permanently clamped in position at the exact focal point vis-à-vis the reflector, and will always be in focus. This greatly simplifies running the spot. Xenon lamps are very expensive up front, but reduced maintenance costs, and not having to buy carbon rods more than offset the expense.

A few theatres and/or arenas may still use carbon-arcs, but most of them have disappeared. Other venues may have lights that were converted from carbon rods to a sealed-beam. However, you can still find an example of carbon-arc technology in large outdoor spotlights that are used to attract patrons to gala openings. The brilliant light beams playing across a nighttime sky are visible for miles. These fixtures require an extremely bright light source that a carbon-arc can easily produce, and since they are operated outdoors, the fumes are less of an issue. They have been around at least since WWII when they were used to search for enemy planes in the sky. They have an incredibly long throw.

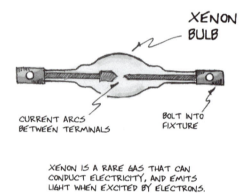

XENON BULB

CURRENT ARCS
BETWEEN TERMINALS

BOLT INTO
FIXTURE

XENON IS A RARE GAS THAT CAN
CONDUCT ELECTRICITY, AND EMITS
LIGHT WHEN EXCITED BY ELECTRONS.

THE GAS IS UNDER PRESSURE, AND
THE LAMPS REQUIRE SPECIAL HANDLING.

Followspots are typically used from a position in the rear of the theatre and require a lamp that is much brighter than that used in a standard fixture, but there are smaller spots that can be fitted with ordinary quartz lamps like the FEL or CYX. It would be possible to run those particular lamps off a dimmer, but brighter arc-type lamps are not dimmable. If the voltage supplied to them decreases below a certain point, the arc will simply sputter out. Instead, most followspots use a mechanical device to vary the light intensity. Other mechanical devices can change the size/shape of the beam, and the color of the light.

Most of the time a followspot has a base that is used to hold up the light from the floor, rather than hanging it from a pipe like other lights. They are generally too heavy to hang and also require room for the operator, and to swing about themselves. One exception to this is the "truss spot." Truss spots are used extensively in the concert business, where they are literally a spotlight that is mounted on top of a section of truss, which is flown out over the stage or audience. An operator sits on top of the truss to run the show. One artistic advantage is that the angle of the light from high above is much more dramatic than the typical flat beam from a spot in the rear of the house. At a concert, haze in the air reveals a shaft of light extending from the truss to the stage. Most of the reason for using truss spots in a concert can be found in the effect created by these moving colored beams.

For a play, a high angle spot is often used when a subtle halo of diffuse light is required to highlight an actor, but it can also be used in a variety of other ways. In a theatre situation, close spots like this are often mounted at a front-of-house lighting position, or from a tower especially installed for the purpose. It is not unusual for a tower of this sort to be located offstage near an "in one" entrance. Sometimes an ordinary fixture like a PAR or ERS is fitted with special hardware, and is used in place of a dedicated spot fixture because of the tight quarters. The bus and truck tours of *Cats* used two old beam projector lights as followspots, and they were suspended from a truss used as the first electric. A series of gel frames were tied to the operator's platform and were individually inserted into the holder to change the color of the light. There was a section of hollow pipe on the side of the light to use as a sight. Crude, but very effective.

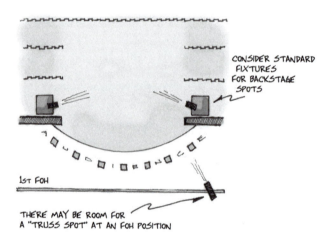

CONSIDER STANDARD
FIXTURES
FOR BACKSTAGE
SPOTS

1ST FOH

THERE MAY BE ROOM FOR
A "TRUSS SPOT" AT AN FOH POSITION

Different followspot models have different mechanical parts, but almost all have the most common few. These include a dowser, iris, stripper, and boomerang.

A dowser is used to vary the intensity of the light output, and to black out the spot so that no light gets to the stage. The dowser is a metal disc that can be rotated into the light beam. This occurs optically in a manner so that the apparent change is a dimming effect rather than seeing an eclipse-like change to the light beam. On some really large spots, the dowser knob controls an apparatus that resembles a barn door of the type used on a fresnel light. The two halves of the dowser plate are pulled in from either side for a more effective mechanical shuttering effect.

On most lights, the dowser control is on the top of the light itself and is a steel rod with a large plastic ball on the end. Different manufacturers arrange the controls differently, but most of the time the dowser is the control nearest the back end of the light.

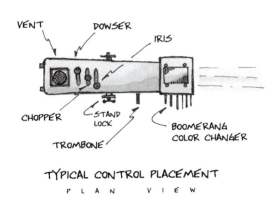

VENT   DOWSER   IRIS

CHOPPER   STAND LOCK   BOOMERANG COLOR CHANGER

TROMBONE

TYPICAL CONTROL PLACEMENT
P L A N   V I E W

Changing the size of the opening varies the size of the pool of light that reaches the stage. If the spotlight is located far from the stage, you will need to iris in for the distance, while being closer will mean a larger opening. The design of the show, and individual cues, may require a larger and/or smaller size as well. The iris control knob is often the closest one to the front of the light.

It is sometimes possible to completely black out the light by closing the iris in all the way. Do not do this. The iris is a delicate device and it is very close to the light source, which is extremely hot. If you block all of the output with the iris, the thin metal plates will heat up very rapidly. They will warp out of shape and be ruined.

TURNING THE OUTER RING
WILL MAKE THE CENTER
OPENING LARGER OR SMALLER

IRIS

You can make small adjustments in the amount of the light beam that is blacked out, but it is difficult to stop at precise points. Some operators make a mark on the housing in order to stop the lever at a predetermined place, but most of the time, a certain value must be intuited by the "spot op". Running a followspot is somewhat more artistic than just punching a button at the lighting console.

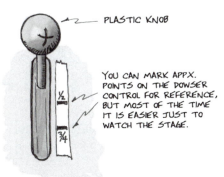

PLASTIC KNOB

YOU CAN MARK APPX. POINTS ON THE DOWSER CONTROL FOR REFERENCE, BUT MOST OF THE TIME IT IS EASIER JUST TO WATCH THE STAGE.

½

¾

Dowsers absorb a lot of heat, especially if they are not opened up for a long period of time during the show. Even so, it is generally not a good idea to turn the spot on and off, as this can actually be harder on the equipment than just leaving it running. Plus, you may have a difficult and noisy time getting it to start back up. Virtually all spots have some sort of fan that cools both the power supply and the light itself. This fan should be allowed to run for a while, even after the spot is turned off, in order to avoid overheating the lamp.

Another commonly found control is the iris. An iris is a system of thin, curved metal plates in a movable housing. The plates overlap one another, and when an outer retaining ring is rotated, the thin plates form a larger or smaller circle. They really act a lot like the kind of ordinary shutters found in a Leko, except that the shape they form is round rather than square. The same kind of mechanism can be found in some cameras.

Some spots have an additional device known as a "trombone" that can also be used to vary the size of the spot. The trombone is a handle on the side of the light that can be pulled back and forth along the length of the spot (hence its name, in action it is like a slide trombone). The trombone works by changing the relationship between the light source and the lens mechanism. Some operators use a combination of the two controls in their work. Most of the time in theatres the distance of the talent from the spot position remains fairly constant, and the trombone is not necessary. The trombone is more often used for arena acts like an ice show where the skaters may move from 300 feet away, to only 100, in a matter of seconds.

The iris can be used to create a variety of spot sizes that are selected because of artistic reasons. The largest is generally the "full-body" size, which is large enough to include the entire body of the actor. Sometime you may need to go larger than this to include two characters standing right next to one another. "Three-quarter" means from the knees up and including the head. It is very rare for a designer to ask for a shot that does NOT include the actors head and face. You should always strive to keep the head in the light no matter what. The next smaller shot is the "waist," and then finally the "head-shot." Sometimes there are special instructions like "head and shoulders, but try and stay off the white guitar as much as possible," which are fairly descriptive in their own right.

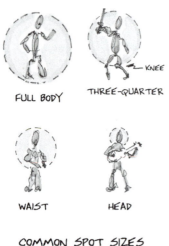

FULL BODY

THREE-QUARTER — KNEE

WAIST

HEAD

COMMON SPOT SIZES

In the light itself, there are six flanges for the frames to slide onto. The flange that is nearest the rear of the light is for frame one. Six goes toward the front end of the light. This is the standard numbering method and it is important to maintain proper orientation so that the correct color will be brought up during the cueing process. The original choice was a somewhat arbitrary selection, but has become the standard method and should be followed.

The "chopper," which is also known as a "stripper," is used to cut off the top and bottom of the light beam so that it is more like a horizontal strip. If you then iris out to a very large size, there will be a strip of light perhaps as wide as the stage. This sometimes happens when a designer wants to have lots of lateral coverage for something like a curtain call. In reality, this effect is rarely used because it is not very attractive.

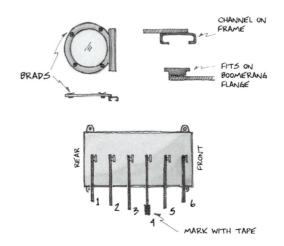

CHANNEL ON FRAME

FITS ON BOOMERANG FLANGE

BRADS

REAR   FRONT

1 2 3 4 5 6

MARK WITH TAPE

COLOR CHANGER OR "BOOMERANG"

EFFECT OF A CHOPPER
ON A CURTAIN CALL LIGHT

Virtually followspots have some sort of color changer. This device is often called by the slang term "boomerang." Normally, six different colors are possible. The gel is loaded into round frames that are designed specially for that particular light. The two halves of the frame are fastened to one another with small brass brads like the kind used to hold papers together, and are also used on other types of gel frames. It is important to do a really neat job of inserting the color media into the spot frames because they must slide smoothly beside one another while in the light. If either the brads or the gel stick out to the side, the frames will have a tendency to get hung up on each other during the show.

There are six levers on the outside of the housing that can be used to bring a particular frame up into the path of the light beam. When a color is up, it filters out all but the precise wavelengths relating to that color. The desired light color passes through, but the remainder of the light waves are stopped and converted into heat energy. Over a period of time, the gel will burn out because of that. There is also a lot of heat from the lamp itself. Gels with heavily saturated colors will last longer if they are placed in the number 5 and 6 positions away from the heat. Most lights have a button you can use to cancel out a gel frame and make it drop back out of the light beam. Alternatively, if you pull a different frame lever all the way down, the first color will be automatically cancelled.

A color correction gel is often used when television is involved, so that the color temperature of the light from the followspot will match the color temperature of the rest of the lights. It might be used all the way throughout a show. The term "no color" is used to indicate that no gel is to be used on a particular cue.

Running a followspot requires a lot of concentration. Professional stagehands are expected to come in and run a show cold, without ever having seen any the action of the piece. Generally, there is a Lighting Director to call the cues for a musical act, ice show, or circus, while in a theatre show, the cues are called by a Stage Manager, or possibly by a spot operator who travels with the show and is familiar with it. There are standard methods of setting up a show and of calling cues, which make it possible for an experienced operator to understand the cues with a minimum of explanation.

The spot-ops are usually given numbers in a clockwise rotation. In an arena, this means starting upstage left and moving around to upstage right. In a theatre show, the house right spot is usually number one and the house left is number two. Traditionally, most theatre shows are designed for two spots, but it is not unusual to have three or even four if the budget will allow it. The numbering system is used to simplify cue calling, and in case of a change in personnel. It is very important for each operator to remember their spot number.

Sometimes the cue caller will assign each spot a "home position," which is kind of like a default setting in a computer. A call to go to your home position is a way for the cue caller to reset the spots in a familiar, predetermined pattern. This happens more often in concert lighting where home positions are things like the lead singer or the stage right guitar player. In theatre shows, the same spots tend to pick up the same characters in the play so that it is easy for them to remember who to hit.

Quite often, there are instructions about the timing of fades, intensity of the light, size of the spot, etc. Very often, cue callers make a blanket statement that fades should be on a one or two count unless there are instructions to the contrary. They might ask for a very long fade like a five count for a very emotional moment, or for the spot to go out all at once on a bump if there is a general blackout. Good spot operators develop an ability to "get in tune" with the tempo of the the show, and adjust their actions intuitively.

Most of the time in a theatre show, a spot will stay with the same gel color for an entire cue, but on occasion it is necessary to go from one frame to another with the light still on. Many cue callers express this by saying "roll to frame # so and so," or sometimes "cross fade." This could be on a bump, but often they want a smooth transition from one color to another. You can do this by slowly engaging the second frame to the point where it cancels the first one. That first frame will want to drop out quickly, but if you catch the lever with your finger you can gently lower the outgoing gel from the light beam in an artistic manner. Running a theatre show is generally a somewhat more subtle enterprise than a concert or circus.

It can sometimes be difficult to locate the next frame lever if you are concentrating on watching the stage and moving the spot to follow an actor. It is helpful to remember that there are six levers, and that quite often number three or four is longer so that you can find it by touch alone. Some operators put tape on number four, for the same reason. It is easy to find numbers six or five by counting backwards from the far end.

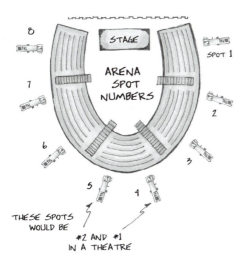

THESE SPOTS WOULD BE #2 AND #1 IN A THEATRE

USE YOUR THUMB AND FINGERS TO ARTISTICALLY CHANGE FROM ONE FRAME TO ANOTHER

A typical spot cue might go like this: "Stand by for spot one to pick up the woman in the red dress up left in a frame one, and spot two on the man in the black suit down right in a frame five. Spots standby and . . . Go." If you are spot one you should push down on the first lever on the boomerang to load frame one. Spot two should do the same with frame five. On the go, both spot ops should run their dowser levers to bring the light up on the target specified by the cue caller. From that point on it is just a matter of staying with the target until the next cue is called.

Most of the time, operators are asked to stay on one person until the light fades out, and then to fade back up on another subject. On occasion, the design calls for the light to move directly from one target to the next. The cue caller may express this by saying, "slide over to so and so," or perhaps "drag your light." In this instance, you simply move discretely from one place to the other. This often happens when there are two actors close together and the idea is to trade one for the other. If you can time it so that this happens as they pass one another, the audience may never notice it, especially if diffusion gel is in use.

A diffusion filter causes the light to change from a sharp edged beam to a soft edged beam, rather like the difference between an ellipsoidal and a Fresnel. There are different values of diffusion so that the edge of the beam can be anywhere from a little bit fuzzy to practically unfindable. It is much more difficult to run a light with a diffuse edge, especially if the stage is bright and the difference in value is hard to see. It is generally easier to keep track of things by choosing to watch the pool of light that has an actor in it, rather than on the actor in a pool of light. A subtle, but very real distinction. If things get really bad, you may have to move your light around a bit to see if you are still on target. If it is that hard for you to see, then probably no one else will notice that you have done it, especially if you manage to avoid running the light off of the actor's face. As a general rule, you should avoid jerking the light around unnecessarily. Stay still even if you are slightly off target, wait for the actor to move some, and then readjust.

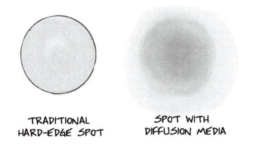

TRADITIONAL HARD-EDGE SPOT

SPOT WITH DIFFUSION MEDIA

It is often difficult to have your spot lined up on the actor when the light comes up. It is very distracting to have a light appear near center stage and then uncertainly wander around until it finds the woman in the red dress upstage left. You can avoid this by using some kind of targeting device. This can be as expensive as a high-powered telescopic rifle sight, or as low tech as a bent piece of wire. There are a number of proprietary devices that are made specifically for this purpose and new ones are developed from time to time. You should try different things and find one that works well for you personally. Using a sight of some sort is a really important step that can enhance the artistic qualities of your spotting work.

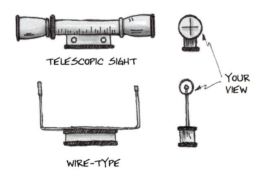

TELESCOPIC SIGHT

WIRE-TYPE

YOUR VIEW

USE A SIGHT TO IMPROVE YOUR AIM

The sight is a personal tool, and you will need to move it from one spot to another each time you work. It is common practice to attach the sight, of whatever type, to a powerful magnet so that it can be easily mounted on the steel housing of the spotlight. Then it is just a matter of adjusting the sight so that it is accurately centered on the light beam coming out of the spot. For best results, make your adjustments at maximum distance, with the iris as small as practical.

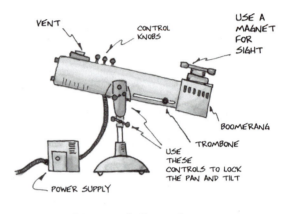

VENT

CONTROL KNOBS

USE A MAGNET FOR SIGHT

BOOMERANG

TROMBONE

USE THESE CONTROLS TO LOCK THE PAN AND TILT

POWER SUPPLY

SIGHT ON A FOLLOWSPOT

There are some rather quirky spot instructions that come up on a fairly regular basis, often enough so that they have actual names. One of these is the ballyhoo. This occurs when the spots criss-cross the audience area in a figure-eight pattern, or perhaps a swirl. This is generally done to excite the crowd, as though the lights are searching for someone. It is even more effective if you change speeds occasionally, as though you are slowly searching, then speed over to another possible target, then slowly search again.

Another technique is to pan back and forth over a group that is too large for one or more spots to cover effectively. This works well for a line of actors at curtain call, or perhaps even a line of elephants on the back track near ring two.

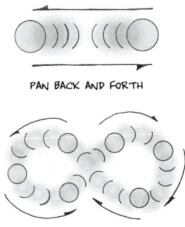

PAN BACK AND FORTH

BALLYHOO THRU THE AUDIENCE

LAMPS

There are many different kinds of lightbulbs used in the theatre, but they all have one thing in common, which is that they are all expensive. Lamps that sell the most tend to be less expensive due to the economy of scale in manufacturing. You may want to consider lamp replacement costs when selecting which brand of lights to buy. Lamps often specify how many hours they are expected to last, and that can can also be a consideration when making a selection. Some Xenon lamps for followspots list for hundreds of dollars and come with a guarantee that they will last for a certain number of hours.

Most lights today use some sort of quartz-type lamp, meaning that the glass used to create the vacuum chamber covering the filament is made of a special quartz glass. This type of glass is able to survive extreme heat, and as a result, the glass envelope can be made relatively small, with the glass close to the filament. This makes it easier to design the structure of a fixture that contains a high-wattage bulb.

A 1,000-watt filament puts off a lot of heat. It is important to remember to never touch a quartz lamp—not when it is hot because you will be severely burned, and not when you are installing it because dirt and oil from your hand will get on the surface of the glass. It will turn black from the heat, and might cause the lamp to explode. The black spot on the lamp will cause more heat to collect on that side and the lamp will fail prematurely. It is usually enough just to wipe a dirty lamp off with a clean cloth, but rubbing alcohol is good if it is really dirty. Avoid highly flamable solvents.

The American National Standards Institute has laid down specifications for lightbulbs so that any bulb of a certain type base will fit into any socket meant for that base, regardless of the manufacturer. The most often used bases in the theatre are the screw base, prefocus, bipost, and the two pin. Most of these bases have different sizes, usually the regular standard, or the much larger mogul. Screw bases have smaller versions, such as intermediate and candelabra.

Each type of lamp has a specific ANSI code, which is its name. For the most part, these are three-letter codes like HPL, BTN, or EHG.

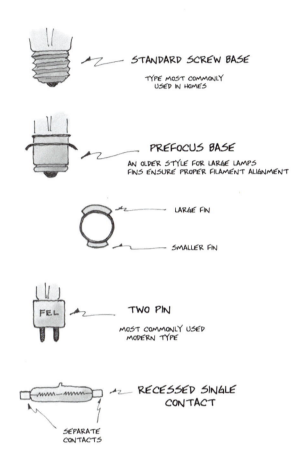

STANDARD SCREW BASE
TYPE MOST COMMONLY USED IN HOMES

PREFOCUS BASE
AN OLDER STYLE FOR LARGE LAMPS
FINS ENSURE PROPER FILAMENT ALIGNMENT

LARGE FIN

SMALLER FIN

FEL

TWO PIN
MOST COMMONLY USED MODERN TYPE

RECESSED SINGLE CONTACT

SEPARATE CONTACTS

CHAPTER 7

HARDWARE

Sometimes it is revealing to look at a word as if it were foreign and to consider the meanings of the root words. When you look at it that way, hardware consists of wares, or products, that are generally made from a hard substance, metal. That could be a fairly good definition of hardware, especially back in the day. Plastics are used now for many hardware items that were once made of steel or brass, but the vast majority of hardware is still metallic in nature. I think that originally the word "hard" was used to differentiate these supplies in name and concept from the wooden structures they were used to connect.

There are literally hundreds of thousands of pieces of different types of hardware available today, for use in dozens of different construction crafts. It would be difficult to be familiar with all of them, and it would be foolish to attempt to cover everything in this type of textbook. Even if the publishers were willing to pay for it, you wouldn't want to read all of it. This chapter is limited to hardware commonly used in the theatre. There are hundreds of hardware items that might be used in the scenery construction, but I will cover only those that seem to be the most basic and useful to the craft, so that these few can get more attention. This chapter is mostly centered on fasteners, hinges, rigging hardware, and a few other items that are peculiarly theatrical.

Most of the hardware in this section was developed for use in building things other than theatre scenery. Stage carpenters have found ways to use hardware that suits their particular craft. Sometimes it is important to know what the original use of the piece was, so that gets mentioned from time to time.

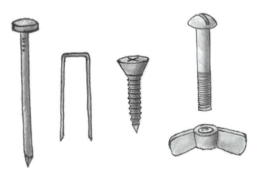

FASTENER TYPES

FASTENERS

Fasteners are used to connect building materials. "Fastener" is the preferred modern term for the hardware group containing nails, staples, screws, and bolts. Each one of these fasteners is definably separate from the others. A nail is different than a staple, and a screw is not the same as a bolt. Sometimes the differences are a bit vague, but there are commonly understood definitions. It is important to know the names and definitions of things not simply to be able to ask for them, but also because knowing how something works can help a technician to understand why it might be important to choose one piece of hardware over another.

NAILS

Nails were some of the earliest fasteners in common use, at least in part because they require very little technology to produce. The Industrial Revolution brought about the ability to use machines to easily manufacture all sorts of things in mass quantities, including metallic hardware. Before that, all metalworking was done by hand one piece at a time. Early nails were made by cutting across bars of flat stock at a slight angle, and this type of nail is known today as a cut nail. Cut nails are triangular in shape, and if laid head to toe and side by side, it is easy to visualize how they were made. These nails are still manufactured in small quantities for historical restorations.

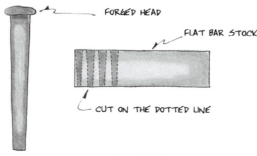

CUT NAILS

The method of categorizing nail sizes was developed over a long period of time, and it is one of those fun things to know about. It is related to a method that was also used to price them when they were produced in England some centuries ago. As you can imagine from seeing how early nails were cut, the larger the nail, the harder it was to produce and hence more expensive. Making cut nails was a labor-intensive undertaking. The present system of sizing is related to the cost of making nails back at that time. The

small letter d is used to represent the word penny in England. When this system originated, one hundred of the larger nails cost 16 cents, which was a great deal of money at that time. Of course, we've had quite a bit of inflation since then. So the larger the nail, the higher the penny number, and the smaller the nail, the lower the penny number.

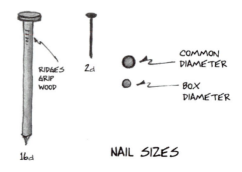

NAIL SIZES

In modern times, a two-penny is the smallest size nail available. The 16d nail is the largest that is commonly used in woodworking. A 2d nail is about one inch long, while a 16d nail is about three and one-half inches long, which should give you some indication of the relative sizes.

Constructing a home requires a considerable number of fasteners. Modern nails are made from wire rather than bars of iron. They are quickly and easily manufactured by large machines that can turn out thousands in a minute. The prices of today's nails are mostly related to the cost of the steel wire and distribution of the finished product. Allowing for inflation, they are quite inexpensive by comparison to the earlier version. Wire nails are easily distinguishable from cut nails because the modern type is round in cross section rather than squarish like the antique cut nails.

Modern, machine-made nails are more precise than a cut nail, yet even so it is not really necessary to be terribly exacting in making them. If a 16d nail is said to be about 3 1/2" long, it might well be 3 1/4" or 3 5/8". The work that they do does not require an exact tolerance. The diameter of the nails is related to the length and is an arbitrary but standard gauge. The longer a nail is, the larger its diameter is. There are two classifications of the diameter gauge size, box and common. Box nails are thinner than common nails. A 16d box nail is skinnier than a 16d common nail, but a 4d common nail is smaller in diameter than a 16d box nail, depending on the manufacture. Box nails are usually best for scenery because they are thinner and tend to split lumber less easily. Most fastener outlets stock nails in even penny sizes from 2d to 16d, although it is certainly possible to find the odd sizes on occasion. Larger than 16d, nails tend to come in even multiples of 10, like 20d, 30d, 40d, and so forth. These larger sizes are not of much use to the scenic technician as a nail per se, but if you bend the head at a 90 degree angle, a nail can become a replacement hinge pin.

Another type of nail is the finish nail. Many people mistakenly think that a finish nail has no head, but in reality it has a very small head that is intended to be driven completely beneath the surface of the wood it is holding down. The small head is large enough to get a grip on the wood, but tiny enough to leave only a minute entrance hole on the surface of the wood. A close inspection reveals that there is a small dimple on the finish nail head that may be used in conjunction with a nail set to "set" the head below the surface of the work. The resulting hole may later be filled and sanded so that it does not show. This technique is how the finish nail got its name, because it is to be used in "finishing" work, such as applying trim to doors and windows.

BENT NAIL FOR
HINGE PIN

Any nail smaller than 2d is generally referred to as a brad, and the length is given in inches such as $^7/_8$ or $^3/_4$. Nails today are most usually sold by the pound, although some hardware stores have them in small boxes of arbitrary amounts. Traditionally, a standard full box of nails weighs 50 pounds. That is a very large number of 4d box nails, but not so many 20d common.

TYPES OF NAIL HEADS

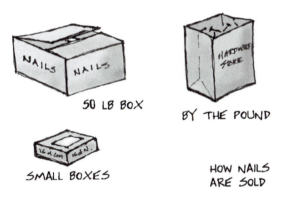

50 LB BOX

BY THE POUND

SMALL BOXES

HOW NAILS
ARE SOLD

There are several different types of nail heads. The most recognizable is the standard flat head. This kind of head is used for most nailing, especially when the heads will not show in the final product. The head of this type of nail is easy to grasp and remove with a claw hammer whenever that is necessary. The nail head serves another purpose that is not so obvious, but is the real reason it exists. The head prevents the nail from being pulled entirely through a piece of lumber. In construction, most of the time a thin piece of wooden material is being nailed to a thicker piece, such as a sheet of $^1/2"$ plywood being nailed to a 2x4. If the nail had no head, movement in the wood could easily work the nail through the plywood, and the two pieces would come apart. The head keeps that from happening. It is important to drive nails all the way down so that the heads are snug to get the greatest holding power from them.

A duplex or double-headed nail looks much the same as a standard nail, except that there are two heads on the shaft about one-half inch apart. The double head approach is meant to secure the wood with one head, and to leave the other head for pulling the nail out at some future date. Double-headed nails are used in situations where the work is known to be temporary, quite often in concrete form work. Some theatres use the double-headed nail for temporary set-ups.

There is another category of nails that are meant to be used in a nail gun. Most nail guns are pneumatic, meaning that they run on air pressure. They are covered in the chapter on tools. Nails of this type must be manufactured to a much closer tolerance than ordinary nails because they need to fit through the gun without jamming. Most often these nails come in some sort of strip, which is glued or taped together as a means of organizing them. Each company has its own patented method of producing nails that is different from everyone else's, so that the nails are usually not interchangeable. In recent years, competing nail manufacturers have sprung up to make generic "brand x" type nails for some of the guns. Some of these will work fine, and some will cause the nail gun to jam frequently. Nail guns have traditionally been sold at a very low price in order to get people to buy them. That guarantees a long-term commitment to buying a particular type of nail, and that is where the money is made. The nails tend to be somewhat expensive. It is best to consider the economic ramifications of nail gun politics when buying a particular type. It is not a good idea to buy a gun that uses inordinately expensive or difficult-to-find nails. Exact brands may differ from region to region.

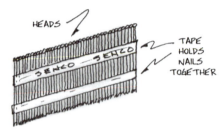

NAILS FOR A PNEUMATIC GUN

A good finish nailer is an indispensable tool in the modern scene shop. Nail guns speed up your work tremendously, and there are some techniques that are almost impossible without one. Most guns will hold a variety of nail lengths from 1 inch to 2 inches, and that should fit most of your needs.

The holding power of small finish nails is not very great. Sometimes that is OK, and other times it is not. Many of the construction methods depicted in this book require that wooden joints be glued together. Glue joints are very strong, but the parts must be closely held together until the glue has a chance to bond. Normally, clamps are used for that purpose, but putting them on is a very slow and tedious process. Pneumatic finish nails are a great way of pinning the joinery together until the glue sets. Even though the tiny pneumatic nails don't have much holding power, they are ideal to use because they are so easy to put in, and they hold well enough for the short time they are needed.

One thing to remember about these nails is that like all finish nails they are meant to be set into the surface of the work about $1/8$". If you are using them to join two pieces of 1-by stock (that are really $3/4$" thick), care must be taken to select a nail that will not go through the far side of the work. The two pieces of wood are 1 $1/2$" thick when placed together. If a 1 1/2" nail is used, the setting of the nail will send it $1/8$" through the wood. A nail 1 $1/4$" thick would be a better choice.

There are nail guns that shoot much larger, common headed nails. They can be used to speed things up if you are building scenery from large framing lumber.

STAPLES

Staples are used in a very similar manner to nails, but there are some important differences. A nail is one metallic shaft, whereas a staple has two legs connected by a top section known as the crown. Everyone is familiar with a desk stapler that uses very small staples to batch together loose sheets of paper. This kind of stapler uses a plate to bend the ends, or legs of the staple over after they have passed through the last sheet. Construction staples are different in that they are a much heavier gauge and are not intended to be bent over. The legs simply go all the way into a piece of wood in the same manner as a nail. Construction staples come glued together in a strip just as desk staples do. They are generally classified by the length of the leg in inches, ($3/4$, 1 $1/2$, etc.) and by the width of the crown. Most staples have a crown that is either $1/4$" or $1/2$" wide. One-quarter-inch wide staples will not fit into a gun intended for half-inch crowns. The manufacturing principles and the sales philosophy of this type of staple are much the same as for pneumatic nails.

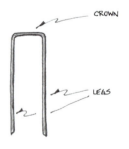

PARTS OF A STAPLE

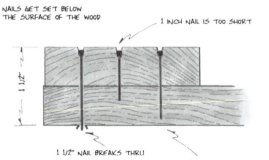

NAILS GET SET BELOW THE SURFACE OF THE WOOD

1 INCH NAIL IS TOO SHORT

1 1/2" NAIL BREAKS THRU

1 1/4" NAIL IS JUST RIGHT

MAKING A NAIL SELECTION

Staples are a better choice for certain applications than nails are. The most obvious example of this is when you must attach very thin pieces of plywood to a thicker substrate. A nail gun nail sets its nails in $1/8$". If the plywood you are using is 1/4" thick, that leaves the nail only $1/8$" to grip of the plywood. It is very easy for the plywood to work its way off of the nail under these circumstances. With a staple, the crown of the staple tends to catch a certain amount of the wood fiber under itself and uses it to hold the thin ply to the framing underneath. Some guns set staples below the surface of the wood, and some do not.

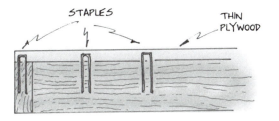

WHEN USING A THIN COVERING MATERIAL, STAPLES GRAB SOME OF THE WOOD AND HOLD IT DOWN RATHER THAN SHOOTING RIGHT THROUGH

Staples are also best suited to other thin materials, such as fabric or cardboard or paper, but a large construction stapler may be too powerful for them. There are also hand-operated, manually-powered staplers that are useful for stapling smaller objects. A fabric stapler is a pneumatic gun that shoots very small gauge staples that are often used in upholstery work.

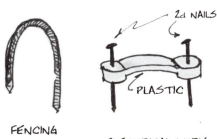

FENCING

ELECTRICAL WORK

Some staples are not intended to be used in a gun. There are fencing staples, which are essentially U-shaped bent nails with two sharp ends, and also insulated staples designed for electrical work. Modern insulated staples are made of two small 2d nails that are connected by a piece of plastic. Plastic is used in this application because it is does not conduct electricity. It is not a good idea to use a metal crown staple on electric wires because of the chance that the staple will be driven too far and cut through the wiring insulation. That would cause a short circuit. Only the insulated staples are approved by the National Electric Code.

SCREWS AND BOLTS

Screws and bolts are fasteners that use threads to hold themselves in position. Threads are the ridges found on the side of the shaft of a screw or bolt. A close inspection will reveal that a thread is really one long ridge that curves around, spiraling from one end to the other.

Sometimes it is easy to become confused about the difference between screws and bolts. Generally speaking, bolts are used with a nut that holds the bolt in place. The nut has female threads that match the male threads on the bolt. On occasion, female threads are tapped into a hole drilled into a metal structure or housing. Then a bolt can be screwed into that pre-threaded opening rather than using a nut. The threads on a bolt are sometimes called "machine threads." Bolts have a blunt end.

Screws have a pointy end and make their own pathway into wood, plastic, or sheet metal. They compress the material on either side in order to form that hole. The male threads of the screw grip the walls of the hole with much more holding power than a nail does.

Even though these descriptions hold true most of the time, some smaller bolts are referred to as machine screws. This is a plot hatched by manufacturers, just to make the whole thing more confusing. But if you recall that bolt threads are called "machine" threads, it is a bit easier to understand.

SCREW   BOLT

Screws and bolts come in a variety of different head types so that you can select a style that works well for the particular job at hand. Perhaps the most common type is the flat head. The flat head is used when it is necessary to maintain a flat surface, with none of the screw head protruding above the surface of the work. This kind of head is often used to attach certain types of hardware, such as hinges, picture hangers, hanging irons, and so forth. The cone-shaped flat head is manufactured to fit into countersunk holes in the hardware just mentioned.

Some screws and bolts have a round head. It is intended to be more decorative and will show above the surface. Round heads are often found on stove bolts, the 1/4" diameter bolts used to hold scenery together. Sheet metal screws have a head similar to the round head, but with a flattened top.

This kind is called a "pan head" because it is the same basic shape as the interior of a cast iron skillet. Sheet metal screws are not intended to sink in flush because the material they are used on will not allow it. The pointy ends of these screws are used to connect pieces of thin sheet steel, and as a result the screws themselves are made from a very hard steel. This theoretically allows them to work their way through the metal without dulling or breaking.

SCREW HEADS

There are two very popular drives used for screw heads, the standard slot and the Phillips. When screws were made by hand, slotted heads were the only type feasible to manufacture, but in the machine age the Phillips drive has all but totally replaced it. The Phillips drive is much easier to use with a power screwdriver, which is the only logical way to drive the thousands of screws it takes to put together a stage setting. In recent years there has been a move toward even more functional shapes, with the most successful being the square drive. The major problem encountered in using a power screwdriver (such as a variable speed drill) is that the driver bit tends to slip out of the screw head. This can lead to deforming the head in such a way as to make impossible to get the screw in or out. The Phillips head handles this problem much better than the slotted head, and the square drive is better than the Phillips. The only problem with the square drive is that they are more difficult to find, and you will most likely wind up with a mixture of half square and half Phillips drive screws. Obviously, production will be streamlined if only one kind of fastener is used, and there is no need to change bits back and forth. Perhaps in the future square drive will overwhelm the Phillips drive in much the same manner as Phillips replaced slotted.

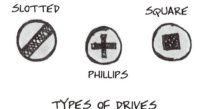

TYPES OF DRIVES

The diameter of a screw is determined by a gauge number that is fairly arbitrary in nature. A common gauge screw for attaching hinges is the #8. To give some basis for comparison, #2 screws are teeny tiny, whereas a #12 screw is about the largest commonly found. The practically microscopic screws used on things like eyeglasses have numbers like 00 or 0000. The length of screws is described in inches or fractions thereof.

Not all screws are manufactured in the same way, or are of the same quality. Ordinary wood screws have a thread that does not extend all the way from the point to the head, but rather stops short of the top, leaving a portion of the shank smooth. Another type of screw known as a tapping screw has threads that are continuous. The tapping screw also seems to have sharper threads, and they are much easier to drive. The size of regular screw used most often in scenery building is the $3/4$", #8 flat head Phillips tapping screw. This screw, or similar longer ones, may be used to install most hardware that requires screws.

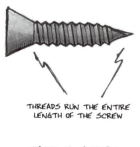

THREADS RUN THE ENTIRE
LENGTH OF THE SCREW

TAPPING SCREW

Another family of screws that are very useful in a theatre scenery shop is the drywall type. Drywall screws were developed (strangely enough) to hang wallboard in houses. These screws are very long and thin, and have a distinctive appearance. They have what is called a bugle head, which looks and works much the same as a Phillips flat head. Drywall screws are most often black in color. They come in two gauges, #6 and #8, with the #6 diameter being the most useful. The lengths are somewhat odd, generally being $7/8$", $1 1/4$", and $1 5/8$" for the shorter screws, and then jumping up into the 2", 3", and even 4" ranges.

Drywall screws are very hard and brittle, so the heads tend to break off if the amount of torque used in driving them is too great. If a drywall screw is sticking through the back of a piece of scenery it can be easily snapped off with a hammer, or even your foot. This would not be even remotely possible with any ordinary type of screw, and serves as a demonstration of how hardness and malleability are inversely proportional. Drywall screws need to be made of especially hard steel because of their length and their thin nature. Some drywalls have a twin set of threads rather than just one long continuous thread.

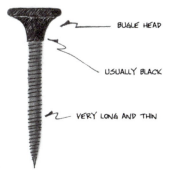

DRYWALL SCREW

Tech screws are a specialty item that is mostly available from a dedicated fastener outlet, although you can find a limited selection of them in some hardware stores.   (If you spell tech with a K, it becomes a well known brand name.) They are intended to drill into thin steel, such as 16ga square tube, and then create their own machine threads that will secure the screw in place. They are at their best when you are attaching wood to metal. Tech screws are usually either #10ga or #12ga in diameter and are available in a variety of lengths. There are three types of heads used, a large flat head, a pan head, and a hex head. All of them are intended to be used in conjunction with a power driver, because tech screws cannot be driven by hand. The hex type is much easier to install, but it leaves a rather large and unsightly head above the surface of the wood. The flat-headed type is harder to spot once the scenery has been painted.

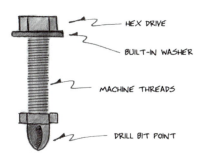

TECH SCREW

As mentioned earlier, the difference between screws and bolts lies in the type of thread that is used. Screw threads are pointy at the end that must start into the wood, and the threads flare outward so that they can gain more purchase on the surrounding material. Machine threads are exactly the same from beginning to end to be in synch with the threads found on a matching nut. Tech screws have a drill bit on the end that creates the hole for it in the steel. The screw then taps its own treads in the metal. Normally, a bolt must have a hole drilled for it in advance, whereas a screw tends to make its own pathway.

Bolts are sized by their diameter and by their length in inches. The diameter is given first and the length second, as in "quarter-inch by three-inches." Metric bolts are not commonly used in scenery building in this country. Very small bolts under $3/16$" in diameter are sometimes referred to as machine screws and given a gauge number starting at #10 and going down.

The threads of bolts are not all the same size, although a standard size has been adopted for most of the commonly used $1/4$" to $1/2$" bolts. Thread descriptions are given in threads-per-inch, or tpi. Each diameter of bolt has a normal number of tpi, but sometimes manufacturers will deviate from the norm for a specific purpose, and you may find that even though your replacement bolt is of the same size, it still will not work properly. If you are buying only $1/4$" and $3/8$" bolts at a hardware store, you may never run into this problem, but power tool manufacturers often use fine threaded bolts. As a rule, the larger a bolt is, the larger its threads will be and the smaller the tpi number. Very small machine screws like the #8 or #6 are often found with a variable number of threads.

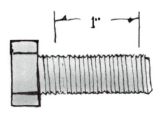

16 TPI
(THREADS PER INCH)

Almost all screws and bolts are threaded right-handed, which means that to tighten them you should turn to the right, or clockwise. To remove, apply force to the left, or counterclockwise direction. Someone long ago came up with the phrase, "Righty tighty, lefty loosey."

The capacity of bolts that must hold an extraordinary amount of weight may be rated with marks on the bolt head. These marks relate to a numbering system for hardness. Rated hardware is guaranteed to hold a certain amount of weight. Grade 8 bolts are the strongest, but the grade 5 are the most common at a hardware store.   Many types of hardware have both rated and unrated versions.

Bolt heads are similar to screw heads with the exception that round heads and hex heads are more common than flat heads. Hex heads are intended to be used with a wrench. The higher torque possible with a wrench will get the bolt much tighter than a screwdriver can. Bolt head sizes naturally correspond to wrench sizes, in inches. The size of the head and the size of the shank of a bolt are two separate issues. The size of a bolt as it is listed at the hardware store refers to the size of the shank, not of the head.

The heads of carriage bolts are entirely different. They have a smooth, slightly rounded head with no gripping surface. The carriage bolt has a bit of square shank just below the head that is meant to be used in conjunction with a square hole in metal surface, or with a torque washer into wood.

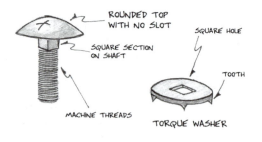

CARRIAGE BOLT

A torque washer has a square hole in the center and teeth on the outside edge. The teeth dig into the wooden surface and prevent the carriage bolt from turning while the nut is tightened. If a carriage bolt is used in wood without a torque washer, and the threads of the bolt are disrupted in some way, it may be impossible to remove the bolt without an angle grinder. Many people like the tight way the heads fit against the side of a platform.

Nuts are most often hex shaped, but some older types are square. A really old bolt might also have a square head. Wing nuts are just about the only other type, and they are very helpful because they can be made "finger tight" without the use of a tool.

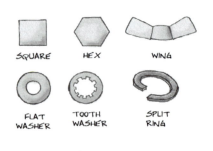

BOLT HEADS, NUTS, & WASHERS

It is generally best to use washers with bolts because this spreads out the holding force of the bolt over a greater surface area for the pieces being bolted together. This makes it much less likely that the bolt will pull itself through the hole and cause the joint to fail. Also, washers keep the action of tightening the nut from marring the surface of the work and make it easier to get the nut tight. You should always turn the nut, not the bolt, especially if the bolt is holding together steel pieces. This helps protect the threads on the bolt from becoming damaged. Split ring washers and tooth washers may be used where vibration is a problem. These types of washers keep tension on the nut at all times and prevent it from working itself loose.

A lag bolt is a hybrid type of screw/bolt. They look like large screws that have a hex head on them. They are sized like a bolt, but go in like a screw. They are most often used to secure large items like lighting towers to the deck. Lag bolts often require a pilot hole for insertion.

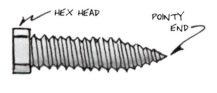

LAG BOLT

In general, screws have much more holding power than nails, and bolts are more secure than screws. Something that has been bolted through and properly washered is very unlikely to come apart unless the bolt fails. Anything that hangs overhead should be bolted for safety reasons, and if there is any question at all about the weight of the piece, but sure to use rated bolts and other hardware. Sometimes you can install hardware items like hanging irons with screws to get the position set, and then come back and put at least one bolt in each iron to safety it off. It is much better to spend a few extra minutes on a process like this than to have an injury accident.

HINGES

Hinges are crucial in the rigging of stage scenery. Except for fasteners, they are used more than any other type of hardware. You are familiar with how hinges work when hanging a door, but in the theatre they are used in a much larger variety of applications. There are many different types of hinges, some of which have specialty uses and are manufactured with that purpose in mind. Hinges are often used in scenery as a fastening or connecting device and not because they can be made to swivel back and forth.

The shaft that holds the two leaves of a hinge together is known as the pin. Some hinges have tight pins that are permanently attached to the hinge. A loose pin hinge can be separated into two halves when its pin is removed. If one leaf of the hinge is connected to one piece of scenery, and the second to another unit, you can disassemble the two units by simply removing the pins.

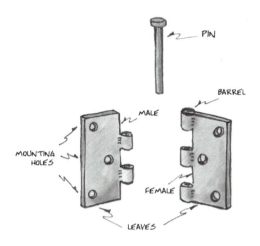

PARTS OF A HINGE

Butt hinges are used to hang doors. The name is derived from the fact that this type of hinge is intended to butt up against the edge of the door. In woodworking, boards that meet at their edges are said to be butting against one another, and when connected in this way the result is called a butt joint. An inspection of any butt hinge will show that the two leaves or sides are much taller than they are wide. If you compare the shape of the hinge to the edge of the door where it is used, the specific shape of the butt hinge makes sense. Butt hinges are meant to be used in pairs, as one alone would not provide much stability when the door swings open. Heavy, or heavily used doors may have three or even four hinges on them. A more complete description of the use of butt hinges may be found in the chapter on doors.

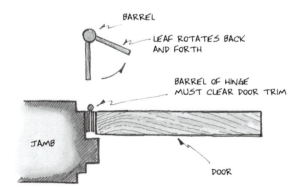

HOW A BUTT HINGE WORKS

Butt hinges are usually sized by the height of the leaf. Three-inch butts are fairly small, while four and one-half or five-inch butts are quite large. The width of the leaves is proportional to the height, with the theory being that heavier doors will also be thicker doors. For theatrical use the three-inch size is large enough for most applications. Some modern-day butts have rounded corners. These corners are to compliment the use of a router and jig in creating the mortise that the hinge fits into. A straight corner hinge is generally more preferable when a jig is not used.

Strap hinges are shaped like two isosceles triangles joined at the base. This type of hinge is intended to be used on gates and other such flat structures. Strap hinges attach to the front of the gate, and the reasoning behind their shape is contingent upon that manner of attachment. Butt hinges are shaped to fit the edge of a door, but strap hinges are shaped to take advantage of the large flat surface of a gate front. Some strap hinges are made of, or to appear as though made of wrought iron. A more practical type for the theatre is made of ordinary steel. Most strap hinges are made as tight pin hinges, which is a limiting factor in their use in a scenic studio. But you can use a grinder to remove the manufacturer's pin and replace it with a bent nail more suited to normal stage use. Strap hinges are best when a large, very heavy-duty hinge is required. Its shape makes it a natural candidate to be bolted to some heavy scenic unit. A close relative of the strap hinge is the T hinge, which is like a strap hinge on one side, and a butt hinge on the other. The unique shape of this hinge can be useful in certain situations.

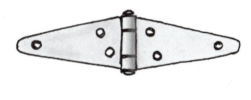

STRAP HINGE

Another type of hinge may be referred to as a "saloon-door," or "kitchen-door" hinge. It is included here because swinging doors are frequently required to facilitate stage movement. Directors love to have doors swing back and forth to reveal characters in a comedy. Mounting a swinging door hinge can be quite a challenge as it is somewhat more complicated than a butt or strap hinge. The common type of swinging hinge operates by using two spring loaded barrels that are located on either side of the door. Rather than having two leaves, as most hinges do, this type has three. The center one serves only to connect the two barrels. This leaf is not attached to either the door or the jamb.

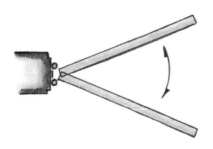

DOOR SWINGS BOTH WAYS

Around the top of each hinge barrel are a series of holes. A steel pin is used to turn the disk where the holes are located. (The manufacturer will most likely supply a special tool, but after you have lost it, a nail with the point ground off will do nicely.) Rotating the disk winds a spring that gives the hinge its ability to swing. A small pin is used to prevent the spring from unwinding. There are two barrels on each hinge, and all of the barrels on all of the hinges must be wound in order for the door to operate properly. It is possible to vary the speed of the closing of the door by adjusting the amount of tension on the springs.

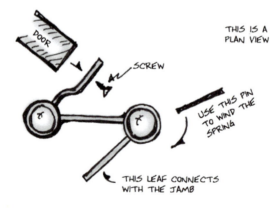

THIS IS A PLAN VIEW

SCREW

USE THIS PIN TO WIND THE SPRING

THIS LEAF CONNECTS WITH THE JAMB

SWINGING DOOR HINGE

This type of hinge comes in a variety of sizes, which mostly have to do with the thickness of the door slab. The hinge must be large enough to properly fit on the edge of the door. If the door is too thick for the capacity of the hinge, there will be no place for the barrels to fit without hacking away a bunch of the door and making an unsightly mess. Several pairs of large swinging hinges are a good addition to the stock of any permanent theatre company. A close relative of the swinging door hinge is the double action hinge that swings

in much the same way, but is not spring loaded. These may be used on folding screens, but are not really sturdy enough to be used on very heavy scenery.

There are a number of different types of cabinet hinges. Some of them greatly resemble butt hinges and are used in more or less the same way, but on a smaller scale. Some are meant to be face mounted like a strap hinge.

The most popular type of cabinet hinge is the self-closing flushmount. These are used for American style doors that do not cover the entire front of the cabinet. On this type of cabinet the face frame and one half of the hinge are visible when the door is closed. This type of hinge attaches to the back of the door, and to the front of the face frame. The modern self-closing type does not actually close the door, but will hold it shut without using any type of catch or latch. Self closing cabinet hinges are very cheap, plentiful, and easy to install without any special tools. An offset, or inset type, is available for doors whose backs are not on the same plane as the front of the face frame, but rather are inset $3/8$" into the opening.

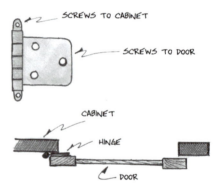

SCREWS TO CABINET

SCREWS TO DOOR

CABINET

HINGE

DOOR

CABINET DOOR HINGES

The backflap hinge is the most useful fastening device (other than nails, screws, and bolts) used in the theatre. It is generally not used in the traditional way — that is, to allow a piece to rotate. The backflap is more often used as a connector that holds scenery together. It allows the scenery to be disconnected and to take the units apart. Backflap hinges are indicative of the kind of methodology that gives scenery its knockdown, pull apart, and reassemble for act three in Peoria nature. There is a definite style to the construction of early-twentieth-century wooden scenery that revolves around this portability factor. Traditional scenery is constructed so that it is lightweight and movable, whether the intent is to tour, or to allow for the production of a play with multiple scenes that must be reset. In commercial theatre, virtually all scenery is built elsewhere and must be trucked in to the theatre. The use of backflap hinges has traditionally been a critical link in this methodology.

When not in use, jacks may be folded over against the back of the flat, or if this is not possible for some reason, the pins can be pulled and the jack removed from the scenery. Sometimes several flats joined together will need to be stiffened so that they do not bend where they are hinged. A stiffener may be hinged to the back of the flats so that they remain rigid. Hinging the stiffener with loose-pin backflaps will make it possible to remove the stiffener and reattach it easily. Even if scenery does not need to be moved during a show, being able to easily assemble/disassemble facilitates things like painting and moving the scenery around the shop.

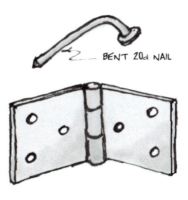

LOOSE-PIN BACKFLAP

You can examine the backflap hinge for clues on how to use it effectively. Notice that the leaf of the hinge is more or less square in nature. This would tend to indicate that it is not meant to be used on the edge of lumber as a butt hinge is, but rather on the face of some framing member. Most backflaps are loose-pin, and the pin supplied is a bent shaft, giving it a small handle to grasp. This points to the need to easily remove and replace the pin. It is this feature that makes the system work.

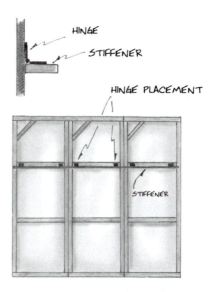

BACKFLAP HINGES
ON A STIFFENER

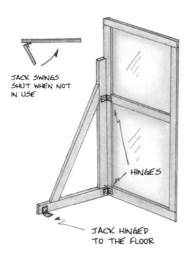

BACKFLAP HINGES USED
ON AN L-JACK

Loose-pin backflaps are often used to join groups of flats or other scenery. Attach the hinges to the backside of the framing so that removing the pins allows you to separate the flats from one another. This hinge may also be used to attach L-jacks to the back of a flat in order to keep it upright.

Another use for this versatile hinge is to connect scenery to the floor. If it is not practical to use a stage weight to hold an L jack to the deck, then a hinge may be used for the same purpose. You can also use this same technique to secure the bottoms of stairs, newell posts, columns, and any other scenic element the hinge will fit onto.

Sometimes it is necessary in the construction of scenery to connect two framing members that do not intersect at a 90-degree angle. Sometimes it is not possible to nail, screw, or glue the joint together effectively. A hinge may be used to securely join the boards together. This technique can work on a right angle like an angle iron, but it will also work when the angle to be joined is not 90 degrees, and other types of hardware will not fit properly. The hinge may be rotated to any angle required. When using a backflap for some purpose where the pin will never need to be removed, it is best to use a tight pin hinge, or to replace the original pin with pin wire. Pin wire can be bent over at the ends to ensure that it does not fall out unintentionally.

In general, it is best to replace original hinge pins with either pin wire or bent nails to ease the assembly process. You might try using the tight fitting original pin to put the scenery together, and then knock it out and replace it with a bent nail. This serves to give the joint just enough slack to fit together easily. Twenty-penny nails are a good fit for the 2" backflap size. Although you can buy pinwire by the pound from a supplier, I have found it less expensive to buy the kind of wire that is used to hang suspended ceilings and to cut my own. This wire is quite stiff and useful for other projects as well.

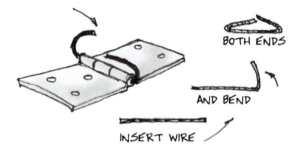

BOTH ENDS

AND BEND

INSERT WIRE

If necessary, backflaps may be trimmed with a grinder to fit an odd shape. Sometimes you may need to bend them with a hammer and vise, or drill holes into them, and this can be done without too much effort. There is a certain brand of backflap hinge that has notches cut into it to make this a simpler process, but they are somewhat more expensive.

Backflap hinges come in several different sizes, running from 1" to 2". There is some merit to having a variety of sizes, but the 2" size is the most effective, so you may wish to stick with those. If you make a habit of buying from one manufacturer, the hinges you buy today will fit the hinges you bought last year. It is easy to recycle hinges, as there is little to go wrong unless they become bent in some way. The two-inch variety is a heavier gauge and will last longer.

HANGING HARDWARE

Oftentimes it is necessary to fly a unit of built scenery. Soft goods are simply tied to a batten using their own tie lines, but built scenery is heavier and requires another approach. There are specific pieces of hardware that may be used for this purpose. Safety is the key to flying scenery, as it should be with all aspects of work in the theatre. Obviously, hanging something over the actor's head requires a bit more attention to detail in its installation, as the chance for disaster

is high if an accident should occur. A further explanation of the use of flying equipment may be found in the chapter on rigging.

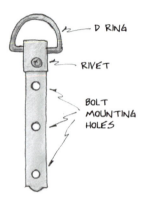

D RING

RIVET

BOLT MOUNTING HOLES

HANGING IRON

Hanging irons come in two main types, straight ones, and another kind with a curved bottom that will fit under and around a thinnish piece of scenery like a soft covered flat. The flat type is probably the most useful to keep in stock, as it may be used in more ways than the curved type. It is basically a length of bar stock, bent over, with a D-ring at one end. The D-ring is used to connect to the hanging cable. There are countersunk holes in the hanging iron for use in bolting the iron to a scenic unit. A hanging iron is actually made from steel, but it is quite common in the theatre to call anything metallic an "iron."

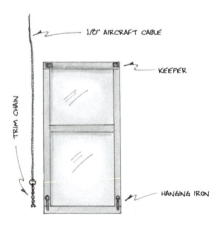

1/8" AIRCRAFT CABLE

KEEPER

TRIM CHAIN

HANGING IRON

PUT THE HANGING IRON AND TRIM CHAIN ON THE BOTTOM FOR EASIER ADJUSTMENTS

Notice that the hanging iron is placed at the bottom of the flat rather than the top. Half of a hinge can be used to keep the line in place at the top. You can find more tips in the "How Do You Make…" chapter.

A D-ring plate is used in a quite similar manner as the hanging iron. However this hanging hardware is shaped differently and may be used in places where a hanging iron might not fit. Most of the time, the hanging iron is used with the D-ring at the top and the iron vertical, while the D-ring plate is used lying flat.

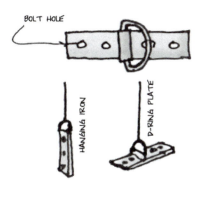

D-RING PLATE

Aircraft cable is used in hanging scenery because it has a very high load rating. Essentially, this is a rope that is made from steel strands. A very large variety is used in arena rigging and is simply called "steel." In the theatre, the weights involved are much less and the size of cable used is correspondingly lighter. Most scenery is hung using $1/8$" cable, which is rated at about 1,000 pounds. The actual amount varies from one manufacturer to the next and is usually stamped on the side of the reel that the cable comes on. If you buy a 500 or 1,000 foot reel at the start of each season there will always be a ready supply on hand. The $1/16$" diameter cable is rated at about 400 pounds while the $1/4$" goes up to 7,000 pounds. These are the breaking strengths, of course, and it is prudent to maintain a safety factor of at least 4, so that the cable strength is 4 times the load.

A rope thimble is used to protect the line from being bent over and kinked. It is very important to avoid a sharp bend when using wire rope. It is less forgiving than a line made from more pliable fibers like hemp or nylon. Kinking the cable will make it more difficult to use and will also greatly reduce its breaking strength. There are different sizes of thimbles for different diameter ropes and cables.

Often called by its trade name "Crosby," a wire rope clamp is used to fasten the aircraft cable around the thimble. Wire rope clamps are quite commonly used to secure lift lines to a stage batten. It is the accepted practice to use two of these clamps when attaching cable to a thimble or a batten, as this better ensures that the connection will hold.

The bottom saddle part of the clamp should be attached to the tail side of the cable. This is often referred to as the "live" end.

WIRE ROPE CLAMP

Swage fittings are used in the same manner as wire rope clamps, but the main difference is that the Crosby is removable, and the swage fitting is not. Once a swage fitting is secured to the cable, it is impossible to get it back off, unless you simply cut off the few inches of cable that are involved. Swage fittings are cheaper than wire rope clamps and they are much neater on the cable. They are also easier to put on but do require a special crimping tool. A different size crimper is needed for each size of cable. Some tools are made with several different apertures that will fit more than one diameter of wire rope. A common trade name for this product is "Nicropress Sleeve."

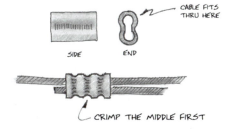

SWAGE FITTING

Trim chains are used to adjust the length of a hanging rig. They typically consist of a welded ring, a two-foot length of $3/16"$ chain, and a snap hook. The trim chain is most often used at the end of the hanging cable that is attached to the D-ring at the bottom of the unit being flown. The chain is used to adjust the length of the cable, and this in turn adjusts the trim of the scenery. When two cables are used, changing the length of one or the other can straighten the unit so that it hangs plumb. Chains are often used at the top to attach the cable to the batten, but this may also be accomplished by using a clove hitch and a Crosby clamp. When a chain is used, it should be wrapped around the batten, and then use a shackle to connect the chain back to itself. Quick links may also be used if they are properly rated. The trim chain at the bottom is used for adjustments. It is much easier to make them while standing on the floor rather than from the top of a lift or ladder. This is fairly easy to do by lifting the low side of the piece and moving the chain up a link or two. Since the chain passes through the D-ring, moving up a one-inch link will raise the side only half an inch. After making a move up, check the trim and repeat the process if necessary.

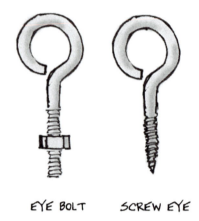

TRIM CHAIN

Screw eyes and eye bolts should be used only when the weight of the item being hung is very low. It is generally unsafe to use this hardware to hang heavy items over the stage. Sometimes, a large diameter rated eyebolt can be used through metal framing, but screw eyes should only be used for small prop items, and never to hang anything weighing more than a few ounces. When using an eyebolt in metal framing, be sure to use a flat washer to avoid having the nut pull through. Eyebolts have a machine thread and are used with a nut. (Like a regular bolt.) Screw eyes have a pointed, screw thread and are intended to be used in wood only. (Like a screw.) Screw eyes come in a wide variety of sizes that are

somewhat arbitrary. Eyebolts are described by the diameter of the rod they are bent from, such as $1/4"$ or $1/2"$. Take the direction of force of the cable pull into consideration when using an eyebolt. Cable pulling at an oblique angle is more likely to cause the eyebolt to fail. Rated hardware has a known load rating and is much safer to use. If the scenery weighs more than a few pounds, rated hardware is a much safer bet.

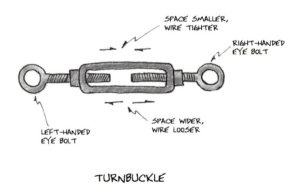

EYE BOLT   SCREW EYE

On occasion it is necessary to make smaller adjustments to a trim than are possible by using a trim chain. The trim chain's smallest increment of change is one-half of the length of one link of the chain, which will most likely be about one-half of an inch. A turnbuckle may be used to affect an immeasurable tiny shortening of a hanging cable. The turnbuckle is essentially a very long nut with an eyebolt sticking out of it at either end. One of the eyebolts has a left-handed thread, and when the center section is rotated the two eyebolts come closer together, or farther apart, depending upon the direction the center portion is turned. Turnbuckles are available in a large variety of sizes, from only a few inches to several feet in length. Most of the time they are not necessary on a simple piece with only two lines, but can really help out on a complicated hanging job where many lift lines are needed.

SPACE SMALLER, WIRE TIGHTER

RIGHT-HANDED EYE BOLT

LEFT-HANDED EYE BOLT

SPACE WIDER, WIRE LOOSER

TURNBUCKLE

An S-hook is a piece of round stock that has been bent into the shape of an S. A pair of pliers is used to close the ends around something you are hanging. This piece of hardware is not easily removed, except with a pair of bolt cutters. They should not be used for overhead hanging because the hook may open up and fail if too great a load is applied. Also, it is not uncommon to see someone forget to bend the ends of the hook closed, and if used in this way the hooks are almost certain to come loose when used on hanging scenery. S-hooks do have a variety of small prop uses.

Shackles are used in much the same way as a quick link, but they are manufactured in much larger sizes, and for much heavier loads. The shackle has a bell and is designed to connect two lines to one, but may also be used for a one-to-one connection. The removable bolt is called the pin, and it is accepted practice to use the shackle with the pin facing down since most of the time a bridle is hung in that way. Shackles are almost always rated hardware and are the best choice for overhead rigging.

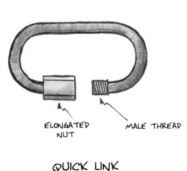

S-HOOK

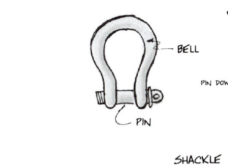

SHACKLE

Quick links resemble an oval chain link, but one side has a nut that may be used to create an opening for the passage of chain links, rope thimbles, and other hardware. When properly closed, the quick link is very secure and will not come open accidentally. Quick links are sized according to the diameter of the link material. It is problematic that the opening in the link is often not large enough to fit over what you would like to attach it to. Some quick links are rated for a specific load, and others are not. If no rating is listed, then there is none.

Snap hooks are used to quickly connect cables or chains. They have a somewhat oval shape, with one end of the oval being larger than the other one. They are very commonly used on lighting safety cables where the load rating is not such a concern. Carabiners are a type of climbing hardware that work in much the same way. Since they are used for climbing they almost always have a load rating, but they are somewhat clumsy to use for most rigging applications. Another type of hook is often referred to as a "dog clip" because it is often seen on a leash.

QUICK LINK

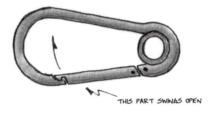

SNAP HOOK

ODDS AND ENDS

Roto Locks are often called coffin locks or casket locks. Rumor has it that they are used to hold caskets shut. Just to know for certain, I called a funeral home to ask, and they tell me that this hardware is indeed used to seal a casket. That makes the name seem quite appropriate.

Casket locks are most often used to lock two or more platforms together, and a full discussion of this process may be found in the chapter on decking. These locks can also be used in a wide variety of applications to join scenic units in much the same manner as loose pin hinges, although the method of attaching the lock is much different. Casket locks consist of a male and a female side, with the male side having the moving parts. The two halves are connected to two different pieces of scenery, and then a $5/16$ hex key is used to lock them together. There is a cam-shaped hook inside the male half that rotates around and grabs two projections inside the female half. Since the hook in the male is a cam, it will draw the female side toward it as it rotates.

nal name. Rota Locks are used to join two pipes together at a right angle. They come in two parts. One is a rod that has been bent into a double U shape and then welded together at the end. The other piece is a spacer that fits in between the two pipes that have been slipped into the U shapes. The spacer part has a bolt on it that may be turned to tighten the joint. Rota Locks are manufactured for all sizes of schedule 40 black steel pipe from 1" inside diameter (id) to 2" id. The only real problem with the use of these clamps is that the pipe must be slipped into the clamp from the very end, and this is sometimes difficult to do.

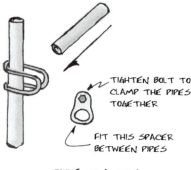

TIGHTEN BOLT TO CLAMP THE PIPES TOGETHER

FIT THIS SPACER BETWEEN PIPES

PIPE CLAMPS

A similar piece of hardware, the Cheeseborough clamp, locks itself around the pipe by means of a bolt and wing nut and has the added advantage of working with the pipe at any angle, not just 90 degrees.

TURN TO LOCK

CAM

HOUSING

MOUNTING HOLE

COFFIN LOCK

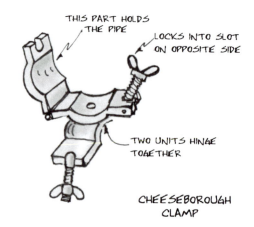

THIS PART HOLDS THE PIPE

LOCKS INTO SLOT ON OPPOSITE SIDE

TWO UNITS HINGE TOGETHER

CHEESEBOROUGH CLAMP

The Rota Lock is another piece of hardware. It has always struck me as odd that there are two pieces of hardware with such similar names and such dissimilar uses. It is convenient that the casket lock is almost never called by its origi-

CLAMP USED TO CREATE A PIPE GRID

Screen door handles come in many sizes and weights. They are quite useful as a "gripping" point when attached to a unit of scenery. They are relatively inexpensive and reusable. (Studio workers who move scenery are called "grips.")

SCREEN DOOR HANDLE

A cane bolt is used to secure rolling scenery to the floor. It is very similar to a barrel bolt used on a door, with the exception that the cane bolt sinks into a hole drilled in the floor or deck. When the bolt is pulled upward and turned to the side, it will stay up and out of the way. When the handle is rotated to the center position, the bolt slides downward and into the hole in the floor.

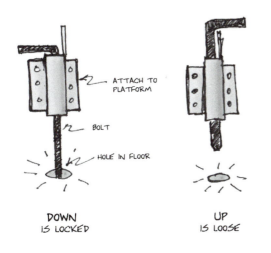

DOWN
IS LOCKED

UP
IS LOOSE

There are several types of flat pieces of steel that may be used to connect wooden framing members. Corner braces form a flat right angle and are especially useful on the bottom corners of stock 4x8 platforms to keep the 2x4s from pulling apart. Angle irons are similar in concept but are made by bending a straight piece of bar stock. Angle irons may often be used in the same connective manner as a backflap hinge, whenever the pieces need not be disassembled. Both come in a wide variety of sizes. You can easily bend an angle iron to an obtuse angle by laying it on a section of steel pipe and tapping it with a hammer.

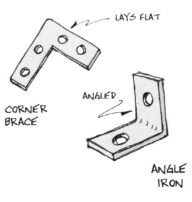

LAYS FLAT

CORNER
BRACE

ANGLED

ANGLE
IRON

CASTERS

Casters are wheels used to roll something. There are many different sizes, types, and styles to choose from, but only a few are really useful for moving scenery. Lots of casters are really intended for use on furniture, and they are not nearly strong enough to move heavy scenery.

The best type of caster for that job has a plate on the top of it and can be bolted to the bottom of a piece of scenery. Casters that fit into a socket like furniture casters are not generally strong enough to fit theatrical needs. Casters are said to be of either the swivel type, or the rigid type. Swivel, or "smart" casters rotate and allow the scenery to be moved in different directions. Rigid, or "dumb" casters are fixed, and will run scenery back and forth along the same pathway. There are some situations that call for swivel, and others that demand rigid casters.

Casters are most often described by the size of the wheel and their load capacity. It is best to be realistic about the load that will be placed on these wheels, and most often to use casters that are rated significantly higher the actual load. This makes for a much smoother ride. It is axiomatic that the larger in diameter the wheel, the easier it will be to move the wagon. Larger wheels are less prone to becoming stuck on or in irregularities of the stage floor. The other side of the coin is that large swivel casters require more clearance room to swivel and this makes it more difficult to stop and reverse direction. You will need to find a happy medium.

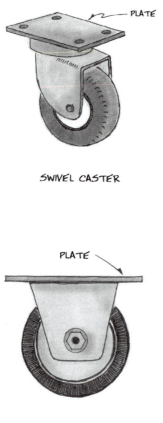

SWIVEL CASTER

PLATE

RIGID CASTER

Manufacturers use a variety of substances to manufacture the wheels used on casters. The best ones most often have a steel center hub and a tire made of neoprene or hard rubber. Plastic wheels or wheels that are made entirely of steel are not generally acceptable because of the amount of noise they create when the unit is being rolled. Plastic casters cannot carry very much weight.

Some casters have a type of locking mechanism on the side that will prevent them from rolling when depressed. While this works just fine for an AV cart or a hospital bed, it is not as useful in the theatre, because it is often very difficult to get under the scenery to operate the mechanism. Locking casters can be useful on occasion.

Casters are a high-dollar investment for most theatre companies. Good casters are somewhat expensive, and they are often required in vast numbers. If your theatre keeps a stock of casters it is best to stick to some standard sizes so that they will all match. Three-inch-diameter casters are a popular size.

One interesting type of caster is the universal type, which has three small wheels on a revolving base. This allows the caster to carry more weight on small wheels that can be fitted into a lower space under the scenery. Quite often it is nice to be able to make a piece that is very low to the ground. Universal casters are also able to swivel in a smaller space. More information about using casters can be found in the "How Do You Make…" chapter.

CHAPTER 8

SHOP SUPPLIES

There are some scenery construction items that are used so often that they are generally kept in stock. That keeps the shop working day to day and avoids delaying production. The items listed in this section are for the most part not really hardware or building materials, but they are consumables that must be replaced from time to time. In order for a shop to work efficiently there must be a steady supply of materials provided to the work force. It is important to look ahead to the requirements for the next day's work, or if items must be ordered from out of town, you must look ahead to next week or next month. Your theatre may have its own special requirements for supplies that are needed for your particular situation.

ADHESIVES

Aliphatic resin glue, which is often called carpenter's glue, is probably the most commonly used adhesive in building scenery. It has a yellow color that makes it easy to differentiate from a white glue like Elmer's. Regular Elmer's is in the family of polyvinyl glues. Either one will do the same job, but the yellow glue bonds more quickly and with greater strength than the white glue. Carpenter's glue is the best choice for most woodworking, but not especially for adhering muslin to a flat. The white glue gives you a bit more time to work before it is too stiff to move the fabric around. White glue also dries clear, which can be an advantage in certain situations. As a rule of thumb, the yellow glue bonds to two-thirds of its holding power in about twenty minutes, while the white glue requires about an hour. To get the maximum hold from either takes 24 hours.

Neither of these glues is a good gap filler, which means that the parts being joined should be smooth, well fitting, and tightly held together in some way while the bond is formed. Jostling the joint while the glue is setting up will greatly reduce the holding power of the bond. When used on wood or some other porous material, the holding power of either of these two glues will generally exceed the strength of the material itself. Hence the wood will pull apart before the glue joint does. It is important to spread the glue evenly over the entire joint surface to achieve maximum holding power.

WOODWORKING GLUE

After a year or so of storage, the yellow glue tends to form stringy clots in the jug that jam up the flow of the liquid. If that starts to happen, the glue is past the point where it is really usable. One of the large, 30-gallon barrels of glue costs less per gallon, but much of will bad if you are unable to use it all soon enough. Recently, manufacturers have developed a Type II yellow glue which is said to be waterproof. This may be a good choice of adhesive if the scenery is to be used outdoors, but it is not normally necessary for a show in the theatre unless your smoke doors are desperately in need of repair.

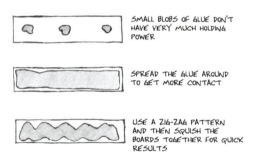

APPLYING WOOD GLUE

Contact cement is an adhesive that works by first bonding to the two separate material surfaces, and then to itself. It is very commonly used to adhere laminates like Formica to a table or countertop. There are two basic types, the original that is quite flammable and really high in VOC (Volatile Organic Compounds — not a good thing), and a newer type that is water-based. Clearly, the water-based type is a wise choice for use in the theatre, although it does not have all the holding power of the original.

It is difficult to tell much difference in quality between the various brands of these two glues, and as a result it makes sense to just buy whatever is the cheapest. Years ago yellow glue was somewhat more expensive than the white, but this is no longer true. You will get a much better value if you buy these glues in gallon bottles. But the smaller applicator-type bottles are a must when you are actually using the glue. Of course you can also fill up other kinds of squeeze bottles and use those as well.

The cement is rolled or brushed onto both of the two pieces to be joined. It makes sense to use the cheapest possible short nap rollers and foam brushes for this purpose because the applicators will be ruined by the end of the project. It is important to let the adhesive dry for at least a half an hour or so, or until it is clear and dry to the touch. Oftentimes it will go on green or tan and dry clear. The contact cement will not bond properly unless it has dried prior to the two surfaces coming together. Exact times and conditions can be found on the label.

It is important to remember that this type of glue bonds immediately on contact. Sometimes if only the least bit of touching has occurred the parts can be yanked quickly apart, but there are no guarantees. It is best to have a means of closely positioning the parts without having them touch each other. When laying countertops, rods are placed on the surface of the counter so that the laminate can be positioned. When all is ready, the rods are pulled out one at a time as the laminate is pressed against the wooden underlayment. It is important to press the two materials together firmly, but clamping is not needed. Laminate is generally cut a bit large and trimmed off later with a router so that exact positioning is not required.

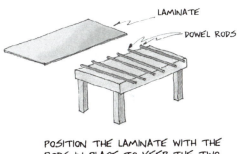

LAMINATE

DOWEL RODS

POSITION THE LAMINATE WITH THE RODS IN PLACE TO KEEP THE TWO SURFACES APART, THEN PULL THE RODS OUT ONE BY ONE

Contact cement is a good adhesive for building up blocks of polystyrene foam for carving. Unlike construction adhesives, it leaves no residue on the inside of the block that is difficult to carve through. The water-based cement will not "eat" the foam, and it makes a very good bond since it connects entire surfaces.

There is one specific product that is a flammable contact cement, but which is often useful for small prop jobs. Barge cement comes in a can with a brush applicator in the cap much like rubber cement. It is a true contact adhesive and must be put on both surfaces. It is an excellent product for emergency repairs.

Construction adhesive is a very thick liquid, or mastic. It is often used to glue together foam pieces. It will also stick foam to wood, steel, aluminum, acrylic sheet, or just about anything else. A longer explanation of its use may be found in the section on working with foam. One of the advantages of this type of adhesive is that it is an excellent gap filler and can be used to connect parts that do not fit well. Normally, this product comes in a caulking tube, but you can also find it in gallon cans. Liquid Nails is a brand of construction adhesive that has been around for many years. Make sure to use the original formula. It will melt a bit of the foam, but it holds much better than any other type. Construction adhesive is also great to use in connecting wood to metal square tubing.

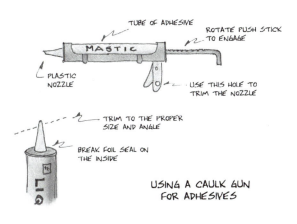

TUBE OF ADHESIVE

ROTATE PUSH STICK TO ENGAGE

MASTIC

PLASTIC NOZZLE

USE THIS HOLE TO TRIM THE NOZZLE

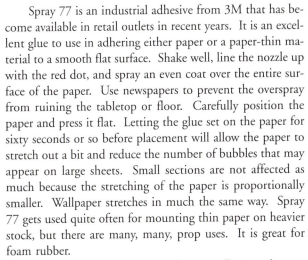

TRIM TO THE PROPER SIZE AND ANGLE

BREAK FOIL SEAL ON THE INSIDE

USING A CAULK GUN FOR ADHESIVES

Spray 77 is an industrial adhesive from 3M that has become available in retail outlets in recent years. It is an excellent glue to use in adhering either paper or a paper-thin material to a smooth flat surface. Shake well, line the nozzle up with the red dot, and spray an even coat over the entire surface of the paper. Use newspapers to prevent the overspray from ruining the tabletop or floor. Carefully position the paper and press it flat. Letting the glue set on the paper for sixty seconds or so before placement will allow the paper to stretch out a bit and reduce the number of bubbles that may appear on large sheets. Small sections are not affected as much because the stretching of the paper is proportionally smaller. Wallpaper stretches in much the same way. Spray 77 gets used quite often for mounting thin paper on heavier stock, but there are many, many, prop uses. It is great for foam rubber.

The 3M company has several spray adhesives that are identified by a number and can be used in much the manner as the 77 is.

SHAKE WELL

ADJUST THE
NOZZLE TO THE
RED DOT

SPRAY 77

USE A NEWSPAPER
TO MASK THE OVERSPRAY

SPRAY GLUE WORKS
VERY WELL ON PAPER
PRODUCTS AND FOAM
RUBBER

pear into the darkness of the backstage void. It is often used on electrical cables (Hence the gaffer connection.) The main advantage of gaff tape over ordinary duct tape is that the fabric nature of the former makes it stronger and more malleable. Duct tape is of course less expensive, but you get what you pay for. There are so many uses for gaffer's tape that it would be impossible to list them all.

ACTI

USE WHITE TAPE AND
A MARKER TO MAKE
TEMPORARY LABELS

GAFF TAPE RIPS EVENLY
ALONG ITS LENGTH

GAFFER'S TAPE

Zap is a brand of cyanoacrylate or "Super Glue" that is sold at woodworking stores. There are several different formulas for specific purposes, as well as a kicker that speeds up the bonding time. This product is not recommended for general woodworking, but it is handy to have around for the occasional odd problem. You can use it to glue small parts together when speed is of the essence. It is important to not use too much or the set-up time will take too long. It really does take just a drop. The kicker causes the glue to set up almost immediately. Be sure to follow the instructions exactly. Generic types of this glue are available just about anywhere, but you will most likely only find the kicker at a specialty woodworking store.

TAPE

The most useful tape for the theatre is gaffer's tape. This is a cloth tape with adhesive on the back that gets its name from its original use by movie electricians. It is available in many different colors, but black and white are the most desirable. You might want to order a case that is half white, half black, so that you have some of each. The most useful size is the 2-inch wide, 60-yard roll. There are several different brands, and many stagehands have a particular brand that they insist is the best. Some are thicker and stiffer than others and might be better suited to your particular situation. Some leave less sticky residue behind when you pull them off. I discovered one night during a load out in Cleveland that "gaff" tape won't stick to anything if the temperature is below 10 degrees Fahrenheit.

One of the great things about this tape is that it can be ripped along its length into very narrow strips when odd sizes are required. The white can be used for putting labels on boxes and hampers, rail linesets, or dressing room doors. It can be ripped into strips to mark sightlines or to be used as spike marks. The black is useful when you need it to disap-

Glow tape is a plastic tape that is impregnated with a fluorescent powder that glows in the dark. The powder soaks up light energy and then releases it when darkness comes. It is often used for spiking the stage floor. "Spiking" means to put marks on the stage floor, or wherever, which indicate placement of scenery or props. The advantage is that, theoretically at least, the tape will glow in the darkness of a scene-change blackout. If you are not careful with it, you may find that there always seems to be either too much of it or too little. The pieces out on the stage floor that are exposed to bright light can seem like airport landing lights in the darkness. On the other hand, the tape used in the wings where there is no light to charge up the chemical will hardly be visible at all. Most of the time small strips of white gaffer's tape work as well or better, although there are times when glow tape is the only solution.

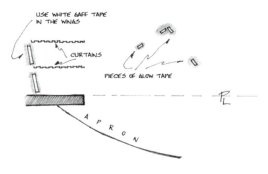

USE WHITE GAFF TAPE
IN THE WINGS

CURTAINS

PIECES OF GLOW TAPE

A P R O N

PL

GLOW TAPE CAN'T CHARGE UP IN THE WINGS
WHERE THERE IS NO LIGHT. IF YOU USE TOO
MUCH OUT ON THE STAGE, IT WILL BE
DISTRACTING IN A BLACKOUT.

Vinyl electrician's tape is used to provide extra coverage for wiring insulation. It is stretchy and easy to bend around uneven joints. It is a good insulator. The most common color is black, but there are many other colors available. Electrician's tape is often used to color code wires or even scenic units. It can be used when there are a great many spike marks on the stage floor, and there is a need to be able to differentiate between them. The most useful colors for electrical purposes are green for the ground, white for the neutral, and black, red, and blue for the hots. You can use the same tape to color code the different lengths of jumpers used for lighting purposes.

Masking tape is a paper adhesive tape that was designed to be used as a temporary mask while painting cars. It works great when you are using a sprayer. It works well for that purpose, but not necessarily any other. Masking tape is very cheap in comparison to other types of tape and is often used when some other type would really be better. Remember that masking tape is not designed to be left on any surface for more than 24 hours. After that length of time the paper and glue begin to dry out, and after a while the tape will either let go entirely, or it will become so permanently stuck that it must be scraped off. It should not be used to mark the floor of a rehearsal space, or for any other semipermanent application.

Teflon tape is a non-sticky type of tape that may be used in the place of pipe dope to secure the threads of a pipe connection from leaking. It is wrapped around the male end two or three times in clockwise direction.

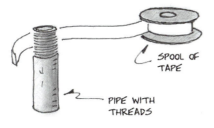

TEFLON TAPE ON PIPE THREADS

Floral tape is a paper tape that uses wax as an adhesive. As the name implies, it is often used in making floral arrangements, especially with silk flowers. It is slightly stretchy and works well for wrapping the stems together. Its green matte finish is more or less invisible when viewed from the audience.

Everyone is familiar with Scotch brand Magic Mending tape as it is used to hold papers together, but this type of tape is also useful on glass or mirrors. On paper, the slightly frosted appearance goes away when the tape is pressed down. On glass, the frosted look stays and can be used to create an etched or beveled look to the surface.

SANDPAPER

As the name implies, sandpaper is a sheet of paper or cloth that has a granular substance (but usually not really sand) stuck to one side. This abrasive side is used to wear away the surface of some other material (most often wood). Sheets of sandpaper are a standard 9"x11" size. Many power sanders use either one-half or one-quarter of a standard size sheet. Belt sanders use an endless belt of sandpaper rotating between two drums. These belts are manufactured to fit a particular size of sander. Random orbit sanders use a round sanding pad with either an adhesive back or Velcro to attach the disk to the sander.

SANDING SUPPLIES

Most sheets of sandpaper are made in either an A or a C weight. The C weight is thicker and heavier than the A. The C weight is typically used for coarser grit sandpaper. The grit number is a measure of the size of the granules on the paper. The 60 grit is very coarse paper that may be used to roughly shape wood or plastic. It is very aggressive and will remove a large amount of wood in a short while, but it leaves a very rough surface. There are many different grits available. A grit of 150 is a reasonably fine number for sanding wood, while sanding coats of finish on furniture might require a grit in the 300 or 400 range. Most wooden scenery is smooth enough for painting after a quick workout with 100-grit paper.

If an extraordinarily smooth surface is required, steel wool may be used. Steel wool is made from very fine steel shavings and is like an SOS pad without the soap. Steel wool comes in several grades from #2 to 0000. The #2 is fairly coarse while the 0000 is exceedingly fine. Steel wool is very handy for polishing metal surfaces like the top of the table saw.

FABRICS

Fabrics are very important in building scenery. Theatres make great use of curtains and drops, as well as fabric-covered flats and other scenery. Fabrics are often used as a means of creating painted scenery that is portable and lightweight.

Scenic muslin is the most often used fabric in theatre. It can also be used in the construction of costumes. Muslin is a lightweight, all-cotton fabric, which makes an excellent surface to paint on. It is often used for painted backdrops or for cycloramas. It is also used to cover the surface of soft covered flats, although when very high strength is required some shops may use canvas for this purpose. Canvas and muslin are both made from unbleached cotton threads, but the threads used for the canvas are larger in diameter, and as a result the fabric is heavier and coarser. It is important that theatrical canvas/muslin be manufactured from 100% cotton in order for the painting and sizing techniques of the theatre to be effective. Canvas tends to come in narrower widths, usually 72" or less, although wider widths are available. The ounce weight of canvas refers to how much the fabric weighs per square yard, so naturally the heavier the weight the thicker and more durable the fabric will be.

Muslin is easily available in widths up to 120", and much greater widths are possible, up to 35 feet in size. The largest sizes are most often used for cycloramas, or for translucent drops where a seam would be unsightly. You should select the width of the fabric in the same way that you would choose the length of lumber being used for a specific project. The width chosen is a function of the width of flats being covered, or of drops being sewn together. The 120" width muslin is more flexible with regard to the sizes you can cut out of it. The weight of the fabric may be light, medium, or heavy, but the heavy weight is recommended for most scenic uses. Canvas is often found in a variety of colors, but muslin is most often the natural off white. Sky cyc muslin is sometimes sold as a light blue color, as this enhances the ability to color the cyclorama a light blue sky hue.

Most theatrical fabrics are available as either flameproofed (FP) or non-flameproofed (NFP). Fabrics are very flammable, especially anything made from jute, and if the fabric is not flameproofed from the manufacturer, it should be treated in the shop.

There are a number of specialty fabrics that are generally available only from a theatrical supplier. One of these is sharkstooth scrim, which is a net-like material with triangular openings. It is often used to create see-through curtains. It may be found in white or dyed black. Scrim is generally

available in widths around the 16- to 18-foot range, or in the 30-foot range. Thus you could construct a scrim that is either 18 feet tall by any width, or a scrim that is 30 feet tall by any width, or a scrim which is 30 feet wide by any height. It is not practical to sew two pieces of scrim together, as the seam would show when the translucent quality of the scrim is put to use.

Bobbinette is a similar material with hexagonal openings that are somewhat larger than those found in a scrim. It, too, can be found in white or black colors. This material may be used for cut drops, and is available only in very large widths. An even larger opening is found on scenery netting where the square openings are 1" in either direction. Netting is also used to create cut drops.

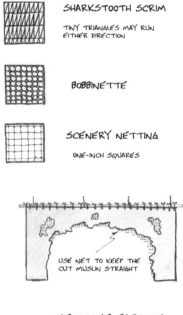

SHARKSTOOTH SCRIM
TINY TRIANGLES MAY RUN
EITHER DIRECTION

BOBBINETTE

SCENERY NETTING
ONE-INCH SQUARES

USE NET TO KEEP THE
CUT MUSLIN STRAIGHT

NET-LIKE FABRICS

Velour is a heavyweight, plush fabric that is used to make curtains. It is most often found as a 54"-wide fabric in a wide variety of colors. Velour has a nap like carpet does, which means that the pile will look different when it runs in different directions. Care must be taken to make sure that the nap on two adjoining panels is running the same way. You can do this by brushing the pile with your hand and seeing how the light reflects off the fabric. Black velour has incredible light- and sound-absorbing qualities, and is an excellent choice for making a basic set of borders and legs. It is often used to cover masking flats, and other parts of scenery that the designer would like to disappear backstage.

A less expensive alternative to velour is duvetyn/commando cloth. Sometimes, this fabric is called duvetyn when it is lighter in weight and commando cloth when it is heavier. Sometimes it depends on which part of the entertainment business you work in. Most people in the theatre call it duvetyn. This fabric has no true nap like velour, but it does have a brushed, textural surface giving it a very matte appearance. Like velour, duvetyn is most popular in black but comes in a variety of colors. The black is very handy for masking flats and can be stapled onto scenery to cover small gaps that were not foreseen in the design process. Duvetyn scraps can also be used to drape things backstage that you do not want the audience to see.

Burlap is a fabric made from jute. Jute is a rough fiber that has an oily resin in it. As a result it is quite flammable and must be heavily treated with a flame retardant. It has a rough texture much like the bags used to hold potatoes or coffee, which are made from the same material. Its natural color is, of course, that of jute, but burlap is also available in a wide range of colors. Colored burlap tends to be of a somewhat more regular weave than the natural. The texture of burlap makes it a favorite with designers.

Cheesecloth is a very lightweight, loosely woven fabric greatly resembling gauze. This material is available from a theatrical supplier, but you may prefer the type sold in fabric stores that comes in a box. It is easier to use for projects like coating foam-built scenery. The theatrical gauze or cheesecloth is much more difficult to apply.

CHEESE CLOTH COMES FOLDED INTO FOUR LAYERS

100 YDS CHEESE CLOTH

IN A BOX

Webbing is a narrow strip of heavy, stiff, woven jute that is used to beef up the edges of a drop or curtain. It is typically used only on the top edge where the grommets are placed. It can sometimes be used in the construction of furniture, or to make straps of one sort or another. Jute webbing is 3 1/2" wide and comes in a roll. There are two red (or sometimes blue) stripes down the length of the webbing, which are useful in lining up the placement of grommets. Grommets are brass rings used to reinforce the holes made in the top of a drop. They allow ties to be used in fastening the drop to a batten. The standard size for this application of grommets is the #2 size. Grommets must be installed with a grommeting hole cutter and setter. They are placed on one-foot centers.

FLAMEPROOFING

It is important to flameproof scenery. It is not that expensive a process and prices have actually gone down as more theatres are flameproofing. Flameproofing means that a treated wooden or fabric material may char but will not support an open flame. "Fireproofing" is another thing entirely. It is generally not possible to accomplish that unless your scenery is built entirely from steel (or perhaps concrete and rocks for an outdoor drama). Many communities have a requirement that scenery should resist burning as an open flame for a certain amount of time when heated with a torch. The fire marshal in your community has the legal authority to make all decisions as to what is allowed on stage.

TWO TYPES OF FLAME RETARDANT

ONE OF THEM MUST BE MIXED WITH PAINT AND THE OTHER CAN BE SPRAYED ON AS A FINAL COATING

There are many different flame-retarding compounds on the market, and they all work well. Some are liquids that get sprayed on after the scenery is painted, and some are additives that you can put in the paint itself. Some are intended specifically for non-porous plastics. Follow the instructions that come with the compound. Retardants are available from most theatrical suppliers.

CORDAGE

Ropes and other lines used for tying are very important when working on stage. The most basic old-style type of rope is the hemp line, so called, but actually made from manila, a similar fiber that is derived from a relative of the banana tree. The rope itself is formed by twisting the fibers into several loose strands, known as yarns, and then twisting the yarns into a rope. This type of line has a definite right-hand twist, known as its lay. The lay becomes a factor when coiling a rope. Ropes of this type come in various diameters that are given in inches. The working strength of a rope is derived from its breaking strength, usually with a safety factor of 4. For example if the breaking strength of a certain line is 400 pounds then the safe working load limit would be 100 pounds. Knots, abrasions, and dirt will all greatly reduce the actual breaking strength, which is why the safety factor is used.

Many modern ropes are made from synthetic fibers such as nylon, polyester, or polypropylene. These ropes are generally more expensive than a hemp rope, but they are stronger and will last longer. Nylon is perhaps the fiber of choice, as it is fantastically strong and lightweight.

Sash cord is a very popular theatrical line. It was originally intended for use on the type of older window that used a counterweight hidden in the wall to balance out the weight of the sash. It is a woven rope, which means that there is an interior core of fibers that are surrounded by a woven casing. Since the fibers are not twisted together, the rope is less likely to become twisted up and tangled. Sash cord is excellent for tying knots, and for lashing together scenery back stage, but it is not especially strong. Nylon ropes are often made by the same technique and are among the strongest lines available. Sash cord has a matte white sizing added to it, while nylon has a shinier appearance. The natural color of nylon is milky white, but it can be dyed any color. Modern-day sash cord has a cotton exterior with synthetic fibers on the inside.

Jute tie line is very inexpensive and is often used to tie up electrical cables on stage. It is not particularly durable and tends to fall apart after a few uses. It is also quite flammable. When cutting ties for either electrics or curtains, it is important to make the tie long enough to work well. Ties for electrics should be about 30" long in order make two wraps around the pipe. Making all the ties the same length will help keep them organized.

A better tie is made from #4 black trick line. This black line is about $1/8$" in diameter and much more stable and tightly woven than is the jute tie line. It can be used in a variety of situations, but it is important to remember that the safe working load of this tie line is only 16 pounds. Double wrapping will make for a more secure load. This kind of black tie line is most often available on a 3,000-foot reel and can be found either glazed or unglazed. The glazed version tends to last longer, but it is harder to tie.

Aircraft cable is not really what most people would call rope, although it is sometimes described as wire rope. It is made from steel wires that are twisted together in the same manner as a hemp rope. This cable is found in increments of sixteenths of an inch in diameters from $1/16$" to $1/4$". Larger diameters are available, but are not commonly used in theatres. Most show hanging is done from $1/8$" cable, and most battens are hung with $1/4$" cable. Aircraft cable is very strong but difficult to tie. Special hardware is used to make connections.

More information about ropes, knots, and aircraft cable may be found in the chapters on knots and stage rigging.

ELECTRICAL SUPPLIES

There are a few electrical items that are so frequently used in the shop that they deserve to be listed here. One of these is the cable tie, also know as a Ty Wrap. These are tough plastic strips with a locking mechanism at one end.

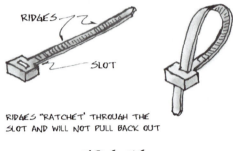

RIDGES "RATCHET" THROUGH THE SLOT AND WILL NOT PULL BACK OUT

CABLE TIE

The plain end of the tie is inserted through a slot in the eye at the opposite end, and ridges keep the strip from coming back out. Pulling on the free end will tighten the loop and firmly band together any wires or other material caught inside the loop. Cable ties are available in a wide variety of styles, sizes, and even colors.

Terminals are metal ends that may be crimped onto the ends of stranded copper wiring, making it easier to connect those bare ends to an electrical device. They are very commonly used when putting on cable ends such as pin connectors. It is possible to attach a pin connector by bending the wire around the screw post, but the wire tends to fray, and if there is enough fraying the resulting resistance created may make the device heat up and catch fire. Terminals cost only a few cents each and are well worth the investment in avoiding accidents, downtime, and possible injury.

RING   FORK

ELECTRICAL TERMINALS

There are many different types of electrical boxes that may be used in the theatre. These range from large disconnects to small boxes used with toggle switches. A commonly required type is the kind used in home construction to house and mount switches and receptacles. Wall switches and receptacles are commonly used when constructing realistic interiors. Most of the time the wall switches are just for show, but quite often the receptacles must actually work to power a lamp or some other prop item. An approved box should be used to wire a receptacle under these circumstances. What you are really making is an extension cord with a box on the female end, which is later attached to the wall.

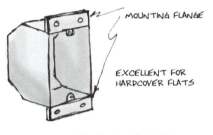

RECEPTACLE BOX

The metal type that is designed to be used with conduit is the easiest to install. Plastic boxes that have nails already on them are problematic. A cable clamp is required to keep the portable type SO or SJ cable from becoming yanked out. Several extension cords with boxes on the end can be made up and kept in stock to be used as required.

Larger metal junction boxes are available to house shop-built electrical devices. They can be used to make fiber optic light sources, disconnect boxes, and in a variety of other applications.

CHAPTER 9

WOOD, LUMBER, AND OTHER BUILDING MATERIALS

Wood and lumber are not interchangeable terms, although there is a direct relationship between the two of them. Wood refers to the species of tree that lumber comes from. Lumber is a product that is manufactured from wood. Lumber has a uniform size and fits into certain categories, so theoretically all 2x4s that are ten feet long are exactly the same size. All lumber is made of wood, but not all wood is made into lumber.

Hardwoods and softwoods are the two divisions of types of trees and the wood that comes from them. You would naturally assume that the wood from a hardwood is higher in density than that from a softwood, and for the most part this is true, although the two divisions are really defined in a way other than just how hard they are. Hardwoods are designated as coming from broad-leafed trees. These are generally deciduous trees that lose their leaves in the winter and then grow a new set in the spring. Hardwoods as a group are usually denser than softwoods, hence the obvious names, but this is not always the case. Well-seasoned (dried) yellow pine varieties can be much denser than some varieties of mahogany.

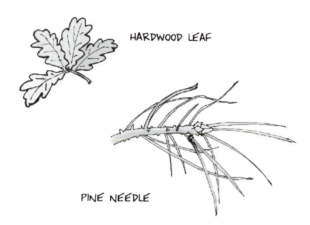

HARDWOOD LEAF

PINE NEEDLE

TREES AND WOOD

Softwoods are coniferous trees that have a needle-like leaf structure. The most common varieties in North America are pine, spruce, redwood, cedar, and fir. Fir, pine, and spruce are the three types of wood most often used in producing lumber. There are many different varieties of pine trees, but they can be separated into two main types, yellow and white. Stage scenery has traditionally been constructed of white pine. White pine is an extremely workable wood for building scenery as it is soft and easy to cut, it has a straight grain pattern, and it is widely available at a reasonable price. Yellow pine is much heavier and is more susceptible to splitting. Fir is quite often used to make interior trims and moldings. It is an excellent wood for this purpose.

At least a cursory understanding of the mechanics of how trees grow can help you understand how wood will react when it is used for building stage scenery. Since trees grow naturally, they are prone to quirks that cannot be entirely eliminated by the lumber milling process.

Trees grow from the outside out and from the top up and not from the center or bottom. Tree bark protects an inside layer of fibers known as the cambium. The cambium layer of a tree is the area where growth rings originate. Everyone has seen growth rings, which are evident when looking at a cross section of a tree trunk. These rings are added to from the outside, which is to say that each year's growth ring, provided by the cambium layer, is added to the outside of the tree trunk, just under the bark. Bark is very much like skin for a tree and protects the cambium layer from weather and disease.

The cambium is the part of the tree that is responsible for transporting water and nutrients from the ground to the leaves. It is really a mass of tiny tubes much like blood vessels. These fibers are very strong and pliable along their length, but they are not bound together all that well. It is possible to strip the fibers from some trees into long strings. This works with other plants as well. Hemp fibers are stripped from the stalk of that plant and then twisted into rope. You may think of a stalk of celery as being indicative of the mechanics of the structure of a tree. The stalk will bend along its length, but will easily snap across its width. After it does, the stringy fibers that make up the stalk are plainly visible.

CAMBIUM

THE CAMBIUM LAYER IS MADE UP OF MANY SMALL TUBES THAT RUN FROM THE ROOTS UPWARD

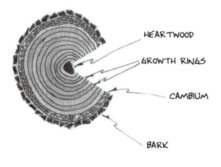

HEARTWOOD

GROWTH RINGS

CAMBIUM

BARK

CROSS SECTION THRU A TREE TRUNK

Celery grows to its full size in one season, so there is no division of growth rings. A tree can grow over hundreds of seasons, and the heartwood, or interior of the trunk, is the remaining evidence of many years' cambium layers. The heartwood is the rigid material that gives the tree its strength and ability to remain erect.

This process or mechanics of growing means that objects on the outside of the tree trunk will eventually be enveloped by it. If a sign is nailed to the exterior of tree trunk, some years later the tree will have grown around it, causing the sign to eventually disappear. The same thing can happen to wire fences and other man-made objects in the forest.

If a limb should die, and fall from the tree leaving a small protuberance or stump, this stump will in time be covered over by the natural growth of the trunk. If this tree is eventually cut down and sawn into boards, the dead limb will show up as a knot or knot hole.

and causes the lower limbs to fall off. As a result the trunk of the tree, which is the source of lumber, is longer and taller. It also has smaller knots. The grain is straighter in a forest tree, and lumber from it is less likely to warp out of shape. Most lumber today comes from farm grown trees which are planted just the right distance apart to get maximum production.

THIS OAK
HAS GROWN AROUND A SIGN

TREE ALL ALONE   TREE IN A FOREST

As you have seen, trees grow from the outside out, but they also grow from the top up. Since the bulk of a tree is added to by the growth of the cambium layer outward, there is no way for the trunk to elongate itself. A tree gets taller when new limbs grow on top of it.

LUMBER

Lumber refers to wood from a tree that has been cut to a specific dimensional size for use in construction. Lumber is called by its nominal size, which is its name size, and not the actual size of the board. When logs are harvested to be used as lumber, they are sawn into planks using a very large circular blade saw. The logs themselves are quite large in cross section and require a blade several feet in diameter in order to get through the entire log. The teeth on such a blade are very big. The resulting cut is rough, and because of the difficulty in making precise cuts in so large and heavy an object, the size of the planks is not very exacting.

HOW THE CAMBIUM
GROWS AROUND A
DEAD LIMB

Limbs on a tree remain at the same distance from the ground for as long as they live. If a limb dies and falls off, the resulting scar gets covered over by new growth. This scar and new growth creates a swirling pattern that is identifiable as a knot in a board. Knots in a live tree remain the same distance from the ground just like a limb does. Most lumber trees will grow taller and straighter if other trees surround them. This forces the tree to grow upward to get to the sun,

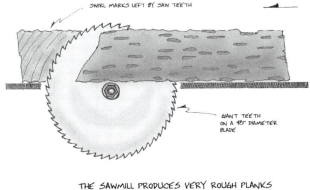

SWIRL MARKS LEFT BY SAW TEETH

GIANT TEETH
ON A 48" DIAMETER
BLADE

THE SAWMILL PRODUCES VERY ROUGH PLANKS
THAT MUST BE MILLED SMOOTH

In an earlier time, methods of home building were designed to accommodate this problem. Lath-and-plaster construction was much more forgiving of uneven walls and rooms that were not exceptionally square. A more accurate dimension size is required for modern construction techniques. Most lumber is really cut for the home construction industry, which is a very large market, and not for the scenery construction business, which is very small by comparison. To accommodate the need for more accurate lumber, roughsawn planks are sent through a planer to smooth and shape them to an exact size. This milling process reduces the size of the lumber by a certain amount and is what causes the milled size to be somewhat smaller than the nominal size. The milled size is the actual size of a piece of lumber.

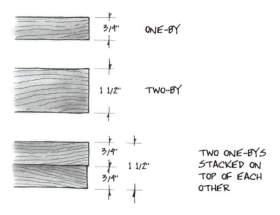

Light construction lumber comes in two main thicknesses. These are most often called by the names "one-by" (1x) and "two-by" (2x), referring to one inch thick by some variable width, or two inches thick by some width. This is of course a nominal size. The milled or actual sizes are $3/4$" for a one-by and $1 1/2$" thick for a two-by. It is interesting to note that twice the nominal size of a one-by is equal to the nominal size of a two-by (1" + 1" = 2'), and that twice the milled or actual size of a one-by is equal to the milled size of a two- by ($3/4$" + $3/4$" = $1 1/2$"). Thus if two pieces of one-by material are placed on top of one another, they will have the same nominal and/or milled thickness as a piece of two by material all on its own. Inch symbols, (") are used to represent the word inches. The symbol for feet is given as ('). The nominal widths of construction lumber are in even numbers of inches beginning with four. The chart shows the thickness and width of common lumber sizes in both the nominal and milled categories.

There are some similarities in the milled sizes that makes it quite easy to remember all of them. As mentioned earlier, all of the 1x thicknesses are actually $3/4$" thick, and the 2x thicknesses are really $1 1/2$" thick. All of the milled widths are $1/2$" narrower than the nominal size except for the 8", 10", and 12" boards, which are $3/4$" smaller. Four rules are all you need to remember to memorize the entire chart.

LUMBER SIZES CHART
NOMINAL TO MILLED

	4	6	8	12
1X	3/4 X 3 1/2	3/4 X 5 1/2	3/4 X 7 1/4	3/4 X 11 1/4
2X	1 1/2 X 3 1/2	1 1/2 X 5 1/2	1 1/2 X 7 1/4	1 1/2 X 11 1/4

Larger sizes of lumber such as 4x4 and 4x6 are available, but they are not commonly used in the construction of lightweight stage scenery.

Dimension lumber is generally available in even numbered feet lengths starting at eight feet long and running through sixteen feet (8', 10', 12', 14', 16'). The written description of specific lumber sizes is given using the formula thickness x width x length, and the feet and inch marks are left off. Thus a one by four that is ten feet long would be expressed as a 1x4x10. If this standard form is used, then anyone familiar with the industry should understand what you mean. The inch and feet symbols are not shown because this makes it easier to write the notation.

Quite often, and especially when building traditional soft covered flats, there is a need for a one-by material that is slightly narrower than a 1x4. As you can see from looking at the chart there is no such size commercially available. It is common practice to rip down 1x12 lumber in order to get a theatrical size called the 1x3. These 1x3s are not available at the lumberyard. The width of 1x3 boards is determined by the largest practical width that can be gotten when dividing a 1x12 into four equal sections. Allowing for the width of the saw blade, this width turns out to be $2 5/8$", so the actual, milled size of a 1x3 is $3/4$" x $2 5/8$". That is an important size to remember when figuring lumber cut lists for flats.

Since lumber is formed from a natural source rather than being manufactured, the quality of individual pieces varies. Some factors that are important to lumber grading are grain structure, dryness, and the type and quantity of knots. Lumber that has a straight grain structure is the best for construction. Grain that appears as swirls, or which varies greatly in size and consistency, indicates a tree that either grew under stress, or perhaps a board cut from a portion of a tree that supported many limbs. These boards are more prone to splitting, breaking, and warping.

Lumber is generally dried in a kiln to remove excess sap, which naturally appears in the wood. An overabundant amount of moisture left in the wood causes boards to warp and shrink. Lumber that is not thoroughly dried before construction begins will tend to shrink after the structure has been completed and make the joints pull apart.

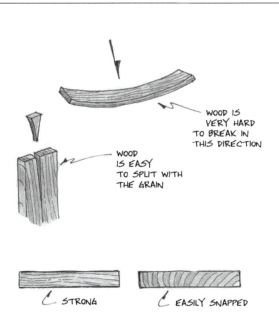

WOOD IS VERY HARD TO BREAK IN THIS DIRECTION

WOOD IS EASY TO SPLIT WITH THE GRAIN

STRONG   EASILY SNAPPED

GRAIN DIRECTION INFLUENCES WOOD STRENGTH

Even thoroughly dried wood will expand and contract in accordance with the amount of moisture in the air. In humid conditions wood grain absorbs water from the air and swells across its width. The length of a board is not similarly affected. It is the absorption of moisture by the growth layers, and their subsequent expansion that causes the lumber to swell, and this is why it is only the width that is affected and not the length.

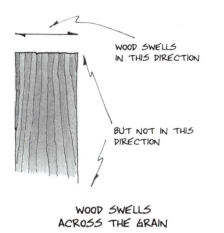

WOOD SWELLS IN THIS DIRECTION

BUT NOT IN THIS DIRECTION

WOOD SWELLS ACROSS THE GRAIN

Knots are formed by limbs that dropped off the trunk as the tree grew. If the knots are small and solid, they will have little affect on the structural soundness of the piece of lum-

ber, but if they are large and loose, quality is greatly reduced. Loose knots are just that; the wood in the center of the knot is easily moved with the fingers, or is missing entirely.

A LOOSE KNOT

A grading system has been established in order to differentiate between various grades of lumber. Obviously, higher grades are more expensive because they are more desirable. In construction grade lumber, the grades are #1, #2, and #3. Number-three grade is sometimes known as utility. Number-one grade lumber is of a very high quality, having a straight grain pattern and a minimal number of small knots. Number-two has more knots that tend to be larger and more pronounced. Number-three lumber contains loose knots that fall out and leave a hole. Number-one grade is quite expensive and rarely available, while number-three is often used in construction work for braces or other members that will not be retained in the finished product. This leaves the number-two grade as the predominant choice for most construction.

Another grading system is used for finish grade lumber. Finish lumber is usually meant to be used in the construction of furniture, cabinets, windows, doors, and other such very exacting work. Finish lumber is much more expensive and is of a much higher quality. Finish lumber is often sold in its rough-cut state, with the customer being expected to plane the boards to a smooth finish. The grades of finish lumber are A, B, C, and D. Sometimes A and B are lumped together as a grade known as first and seconds. Professional scenery building shops often use finish lumber because very high labor costs make the proportional share of money spent on excellent materials less of a concern. Expectations of the client are also higher.

Finish lumber that is sold without the benefit of having been planed is generally known as rough cut lumber. Rough cut lumber of this type has no standard dimensional size like regular construction lumber. In order to make the most efficient use of the tree, the lumber is left as wide and as long as it is possible, and there are no sizes given other than thickness. The thickness of rough cut lumber is given in quarters. A rough-cut board that is two inches thick is called an 8-quarter board. A one-inch thick board would be a 4-quarter board.

USING THE QUARTER SYSTEM,
A THREE INCH THICK BOARD IS
EQUAL TO 12 QUARTERS

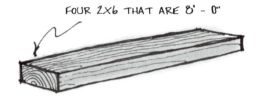

FOUR 2X6 THAT ARE 8' - 0"

FIRST DETERMINE HOW MANY
RUNNING FEET OF 2X6 ARE EQUAL TO
ONE BOARD FOOT.

12 DIVIDED BY 2X6 = 1

IT TAKES ONLY ONE RUNNING FOOT OF
2X6 TO MAKE UP ONE BOARD FOOT

THERE ARE 4 PIECES OF LUMBER, AND
EACH ONE IS 8'-0" LONG.

4X8= 32 TOTAL RUNNING FEET
32X1= 32 BOARD FEET OF LUMBER

Quite often, lumber is priced by a volume measurement known as the board foot. When this type of measurement is used with construction lumber, it refers to the nominal, or name size of the board. One board foot is equal to a volume that is one inch thick by twelve inches square. Another term is the running foot, which refers to the total length of all boards involved without regard to their width or thickness. If you have ten 1x4s and each one is twelve feet long, then you have 120 running feet of 1x4. If you have twenty pieces of 1x6 and each is twelve feet long, you have 240 running (or linear) feet of that material.

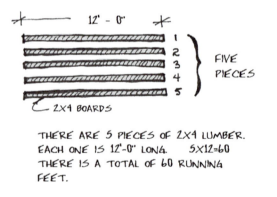

12' - 0"

1
2
3
4
5

FIVE
PIECES

2X4 BOARDS

THERE ARE 5 PIECES OF 2X4 LUMBER.
EACH ONE IS 12'-0" LONG.   5X12=60
THERE IS A TOTAL OF 60 RUNNING
FEET.

Back in the day, it was quite common for lumber yards to list their prices by the board foot, but stick pricing is much more common today. A "stick" is one piece of lumber. A price is given for each length of each type of board of each grade. Rough-sawn lumber is still sold by the board foot because the pieces are not uniform, and contain different volumes of wood.

It is easy to calculate the number of board feet by adding up the total number of running feet, and dividing that number by the number of running feet of any particular dimension that are required to make up a board foot. The number of running feet required to make up a board foot can be determined by dividing 12 by the width of the board in question. Thus for a 1x4, the answer would be 3 running feet in one board foot.

For a 1x3, it would take 4 running feet to make up a board foot. For a board that is two inches thick, double the amount being used as a divisor. When calculating a 2x4, the divisor would be 8. An easier form of 12 divided by 8 is $3/_2$. Multiply the total number of running feet by 3 and divide by 2 to get the correct answer. Multiply the total number of board feet by the price per board foot to get the total cost of the materials in question.

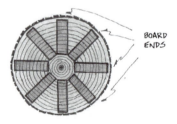

BOARD
ENDS

QUARTER-SAWN BOARDS HAVE
THE MOST STABLE GRAIN PATTERN

MOST LUMBER IS CUT THIS
WAY BECAUSE IT IS MORE
ECONOMICAL

There are three very common defects found in lumber that refer to the straightness of the boards. Each one of these defects can be overcome during the construction process, but the approaches to doing that are different. It is helpful therefore to be able to tell them apart.

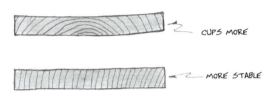

END GRAIN DIFFERENCES

The first of these defects is cup. Cupping is most pronounced when a board is harvested across the center of the trunk, just to one side. Unfortunately, this is the most common location for cutting 1x12s used in building scenery. As a result, the growth rings appear with a preponderance of the softer, lighter colored wood on one side of the board. That side will shrink a bit more in the drying process, and the board will curl some to that side as a result. Cupping occurs across the grain. It tends to happen more frequently and severely in wide boards like the 1x12 stock often used to make 1x3s. The effect of cupping is reduced when lumber is cut into narrow strips. When the amount of the curve is divided between the boards it becomes proportionally smaller and may virtually disappear.

THIS BOARD IS CUPPED

The second defect is known as bow, which occurs along the length of the grain. It is seen as either a turn to one of the flat sides, or to one of the edges. If the bow is a gentle curve along the entire length of the piece, then it can often be worked out as a consequence of internal bracing as in a soft cover flat with toggles. If the bow is the result of a large

knot, causing the board to take a sudden turn, it is usually better to try to cut around the knot, and use the board for two shorter pieces.

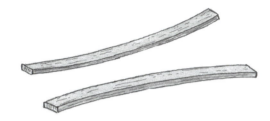

THESE BOARDS ARE BOWED

Warp is used to describe the lateral twisting of a board from one end to the other like a licorice stick. It is very difficult to remove this defect by using internal bracing. It is best to use this sort of board for very short pieces of stock where the proportional amount of warp is reduced.

THIS BOARD IS REALLY WARPED

PLYWOOD

Plywood differs from dimension lumber in that it is a product manufactured from wood rather than being simply cut down from it. The main advantages of plywood are that it comes in large sheets, it is very strong, it is less prone to splitting, and it is less expensive than dimension lumber.

The standard size of a sheet of plywood, and most other sheet goods, is 4'- 0" by 8'- 0". By comparison, the widest commonly available lumber is only 12" wide. However, lumber comes in much longer lengths than plywood. So the choice between plywood or lumber can often be made on the basis of what size pieces you need for a particular project.

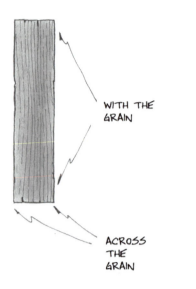

WITH THE GRAIN

ACROSS THE GRAIN

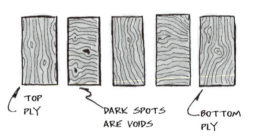

TOP PLY

DARK SPOTS ARE VOIDS

BOTTOM PLY

ALTERNATING WOOD GRAIN IN PLYWOOD

Plywood is made by peeling layers of wood off of a large log in much the same way that a hand held pencil sharpener shaves tiny layers of wood off the end of a pencil. This method of forming plys is known as rotary cutting. Sometimes the plys are called veneers. The layers of wood are glued together to form large sheets.

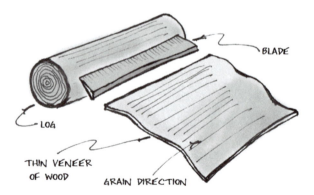

BLADE

LOG

THIN VENEER OF WOOD

GRAIN DIRECTION

PEELING VENEER FROM A LOG BY THE ROTARY METHOD

Plywood develops its great strength from the way that the grain of various layers is oriented. You have seen that the strength of wood lies along the length of the fibers. The fibers are much stronger and more pliable along their length than are the bonds that hold them together. It is fairly easy to split the fibers apart from one another, but it is much more difficult to break them lengthwise. If the grains of the various sheets of veneer that make up the plywood are oriented at right angles to one another, the resulting plywood will have extraordinary strength in both directions.

That is how plywood is formed, by gluing together the layers of shaved wood with the grain of adjoining plies running in alternating directions. The exterior plies on a sheet are oriented so that the grain of the wood is running along the eight-foot length of the sheet. This means that there are normally an odd number of plies, no matter what the exact number is. The grain pattern of rotary cut veneers is always rather extreme because the cutters are constantly weaving in and out of the various growth rings. On occasion this is called a "flame" pattern. Sometimes this will make it difficult to determine exactly which way the grain runs, but if you look closely you will be able to see it.

The plies are stacked up with a layer of glue sprayed between each one. It is a special glue that sets up quickly in the presence of heat and great pressure. A press is used to squeeze the assembly together until the glue bonds. After the plies are securely joined together, the sheet is cut to its 4x8 size, and if the grade of plywood calls for it, the surface is sanded smooth and to an exact thickness.

Plywood is made from many different types of trees, both hardwood and softwood. Most common construction-grade plywood is manufactured from either yellow pine or fir. The type and quality of wood used to make plywood is reflected in its grade.

Plywood is graded with the letters A, B, C, and D. Since there are two distinct sides to a sheet of plywood, two letters are used to describe the sheet. For example, A/C or C/D. Statistically it appears that there could be a maximum of 16 grades of plywood possible with this method. In reality there are many less, because not all of the possible combinations of letters exist as grades of plywood. Most commonly found are A/C fir ply, which has been sanded smooth on one side with unfilled knot holes on the other, C/D yellow pine ply, which is rough on both sides, and B/C yellow pine ply, which has been plugged and sanded on one side and is rough on the other. The type of plywood to use depends on your budget and the kind of work being done. There are a number of factors to determine when making a selection.

Fir plywood is much lighter than yellow pine and tends to warp less. Yellow pine plywood is less expensive. A/C fir has one excellent side that is very smooth, but the good side of B/C yellow pine is almost as smooth. If the plywood is to be covered over with a layer of Masonite, then it may not matter what the surface is like, and perhaps C/D can be used.

When a very good grade of plywood is needed, A2 cabinet grade ply may be the answer. This type of plywood has two sides graded A. It is usually made from birch or some other similar wood. Sometimes, A2 plywood has an inner core of birch veneers and an outer skin of a more exotic wood. This material is quite dense and is very heavy as a result.

A2 is often touted as being very solid and having no voids. A void is an empty space on one of the interior plies of a sheet of plywood. They are quite common in construction grade plywood and usually show up as a slot on the edge of a sheet after it has been cut. They are most often caused by a knothole or some other defect in one of the plies. A2 is generally sanded very smooth on both sides.

Fir and yellow pine plywood sheets come in a variety of thicknesses from $1/4$" to $3/4$" in $1/8$" increments ($1/4$, $3/8$, $1/2$, $5/8$, $3/4$). Some other thicknesses are available by special order. Sometimes the thickness of a sheet is a bit different from the stated dimension, especially in the lower grades. Generally, $5/8$ C/D is actually $19/32$ and may be marked so, but this slight difference will most likely not matter in what you are building. A/C fir ply is usually only found in thicknesses of $1/4$, $1/2$, and $3/4$ inches. It is truly the thickness stated. Plywood can generally be depended on to be exactly four feet by eight feet and exactly square. It is often useful as a squaring-up device in constructing scenery.

In years past, A/C fir plywood was a mainstay of scenic construction because of its high quality and light weight. B/C ply is much heavier and tends to warp. But market forces in recent years have made A/C very expensive and difficult to find. It may soon disappear altogether. Shops have been forced to be much more creative in plywood selection. There are many different import varieties that seem to come and go. Manufactured products that are similar to, but structurally different from plywood have become popular.

Lauan is a mahogany plywood variety that is imported from the Pacific Rim. The major advantages of lauan are that it is often less expensive than American plywood and has a much smoother finish that takes paint well. It is, however, not nearly as dense as domestic plywood, and that makes lauan not as sound structurally.

This material is most commonly available in its $1/4$" thickness, but may also be found in $1/2$" and $3/4$" varieties. The $1/2$" variety is especially good for small profile pieces that must be cut out with a jigsaw because it is much sturdier than any type of $1/4$" board. Since this material is made in countries where the metric system is used, the sizing can be a bit off, but the sheets are generally just as square as any other type of plywood. The thicknesses mentioned here are actually 6, 12, and 16 millimeters.

OTHER MATERIALS SOLD IN LARGE SHEETS

There are a number of other building materials that are sold in sheet form. These include hardboard, particleboard, MDO, OSB, foam insulation, and acrylic sheet.

Hardboard is often called by its trade name Masonite. It is made from finely ground wood particles that are glued together into a very dense cardboard-like material. The tempered version is semi-waterproof. Hardboard comes in $1/8$" and $1/4$" thicknesses. Sometimes there are two slick sides, and sometimes one side has a burlap-like texture. The lack of a grain structure greatly reduces the strength of this material and is a serious drawback. It is also very heavy, but it is quite often used as floor covering where those shortcomings are not as important. Hardboard can stand up to the punishment of casters, and the weight is not so much of a problem once it is on the floor. Hardboard is also used to make pegboards of the sort used in retail stores and closets.

TOOLS ON PEGBOARD

Oriented strandboard (OSB) is made from wood chips that are arranged so that they overlap one another. The overlapping nature of the wood fibers gives OSB a structural integrity not found in particleboard. It develops a great deal of tearout, but has the advantage of maintaining a flat stability that is not usually found in B/C yellow pine plywood.

ORIENTED STRANDBOARD

Particleboard is similar to hardboard in that it is made from sawdust that has been glued together into sheets. The particles are larger, and the sheets are much thicker. It is often used for countertops or speaker enclosures where a very dense material is actually a plus. Particleboard is usually not suitable for scenic use because it is extremely heavy, and because it is completely lacking in strength due to the absence of any sort of grain structure.

MDO, or Medium Density Overlay, is a yellow pine plywood product that has been surfaced with a layer of thick, dense paper giving it a very smooth surface. It is quite water-repellent and is often used for outdoor signs. It can have a number of scenic uses. It is very strong, and the surface of the paper is as slick as tempered Masonite.

The non-grain plywood substitutes are fine for many projects, especially when full or nearly full sheets are used. They are not as successful when cut into strips and used as a substitute for dimension lumber. Care must be taken to consider what the limitations of particleboard and OSB are when selecting materials for a certain projects. As it has become more difficult to find quality lumber it has become more common to use plywood as a replacement for one-by lumber, and even two-bys when the material is laminated together. The nature of lumber is for it to be used in long, slender pieces. Plywood can work fairly well in some of these applications, but particleboard is generally a very poor choice.

PLASTICS

Foam insulation can be found in two main types. Expanded polystyrene is made from tiny plastic beads that are expanded and fused together to form large hunks of foam, which are then sliced into sheets. It is white in color, and when carved with a surform or wood rasp, will come apart into small beads. It comes in a variety of thicknesses and widths.

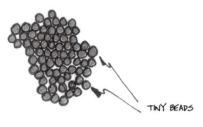

EXPANDED POLYSTYRENE IS
MADE UP OF MANY TINY BEADS

Extruded polystyrene is manufactured by the Dow Chemical Company under the name Styrofoam. It does not flake off in beads, but it has a more homogenous texture that is something like a sponge. It is more difficult to carve, but it is better at maintaining sharp edges. Real Styrofoam is always blue or gray. A competitor's product is pink. More information about foam products can be found in the "Working with Foam" chapter.

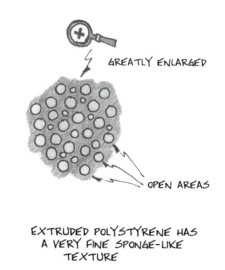

GREATLY ENLARGED

OPEN AREAS

EXTRUDED POLYSTYRENE HAS
A VERY FINE SPONGE-LIKE
TEXTURE

Acrylic sheet is often referred to by the trade name Plexiglas. It comes in clear, mirrored, white, black, and a variety of colors. It is rather expensive, but it's much safer than using glass on stage. Acrylic sheet will break, but does not shatter like glass, and the resulting pieces are not nearly as sharp or dangerous as real glass. Acrylic sheet can be found in a wide range of thicknesses from $1/16$" to several inches, but the $1/16$", $1/8$", and $1/4$" sizes are by far the most common and usable. Mirrored Plexiglas is also available. Acrylic sheeting will bend quite easily when it is thin and will automatically return to its original flatness. If acrylic sheet is heated to near its melting point with a heat gun or heat tape, it can be bent at a sharp angle, and that angle will be retained when the plastic cools. It can be cut and drilled with ordinary woodworking tools, but care must be taken, as the material is very brittle. The main drawback to acrylic sheet is that it scratches so easily.

CHAPTER 10

HAND TOOLS

This chapter on hand tools is presented in several parts. The first section covers tools used to measure and mark materials. The second relates to wrenches and screwdrivers, which are tools often used with fasteners. The third category consists of hammers and the fourth with different types of clamps. Naturally, this is a gross oversimplification of the thousands of different types of hand tools, but it seems best to create some sort of organizational structure. Some of the tools shown don't really fit into any of the sections exactly, so I've just plugged them in at the most convenient spot.

Once upon a time, when speaking to my class about tools, I would begin my remarks with the statement that tools are really just an extension of our own bodies. And then continue with how our fingers can grasp things but a wrench or a pair of pliers can do it with more force. One year as I was standing before the class prepared to say just that, a student remarked, "You're not going to tell us that tools are an extension of our own bodies, are you?" and of course I said no. At least until now. I guess I wasn't the first person to think of that. But you can easily see the meaning of the statement.

MEASURING AND MARKING TOOLS

Undoubtedly, the most commonly used measuring tool is the measuring tape. It is a tool that seems so obvious and self-explanatory at first glance, but it is actually much more complex than that. Physically, the standard type consists of a thin metal strip that is rolled up inside a plastic or metal housing. This strip is called the 'blade," and it is connected to a wind-up spring that retracts it into the housing. The blade is curved from side to side so that it has a certain rigidity when extended. That is to say that it stiffens and can be played out to a distant point. The width of the blade (the best are one inch wide) governs the effectiveness of its ability to be extended in this manner, and narrow blades will not go as far. Generally, there is a button or catch of some sort that locks the blade in an extended position.

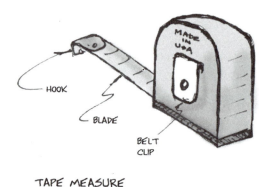

TAPE MEASURE

There is a small metal piece attached to the end of the blade that is used to hook over the end of a board that you are measuring. On close inspection, the hook will appear to be quite loose, and the casual observer might attribute this looseness to shoddy workmanship on the part of the manufacturer.

There is, however, a method to this madness. The hook is intended to shift position in order to accommodate both inside and outside measurements, while adjusting itself to account for the thickness of the hook itself. When used for a measurement to the inside of a space (such as the inside of a cabinet) the hook will slide toward the user, making its outside the point of absolute zero. When hooked over the end of a board it will extend outward, making its inside the point of absolute zero.

Another method of enhancing the accuracy of a tape measure is by adjusting the hook through bending. Using a pair of pliers, it is possible to bend the hook until the tape reads accurately when tested against an object of known size. If the hook has been flattened out by stepping on it or some other misadventure, it should be readjusted before further use.

The blade is marked with a series of numbers and lines that are used to reference measurements. Most tapes can measure an object down to the closest sixteenth of an inch. That is the distance between the closest-together marks on the blade.

The fractional sizes used in woodworking may seem quite odd at first, but they are actually derived in a very logical way that comes from dividing distances in half. The largest mark between any two of the inch designations is used to indicate one half of an inch. The two next-longest marks indicate one-half of that distance, or four one-quarters of an inch. Next is one-eighth of an inch, and finally the smallest lines are used to measure one-sixteenth of an inch. One-sixteenth is equal to half of a half of a half of a half of an inch. If you are unsure which lines represent which fraction, simply look in the middle of the inch to find the half, the middle of the half to find the quarter, the middle of the quarter to find the eighth, and the middle of the eighth to find the sixteenth. Or count how many of a particular size space are between two inch marks. If there are eight of them, then those are the $1/8$" spaces and/or marks. (Actually, seven marks make up eight spaces because there are already beginning and ending marks. That is the sort of concept that algebra teachers live for. Spaces = lines – one.)

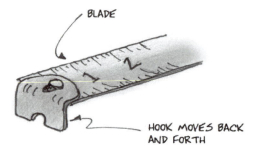

BLADE

HOOK MOVES BACK AND FORTH

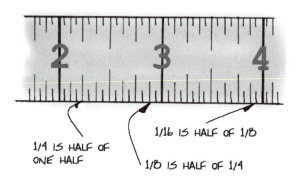

1/4 IS HALF OF ONE HALF

1/8 IS HALF OF 1/4

1/16 IS HALF OF 1/8

Notice that the numbering system on a tape measure has two different sets of numbers, one along each edge of the blade. One consists of numbers that are all inches. Twenty-five feet is equal to 300 inches. On the other edge both feet and inches are shown, so that you have measurements such as 10 feet 2 inches. That also equals 122 inches. Look from side to side on the blade to convert systems. Dimensions listed on a plan sometimes use one method and sometimes the other, so the tape is manufactured to accommodate either one. If you are ever looking at a plan, and would like to convert feet and inches to just inches, you can look up the answer by cross referencing it on the tape.

There is also a series of numbers printed on the tape with red ink. They start at 16 and continue onward to include 32, 48, 64, 80, 96, and so forth. These numbers are, of course, multiples of 16. They are printed red to make them easy to locate. Sixteen inches is the normal center spacing for framing members like studs in the wall of a house. Most tools are designed for the home construction market rather than for scenery building. This can sometimes leave us with extraneous information, but in this case you may find occasions to also frame scenery on sixteen-inch centers.

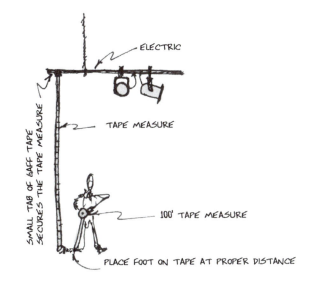

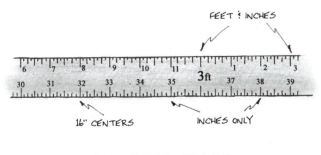

TAPE MEASURE MARKINGS

There is another type of tape measure that is more often used in the theatre itself rather than in the shop. A fifty- or one-hundred-foot cloth or steel tape that can be reeled in like a fishing rod is helpful for laying out the locations of large units of scenery. This kind of tape is also used for measuring the trim heights of battens by lightly attaching the end of the measuring tape to the batten with adhesive gaffer's tape and then flying the batten out. Hold the correct distance marking to the floor with your foot, and when the tape becomes taut, the proper height has been reached. It is fine to step on this kind of a tape measure because it is already flat. Repeatedly stepping on a tape with a curved blade will eventually ruin it.

A framing square can be used for both measuring and marking. This square is so named because it is often used in laying out the framing (or structure —studs, joists, and rafters) of a house. This is another example of how most tools and materials are really made to be used in the home construction industry. A good framing square is made of aluminum so that it is lightweight and rustproof. There are inch markings along all the sides.

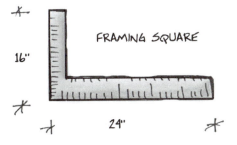

Because this tool is often used to compute roof pitches, some of the markings may be in twelfths of an inch rather than in sixteenths of an inch. Roof pitches are expressed by stating a rise and a run in twelfths of an inch, such as 9/12 or 12/12. Twelfths of an inch will not work if you are measuring sixteenths or eighths. You should be aware of this when using this square as a measuring tool. The framing square is most often used to check or create 90-degree angle corners.

A relative of the framing square is the "Speed Square" that is used in much the same manner. Speed Squares are smaller and sturdier than their larger cousins and also have a lip along one edge to make it easier to line them up with a board. They are very commonly used to mark the alignment of framing members. Speed Square is capitalized because it is a name of a specific product. There are knock-off brands with names like "Rapid Square."

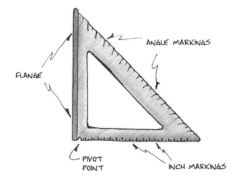

SPEED SQUARE

A very large type of square is the drywall square. Drywall squares look like a large metal version of the T-square that was once used for drafting. They are not terribly accurate, but they make excellent straight edges and are also useful for jobs such as laying out where nails should go in order to run into hidden framing when you are building hardcover flats or platforming.

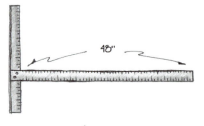

DRYWALL SQUARE

The chalk line is an excellent tool for marking long straight lines. This tool consists of a fishing-type reel housed in a box filled with chalk dust. String on the reel becomes coated with the chalk. If the string is stretched between two points it will form a straight line, and snapping (pulling the string up slightly and letting it go) the string will leave chalk dust on the surface of whatever you are marking. Be sure to stretch the string tautly, in order to assure that the line is really straight.

It is often easier to run the string past the two marks so that the line is longer than you really need. If the points are extremely far apart, have a third person hold the center of the string, and snap the line twice, once from either side.

Shake the box and hold it with the pointy end down to get extra chalk on the string as it comes out of the tool. Chalk is usually blue, but other colors are available. The red is meant to make semi-permanent lines in concrete, so you may have trouble getting that color off if you use it for woodworking. Painters like to use powdered charcoal instead of chalk.

CHALK LINE

A large wooden compass is essential for marking circles. You can easily make this one from scrap lumber and a bolt.

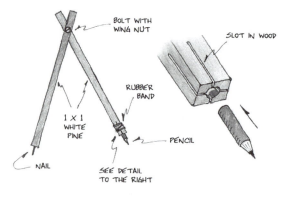

LARGE SHOP-BUILT COMPASS

For even larger circles, trammel points are used. These are essentially small clamps that can be attached to a wooden slat. One of the clamps forms a pivot point while the other holds a pencil. Many slats of wood can be joined together if necessary. This type of rig is much more accurate than the old "string and a pencil" method. If trammel points are not available, a very satisfactory shop-built compass can be put together with slats of wood, a nail, and a hole drilled for the pencil. This alternative method is not quite as easy to use, but it can give excellent results.

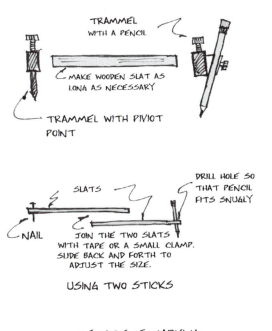

TRAMMEL
WITH A PENCIL

MAKE WOODEN SLAT AS
LONG AS NECESSARY

TRAMMEL WITH PIVIOT
POINT

SLATS

DRILL HOLE SO
THAT PENCIL
FITS SNUGLY

NAIL

JOIN THE TWO SLATS
WITH TAPE OR A SMALL CLAMP.
SLIDE BACK AND FORTH TO
ADJUST THE SIZE.

USING TWO STICKS

TWO METHODS OF MARKING
LARGE CIRCLES

WRENCHES, PLIERS, ETC.

These tools are used for gripping and turning and come in a multitude of varieties for special purposes. Choices should be made as to which tool is most appropriate for a particular task. Using the wrong tool can be very frustrating, while using the right one will make any job easier. Remember that virtually all fasteners tighten in a clockwise direction and loosen in the opposite. direction. As the saying goes, "Righty tighty and lefty loosy."

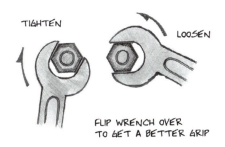

TIGHTEN

LOOSEN

FLIP WRENCH OVER
TO GET A BETTER GRIP

Levels are used to check objects to see if they are level to the horizon, or plumb with a line that is perpendicular to the horizon. Those are the proper terms, level being flat, and plumb being upright. Most levels have several small vials with air bubbles inside of them. The vials are placed so that they are either in line with the length of the tool or perpendicular to it. That facilitates using the level either horizontally or vertically. A level with a longer body is more accurate but often more difficult to use.

Each vial has two marks toward its center. The middle of the vial bulges slightly to help steady the bubble inside. When the bubble is directly between the two marks, the level is in proper alignment.

The most commonly used wrench in most theatres is the crescent or adjustable wrench. The Crescent tool company invented this type of wrench, and in modern usage any brand of adjustable wrench is often referred to as a crescent or "C" wrench. A crescent is identifiable by its peculiar half-moon shape. The jaws of the wrench can be adjusted to different sizes by turning a screw-threaded device with your thumb. A crescent wrench is essential for use in hanging or focusing lighting equipment, since lighting equipment uses so many different sizes and types of bolts.

ADJUSTABLE

CRESCENT WRENCH

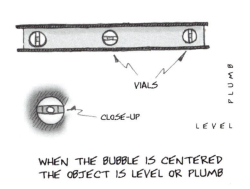

VIALS

PLUMB

CLOSE-UP

LEVEL

WHEN THE BUBBLE IS CENTERED
THE OBJECT IS LEVEL OR PLUMB

An open-end wrench is similar in appearance to a crescent wrench except that it is not adjustable. A set of these wrenches is usually required in order to possess the correct size. Quite often there are actually two different sizes incorporated into the same wrench, one at either end. Notice that the ends are fixed at an angle to the body of the tool. This allows you to get a wider range of motion when using the wrench in a tight space. You can get a better angle to start from if you flip the wrench over each time you reposition it.

OPEN END WRENCH

A box-end wrench entirely wraps around a hex headed bolt and makes for the best possible gripping force. If a wrench should slip off while you are turning a bolt, the head will be damaged. It may get to a point that the faces of the bolt or nut are so rounded off that it is no longer possible to turn it with the wrench. Box-end wrenches are less prone to slipping and damaging the bolt. They generally come in sets that are double ended, just like the open-ended wrenches.

BOX END WRENCH

Socket wrenches are very similar to box-end wrenches in the way that they grip a bolt head. The difference lies in the method of attaching a handle.

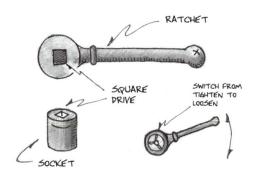

SOCKET WRENCH

Sockets typically use a ratchet type of handle that can be set to turn freely one way and grip in the other. This negates the need to remove the wrench from the bolt head in order to gain fresh purchase. This makes for especially speedy tightening and loosening. Deep sockets are good when the end of the bolt protrudes a good distance through the nut and might cause the wrench to bottom out with a normal socket.

The "drive" of the ratchet refers to the size of the square nub that fits into the top of the socket. The most common drive size is $3/8$".

Pliers are the most quintessential gripping tool, and the most likely to be considered an "extension of the human body." Most pliers are not designed to be used on bolt heads, and indeed will often scar a bolt or nut and make it difficult to deal with later on. Some types of pliers are really meant to be used as cutting tools and not with any type of fastener at all. There are some new types of gripping pliers marketed to automatically change size and get a really strong grip on a bolt. They are very hard on the metal and should be used only as a last resort.

Slip-joint pliers are the most common type. They can be used for gripping and holding different-sized objects when fingers are not strong enough. The slip-joint part comes from the fact that the rivet holding the two halves together can be adjusted, allowing the jaws to accommodate either very small pieces or very large pieces, depending on the placement of the rivet. This tool has a wide range of uses, such as gripping small wires or crimping together an S hook.

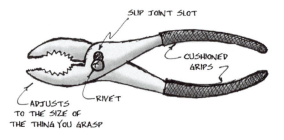

SLIP-JOINT PLIERS

Needle-nose pliers have a long, pointy snout for small objects.

NEEDLE-NOSE PLIERS

Vise Grips (another brand name) are specialized pliers that can clamp and lock into place with great force. They are adjustable for a wide range of sizes. Vise Grips have an amazingly large variety of uses when you need a tool that can be clamped in place. They are particularly handy for removing stripped-out screws when there is enough of the head or body sticking out to get a grip on it.

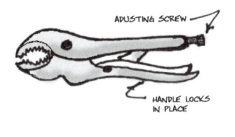

VISE GRIPS

Diagonal pliers or "dikes" are actually intended to cut pieces of wire or small metal hardware like pins or nails. You may also find them to be an excellent tool for misapplied pneumatic nails or staples. Use them to grip, rather than cut through the nail, and then twist the dikes and pull the nail out. Use a twisting motion to gain leverage, just like a claw hammer. Of course this won't work on larger sizes of hand driven nails because the amount of required force is too large.

DIAGONAL PLIERS

Bolt cutters. These really aren't pliers at all, but they are kind of similar in appearance. As the name implies, this tool can be used to cut off bolts, but also chain, metal rods, and the occasional padlock.

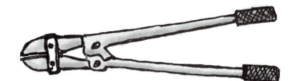

BOLT CUTTERS

Locks are made with hardened steel and will ruin your bolt cutters after a short while. You can get much more leverage on the cut if you place the bolt as far as possible into the jaws of the cutters, close to the pivot point.

Pipe or "monkey" wrenches are intended to grip a round object, most often a pipe. They are adjustable to fit different pipe sizes. Pipe wrenches only grip in one direction at a time and thus must be repositioned in order to go from tightening to loosening. (So any monkey wrench can be left-handed if you just turn it over.) If you are connecting two pipes with a coupling, use two wrenches facing in opposite directions.

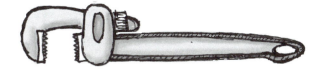

PIPE WRENCH

Cable cutters are really the only tool choice for cutting aircraft cable, and that is the only thing you should do with them. Felco is the most common brand. Cable cutters are quite expensive and will be seriously damaged if used to cut anything else. The jaws are angled so that the front part comes together first, which forces the cable together and greatly reduces the amount of fraying that occurs when making the cut. An ordinary pair of dikes won't do that. The 7" size cutters are big enough for the $1/8$" aircraft cable used to hang most theatre scenery. You will need something larger for the $1/4$" cable used to rig battens.

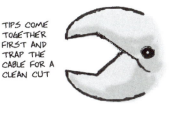

CABLE CUTTER JAWS

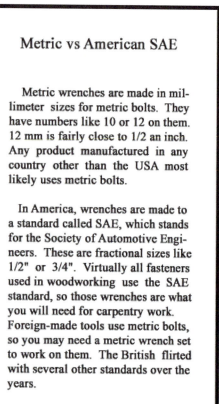

Metric vs American SAE

Metric wrenches are made in millimeter sizes for metric bolts. They have numbers like 10 or 12 on them. 12 mm is fairly close to 1/2 an inch. Any product manufactured in any country other than the USA most likely uses metric bolts.

In America, wrenches are made to a standard called SAE, which stands for the Society of Automotive Engineers. These are fractional sizes like 1/2" or 3/4". Virtually all fasteners used in woodworking use the SAE standard, so those wrenches are what you will need for carpentry work. Foreign-made tools use metric bolts, so you may need a metric wrench set to work on them. The British flirted with several other standards over the years.

Good Luck!

HAMMERS AND MALLETS

There are basically two different categories for hammers: those used for driving nails, and all others. Nail driving hammers are of course the most common in a woodworking shop. Other types include rubber mallets, sledge hammers, wooden mallets, and ball peen hammers. This second grouping is used for various tasks like demolition and metalworking.

The standard nail-driving hammer has a 16-ounce head, although they are also manufactured in lighter and heavier weights. There is a curved claw version and a straight claw type. The claw is the opposite side from the portion used to pound in nails. The curved claw is best for removing nails, as it allows the user to rock the hammer along the claw to gain leverage and more easily pry out the nail. A straight claw is easier to slip in between boards and pry them apart. Either one is about the same when it comes to driving nails.

There is a definite difference in the quality of various hammers. The steel used in the head of the hammer should be hard enough not to wear away or be deformed by nails. You may have seen cheap hammers made from very soft steel whose claws have been bent and twisted from the force of removing nails. On the other end of the spectrum, if a hammer is made from steel that is too hard, it may be brittle as a

result. Chips of the hammer head itself can shatter and fly away and are very dangerous. Some years ago, OSHA came up with guidelines for manufacturers about grinding some steel from the striking area of hammers to make them less likely to chip. You can see that the edges of a hammer are chamfered at a 45 degree angle.

The handle of a hammer is also important. It should be sturdy and unlikely to break, as again, the prospect of an entire head breaking loose and flying through the air is not a happy one. Steel handles are unlikely to break, but they are prone to transmitting a high degree of shock and vibration to the elbow. Prolonged use may result in tendonitis. Wooden or fiberglass handles are really the best.

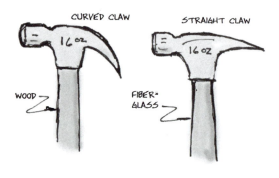

WOODWORKING HAMMERS

When using a hammer, try to keep in mind that it is intended for driving nails and not for pounding concrete or steel beams or other such items. Using a hammer to drive nails takes a moderate amount of skill gained through practice. Holding the handle near its end will increase the amount of leverage and hence force that is transmitted to the driving of the nail. However, the same statement can be applied to the striking of your thumb if your aim is not very good. Your thumbs will no doubt appreciate choking up a bit on the handle until your hand-eye coordination catches up with your enthusiasm. In this modern age of pneumatic nailers and staplers the use of a hammer has become somewhat outmoded, but skill with this basic tool is still a fundamental requirement.

Rubber mallets are used when a soft, cushioned blow is required. The same is true of plastic or wooden types. Forcing together mortise and tenon joints, or using a chisel, or putting the lid on a can of paint are all examples of this concept. Sledgehammers (some of which are steel and some rubber coated) are used primarily for demolition, although a large, rubber coated Deadblow (trade name) is excellent for forcing decking pieces into place. Ball peen hammers are intended exclusively for the shaping of sheets of metal. You probably won't have much need for them unless you are crafting props or some other specialty item.

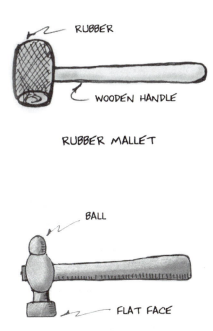

RUBBER

WOODEN HANDLE

RUBBER MALLET

BALL

FLAT FACE

BALL PEEN HAMMER

Wooden clamps are useful because they have very deep jaws and can clamp the interior of an item far from the edge of the piece. They are also the most adjustable for clamping at odd angles, but learning to operate the jaws can take a bit of practice. This clamp is less likely to leave depression marks on your work.

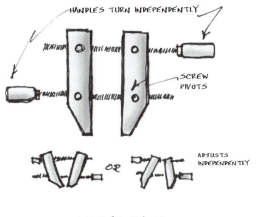

HANDLES TURN INDEPENDENTLY

SCREW PIVOTS

ADJUSTS INDEPENDENTLY

WOODEN CLAMP

CLAMPS

Clamps are used to hold things together. There are many various types, because there are many different kinds and shapes of things to hold together. The most common type is the C-clamp. The origin of the name should be obvious from its appearance. These clamps come in many sizes, but the 4-inch variety seems to be the most useful in a theatre shop. This type of clamp has very great holding power, but it may leave indentations on soft materials such as white pine lumber. If this is likely to be a problem, use some small blocks of scrap lumber as pads.

Pipe and/or bar clamps are useful for clamping items that are very wide or long. They can be used for squeezing in or adjusting the framing of platforms or flats. A bit of room is required in order to turn the handle and tighten the clamp. Pipe clamps are made from a length of $3/4$" steel pipe and some commercially manufactured ends. You can make up virtually any length of clamp since this type uses pipe ordinarily found lying around the shop. Oftentimes it is handy to have a clamp longer than an 8-foot sheet of plywood, and a pipe clamp of that size is easily made up. When a less cumbersome size is required, you can exchange the long pipe for a shorter one. Bar clamps work the same way, but you are stuck with the length of flat bar that came with the clamp.

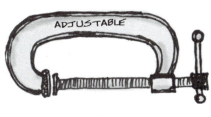

ADJUSTABLE

C CLAMP

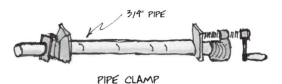

3/4" PIPE

PIPE CLAMP

Belt clamps are often used when it is necessary to tighten around the circumference of an entire object. One example is the legs of a chair. This clamp works somewhat like a ratchet strap used in truck loading, and the loop formed by the webbing cinches in to enclose and tighten around whatever is inside.

TIGHTEN HERE

BELT CLAMP

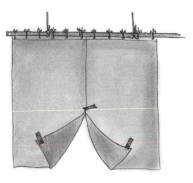

USE SPRING CLAMPS TO HOLD
THE CURTAINS OPEN

Vise Grip clamps are very easy to put on and have a great amount of holding power. The somewhat pointy ends of the clamp can be useful when the item being clamped is small. Once the size of the opening has been properly set, it is very easy to apply and/or remove this clamp. They are great for welding tabs and/or hinges onto square tubing. The mechanics of the handles are just like the pliers, but the jaws have been replaced with a clamp shape.

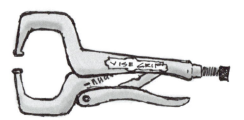

VISE GRIP CLAMP

Spring clamps are somewhat like giant clothes pins. They do not have a terrific amount of holding power but are very easy to attach. They are quite popular for pinning back stage draperies and other lightweight chores.

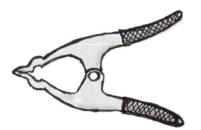

SPRING CLAMP

HAND-HELD POWER TOOLS

This section is divided into two basic types of small power tools that are categorized by the kind of power used to operate them. Tools that are powered by compressed air are known as pneumatic tools. The other is, of course, the type powered by electricity. There are pneumatic versions of virtually all tools. They are intended for environments where sparks from electric motors might cause a dust explosion. Some types are not nearly as efficient as their electric counterparts. On the other hand, because of the type of work that they do, nailers and staplers are much more efficient in the pneumatic versions. Of course you need an air compressor to use them. A compressor and its delivery system of pipes and hoses represents a sizable monetary investment, but one that is well worth the investment when compared to the resulting savings in time and labor.

A LARGE CAPACITY AIR COMPRESSOR

AN ELECTRIC MOTOR DRIVES A PISTON
THAT COMPRESSES AIR INTO THE TANK

ELECTRICAL TOOLS

At its most basic level an electric hand drill consists of a motor, a trigger or switch that turns the motor on, and a chuck that is used to clamp a drill bit to the motor. The chuck rotates to move three jaws placed inside of it.

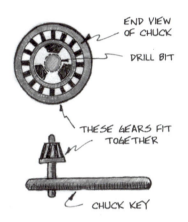

They come together or apart, depending on the direction you rotate the chuck. When a drill bit is placed inside, the chuck is rotated until the jaws are firmly seated against it, and then the chuck key is used to lock the bit in place. There are gear teeth on the chuck that correspond to teeth on the chuck key. These teeth make it possible to lock the chuck very tightly.

Some drills have a "keyless" chuck. The chuck itself is covered with a large rubber grip so that you can tighten it with just your two hands, and a key is not required. They make changing bits a very quick process and hold the bit securely enough for most jobs.

There are different sizes of chucks. The power of the drill motor dictates the permissible size of the chuck. A $^3/_8$" chuck will accommodate a bit shaft of up to that size.

The $^3/_8$" drill is the most popular size, with the $^1/_4$" rating applied to very small, low-powered drills. Half-inch drills are much more powerful, but often somewhat unwieldy, drills. You should select the size of drill to match the purpose of the work.

Another descriptive clue as to the workings of a power drill is found in the motor control switch. The best type of switch to have is the variable speed reversible. This feature is more or less required if the drill is to be used as a power screwdriver. Variable speed means that if the trigger is depressed only a small amount, the drill will turn at a slow speed, whereas pulling harder on the trigger will cause the drill to rotate at a higher speed. This is much like the gas pedal in a car. Reversible indicates that the direction of rotation can be changed, allowing screws to be removed as well as put in. When using a drill to install screws, remember to "push hard, turn slowly." If you depress the trigger switch all the way,

the drill will turn far too fast for you to control it. Pushing hard ensures that the driver bit stays firmly seated in the screw head. It is also usually best to use a slower speed when drilling through steel or other metals in order to avoid overheating and damaging the bit.

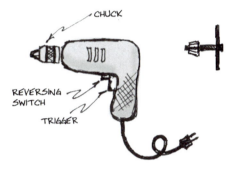

3/8" VARIABLE SPEED REVERSIBLE DRILL

Hammer drills are a variation the standard type. They not only turn, but also pound the bit in and out. That only works for drilling into concrete, which is a material not often used for stage scenery. You might need to use a hammer drill on occasion when installing scenery or equipment in the theatre itself.

In recent years there have been major improvements in the rechargeable batteries used in a variety of power tools. Battery powered drills and/or screw guns are the most popular, with the obvious advantage being a greater freedom of movement when the tool is free of a power cord that must be dragged about. This can be a most convenient feature, especially for quick jobs in odd locations. Battery powered drills possess an amazing amount of torque (driving power) for their size. You may still need an older, corded drill for heavy jobs. The voltage rating of a battery drill makes a big difference in how well it cuts through difficult materials. The higher the voltage, the greater the torque. Most of the new types have a racheting chuck that works really well without a key. This class of battery-powered drills often has a torque setting on the chuck that allows the user to select the exact amount of force that is applied. This will allow you to stop screws from damaging soft materials like sound-deadening insulation.

There are a number of different types of drill bits. The most common are the twist drill, the spade bit, and the hole saw. It is important to know something about how the different types work so that you can choose the right bit for a particular job.

A twist drill has a spiral shape, as the name implies, and is intended for use in wood, metal, or plastic. (Only a special masonry bit should be used in concrete.) These bits are somewhat difficult to resharpen and are quite expensive in larger sizes. For bits over $^3/_8$" in diameter, it is common for the end that fits into the chuck to be made a smaller diameter so that it will still fit into a $^3/_8$" drill chuck.

TWIST DRILL BIT

Spade bits are flat pieces of metal with a round spindle that fits into the chuck of a drill and are only meant to be used in wood or other soft materials. They somewhat resemble a garden shovel, hence the name. Spade bits are much easier to manufacture than are twist drills and are as a result much less expensive. Since the size of the cutting part of the bit is not in any way bounded by the size of the shank that fits into the drill chuck, it is easy to find quite large spade bits, all with 1/4" shanks. It is common to find this type of bit up to a 1 1/2" diameter. For anything larger than this a hole saw should be used. Spade bits are also known as paddle bits.

SPADE BIT

As the name implies, the hole saw is actually a round-shaped saw blade that is rotated by the drill. Hole saws vary greatly in quality and price, and can be found in sizes up to 6" in diameter. The larger sizes should be used in a more powerful 1/2" drill.

HOLE SAW

It should be noted that all drill bits are intended to cut only when the drill rotates in a forward, clockwise direction.

Belt sanders consist of a motor, a switch, and a belt of sandpaper moving on two revolving drums. There is generally a mechanism on any belt sander that will shift the two drums closer together to allow for belt changing. There should also be an adjustment knob that makes very small changes in the alignment of the front drum in order to make the belt "track" properly. This alignment prevents the belt from running to the edge of the drums and coming off, and/or from getting jammed against the other side.

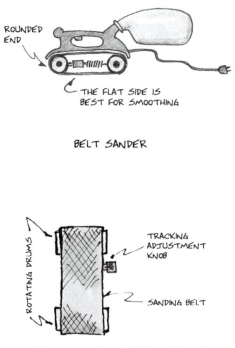

BELT SANDER

BOTTOM VIEW OF BELT SANDER

Sandpaper grits are an indication of how rough the paper is and how aggressively it will wear away any material you are sanding. A 40 grit belt is extremely rough and effective, while 100 grit is more suitable for sanding smooth to a paintable surface.

When using a belt sander, it is important to remember this rule of thumb: if you want to sand something so that it becomes flat, be sure to use the flat part of the sander. You can find that on the bottom of the machine. If you wish to intentionally leave a surface with undulating dips and mounds, it is OK to use the rounded front of the sander. (That does happen from time to time when distressing something. Never say never in the theatre.) You may notice after a bit of practice with a belt sander that the rounded front edge is more aggressive in removing the wood. So it is tempting just to use it all the time, but experience will show you that it is very difficult to get a smooth finish using the round end.

At first glance a random orbit sander looks like it just spins in a circle, but in fact this sander has a system of gears that moves the sanding pad along a random path. They work amazingly well, especially on curved surfaces. They are very aggressive, but because the sanding pad moves in a random orbit rather than just spinning, it leaves no "swirl marks" behind. An ordinary orbital sander often leaves sanding marks that look a lot like the curved scrapes left behind by a circular saw blade. The random orbit sander is much easier to manipulate than a belt sander and can be used in tight situations.

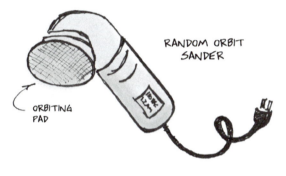

RANDOM ORBIT
SANDER

ORBITING
PAD

A good jigsaw is an essential tool in any theatre shop because of the preponderance of odd-shaped items that scenery work demands. Jigsaws use a "bayonet" type of blade. This is a flat piece of metal with saw teeth that is connected to the saw at one end. The jigsaw moves the blade up and down, thus creating the cutting action.

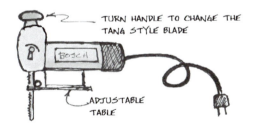

TURN HANDLE TO CHANGE THE
TANG STYLE BLADE

BOSCH

ADJUSTABLE
TABLE

JIGSAW

The best jigsaws have several features to look for that make them much easier to use than cheaper varieties. One of these is the tang style of blade that can be inserted into its holder and held in place by a set-screw from the top. Some brands use a set-screw that is placed through a hole in the blade itself. This hole in the blade is of course a weak spot that can cause premature blade breakage. The tang-style blades are much easier to change.

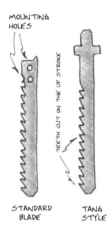

MOUNTING
HOLES

TEETH CUT ON THE UP STROKE

STANDARD
BLADE

TANG
STYLE

JIGSAW BLADES

Another feature to look for is the ability to adjust the blade to kick outward as it travels up and down, leading to a much more aggressive cutting stroke. As with any saw blade, the more aggressive your cutting becomes, the more splintering or tearout will result. It is good to be able to adjust blade kick to a particular material and work situation.

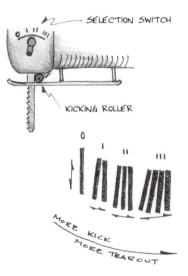

SELECTION SWITCH

KICKING ROLLER

0   I   II   III

MORE KICK
MORE TEAROUT

SELECT THE PROPER AMOUNT OF
KICKING ACTION FOR YOUR JOB

Jigsaws can be used to cut out curved and otherwise odd-shaped pieces. Since the blade is free at one end, it can be inserted into a hole drilled in the interior of a piece and then used to cut out a shape in the middle of it. There are many kinds of blades for different types of materials, such as wood, plastic, and metal.

On a bandsaw, the size of the blade from front to back makes a great difference in the turning radius of the blade. The same is true here. Some jigsaw blades are very small from front to back, and this allows them to cut very tight curves. Of course the smaller the blade, the more likely it is to break.

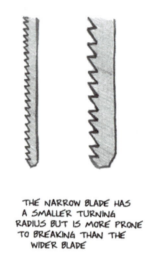

THE NARROW BLADE HAS
A SMALLER TURNING
RADIUS BUT IS MORE PRONE
TO BREAKING THAN THE
WIDER BLADE

The basic moving parts of a router are a very high-speed motor, a base that can be adjusted up and down, and a collet. The collet is similar to a drill chuck and is used to clamp router bits in position. Unlike drill bits, router bits are intended to cut from the side of the bit rather than from the end, as when drilling a hole. There are many different types of router bits that may be used to cut profiles along the edge of a piece of wood.

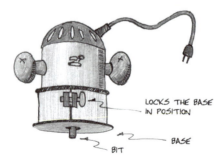

LOCKS THE BASE
IN POSITION

BASE

BIT

PARTS OF A ROUTER

Routers are manufactured with 1/4" and 1/2" collets. That size indicates the diameter of the shank portion of the router bit, which is the part that is fitted into the collet. This is very similar to the way a drill is sized. Half-inch bits are generally more stable and give a better cut. The horsepower number of a router is relative to the strength of the motor.

The router base is adjustable up and down, allowing the operator to extend a variable amount of the bit below the surface of the base. Only the portion of the bit that has been extended below the base will actually cut anything. Varying the amount of bit will alter the profile that can be cut.

It is very common to use a router that has been set up with a flush trim bit to trim the edges of hard cover flats, or other scenic elements. There are many different types of router bits you can buy to form a decorative edge on wood trim. Roundover bits are very popular to give wooden structures a finished appearance and to remove unwanted, sharp, and splinter-prone edges. Remember that the bit represents the negative shape of the profile that will actually be created.

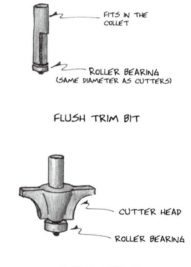

FITS IN THE
COLLET

ROLLER BEARING
(SAME DIAMETER AS CUTTERS)

FLUSH TRIM BIT

CUTTER HEAD

ROLLER BEARING

ROUND-OVER BIT

A hand-held circular saw is most commonly called a Skil saw because the Skil tool company was an early manufacturer. (That seems to happen an awful lot.) Many other companies now manufacture what is generically called a circular saw, which does, in fact, use a circular blade very similar to that used on other, larger, shop saws. This blade is usually smaller, since the tool is intended to be guided by hand. There is much more information about circular blades in the next chapter.

Most of the cutting in home building is done with a Skil saw. In a theatre shop that is equipped with stationary cutting tools, this saw is not used as much, but it can still be very handy for cuts that are difficult to make on the larger tools. That most commonly occurs when making straight cuts in plywood that are not at a right angle to the edges, and/or when the sheet cannot be fed into the table saw for some other reason. Many times it is much easier to maneuver the saw through a large piece of work than to maneuver the work through a saw. You can find instructions for making a Skil saw guide in the How Do You Make... chapter. The guide is very useful for making more accurate long cuts in plywood.

THIS CIRCULAR SAW HAS A TABLE ON THE BOTTOM. THE GUARD RAISES UP AS YOU ENTER THE WORK

The Sawzall tool was named by the Milwaukee tool company. It is generically known as a reciprocating saw. It is often more of an "anti-tool," because it is frequently used to tear scenery apart after the show is over with. The blade on a reciprocating saw is very much like a larger version of the jigsaw. It is at its best when there are large, oddly shaped pieces that must be dismembered in a hurry without much regard for accuracy. You can buy different types of blades to use on either metal or wood. The metal blades are especially nice for tearing apart scenery made from steel square tube. Sometimes the reciprocating saw can be used in construction to make odd angled cuts that are larger than 45 degrees. But the accuracy is generally not that great because the blade tends to flare off to the side.

PNEUMATICS

Some tools are best powered by compressed gas, and nailers/staplers definitely fit into this category. Most of these tools are pneumatic and use an air compressor to provide power to the tool. It is dangerous to use bottles of other compressed gasses, such as the oxygen used in some types of welding. There are some electric versions of nailers, but they do not work nearly as well as the pneumatic ones. Remember that staples are different from nails because they are manufactured with two prongs connected by a crown across the top. Nails are simply one single shaft. There are several manufacturers of pneumatic guns, and each one produces equipment in its own style. Although the guns are somewhat different in their specific mechanics, the basic concept of how they propel a fastener is the same.

A piston inside the gun drives a shaft, which in turn forces a nail or staple down into the wood. (They are not intended to be used in metal or concrete.) The nails are connected together either with glue, tape, or plastic retainers. There is generally some sort of magazine to fit the nails into.

The nails are fed through the magazine toward the drive shaft by means of a spring mechanism that creates a semi-automatic type of firing sequence. Both staplers and nail guns are equipped with a safety at the point where the nail or staple fires out of the gun. The safety must be pressed against a solid object in order to fire, preventing the user from accidentally shooting a nail into the air and possibly hitting another person. The safety is not entirely foolproof, and if it becomes bent or coated with glue it may stick in the fire position. So be careful not to leave your finger on the trigger when moving the gun around the shop. Of course, you should never stick anything into the linkage to purposely circumvent the safety.

TWIST KNOB
TO CHANGE BLADE

VERY LARGE
BLADE

KEEP THIS REST
AGAINST THE WORK

HEAVY DUTY MOTOR

RECIPROCATING SAW

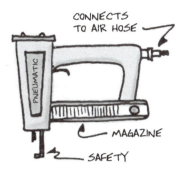

CONNECTS
TO AIR HOSE

MAGAZINE

SAFETY

TYPICAL STAPLER

A major cause of nail gun accidents occurs when a nail comes out the side of a board and strikes a finger. This can be a common problem if you are holding two boards together and fail to shoot the nail in straight. Sometimes a nail will curve out the side when it strikes a dense area inside the board, and there is really no way to predict when that will happen. It is a good practice to avoid putting your fingers anywhere a nail could conceivably shoot out the side of your work. Since it is also common for carpenters to use their fingers to judge when joints are lined up properly, you should make it a habit to line up the joint, and then move your finger before firing.

NAILS CAN COME OUT THE
SIDE OF THE LUMBER

OUCH! BE CAREFUL!

Staplers and finish nailers typically set nails below the surface of the board, with the theory being that filler will later be used to make the point of entry invisible. When selecting a length of fastener to be used, it is important to take this fact into account. If you want to nail two pieces of one-by material together (a total thickness of $1\,^1/_2$"), and a $1\,^1/_2$" fastener is used, the $^1/_8$" deep setting of the nail will cause it to extend that same $^1/_8$" beyond the back of the second board. Selecting a $1\,^1/_4$" fastener will ensure that the nail does not come out the far side. If your hand or leg or some other body part is in contact with the backside of the work, a too-long nail will come through the wood and into your flesh. So it is a good idea to avoid putting any part of your body under the board.

There are numerous other tips for the use of nail guns contained in the chapters on construction.

Be sure to read, understand, and follow all of the safety rules that come with any power tool. Always wear safety glasses when using power tools.

CHAPTER 11

SAWS AND WOODWORKING

Constructing scenery requires excellent woodworking skills. Carpentry in the theatre has more in common with cabinet work than it does with most home construction. Cabinet work is very exacting, and it results in freestanding units that are transported to the work site for installation. Houses are stationary, and for the most part it really doesn't matter how heavy they are, or if they can be moved. The framing for a house is extremely heavy, and those methods are really not workable in a theatre. Scenery must be lightweight enough to at least move from the shop to the theatre and quite often, from one theatre to another. Scenery is built in parts, or units, that later on are put together in the theatre. Many times scenery must also be moved during a show, either hand carried, rolled, or flown out on a rigging system. Moving scenery puts extra stress on the structure and that must be taken into account when the structures are designed. In truth, building scenery is not like anything else you could possibly think of. Stage carpenters are called on to build very complicated units within a very short time span. There are often requirements for "magic" tricks, like an actor who gets sucked into the floor, walls that fly out on cue, or a bed that folds up into a table. If you asked a framing carpenter for a bridge that flies out of the way for Act II, you would most likely receive a blank stare in return. A theatre carpenter will ask how fast and how high.

On occasion, the designer will provide drawings that include detailed instructions on how scenery is to be built. Most of the time these duties fall to a shop foreman or technical director, and they are responsible for working out the structural details of how the scenery should go together. A stage carpenter is generally not expected to determine things like platform loading limits, but there are many standard construction practices that you should understand in order to be efficient in building scenery. The following chapters go into very specific detail about how to construct some of the most common scenic units.

Marking lumber and cutting it to size is an essential skill in any woodworking shop. There are many small techniques that you will need to master in order to become a proficient carpenter. You may wish to keep this book handy in the shop so that you can refer back to it as you go along. It would be difficult just to read through this material and jump right into carpentry work. An apprentice period of working in the shop is required in order for you to work safely and efficiently. There are dozens of different woodworking tools in most theatre shops. Some of them were mentioned in the last chapter. The tools in this chapter are so commonly used and so complex that they deserve some special attention. Chapter 11 goes into detail about the table saw, the radial arm saw, the power miter saw, and the band saw. It also covers some general terms about woodworking.

There are three main types of basic joinery cuts that comprise 90% of woodworking. Ripping wood means cutting it along the length of the grain. Since the grain in a piece of lumber generally runs along the length of the board, ripping tends to be very long cuts. Cross cutting is done across the grain, at a 90-degree angle. It is often associated with trimming boards to length. Miter cuts are used to shape boards to some angle other than 90 degrees. The most common of these would be a 45-degree angle cut, such as might be used to make a picture frame. There are many, many combinations and permutations of these types of cuts, but it seems helpful to begin with some way of organizing these different concepts to make them easier to remember. The remaining 10% of sawing involves making curved cuts, such as can be done on a band saw, or using a jigsaw.

When the edges of two boards are placed together, they are butting into one another, and if you nail them together like that, it will create a butt joint.

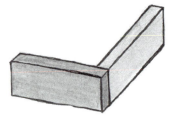

BUTT JOINT

If you connect two boards together so that they are overlapping one another, this creates a lap joint. If you cut away half of the material from either board so that the overlap then keeps the faces of the two boards on the same plane, you will have a half lap.

LAP JOINT

HALF LAP

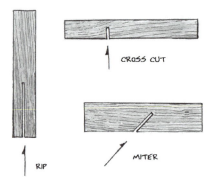

CROSS CUT

RIP

MITER

THREE TYPES OF CUTS

If you connect two boards by using a small piece of plywood, you have a covered joint. If you lengthen a board by using another piece of the same material, and then join the two sections with a third piece, the covering piece is called a scab.

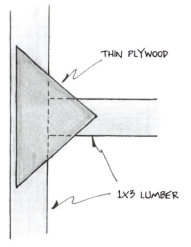

COVERED JOINT

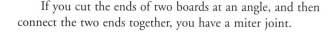

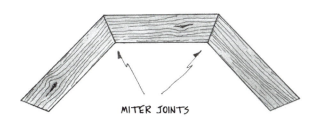

SCAB JOINT

If you cut the ends of two boards at an angle, and then connect the two ends together, you have a miter joint.

MITER JOINTS

There are lots of other joining techniques, such as mortise and tenon, dovetail, dowels, and finger joining. These joints are much more difficult to produce, and since scenery is usually built in a short time frame, they are not so commonly used in a theatre shop. "Joiner" is an archaic term for a carpenter. One of the mechanicals in *Shakespeare's Midsummer Night's Dream* is Snug the Joiner.

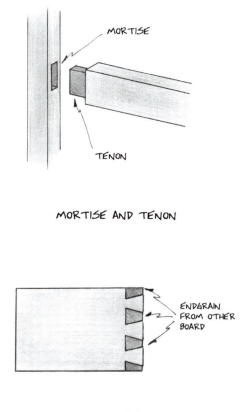

MORTISE AND TENON

DOVETAIL

CIRCULAR SAW BLADES

Just to be clear, it is the blade that is circular and not the saw. As the name indicates, a circular saw blade has a round shape with teeth located around the outside edge. This type of blade cuts when it is rotated at a high speed and the teeth are pressed against the wood you are cutting. They are used in many different types of saws. Circular saw blades are sized according to their diameter in inches, so a 10-inch blade is therefore 10 inches in diameter. Small teeth on a circular saw blade result in a finer cut with less tearout. Tearout is the splintering that occurs in wood as the blade passes through it. Blades with large teeth are commonly referred to as ripping blades, and those with smaller teeth as cross cutting blades. Larger teeth are fine when ripping lumber, because the wood is less likely to splinter when it is cut with the grain. Larger teeth are more aggressive and better suited to making the long cuts that are associated with rip sawing.

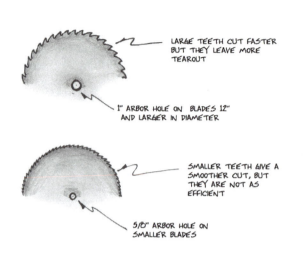

LARGE TEETH CUT FASTER BUT THEY LEAVE MORE TEAROUT

1" ARBOR HOLE ON BLADES 12" AND LARGER IN DIAMETER

SMALLER TEETH GIVE A SMOOTHER CUT, BUT THEY ARE NOT AS EFFICIENT

5/8" ARBOR HOLE ON SMALLER BLADES

CIRCULAR SAW BLADES

Saw teeth are either the traditional type, or are built with tips made from carbide steel. Traditional blades require that the saw teeth be slightly bent over at the tip. This is known as "set" in the blade and is an integral part of the way the blade works. We are all aware that friction causes heat, and if there is any doubt, rubbing your hands together rapidly will prove the point. When a circular saw blade is spinning at high speed (which it must do in order to cut) a great deal of heat is generated by the blade rubbing against the piece of wood that it is cutting. Set in the blade teeth is used to minimize this friction by separating the wood from the body of the blade by a slight amount. Saw teeth are bent to the side in an alternating pattern, first to one side and then to the other. Since it is really the tips of the teeth that do all of the cutting, setting the teeth will ensure that the pathway that they cut through the board is a small amount larger than the body of the blade. This reduces friction and heat.

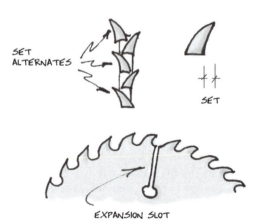

SET ALTERNATES

SET

EXPANSION SLOT

SET IN A SAWTOOTH

If the body of the blade gets too hot, it will tend to waffle and warp out of shape. This happens because the circumference of the outside part of the blade is much larger than the circumference of any interior part of the blade. As the blade warps, more friction is created and the heat build-up gets worse. Some blades have slots cut into them in several places around the outside circumference so that the blade can heat up and expand a bit without deforming.

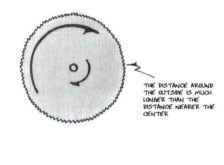

THE DISTANCE AROUND THE OUTSIDE IS MUCH LONGER THAN THE DISTANCE NEARER THE CENTER

SAW BLADES CAN "WAFFLE" IF THEY GET HOT ENOUGH

HEAT CAUSES EXPANSION OF THE BLADE

The pathway cut through the wood by the blade is called the kerf, and this part of the wood is reduced to sawdust in the cutting process. If you were to cut halfway through a plank and then stop, the kerf is the leftover slot in the wood. The kerf disappears when you have finished cutting, just like your lap disappears when you stand up.

KERF

In recent years circular saw blades have become increasingly "high tech" as advances in technology have made it possible to manufacture them with ever increasing precision. You may have noticed that some blades have teeth that are not bent at the tips, but rather seem to have an entirely different piece of metal attached at that point. These blades are known as carbide blades, because the metal used to make the blade tips is comprised of carbide steel.

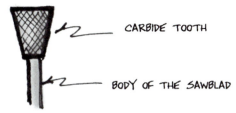

CARBIDE TOOTH

BODY OF THE SAWBLAD

There is a scale known as the Rockwell Scale that lists the density or hardness of a variety of different types of steel. They are not all the same. It is axiomatic that the harder something is, the more brittle it is. Carbide steel, being very hard, can be honed to an incredible sharpness and can retain that edge for a very long time. Those are excellent qualities for a saw tooth. Conversely, this variety of steel is brittle and quite easy to shatter, which is not a quality you would ask for in a large chunk of metal spinning at high speed. As a result, manufacturers have chosen to construct blades with the carbide steel used only in small amounts that are welded onto the tips of the teeth, like caps.

The body of the blade is comprised of regular tool steel that is much more malleable. In this way, each part of the blade is made from the ideal material for that part. Carbide teeth are often ground into very advanced shapes at the factory, and these enhance their cutting abilities. They do not have set in the traditional sense, but rather each of the carbide tips projects to both the left and right sides.

One drawback to carbide blades is that they are much more expensive and often impossible to resharpen effectively because of the intricate nature of the shape of the teeth. The greatly increased efficiency of these blades more than offsets the added expense. They stay sharp much longer than an ordinary blade.

Although circular saw blades have been mentioned specifically, the concept of set in the teeth and the way a kerf is formed is true of all types of blades.

THE TABLE SAW

The table saw gets its name from its basic shape, which does indeed resemble a small table. The horizontal metal surface is itself referred to as "the table," and is the most easily recognized feature. Another important part is the rip fence or guide. This is the metal and/or wooden structure that runs from the front of the saw to the back and is adjustable as to its distance from the saw blade.

The table saw uses a circular saw blade that is engineered to run parallel to the rip fence. Probably by now you have

realized that the word "rip" keeps cropping up in this writing, and predictably, the table saw is most commonly used to rip lumber or plywood to a specific width. Basically, this involves taking long boards or sheets of plywood and feeding them through the saw to create long, thin strips of material, such as a 1x3.

There are several adjustable features on any table saw. These are: the rip fence, the angle of the blade as it intersects the table, and the height of the blade above the top of the table. There are wheels or knobs of some sort on the front and/or side of the saw that operate the blade moving mechanisms. The specific workings of a table saw differ from one manufacturer to another, but these features are a requirement of any table saw.

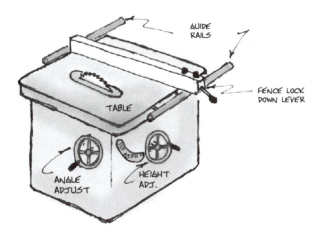

GUIDE RAILS

FENCE LOCK DOWN LEVER

TABLE

ANGLE ADJUST

HEIGHT ADJ.

PARTS OF A TABLE SAW

It is important to be able to raise and lower the blade so that materials of varying thicknesses may be cut. It would be quite dangerous to leave the blade extended to its full height at all times. The normal rule of thumb is to set the blade to rise above the work about half an inch or so, enough to cut efficiently, but not so much as to be a hazard.

ONLY LEAVE ABOUT 1/2" OF BLADE EXPOSED ABOVE THE WORK

There are some types of cuts that will only work if the saw blade does not cut all the way through the work, and you must carefully measure how much is sticking up from the table.

The blade can be angled to produce a beveled edge along the side of a ripped board.

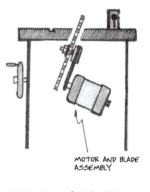

MOTOR AND BLADE
ASSEMBLY

TILTING THE BLADE FOR AN
ANGLED CUT

The rip fence is the most commonly adjusted feature of the table saw. The fence determines the size or width of the material being ripped. You set this by measuring between the face of the fence and the sawblade. Many shops add a better surface to the rip fence than was supplied by the manufacturer. A good cover might be composed of a length of 5/4 poplar surfaced with high-pressure laminate. This provides a very stable and smooth surface for steadying lumber as it travels through the saw.

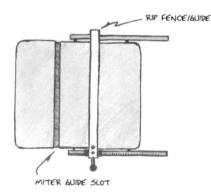

RIP FENCE/GUIDE

MITER GUIDE SLOT

SLOT AND FENCE SHOULD BE PARALLEL

The standard fence has an adjustment feature that allows you to realign it so that it remains perfectly parallel with the blade. If the blade and fence are not true, it is very difficult to feed work through the saw. A stable and secure rip fence is really important on a table saw. Aftermarket products are available to enhance the performance of most saws.

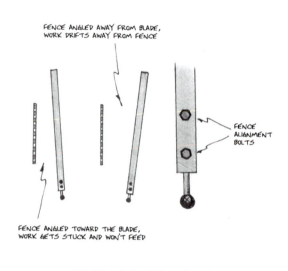

FENCE ANGLED AWAY FROM BLADE,
WORK DRIFTS AWAY FROM FENCE

FENCE
ALIGNMENT
BOLTS

FENCE ANGLED TOWARD THE BLADE,
WORK GETS STUCK AND WON'T FEED

RIP FENCE ADJUSTMENTS

It is important to use a guard on your table saw. On newer equipment, the saw has been engineered so that the guard is attached to the motor rotation shaft, and a thin metal plate extends upward to the table. When wood is ripped on this type of saw, the metal plate holding the guard is aligned with the kerf coming out of the saw. Wood passes on either side of the plate. On older models, a guard extends from the back and fits on both sides of the blade. One problem with this type of guard is that it tends to obstruct the passage of large sheets of plywood when they are being ripped on the saw. Sometimes there is an arm that extends from the ceiling or wall, and the guard rests on that and the guard is not so much in the way.

With most types of woodworking equipment, the material being cut is marked in some way, and then the cutting tool is aligned with that mark in order to make the cut. The table saw is different.

MEASURE TO THE SIDE OF
THE TOOTH THAT IS
CLOSEST TO THE FENCE

With the table saw, the fence is adjusted to a specific point, and it is the gap between the fence and the blade that determines the size of the finished product. In order to be precise, you measure between the fence and the part of the blade that is closest to the fence. You can use an ordinary tape measure for this.

Put the hook up against the fence and move the fence and tape both until the correct distance reads against the blade tooth. If you check the discussion of blade tooth set, you will realize that the closest point will be either the extreme edge of one of the carbide teeth or one of the teeth that has its set bent in the direction of the rip fence. If you should measure to the middle of the blade instead, the resulting rip will be too narrow by half the width of the saw kerf. If you measure to the far side of the blade, the rip will be too narrow by the width of the entire kerf, most likely about $1/8$ of an inch. In woodworking, $1/8$ of an inch is a whole lot, and anything you build so sloppily will be rather poorly done.

Most saws have some sort of built-in measuring device. If yours is properly calibrated it will work just fine, but if you are unsure about that, the measuring technique just mentioned always seems to work effectively. If you change the blade on the saw, you may need to recalibrate the built in device if the replacement blade has a significantly different set to its teeth. If your saw has a shop-built cover added to the fence, the saw's factory installed measuring device will probably be completely inaccurate.

When ripping material on the table saw, you should begin by standing in front of the saw with your feet a comfortable distance apart. Most saws are set up for a right-handed person, and the fence is to the right of the blade. Stand to the left side of the board you are ripping. It is very important to keep the work firmly planted against the fence as you pass it through the saw. If it drifts way, the result will be too narrow. Also, drifting away from the fence increases the chance of a kickback. When the board is fed through far enough to reach the far side of the saw table, your partner can pull it on through the saw. It is best to work with a partner until you have had enough experience and guidance to be safe and confident in your use of the saw.

It is a good practice to use a push stick to help feed the work through the saw, and this is always true when the piece you are cutting is small and brings you too close to the blade. Be sure to use any guards and/or hold downs that are required for your particular tool.

USING A PUSH STICK

Using the table saw should not require a great deal of strength, but rather is more of a balancing act, especially when the work is deftly fed through a well maintained saw. If there is a great deal of resistance to the work passing through the saw, you should check to see that the fence is in proper alignment to the blade, that the blade is in good condition, and that you have properly held the board against the rip fence.

Most table saws have a slot milled into the top of the table that allows for the passage of a miter guide. This is sometimes referred to as a T-square. The miter guide slides back and forth in the slot and can be used to cross cut and/or make miter cuts. This is a somewhat cumbersome undertaking, and it will work for only relatively short boards. Longer pieces are much more easily cut on the radial arm saw.

STAND ON THE LEFT, SO THAT YOU CAN
SEE THE WORK AGAINST THE FENCE

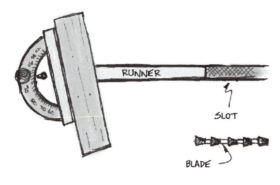

MITER GUIDE

Tool manufacturers like to make their products do as many different jobs as possible so that they are more attractive to buyers. Just because it is possible does not mean that it is a good idea.

The saw blade arbor should be aligned with the table at the factory or when you initially set up the tool, and it will rarely need adjustment. You can use the miter guide slot to check the alignment of the fence to the blade by sliding the fence next to the slot and seeing if the two are parallel. If they are not, then adjust the fence so that it matches the slot. In reality, you may find that the saw is easier to use if there is just a tad more room at the side of the blade away from the front. This allows the work to pass through more easily. If the blade is not parallel to the table, consult the manufacturer's instructions about truing up the blade.

Some shops install an auxiliary table around the saw's own table so that it is easier to cut large pieces of plywood. In this way, you can cut through a section of plywood without worrying about the scrap part sagging and hitting the floor. This auxiliary table will use up a great deal of floor space and may not be appropriate for all shops.

Never try to cut anything on a table saw without using one of the guides. This is called free handing, and it is a good way to get injured by a kickback. A kickback occurs when the wood being cut gets jammed onto the blade, usually because the wood is turned a bit as it passes through the saw. When the blade becomes jammed in the kerf, it will shove the wood outward with tremendous force, and can cause serious injury. Never use the miter guide and the rip fence on the same cut, because a similar situation may develop. Be sure to wear safety glasses. Do not wear any clothes like a tie or gloves, or bulky sleeves that might get caught on some part of the saw. Make sure that long hair is kept in a pony tail.

RADIAL ARM SAW

The radial arm saw is sometimes known as a bench saw or overhead arm saw. The three different names taken together actually help to describe how this saw works. The radial arm saw is best suited to cross cutting long pieces of lumber such as 2x4s or 1x3s. Usually, the saw itself is fitted with a long table or bench that extends to either side of the saw. It is used to support the length of the boards being cut. The actual motor and saw blade are mounted on an overhead arm, which allows that assembly to roll back and forth when pulled over the bench holding the piece you are cutting. The overhead arm can be pivoted radially from a point in the back of the saw in order to make miter cuts.

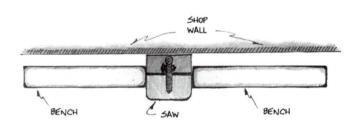

PLAN VIEW OF A RADIAL ARM SAW

The surface of the cutting table that comes with the saw is made from plywood or particle board because it is necessary for the blade to cut slightly into this surface in order to cut all the way through your work. Toward the rear of the table is a fence that is used to align the work (material being cut). The track of the sawblade is at a right angle to the fence. The wooden fence will most likely need to be changed once a week or even more frequently if the saw gets heavy use. Changing the fence is an easy thing to do, and it will increase the accuracy of your cuts. A badly cut-up fence can be a safety hazard.

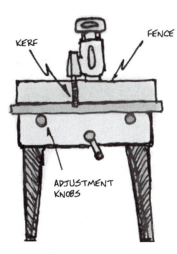

RADIAL ARM SAW

Most often there is a pair of clamps on the bottom of a radial arm saw that are used to easily remove and replace the rear fence. If you cut a new section of 1x3 or 1x4 to the width of the saw table, it is an easy matter to remove the old fence and put in the new. Of course you should wait until the blade stops moving before loosening the clamps. This may take longer than you would think, unless the motor is equipped with a centrifugal brake.

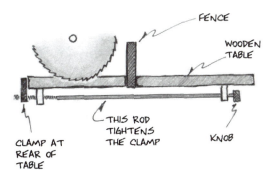

SIDE VIEW OF CLAMPING MECHANISM

In front of the saw should be a crank of some sort that is used to raise and lower the blade. It is common practice to operate the saw with the blade lowered into the table about an eighth of an inch, enough to clearly cut through the work, but not so much as to cut too deeply into the table. It will be necessary to raise and lower the saw motor/blade assembly when changing blades, and also if you need to change the angle of the blade for a miter cut.

The "radial" part of the saw name refers to the way this saw can be adjusted to rotate to an angle other than 90 degrees. On most saws there is a locking mechanism that, if

disengaged, will allow the operator to turn the arm to any point up to 45 degrees. This would, of course, be a miter cut rather than a cross cut. The mechanism is different on various machines, but the basic principle is the same. There should be some kind of marking dial that will let you know the precise number of degrees the arm has been pivoted to.

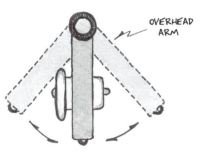

SAW ARM PIVOTS

Some saws allow the user to also turn the motor and blade assembly to an angle other than vertical. When both of the pivoting features are used in conjunction with one another, the resulting cut is known as a double miter. Naturally, these types of cuts take a toll on the wooden fence and table. Each new angle will leave a new cut mark in the fence and on the wooden surface of the table, and will require frequent replacement if you do it often.

The most common size radial arm saw is the 10-inch, meaning that the blade is 10 inches in diameter, but it is possible to buy an industrial model that is 12, 14, or even 18 inches in diameter. Up to a point, the larger and heavier a saw is, the more stable it is. That is a good thing when you leave the arm set at 90 degrees to the fence, but readjusting a 14-inch saw to various angles can be a real bear—not to mention that the large table is somewhat difficult to replace (and expensive). Rather than use this saw for making miter cuts, you may consider a comparatively inexpensive power miter saw to cut small trim pieces. A power miter saw is designed specifically for the purpose of cutting angles and is much more efficient at it. If the pieces you have to cut are really wide, you may have to use the radial arm saw.

The radial arm saw is at its best when there is a table or bench on both sides of the saw. The tables support the length of lumber that you are cutting. In the ideal situation, it is best to have an entire 16 feet on both sides of the saw. The longest commonly found lumber is 16 feet long, and a table that size on both sides will give you complete flexibility in cutting. If that is not possible, most right-handed carpenters like to have a longer bench on the left-hand side so that the piece they are measuring and cutting will wind up on the right-hand side.

Some carpenters use a jig along the bench that has been marked with measurements back to the blade. That allows them to line the end of the board up with preset marks and avoid having to measure with a tape each time. If you are working in a shop with many other people with varying skill levels, it may be difficult to keep a jig like that properly calibrated. Your shop probably has its own policy set, and you can just follow those guidelines.

Before cutting a piece of dimension lumber to length you should trim one of the ends of the board so that it is perfectly square and even at that end. Most lumber from a sawmill is cut to only an approximate length, and the mill workers are not known for using the utmost care in trimming the ends.

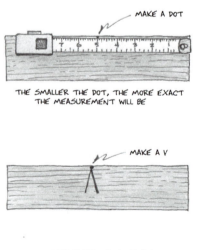

TRIM THE END OF A BOARD
TO STRAIGHTEN IT AND
REMOVE CHECKING

Typically, boards are about 1/2" longer than the stated amount and cut at a small angle. There are often cracks at one the end of a piece of lumber that are caused by the board drying out more at the end while banded together in a unit. This very common defect is known as checking. Trimming the end will get rid of this also.

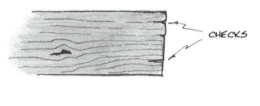

THE SMALLER THE DOT, THE MORE EXACT
THE MEASUREMENT WILL BE

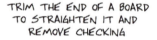

MEASURING A BOARD

After trimming one end, flip the board around to access the opposite end if necessary. If there is enough room on the bench, slide the board to the other side of the sawblade. Use

a tape measure to mark the length of the cut. Take care to measure the board along one side rather than diagonally. This is all the more important on wider boards where the diagonal will cause your measurement to be much shorter than it should be. Mark the cutting spot as close to the edge of the board as possible so that the mark will be easy to align with the blade. For the utmost in accuracy, make a tiny pencil dot on the very corner of the board, and then enlarge the mark by making a "V" with the dot being the apex. This V mark is sometimes called a crow's foot, and it is used by all types of carpenters to mark the exact placement of a cut. The dot by itself would be difficult to find. A line on the board can be misleading if it is not exactly straight, and you are unsure which part is the true length. The point of a V mark is unambiguous.

Having a new fence in the saw will make easy to line your cut mark up with the blade. The kerf in the fence will be exactly the same size as the blade. Therefore you need only to line the V mark up with the proper side of the kerf. Once you have had occasion to cut several hundred flat framing parts from a giant cut list, you will appreciate how easy it is to line the mark up to the fence when there is a clean set-up.

One of the most commonly made errors in using the radial arm saw is lining the board up with the wrong part of the kerf. Let us say that you have marked a board to be cut to 1'- 0". You have made your tiny dot close to the edge, and then made the dot into a V. You have marked the board from the right-hand side, so as a result the portion of the board you want to keep is to your right. To which part of the fence kerf should you align the cut mark, the left side, the center, or the right side?

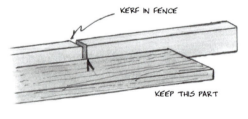

LINE THE V UP WITH THE
PROPER SIDE OF THE KERF

The answer is found by considering what happens when the blade cuts through the wood. The blade is not like a knife, which merely parts the two sections without a reduction in the overall amount of material. The blade cutting through the wood reduces a portion of it to sawdust, and for our purposes it simply ceases to exist. You must not allow any or all of the kerf line space to occupy any of the portion of the keeper part of the board. After all, you have gone to great lengths to ensure that the measurement you made was very exacting. If the measurement is exact and you later shorten the piece with the saw blade, then by definition it cannot be the right size. Align the cut mark with the kerf so that none of the keeper is lost. If your keeper board is to the right side of the fence kerf, then you should line the V mark up with the right side of that kerf. If, on the other hand, the keeper piece were on the left-hand side, then you would need to line the V mark up with the left side of the fence kerf. The center of the kerf is never an option.

You will often have occasion to cut a number of short pieces from the same board. It is tempting to simply measure all of the pieces at one time down the length of the board, but this method does not work. It does not allow for the passage of the saw blade and the creation of the kerf. Measuring that way will cause each succeeding section to be just a little bit smaller than it should be, about the same width as the blade.

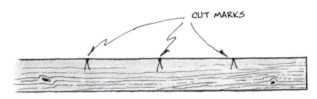

IF YOU MAKE A SERIES OF CUT MARKS
ALL AT THE SAME TIME
EACH PIECE WILL BE TOO SMALL

A good method of cutting a large number of same size multiples is to use a "stop block." This is a small block of wood that is clamped to the fence of the radial arm saw, or if the length of the cut is too long, the block can be screwed to the bench with drywall screws. First mark a board in the usual manner, and place your mark up against the fence as you normally would, but do not cut it. Take a scrap piece of lumber and clamp it to the fence in the appropriate place so that it is at the immediate end of the keeper piece. You can cut this piece and a virtually unlimited number of others without measuring again. Simply gently slide the raw stock over against the stop block and cut each piece in turn. If the board that you are cutting the parts from is large, and you bang it into the stop block very hard, the block will move from its intended position. A Vise Grip clamp is excellent for holding the stop block because it is so easy to operate. It is a good idea to spot check the size of the completed parts with a tape measure. The only thing worse than cutting a board to the wrong length is cutting a hundred or so parts to the wrong length.

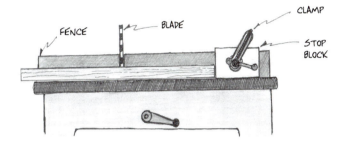

USING A STOP BLOCK

Care must be taken when using a stop block, so that parts do not get trapped between the blade and the block and get kicked back. This can happen when the already cut piece gets loose and turns at an angle. Of course, when the piece is at an angle, the length is increased on the diagonal, and it will tend to become jammed at first and then thrown clear by the spinning blade. This tends to be more of a problem with small pieces. You can lessen the problem by cutting the stop block at an angle to the work, so that only the point is touching.

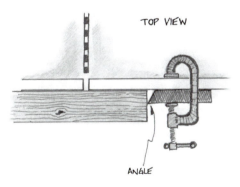

LEAVE AN ANGLE ON THE STOP BLOCK
TO REDUCE KICKBACK

However you have measured your cut, the method of actually sawing the board is the same. Make sure that none of your fingers are in the path of the blade as it crosses the table, firmly press the board against the fence, and steadily draw the saw across the board until it is completely cut through. It will take a bit of practice to learn the exact speed to use in manipulating the saw, but here is a rule of thumb. If the motor becomes bogged down and slows, you are cutting too fast. If there is excessive smoking from the blade, you are most likely going too slowly, and the rubbing of the blade in the same location is resulting in excessive heat buildup. (Of course the latter might also be an indication that the blade is dull and should be changed and/or sharpened.) Do not pull the blade much farther toward you than is necessary to cut the board, as doing so will greatly increase the possibility of a kickback. Most saws have an automatic return spring that pulls the blade and motor rearward to its resting position. It is much kinder to the equipment to gently return the saw to its starting position than to allow the spring to slam it back there.

There are several different types of anti-kickback devices manufactured for radial arm saws. Be sure to read the manufacturer's safety instructions for the particular saw you are using.

The Power Miter Saw

Sometimes this tool is known as a power miter box. That is because of how it was developed from an earlier, non-powered tool. Like many names, this one came about over a period of time and has been expanded to reflect changes in technology. Miter boxes have been around for thousands of years and were originally intended to be used with a handsaw. They consist of a wooden box with saw kerfs at common miter angles.

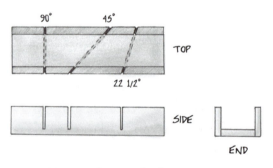

OLD WOODEN MITER BOX

A section of wood trim is placed inside the box, and a saw is used to cut the trim along the same lines as the preexisting kerf. The saw blade is held true to the desired angle by the wood surrounding the kerf.

While this type of low-tech solution is inexpensive and straightforward, it is also not terribly effective. It is difficult to secure the trim inside the box. Using a handsaw is, of course, slow and difficult when compared to a modern power saw. The miter box is limited to a small number of predetermined angles, and as such is not very flexible. Theatre work requires the use of many odd angles, much more so than ordinary home construction, where right angles are generally interrupted only by the occasional 45-degree angle. Theatre settings abound with odd shapes, raked stages, and other such interesting looking, but difficult to build structures.

The power miter saw is easily and quickly adjustable to any angle up to 45+ degrees. It has a fence in the back that may be used in the same way as the fence on a radial arm saw. Naturally the electric motor makes the actual cutting quite easy to do. Some saws are capable of adjusting not only to miter to one side or the other, but also on the opposing axis, making it possible to double miter.

POWER MITER SAW

A power miter saw usually operates by pivoting from the rear. The blade goes through a slot in the surface when cutting, and the entire table, motor, and blade assembly rotates when changing the angle, making a consumable wooden top unnecessary. Most have a degree marker in front to use in adjusting the saw. The rotation mechanism itself has automatic stops at 90, 45, and 22 $1/2$ degrees, because these are the most commonly used angles. When aligning a cut mark, you must bring the blade down so that it is almost touching the wood, as there is no kerf in the fence to use as a reference point. Since there is no kerf in the fence to line up the cut, and since the blade comes down in the middle of the work, it is really better to mark the wood in the middle rather than on the edge. It is not always possible to do that, but if necessary you can use a square to mark a line all the way across the work, and line the blade up with that.

Some of the newer saws have a laser light that comes on to illuminate a line along which the blade will cut. This light may therefore be used to line up the cut.

Rather than having a hinge point, some miter saws slide along two bars when you are making a cut. The method for aligning one of these saws is more like you would expect on a radial arm saw.

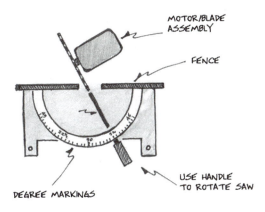

CHANGING THE ANGLE ON A
MITER SAW

Be very careful when using a power miter saw. There is a great temptation to hold on to pieces that are too small. Don't do that. Instead, use a large section of trim, cut the desired angle on the end, and then cut the other angle while holding onto the large leftover section. This way your hand will not come near the blade.

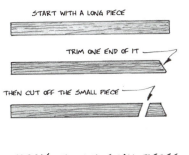

SAFELY CUTTING SMALL PIECES
ON A POWER MITER SAW

HELPFUL HINTS FOR CUTTING ANGLES

Cutting angles confuses many people. You may find it difficult to decide how to measure an angle, and from which point. In reality, there are a few simple rules to follow that will make the entire process clear, or at least translucent.

It may be helpful to picture the angle on the end of a board as being formed by two radii from the center of a circle. The number of degrees in the angle that is created by the end of the board, and a line perpendicular to its length, is the angle of the miter cut.

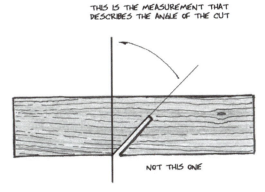

A circle is made up of 360 degrees. You can subdivide that into four quadrants. When two lines intersect each other perpendicularly, four right angles are formed, each being 90 degrees.
(4 x 90 = 360)

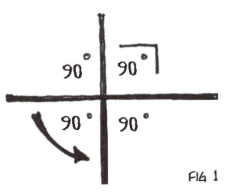

FIG 1

If you shift the intersection of the lines so that they are not perpendicular, but are at any other angle, you have a figure with supplementary angles. A pair of supplementary angles equals 180 degrees when added together.

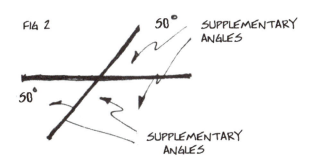

A 90-degree angle quadrant may be divided into two angles that together are complements of one another.

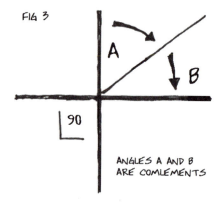

FIG 3

ANGLES A AND B
ARE COMLEMENTS

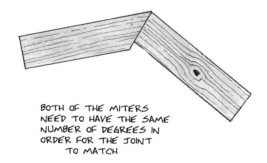

BOTH OF THE MITERS
NEED TO HAVE THE SAME
NUMBER OF DEGREES IN
ORDER FOR THE JOINT
TO MATCH

In Figure 1, note that there are two straight lines that intersect one another. If the top left angle is 90 degrees (which it is), then the bottom right angle will also be 90 degrees. In Figure 2, the angle opposite to the one marked 50 degrees will also be 50 degrees, and both of the remaining two angles will be 130 degrees each.

A rudimentary knowledge of geometry can save time when working with odd shapes. An understanding of how complementary and supplementary angles interact will make it clear how many angles in a construction problem are actually be the same. Look at the trapezoidal structure. Assume that the shape is regular, and that the left side is the mirror image of the right side. The top and bottom lines are parallel to one another. If you are given the span of one angle, you can determine all the others by using simple geometry.

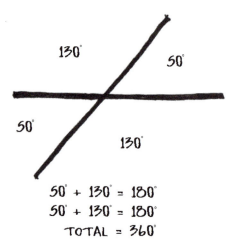

50° + 130° = 180°
50° + 130° = 180°
TOTAL = 360°

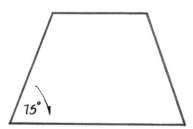

TRAPEZOID WITH EQUAL SIDES
AND A PARALLEL TOP AND BOTTOM

The next drawing shows how supplementary angles are derived from the one angle that was originally given.

When joining two angled pieces together so that the mitered ends match, the two ends must be cut to the same number of degrees in order for them to fit together properly. If the overall angle is 90 degrees, the angle of each member will be 45 degrees. If the overall angle is 120 degrees, each individual piece should have an angle of 60 degrees. If the angles of the two boards are not the same, the beveled ends will be different sizes and the mismatch will be noticeable.

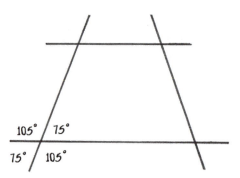

Develop the concept further until the angles of the bottom are extended to the top left. Remember that the top and bottom sides of the trapezoid are parallel to one another.

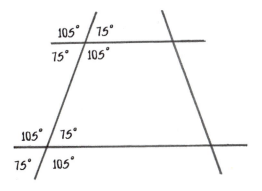

If the left and right sides are mirror images of one another, angles for both sides are inferred to be the same.

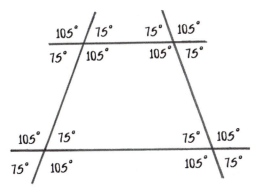

All of the angles in the trapezoid have been described from a starting point of just one.

Angles such as many of those shown here are often greater than 45 degrees, and it has already been determined that most power miter saws will not cut an angle greater than 45 degrees. Neither will most radial arm saws or table saw miter guides. The secret is that you are usually not really cutting the larger number of degrees, but rather the complement of the angle.

Referring back to Figure 3, note that the complement of an angle is the angle that would help the original angle reach 90 degrees. In the present case, an angle of 75 degrees on the drawing is actually the complement of the true angle of 15

degrees. The complementary angle is used because the trapezoid drawing shows an angle measured from one side, whereas the degree markings on your miter saw are measured from the end of the board. The saw is set up so that it is operating from a starting point that is already at a right angle to the length of the section of lumber you are about to cut.

It is convenient that the trapezoid illustrated here can be built with boards cut all at the same angle, because you can cut all of the pieces without resetting the saw.

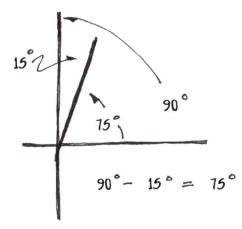

$$90° - 15° = 75°$$

Mistakes occur. If you have determined an angle and it does not fit, the simplest thing to try next is to subtract the angle you have from 90 and try again. This quite often works when you become confused, at least it works for me when I do. Subtracting from 90 will give you the number of degrees in the complementary angle.

It is not unusual to receive drawings that have no degree markings at all, but rather size dimensions only. This is not necessarily a problem and has to do with the way a show is drafted. Quite often designers work with 4x8 multiples in order to take advantage of the natural size and shape of a sheet of plywood. Many times degree markings on a plan are not terribly accurate, especially if they are scaled off a proportionally small drawing. It is prudent not to trust drawing dimensions too far. It is better to make sure that scenic units fit together well. More about that in the chapter on full-scale patterns. There is an easy method of marking angles without knowing what the angle degrees actually are.

First lay out a pattern of the perimeter of the shape. This may well occur as a natural consequence of laying out the platform top or some other construction. If not, you can draw the shape on a large piece of paper, or on the floor. There is a lengthy discussion of this technique in chapter 16.

Lay a length of lumber along the edge of one of the lines of the full scale pattern you have drawn. Mark the end of it with a pencil by holding a section of scrap along the intersecting line. Take this marked piece to the power miter saw and align the saw blade with the pencil mark you've made. If you cut the board and save both parts, you can lay them in place on your pattern and see if they fit. This is a very expedient method of working with angles, and much faster than using a protractor or bevel gauge. You may never need to know the number of degrees for any of the angles, but if you do, you can read them off the saw gauge. This method is very accurate because it uses a proportionally large scale to figure the angles. A full-scale pattern is 24 times larger than a $1/2$" scale drawing.

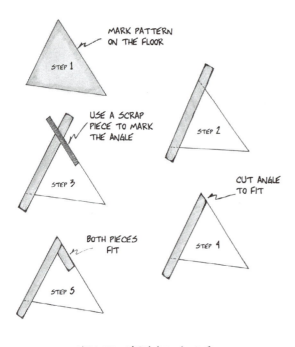

MARK PATTERN ON THE FLOOR — STEP 1

USE A SCRAP PIECE TO MARK THE ANGLE — STEP 2

STEP 3

CUT ANGLE TO FIT

BOTH PIECES FIT — STEP 4

STEP 5

HOW TO MARK AN ANGLE
WITHOUT KNOWING THE DEGREES

THE BAND SAW

Band saws are at their best cutting curves and other odd shapes, although they often have rip fences and miter guides as well. However, unlike the table saw and the radial arm saw, the band saw can be used freehand. This means that the piece you are cutting does not need to be guided by a fence or other such implement, but rather may be manipulated by hand. It is possible to rotate the work through the saw in ways that would be extremely dangerous with a circular saw blade.

The name "band saw" is derived from the type of blade used. Band saw blades are exactly what the name implies, a thin metal strip that has been welded together to form an endless metal band with teeth on it. There are many different styles of blades for various cutting situations. The two main variables in band saw blade manufacture are the number of teeth per inch and the width of the blade from front to back. As with any saw, the larger the teeth (and the fewer per inch) the more aggressively the blade will cut, and also the

rougher that cut will be. Six teeth per inch (TPI) is a blade with very large teeth, while 32 TPI is very fine. You may find that 10 or 12 TPI is the best for general-purpose work. Large teeth create a higher degree of tear out (splintering), and the sides of the wood that have been cut by the blade will have a rougher texture to them. Smaller teeth will of course result in a much finer cut, but the cutting will be slower and more difficult.

Band saw teeth need to have a fair amount of set to them in order to make cutting curves easier. The extra set allows the blade to cut to the side better. Carbide blades are rare because of the very large number of teeth involved. Another factor in cutting curves is the width of the blade from front to back. The smallest size is usually $1/8$", and the largest can be $1 \ 1/2$" or so on a very large industrial machine. The thinner the blade, the tighter the possible cutting radius will be.

The largest blades are not usually intended to cut curves, but rather are designed for cutting thin slices off of very thick lumber, a process known as resawing. The bandsaw is well suited to this type of thick work that requires a large amount of blade exposure. For a table saw to cut through a 6" thick board would require something like an 18" blade, which is kind of frightening just to think about in a theatre shop—especially one in a university.

The best size of blade for general work is either $3/8$" or $1/2$". These sizes allow the cutting of reasonably small radii, but they are large enough to stand up to some fairly hard use with out breaking prematurely. Band saw blades are made by cutting a strip of blade material to a specific length and welding the two ends together to form the band. The weakest point in this structure is the weld, and if it is not executed properly, the blade will easily break.

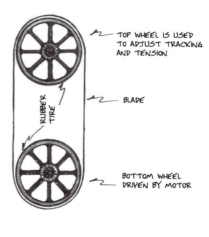

TOP WHEEL IS USED TO ADJUST TRACKING AND TENSION

RUBBER TIRE

BLADE

BOTTOM WHEEL DRIVEN BY MOTOR

BAND SAW WHEELS

The thinner the blade, the easier it is for the weld to come apart. The length of the strip is determined by the size of the saw itself and must be known when new blades are ordered. The easiest way to measure the blade length is from an old blade that fit, but you can measure the inside of the saw itself.

A band saw operates by spinning the blade over two (sometimes three) wheels inside the housing of the saw. The wheels have rubber tires on them to cushion the blade as it rotates. The tires have a slight crown in the middle, which causes the blade to center itself there. Outwardly focused inertia, sometimes called centrifugal force, causes the blade to seek the largest possible diameter of orbit around the wheel, and the blade will therefore center itself in the middle of the tire.

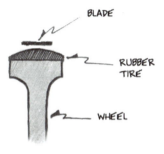

THE CURVATURE OF THE TIRE CAUSES THE BLADE TO CENTER ITSELF ON THE LARGEST DIAMETER

TOP OF A BAND SAW

The bottom wheel is usually the drive wheel and is connected to the motor via a belt. The top wheel has a pair of adjustment knobs to keep the blade tracking properly. One knob tightens the blade by increasing the distance between the two wheels. The other is used to tilt the top wheel so that it is in proper alignment with the bottom one. This process is similar to the one used to adjust the belt on a belt sander. These adjustments are amazingly forgiving, but a saw too far out of whack will result in excessive vibration and blade wear, in much the same way that improper front end alignment will affect a car.

The band saw has a table that is used to support the work. This table is generally similar to that on a table saw, but smaller. There may be a means of attaching a rip fence, and you will most likely find a slot for a miter guide. The rip fence comes in handy when cutting foam. Most band saw tables will rotate to an angle, making it possible to cut bevels on the machine. On the band saw, the table rotates, rather than the blade as on a table saw. It is not practical to turn the two large wheels.

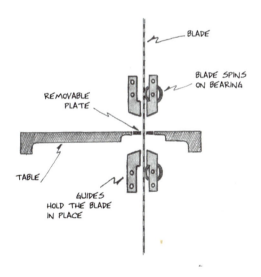

BAND SAW BLADE GUIDES

Just below the surface of the table is a blade guide. There is a similar guide on the guard that slides up and down to cover the blade. These guides are very important to the proper operation of the saw, and without them it is not possible to use the saw with much accuracy. The actual workings of these two guides is different from one brand to another, but the basic concept is the same. The function of the guides is to prevent the blade from flaring to the side when a piece of work is fed through the saw. They are especially important for cutting curves. The pressure of cutting curves will bend the blade way out of alignment and make precise work impossible if the guides are not in good working order.

The guides should fit close to the blade to hold it steady, but they should not touch enough to deflect the blade at rest, as this would create a high degree of friction and heat. There are most likely some type of removable leaves that make it possible to alter the thickness of the guides from front to back in order to accommodate the thickness of the blade. Obviously, the guide will need to be thicker for a $3/4$" blade than for a $1/8$" blade. There should be some kind of roller bearing to the rear of the guide that the back of the blade can press against when resistance is met in cutting wood. A roller bearing is used, so that it spins rather than allowing the rear of the blade to cut into its surface. Setting up a band saw so that all the parts are in alignment is a time consuming task, but you will be very happy with the improvement in cutting ability that results.

Installing a band saw blade is a matter of threading the blade through the machine and into its proper position. Of course you should disconnect the saw from power before opening it up. Use the top wheel adjustment knob to move the two wheels closer together. After the blade has been put into position around the wheels, use the same knob to increase the distance and tighten the blade. Most likely there is some sort of gauge to tell you when there is sufficient tension on the blade. If not, tighten the blade and pluck one side like a string on an upright bass. It should be taut enough to make a musical note. Trial and error will teach you the tone to listen for as an indication that the proper tension has been reached. If the blade is too tight, the saw will often make a squealing noise when you start it. If it is too loose, it may slip on the tire and slow down when cutting thick material.

It is possible to install the blade inside out, so that the teeth are pointed up rather than down. It makes sense that the saw cuts downward because that presses the work against the table. If the teeth are pointing up, flip the blade inside out to reverse their orientation.

The band saw is one of my favorite saws to use because it is so much quieter than any other and because most of the sawdust comes out at the bottom of the saw rather than hitting you in the face. There is hardly any danger of kickback, as may be a problem with a circular saw. It is often fun and relaxing to cut odd shapes on the saw. Do not be lulled into some false sense of security, as the band saw can be just as dangerous as any other saw. Remember to wear safety glasses and to observe all the safety tips for your particular saw. One of the most important rules is appropriate use of the guard that covers the upper portion of the blade. It is adjustable up and down. Never leave more than an inch of blade exposed above the material you are cutting. Actually, this is a matter of craftsmanship as well, because the closer the blade guide is to your work, the more accurate it will be.

The band saw is an excellent choice for cutting lightweight materials such as polystyrene foam. Foam is so light that it tends to vibrate too much in a table saw, and on occasion the vibration will create a kickback. This will not happen on a band saw.

There are a few things to remember when cutting curves on a band saw that will make your work more accurate. One of these is to start a curved cut with the "soft" side of the cut. If you have a curve that must gently begin at one straight side, this is the soft side. Begin with the side of the work parallel to the blade and gently turn the wood into the blade. If you do not cut enough material off the first time, go back and try again. It is much better to cut too little than too much.

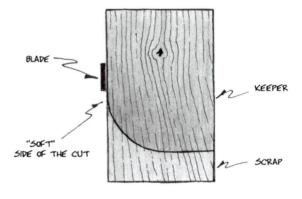

START YOUR CUT FROM THE SOFT SIDE

It is very common to cut circles on the band saw. Most of the time you can simply mark out the curve with a compass, and freehand the circle on the saw. It is difficult to get a really perfect cut when making a regular shape such as a circle because the human brain can pick out imperfections in a geometric pattern more readily than it can from a more organic shape. This is a jig that will allow you to make really exacting curves. It takes a bit of time to get the saw set up for the first circle, but from then on they go really quickly.

You need to install a wooden top on the band saw table. If your bandsaw has rails for a rip fence, you can easily make something that slides on and off of the table. If not, you may need something that covers the entire saw table.

Cut some squares to the same size as the diameter of the circles you want to cut. Find the centers by marking across the corners diagonally. Put a pin through the center where the two marks cross each other. This can be as simple as driving a nail through the wood, if having a small hole in the middle is not problematic. Place the work on the saw table and press the pin down into the surface of the added-on wooden cover. Make sure that the pin is directly across from the blade, and that the edge of the plywood square is touching the edge of the band saw blade. Start the saw, and rotate the work 360 degrees to make a circle. To cut multiples, place the squares on the table one at a time and cut.

If you are cutting a small or lightweight piece, put your thumbs and forefingers on the work, and your other fingers on the saw table. This will help keep the piece steady and decrease vibration as you rotate it through the saw. It also keeps your fingers farther from the blade. There are limits to this. If the piece is too small, the danger of cutting your finger is too great to risk it. If you are not sure if the piece is too small, it probably is.

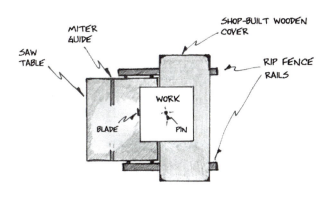

MAKE A WOODEN INSERT THAT YOU CAN NAIL INTO. PUT A PIN THROUGH THE CENTER OF THE WORK, AND ROTATE THE WOOD THROUGH THE SAW.

MAKING MANY PERFECT CIRCLES

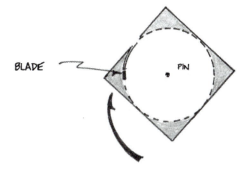

ROTATE THE WORK THROUGH THE SAW ALL THE WAY AROUND

If you need to cut out a notch, cut one side, pull the work out, and then cut the other side. Use the blade straight in to "nibble" away at the bottom of the notch.

Sometimes you need to cut a curve that is very close to the turning limits of the blade. It may be that the saw comes close to cutting a particular curve but binds just a little too much to be workable. In this case you can cut a curve near the one you need, but leaving about $1/8$" or so along the outside. If you then come back and cut the original curve, the blade will bind less because the small strip of wood is more easily deflected than the solid piece that was there. Leaving the small $1/8$" strip makes the finish cutting more stable. If the curve is way too tight for the blade, you can try cutting many small lines that are tangent to the curve. These methods only work on outside curves and not on inside curves.

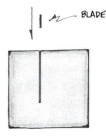

MAKE THE FIRST CUT STRAIGHT IN, THEN PULL THE WORK OUT

MAKE THE SECOND CUT IN

PULL BACK JUST A BIT, AND THEN CUT OVER TO THE FIRST CUT

CUT STRAIGHT INTO THE SLOT AS MANY TIMES AS NECESSARY TO CLEAR THE NOTCH

CUTTING A NOTCH WHEN THE BLADE IS TOO LARGE TO TURN

CHAPTER 12

CONSTRUCTING FLATS

There are two main types of flats, the traditional type covered with a soft material such as muslin or canvas, and an alternate type that has a hard plywood covering. The two different approaches are called soft, and hardcovered flats respectively. Hardcovered flats are often called TV or Hollywood flats because they are used in those industries. In either case, any kind of flat is constructed around a framework that delineates the outside profile and that provides enough internal support to maintain the structural integrity of the flat. This structure, usually unseen by the audience, is called the framing.

The basic rationale behind building flats is to provide a lightweight structure with a surface that represents a large flat area such as a wall. In earlier times, flats were essentially a large artist's canvas onto which all decoration such as windows, doors, wallpaper, and sometimes even furniture were painted. Lashing the flats together to form a room was a method of constructing stage sets that were inexpensive and easily transported. In this modern era, audiences expect to see a more realistic and three-dimensional setting.

The skills that you learn in building flats are easily transposed into building more complex units. Flat-like structures are used in building all sorts of things. The basic techniques of measuring, cutting, and joining are essential no matter what you are making. Cut lists are used in all construction projects, whether you are using wood, plastic, or metal. It is important to learn to visualize how units fit together, and how that interaction dictates the sizes of the individual parts.

FLATS DON'T HAVE TO BE JUST RECTANGLES

SOFTCOVERED FLATS

The most common softcovered flat is a rectangular structure covered with fabric. The covering is usually muslin, an all-cotton fabric that can be purchased in quite large sizes from theatrical suppliers. (See the chapter on shop supplies.) The name "muslin" is quite an odd one that is difficult for many people to hear properly. It is helpful to remember that muslin is a fabric, whereas a Muslim is a devotee of Islam. Do not use muslin from a retail fabric store that may have synthetic fibers in it. This type will not shrink properly during the sizing process. Softcovered flats may be covered with scenic canvas instead when extreme durability is required. Sometimes duvetyn, velour, or some other type of specialty fabric may be used. Black duvetyn or velour can be used to make excellent masking flats. Even so, heavyweight muslin is the standard type of covering for a painted flat. Scenic muslin is usually made in Asia and can be purchased from one of many different supply houses.

The framing for a softcovered flat of this sort is joined together in a traditional way, using framing parts with names derived from general woodworking practice.

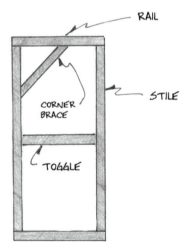

PARTS OF A FLAT FRAME

Any horizontal member is known as a rail. Any vertical member is a stile. (Style is a matter of personal preference, but a stile is an upright piece. Perhaps these mnemonics are corny, but they do help you to remember the proper names.) Internal framing members that help to brace the rails or stiles are called toggles, whether they run vertically or horizontally. Quite often these are referred to with both names, such as in "toggle rail." A brace that runs diagonally across one corner of a flat is called a corner brace. This brace is used to reinforce the squareness of the flat and to keep it from deforming into a parallelogram.

The corner brace creates a triangular form at the corner of the flat. Triangles are a very strong structural form because there is no easy way to deform the shape. In order to do that you must change the size of a leg, or bend it in some way. The corner brace triangle is used to stiffen and reinforce the larger rectangle. If one corner of the rectangle is held rigid at 90 degrees, the other three corners must follow suit. In reality, corner braces are seldom used unless the flat is very large.

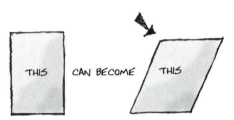

WHEN FORCE IS APPLIED AT AN ANGLE

ONE TRIANGLE WILL STRENGTHEN ALL THE CORNERS

The rails, stiles, and toggles of this type of flat are joined together using thin pieces of plywood that are fastened to the rear faces of the boards. It is easy to see why when a flat is viewed from the edge.

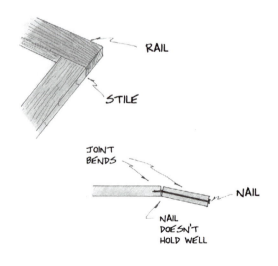

There are two obvious problems in nailing through the rail into the stile. There is a high probability that the wood will split because of the nail, and/or that the nail will bend. This joint would be weak and prone to failure in either case. You could turn the wood on its side and form the butt joint that way. But the muslin covering of the flat would tend to bow the sides inward when it shrinks in during the sizing process.

Thin plywood blocks attached to the rear of the framing are an excellent way of avoiding all these problems. The 1/4" plywood pieces are known as corner blocks and keystones. They form a covered joint. It is easy to understand the derivation of the name corner block, but the origination of keystone is a bit more obscure. It comes from the shape of a stone block that forms the top of a Romanesque archway. These blocks are generally cut into the shape of a trapezoid and are used as a decorative and functional flourish.

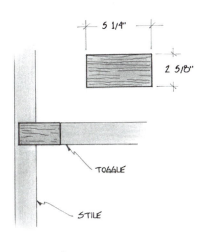

KEYSTONE PLACEMENT

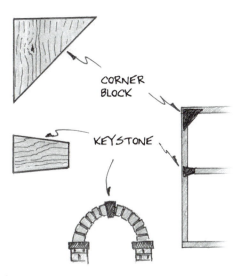

Traditional keystones for flat building are made into this shape so that the wide portion of the keystone is attached to the stile, and the narrow portion (which is the same width as the toggle) attaches to the toggle rail. In that way, there is more surface area that may be glued to the stile and less where the toggle is smaller anyway. However, the trapezoid shape is difficult to cut, because the sides are not parallel, and the angle of the saw must be changed repeatedly. Many shops forgo the traditional keystone shape and use a plain rectangle for the keystone.

That is quite a long explanation for just a name, but it does give you some interesting historical information. The theatre world has a very rich sense of tradition, and it is good to know as much as you can. It gives you a sense of why what we do is important.

On a flat, the top and bottom rails always extend to the very edge of the framing, covering the ends of the two stiles. This is done to protect the stiles when moving the flat. It keeps the wooden framing from splitting if the flat is dropped on its corner. Having the top and bottom rails extend all the way from side to side is such a hard-and-fast rule that the orientation of a flat can be determined just by observing the manner in which the framing pieces are overlapped. This is helpful when there is a mix of different flats and some of them are wider than they are tall.

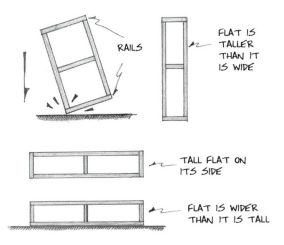

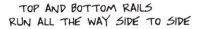

TOP AND BOTTOM RAILS
RUN ALL THE WAY SIDE TO SIDE

A center support or toggle is used to maintain the shape of a flat. Sometimes, especially on larger units, the side stiles tend to curve inward when the flat's covering is attached and stretched. One or more toggles will prevent the stiles from bowing toward the center.   The rule of thumb is to place a toggle every four feet or so.

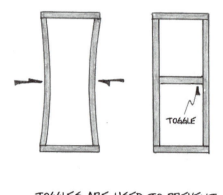

TOGGLES ARE USED TO PREVENT
THE SIDES OF THE FLAT FROM
BOWING INWARD

All of the framing members of a flat are cut from one by material, traditionally white pine. In many shops, softcovered flats are constructed from 1x3, unless they are quite large, and then 1x4 is used. In most professional shops 5/4 material is used, but the cost of 5/4 clear pine is higher than most university budgets will allow. Also, the short duration of the use of our scenery makes the added expense of beefier framing generally unnecessary. Well suited to touring shows, 5/4 construction is very sturdy, but is not necessarily required for a show that just sits down for a few weeks.

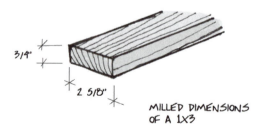

MILLED DIMENSIONS
OF A 1X3

The 1x3 has odd dimensions. As you may recall from the chapter on lumber, all nominally 1-inch thick boards are actually 3/4" thick after they have been through the milling process. If you go to the lumber yard, the widths of one-by material are all even measurements like 4, 6, 8, 10, or 12. So a 1x4 is the smallest commercially available size. That turns out to be somewhat heavier than is actually required for most flats. The added weight makes the flat structure weaker when

the flats are moved around. The weight of the flat makes it more likely that it will get twisted out of shape enough for the joints to come loose. A 1x3 can be made by ripping down a 12-inch wide board into four equal pieces that are 2 5/8 inches wide. Four times 2 5/8 is actually only 10 1/2, but remember that the saw kerf takes away some of the material. You could probably actually have boards 2 11/16" wide, but the 2 5/8 number is easier to work with.

Rectangles that are taller than they are wide are undoubtedly the most common type of softcovered flat. They are typically the most well suited for use as wall sections. This does not mean that this is the only type of unit that can be constructed. On the contrary, the variety of flats is virtually limitless. An often used variation are door and window flats.

DOOR FLAT   WINDOW FLAT

The next step in learning about flat construction is to develop an understanding of how framing is used to form a specific profile or outline. There are several basic concepts used to determine how a flat will be framed. Begin by determining which parts will form the outside profile of the flat.

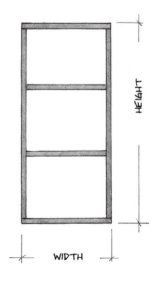

THUMBNAIL SKETCH

It is good to make small thumbnail sketches of scenic units on sheets of paper as you go along. The sketches are used to make up cut lists of the individual parts that will be needed and also serve as a construction guide during the assembly process. Some shops do a whole series of technical drawings that are really just drafted versions of these same sketches.

You may find that it is easier just to make up these hand drawings as you go along. There will be quite a few when you are working on an entire show, and it is good to keep them stapled together for handy reference. It is easy to redraw the sketches for any of the change orders that are often required.

Visualizing each flat or platform or stair unit as a separate entity makes it easier to focus on the construction of each one as a single unit. It is important to think of and construct scenery as individual parts, because that feeds into the requirement that stage scenery be portable. If you build an entire wall as one huge unit, you won't be able to move it anywhere later on.

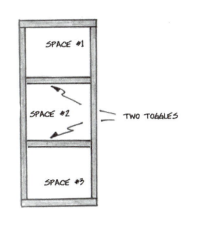

TWO TOGGLES MAKE THREE SPACES

As another example, imagine that you have been requested to build a window flat six feet wide and ten feet tall. The window inside the flat should be three feet wide and four feet tall. The window is centered side to side in the space, and the bottom of it is three feet from the floor. It is easy to sketch out the flat using just this information. Begin with the outside profile, then continue with the inside profile of the window opening.

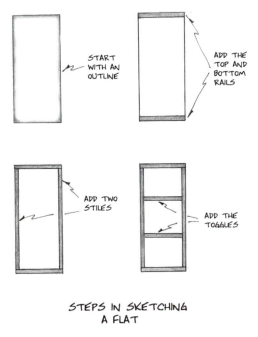

STEPS IN SKETCHING
A FLAT

Sketch a simple flat by starting with a rectangle delineating the outside profile, and then put in the interior parts. Support the stiles with a toggle at least every four feet. Since this unit is ten feet tall, two evenly spaced toggles have been sketched in. One toggle would have left two spaces five feet tall. Two toggles will leave three spaces, each about three feet four inches tall. There is no answer that works exactly, but the closest answer for the number of toggles is two.

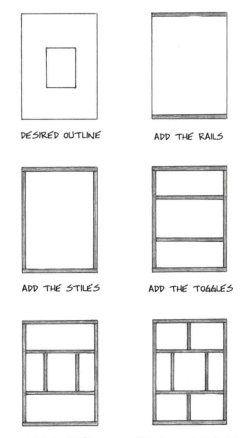

DESIRED OUTLINE   ADD THE RAILS

ADD THE STILES   ADD THE TOGGLES

WINDOW SIDES   BRACE TOP AND BOTTOM

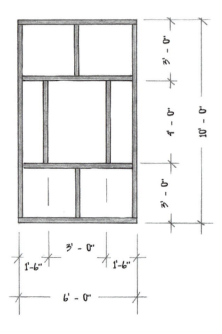

A DIMENSIONED SKETCH

ARCHED DOORWAY

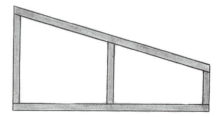

3/4" PLYWOOD IS THE SAME
THICKNESS AS THE 1X3 SO
IT WORKS WELL FOR A SWEEP

One thing to keep in mind is that your sketch should be of the back side of the framing. If the flat is symmetrical from left to right there is no difference, but if not you must be sure to show the correct view. It will not be possible to install the keystones and corner blocks later on if the flat is laid out face up.

There is a non-structural reason to place the toggles for this flat in a specific location. Rather than simply divide the available space into thirds, the two toggle rails are positioned so that they become the top and bottom of the window opening. Because the flat is more than four feet wide, two additional toggle stiles are used to brace between the toggle rails and the top and bottom rails.

Door flats are framed in a similar fashion, excepting that the opening extends all the way to the floor, and the bottom rail is split into two parts. Toggle placement is used to delineate the top of the door opening.

All of the flats presented so far have been rectilinear, but flats are not limited to that shape. One easy variation is to use a framing piece known as a sweep. Sweeps are used to create a curved profile, most commonly at the top of a window or doorway. Sweeps are cut from 3/4" plywood so that the thickness of the sweep matches the thickness of the one-by used to frame the flat. Sometimes the plywood is left whole when the sweep is very small, but more often the material around the curve is trimmed away to reduce the weight of the unit. Use a large wooden compass or a set of trammel points to mark the curve. Connect the sweep to the main structure using keystones or specially cut shapes as required.

There is no reason why flats must be composed of straight lines and 90-degree angles, other than the fact that these are the easiest flats to build. The framing members can be cut at any angle and joined together with blocks and keystones cut to match.

EXAMPLE OF A FLAT THAT
IS NOT A RECTANGLE

Sometimes designs require flats that mirror an object with a completely irregular shape. To construct this type of flat, begin with an interior comprised of straight lines that fill most of the space. Then add to the profile with 3/4" plywood, much like when installing sweeps. The principle is the same; the shapes are simply more complex. The profile edges can be attached with straps or with 1/4" ply that has been cut to the specific size and shape of the profile.

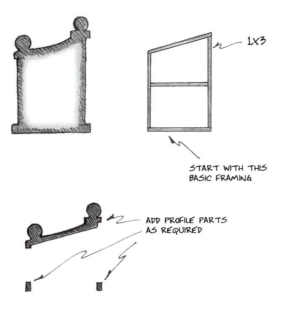

START WITH THIS
BASIC FRAMING

1X3

ADD PROFILE PARTS
AS REQUIRED

A PROFILE FLAT

CUT LISTS

A cut list is essential to build just about anything. You make a cut list the same way for any project, although the sizes of lumber and other materials change from job to job. Making a cut list involves using feet and inches, as well as fractional parts of inches. Fractions of an inch were covered earlier when talking about tape measures in the chapter on tools. The divisions of the tape relate to repeatedly dividing an inch in half. One quarter is equal to half of a half, one eighth is half of that, and so on. Before beginning an in depth study of how to figure cut lists, here is a short review of adding and subtracting fractions.

FRACTIONS AND ENGLISH-STYLE MEASURMENTS

Fractions are an indication of an amount that is divided by another amount. The symbol / actually means "divided by," so that the fraction 1/2 really indicates 1 divided by 2, that is to say, a whole that is split into two equal parts. The fraction 1/4 represents a whole that has been divided into four equal parts. One quarter could also be expressed as the

decimal equivalent of 0.25, which is the number you will get when you divide 1 by 4 on your calculator. There are lots of math problems that are much easier to work when using decimal equivalents of fractions. The math problems that you will use in determining cut lists are not among them. Woodworking is always done using fractions. It is important not to mix the two up in construction work, because it makes the lists harder to do. Many times fractions are actually easier to work with than decimal points, and you can do the math in your head rather than needing a calculator. At any rate, any answers you come up with must be measured with a tape that is marked in fractions, not decimal equivalents. Calculators are available that operate in feet and inches rather than decimals. You may wish to try one but will probably find out that you don't really need it after a short while because the problems are so easy once you get the hang of them.

$$1/2 = 2 \div 1 = 0.5$$

THE SLASH MARK
MEANS "DIVIDED BY"

The top number in a fraction is the numerator, and the bottom is the denominator. In order to add fractions together you need to make sure that they have a common denominator. Before 1/4 and 1/2 may be added together, you must change the 2 in the denominator to a 4 so that a commonality is achieved. You can do that by multiplying the fraction 1/2 by the fraction 2/2. Two halves is equal to 1 and will not change the value of 1/2. Multiplying any number by 1 will not change its value. To multiply fractions you simply multiply the two numerators and then the two denominators.

$$\frac{1}{2}$$ NUMERATOR

 DENOMINATOR

$$1/2 \times 2/2 = 2/4$$
$$1/4 + 2/4 = 3/4$$

Subtracting fractions is essentially the same process of finding a common denominator, and then subtracting the numerator. If you want to subtract $1/4$ from $1/2$, then 4 will again be the common denominator, creating the equation $2/4 - 1/4 = 1/4$.

Another example:

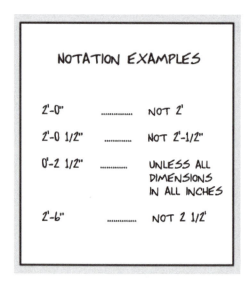

Cut lists for a construction project have the added complexity of being large enough to require adding and subtracting whole feet and inches as well as just fractions. Although fractions are used to subdivide inches, you should never express foot measurements in fractional portions such as "two and one-half feet." Rather, you should say, "two feet six inches."

There is a shorthand method of expressing feet with an apostrophe ', and inches with quotation marks ". (of course you don't call them that in measuring, they are just inch marks and feet marks) Two feet six inches is written as 2'- 6". Two feet, six and one-half inches is written 2'- 6 $1/2$". Always insert a dash between the feet and the inches, but not between the inches and the fraction.

If the measurement is an even two feet the notation should be 2'- 0", with the zero inches included to make the reader certain that there are actually no inches included rather than that the writer has neglected to write the number of inches down. On occasion, you will need to express a measurement that includes a fractional portion of one inch, but no whole inches, such as 2'- 0 $1/2$", and you are seeing the proper notation method written here.

Sometimes measurements are given in all inches rather than in feet and inches. A tape measure is equipped to deal with that because one side of the blade is in feet and inches and the other side is in all inches. Traditionally, if no part of what you are building is larger than eight feet, then all dimensions are given in inches. Flats are almost always at least that size, and as a result flat cut lists are usually done in feet and inches. If you are building step units, or some other smallish scenery, it may be easier just to use all inches. There may be a specific reason to choose one method over the other, but once you have, stick with it. Never mix all inch dimensions with feet-and-inches dimensions because it is very easy to get confused about the numbers. Twenty inches (20") and two feet (2'- 0") tend to look very much alike, and they are very close in actual length. You cannot tell just from looking at the size on a scale drawing which one you have. It is often difficult to read feet and inches marks when they are written in pencil on a scrap board. If you make it a habit to use one system for an entire project you will have fewer mistakes.

Here are a few practice examples of adding and subtracting feet and inches:

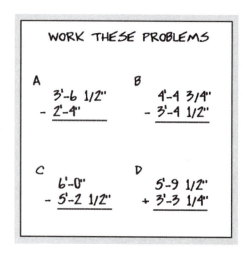

The first problem is fairly easy since it is possible to subtract the 4 inches from the 6 $1/2$ inches cleanly and arrive at an answer of 2 $1/2$ inches. Three feet minus two feet leaves one foot, and therefore the answer to the first problem is 1'- 2 $1/2$".

The second problem is a bit more of a challenge, as you must first convert the fractions so that there is a common denominator. Multiplying $1/2$ by $2/2$ results in a fraction of $2/4$. Two fourths subtracted from three fourths is one fourth. The rest of the second problem is straightforward and the answer should be 1'- 0 $1/4$". Note that a 0 is used to denote the absence of any whole inches.

The third problem involves shifting feet to inches in order to work the problem. The figure 6'- 0" is a whole number of feet, and therefore no inches are present to use in subtracting the 2 $1/2$". Before the problem can be solved, you must convert one of the feet into inches. You can do this by borrowing one foot from the feet column and increasing the number of inches by 12. Since there are 12 inches in a foot, you have neither lost nor gained anything by re-expressing the amount as 5'- 12". You must go a step further to convert one of the inches into a fractional amount so that you have something to subtract the half-inch from. Now the number is written as 5'- 11 $2/2$". From here you can do the normal math and arrive at a length of 0'- 9 $1/2$" for the third problem. Again, you can see that a 0 has been used to indicate that the number of feet is nil rather than simply missing.

The final problem is one of addition rather than subtraction and is distinguished by the fact that in adding the two-inch amounts together, a sum greater than 12 is reached. It is then proper to reduce the number of inches by shifting them over to the foot column, adding 1 to that total. The answer to problem four is 9'- 0 $3/4$".

Cut lists are made from dimensioned drawings of scenery. Someone, most of the time the scenic designer, has drawn out elevations of what the scenery looks like. These are scale drawings that show the shape and size of flats that must be constructed. Of course, flats are just one type of unit used in scenery, but since they are the topic of this chapter that is what will be discussed. If the size and shape of the flat is given, a carpenter should be able to work out a cut list for constructing a standard flat without much more information. In order to form a cut list, it is necessary to make a drawing of the structural framing of the sort that was talked about in the first part of the chapter. It is not generally essential that this type of drawing be to scale, though they often are. As stated earlier, you may wish to make small sketches of technical ideas for individual units rather than drafted plans because the sketches are easier to do. You can use them to generate a cut list. It is important to indicate on the sketch exactly how the framing pieces intersect one another. Basically that means which pieces overlap the others. Dimensions are given to the outside of the structure. If butt joints are used with the 1x3 lumber, only one of the pieces will extend all the way to the outside edge. Any other piece intersecting it will have its length shortened by the width of the 1x3. The math part of making a cut list is mostly about deciding which are the boards that get shortened, and then subtracting some amount from their length.

HOW TO CONVERT FEET TO INCHES
AND INCHES TO
FRACTIONAL NUMBERS

CONSIDER THE PROBLEM

6'-0"
- 5'-2 1/2"

6'-0" = 5'-12"

5'-12" = 5'-11 2/2"

THEREFORE:

5'-11 2/2"
- 5'-2 1/2"
0'-9 1/2"   ANSWER

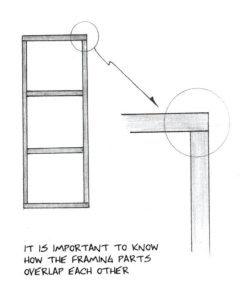

IT IS IMPORTANT TO KNOW
HOW THE FRAMING PARTS
OVERLAP EACH OTHER

The next drawing shows that the top rail and the bottom rail run continuously from side to side, while the two stiles stop short of the top and bottom. Also, the center toggles do not run all the way to the outside, but are shortened by the width of the two stiles. This drawing has been dimensioned, and you can see the lines and numbers used to give the overall size of the flat. The dimensions in this drawing are to the outside of the object. Extension lines are used to indicate the exact point where the dimensions apply. If you are unsure what part of a drawing a dimension refers to, lay your pencil on the drawing and use it as a straight edge. If you line the straight edge up with the edge of the drawing, it is easier to see what lines up with it. Of course if you made the sketch yourself, you know what the dimension includes.

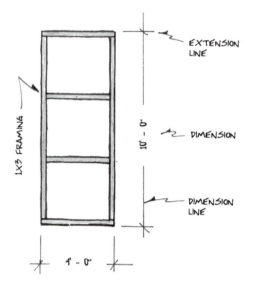

In the drawing above is a flat that is 4'- 0" wide and 10'- 0" tall. There are two toggles. The framing is to be cut from 1×3 #2 white pine. When forming a cut list begin by listing the longest required pieces first and work your way down in order to the shortest. The parts are ranked that way to ensure that they will get cut out in the same order. The importance of that will come later in the chapter. Looking at the drawing, it is apparent that the longest pieces you will need are the two stiles. The stiles are often the longest pieces if you are making wall flats for a box set. Most of the time flats are taller than they are wide.

The first order of business should be to determine the lengths of these two pieces. They will both be the same size. It is normal to assume that the top and bottom of the flat are parallel with one another unless there is information to the contrary. It is apparent that since the two stiles do not reach either the top or bottom that their overall length should be decreased by twice the width of the framing material. It was stated in the instructions that the framing is cut from 1×3 that has an actual milled size of 2 5/8" wide. The number to subtract from the overall height is twice 2 5/8", or 5 1/4".

Knowing the exact size of whatever framing lumber you are using at the moment is not as important as understanding the process that calculations are made on the basis of whatever that size is. Sometimes 1x4 framing is used on flats, and of course in that case the milled size of the framing lumber would be 3 1/2". Whatever size you are using, it will be necessary to subtract the width of the two pieces of lumber from the overall height of 10'- 0" in order to arrive at the proper length of the two stiles.

In our example, subtract 2 5/8" + 2 5/8" from the 10'-0" measurement. 2 5/8" + 2 5/8" = 5 1/4". When that amount is subtracted from 10'- 0" the answer is 9'- 6 3/4". On the list you should make a notation of 2 @ 9'- 6 3/4". This, of course, indicates that two pieces at this length are required to build the flat.

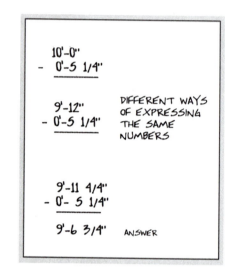

Years ago, it was necessary to explain that the @ symbol means "at," but thanks to the miracle of the Internet and e-mail, that explanation is no longer needed!

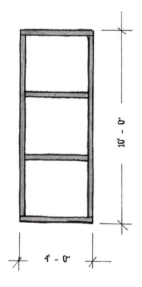

The next longest pieces are the top and bottom rails. You can see from the drawing that these two parts are continuous from side to side, and the dimension listed is 4'- 0". Therefore the next item on our list is 2 @ 4'- 0". Again, you can presuppose that the flat is square and with equal sides unless there is a note to the contrary.

The final items to be listed are the two center toggles. Again you can note that these do not run all the way from side to side, but rather dead end at the inside of the stiles. Again you need to add 2 $^5/_8$" and 2 $^5/_8$", and again the sum will be 5 $^1/_4$". I have added these two numbers together many, many times over the years and somehow the answer is always the same. I'm sure that after you have worked a few of these problems, you will simply remember some of the most common math answers. After subtracting the 5 $^1/_4$" from 4'- 0", the answer is 2 @ 3'- 6 $^3/_4$".

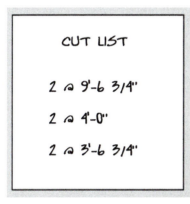

CUT LIST

2 @ 9'-6 3/4"

2 @ 4'-0"

2 @ 3'-6 3/4"

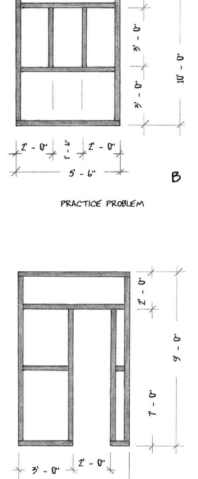

PRACTICE PROBLEM

Please work up a cut list for each of the practice problems. The answers can be found at the end of the Helpful Hints section.

PRACTICE PROBLEM

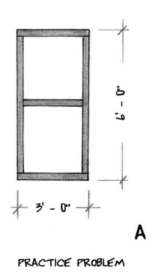

PRACTICE PROBLEM

HELPFUL HINTS

Remember to work from the longest to the shortest pieces.

In order to keep track of what parts you have finished, make an x on the drawing over the appropriate part after you have listed it.

Use a straight edge if you are uncertain about where an extension line is pointing.

If these problems have been difficult for you, make up some more and work them on your own. It is essential that you develop the skill of making cut lists in order to progress to the next level.

ANSWERS

A
2 @ 5'-6 3/4"
2 @ 3'-0"
1 @ 2'-6 3/4"

C
2 @ 8'-6 3/4"
2 @ 6'-9 3/8"
1 @ 6'-0"
1 @ 5'-6 3/4"
1 @ 3'-0"
1 @ 2'-6 3/4"
1 @ 1'-0"
1 @ 0'-6 3/4"

B
2 @ 9'-6 3/4"
2 @ 5'-6"
2 @ 5'-0 3/4"
2 @ 3'-0"

D
2 @ 8'-0"
3 @ 2'-6 3/4"

FLAT CONSTRUCTION

Now that you are armed with the ability to create a cut list from a drawing or sketch, it is time to bring together the skills learned in several different sections and try a construction project. Before using power tools in the shop it is important to review some safety issues.

I don't think that it is possible to talk about safety too much. It is important to wear safety glasses with any type of cutting tool, and hearing protectors with any tool that is loud enough to be annoying. Is it necessary to wear safety glasses

and a hearing protector when using a screwdriver? Probably not, but if someone else is using an angle grinder right next to you, the answer would be a definite yes. The most important aspect of safety is common sense. If you think that something is dangerous, then it probably is, and you should take precautions. Sometimes there are dangers that are not so obvious.

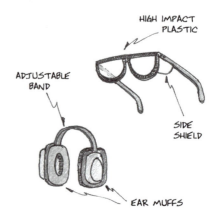

SAFETY GLASSES AND HEARING PROTECTOR

That is why it is important to read and understand all the safety procedures outlined in the instructions that come with any tool. Although many tools are similar, individual examples have eccentricities that you may not know about unless you read the instruction book or receive specific instruction in the use of that tool from a qualified person. The most important safety consideration is to pay attention to what you are doing. Most accidents seem to occur when a worker has a lapse of concentration in using a tool.

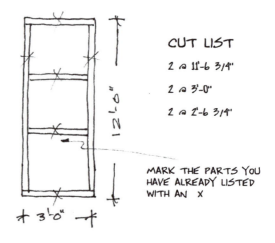

CUT LIST

2 @ 11'-6 3/4"

2 @ 3'-0"

2 @ 2'-6 3/4"

MARK THE PARTS YOU HAVE ALREADY LISTED WITH AN X

TYPICAL ROUGH SKETCH AND CUT LIST

The first requirement for building anything is a cut list. For this project, suppose that you have a drawing for a flat that is three feet wide and twelve feet tall. The cut list has been worked out to the side. If you are actually building this project, you may wish to use some other dimensions; just work up a sketch with sizes that meet your needs.

You want to begin by cutting the longest parts of the flat first, the two stiles that are each 11'- 6 $^3/_4$" long. Use #2 white pine 1×3 for this project. As 1×3 is not a product that is available from the lumberyard, you will need to rip some down first. The odd size of 2 $^5/_8$" is derived from the largest width that can be cut when 4 pieces of 1×3 are cut from a 1×12 that has a milled width of 11 $^1/_4$". Rip down a 1×12 to get enough stock to build this flat. Of course, the 1×12 you start with will need to be at least 12 feet long, or the 1×3s that you rip down will be too short to cut to the proper length.

Unless by some miracle you just happened to come across the finest #2 white pine in the known universe, it is most likely that the 1×3 laying on your shop floor has some imperfections in it. The process of sorting lumber according to quality is known as culling. The culls are the pieces deemed unusable for a particular purpose however, remember that a length of 1×3 that is totally unsuitable for a long stile might be just fine for a shorter rail. This is why it was important to list the parts of your flat in order from longest to shortest.

Some pieces are obviously too bowed or warped to use. (Cupping is not usually a problem with such narrow strips.) To get a good view of how distorted a certain board is, hold one end up to your eye and sight down to the end of it as though you were looking down a pool cue. This makes it easy to determine how much bow or warp there is over the length of the board. If the defect involved is a gentle bow, it can easily be removed by correctly positioning the flat's toggles. If there is a sharp bend where a knot is located, that piece is probably not going to be usable. Cull through all of the pieces, and set aside the ones that are best suited to cutting the long stiles.

Use the radial arm saw to cut the two stiles to length. Remember to trim off the end of the 1×3 first so that you have a nice square starting point. Trimming will also remove the small drying out cracks, or checks, that often appear at the very end of a board. There should be plenty of length to do this even if you are using 12'- 0" stock because the boards from the lumberyard are just a bit longer than that. Also, the stiles are shorter than 12'- 0" because of the way they are interrupted by the top and bottom rails.

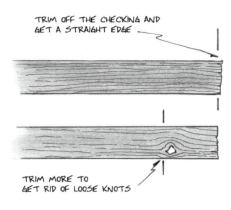

TRIM OFF THE CHECKING AND GET A STRAIGHT EDGE

TRIM MORE TO GET RID OF LOOSE KNOTS

TRIM THE END OF THE BOARD BEFORE CUTTING A PIECE TO LENGTH

Next cut the 3'- 0" rails, and then the two toggles. Cut around large knots wherever it is possible. Refer back to the chapter on woodworking and saws for more information on measuring and marking for the radial arm saw. If a RAS is not available, a power miter saw is the second best choice.

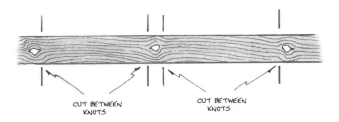

CUT BETWEEN KNOTS   CUT BETWEEN KNOTS

CUT SHORTER LENGTHS FROM LESS DESIRABLE MATERIAL

Now you are ready to cut and prepare the corner blocks and keystones. The best material to use is $^1/_4$" A/C fir plywood, but that material is becoming increasingly difficult to find. It is not a good idea to substitute lauan or Masonite for your corner block material. The lauan is far too spongy and will quite easily break under stress. Masonite is stiffer, but its lack of grain structure is a major fault. There seems to have been a general shift toward using B/C pine plywood, and even though this material is somewhat heavier than the fir, it is a reasonable substitute if $1/4$" thick A/C Fir is not available. The small size of the blocks makes the weight somewhat of a non-issue, and even the high degree of warp found in yellow pine plywood is not such a problem, also due to the size. B/C yellow pine plywood is very strong, much stronger than either lauan or hardboard.

The size of corner blocks is somewhat flexible but should be somewhere in the neighborhood of 12 inches. Something slightly smaller than one foot, such as 11 $3/4$" is an excellent size when you consider the 4x8 size of a sheet of plywood. You can rip four strips of 11 $3/4$" plywood on the table saw, and then cut the strips into squares with the radial arm saw. If you were to make the blocks exactly 12" square, only three strips could be made from a 4'- 0" wide sheet because of the loss incurred when the saw kerf is taken into consideration. Use a stop block on the radial arm saw to ensure that all of the blocks are perfectly square. The band saw is used to slice the squares from corner to corner, creating the triangular shape required for a corner block.

RIP SECTIONS OF 1/4" PLYWOOD TO A WIDTH OF 11 3/4"

USE A STOP BLOCK ON THE RADIAL ARM SAW TO MAKE SQUARES

MARK A DIAGONAL FROM CORNER TO CORNER

USE THE BAND SAW TO CUT THE TRIANGULAR BLOCKS

CUTTING CORNER BLOCKS

Wood has much more strength along the length of its grain than it does across the grain. That is why plywood is manufactured with the grain of the various plies running in opposition to one another. As a result plywood is very strong in all directions. When using $1/4$" plywood, this theory must be modified a bit to accommodate the fact that this thin

material has only three plies. Obviously, there are two plies running one way and only one in the opposite direction. Therefore $1/4$" plywood has much more strength in one direction than in the other. When using it for a corner block you should make sure that the two grains that are visible on the top and bottom run across the crack resulting from the joining of the stile and rail. The tendency of the two boards is to flex at the joint so that they bend with the crack as the corner of the bend.

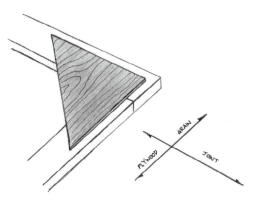

RUN THE PLYWOOD GRAIN AT A 90 DEGREE ANGLE TO THE DIRECTION OF THE JOINT

If the grain of the block runs in the same direction as the crack, the joint will not be nearly as strong. You can see from the drawing that the two blocks shown cannot be cut from the same square unless one of them is flipped over after cutting. That would put the bad side up. It is craftsmanlike to show the good side of the plywood (A or B) as the exposed side, the one you can see from the back. If you flip the triangle over, one of the sides will have to be the rough side.

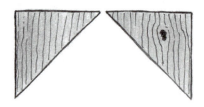

IT TAKES CUTTINGS FROM TWO DIFFERENT SQUARES TO MAKE A PAIR OF LEFT AND RIGHT HANDED CORNER BLOCKS

You can avoid this by making a set of left and right handed blocks when you cut them on the bandsaw. Do this by scribing your diagonal cut lines in opposite directions. When making a large number of corner blocks, it is more efficient to cut a number of them at one time by stacking the blocks together and cutting through all the layers at once. When using this method it is possible to organize the left and right handed blocks by stacking the squares so that the grain on them is alternately vertical and horizontal. When a stack such as this is cut, there will automatically be an even number of left- and right-handed blocks.

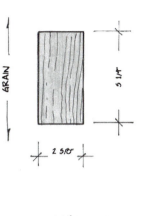

KEYSTONE

Keystones are manufactured in a similar process, except of course that they are a rectangular shape rather than a triangle. Making the traditional trapezoid shape is usually too time-consuming for the amount of extra strength it allows. Some people call the rectangular version a strap. Rip down some of the $1/4$" plywood into strips that are $2\,5/8$" wide. Cross cut these strips into pieces $5\,1/4$" long, and then chamfer the edges of the good sides. Not much can go wrong here as long as you remember to keep the grain of the plywood running the length of the keystone. That keeps the strength of the grain running across the joint as it did on the corner blocks. If for some reason you are building a structure that requires extra strength, use a corner block in place of a keystone.

TO MAKE LOTS OF CORNER BLOCKS STACK THE BLANKS UP WITH THE GRAIN ALTERNATING AND CUT THEM ALL AT ONE TIME

There is one final preparation to make the corner blocks ready for use. It is common practice to chamfer the edges of the plywood blocks in order to keep them from splintering later on. This is easiest to do on a stationary belt sander. A stationary belt sander is the same as a hand held one, except that it is larger and you are meant to move the work in relation to the tool rather than the tool in relation to the work. If the stationary version is not available, you can do almost the same thing by turning the hand held belt sander upside down and depressing the constant run button next to the trigger. Just be sure that your particular sander can do this safely, and be aware that it may move around a bit due to vibration. It is easier to bring the work to the tool when the part you are sanding is so lightweight that you would have to hold it in place anyway. Sanding the corners should be a rapid process requiring no more than a few seconds for each block. Only the good side of the plywood needs to be chamfered, as the rough side will be pressed against the framing of the flat, and doing that side will just create an unsightly crack between the two pieces. Sanding will help to give your work a finely crafted appearance.

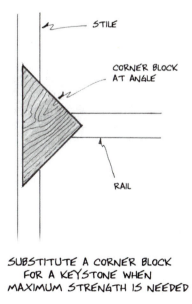

SUBSTITUTE A CORNER BLOCK FOR A KEYSTONE WHEN MAXIMUM STRENGTH IS NEEDED

A template table makes it much easier to assemble the parts of a flat. A template is a set of guidelines used to shape something else. Templates are used in such diverse pursuits as drafting and setting up word processing documents.

In flat building (and other types of construction) they are used to square up the framing as it is put together. Many shops have constructed a large wooden table to use as a template, but a wooden floor works just as well and takes up less room in the shop. If your shop has a concrete floor you have very little choice in the matter. It is imperative to be able to nail into the surface of the template in order to hold your parts in alignment while working on the flat. You can also use a number of platforms laid edge to edge for this purpose. That can come in handy when the flats you are making are too large for the regular template table and no wooden stage floor is available.

A table 6'- 6" wide and 18'- 0" long is a good size. This is somewhat larger than the 6'x16' size that is generally the largest practical limit for a flat. Along one end and one side of the table are screwed 4/4 blocks of hardwood at regular intervals. This guide is used to capture the framing and hold it in place. The resulting corner should be as square as possible so that it is appropriate for squaring up flats and other units built on the table. A sheet of plywood works well as a square, or you can use the "magic triangle." Any triangle with sides that are multiples of 3, 4, and 5 will form a right triangle. A framing square is not a good choice because it is very small in proportion to the size of the table, and as a result will not be very accurate.

The first step in laying out the parts for assembly is to place the bottom rail against the bottom of the template. If there is any bow (crown) in the board it should point toward the inside of the flat so that the structure will not rock when it is in its upright position. There should not be very much bow in such a short piece of 1x3. Next place one of the stiles along the side of the table where the positioning blocks are. Make sure that the crown of this piece is pointed toward the inside of the flat as well. (Crown is another word for bow.) Using 6d finishing nails, secure these two pieces to the table, taking care to straighten them out along the blocks as you go. Try not to put any nails in the places where the corner blocks and keystones will need to be connected. Do not drive the nails in all the way, but rather leave the heads up some so that it will be easier to remove them later on. Use the fewest nails possible to accomplish your purpose.

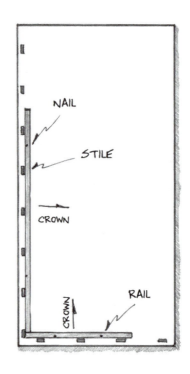

SECURE THE STILE AND RAIL
BUT DON'T PUT NAILS WHERE
THE CORNER BLOCKS WILL GO

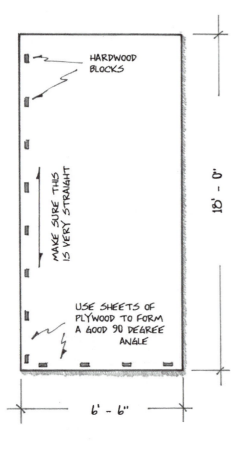

A TEMPLATE TABLE

Set the remaining stile and rail in position, making sure to again point the stile's crown toward the interior of the flat. Adjust all corners so that they are flush with one another and nail down these last two pieces. When tacking down the second stile it is important to use nails only at the very ends of the piece, and close to the edge, where they will be out of the way of the corner blocks. This is necessary to allow for movement in the stile as its bow is removed. If the nails are too far from the end, the joints will be dislocated when the stile is straightened. Using very thin 6d finishing nails will make it less likely that the 1x3 will split when you nail so close to the end. Place the toggles in position and use them to press the second stile outward. If all of the pieces have been cut to the right sizes, the bow or crown should be removed and the flat should now be straight, square, and true.

If the amount of bow in the two stiles is relatively the same, it will have almost no effect on the finished product because the force of one side pushing in is an equal but opposite reaction to the force of the other side. If you are making just one flat you will have very little choice in the matter. But if you are making flats for an entire show at one time, there will most likely be a number of same-length stile pieces to choose from, and you can pick matching pairs for the various units. It is much easier to make many flats all at once than to cut and assemble them one at a time. In industry that is often referred to as an "economy of scale," meaning that if you spread the cost of preparing to build a product over many multiples, the cost per unit is reduced. That philosophy works for building all sorts of things. It is very efficient, but of course, not nearly as much fun as making things one at a time.

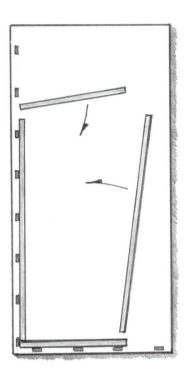

LINE UP THE CORNERS OF THE
REMAINING RAIL AND STILE

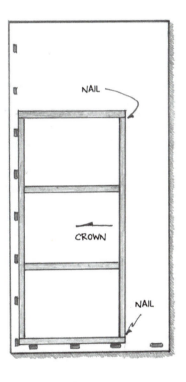

TOGGLES SHOULD BE EVENLY SPACED

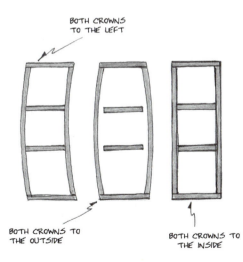

BOTH CROWNS
TO THE LEFT

BOTH CROWNS TO
THE OUTSIDE

BOTH CROWNS TO
THE INSIDE

FOR BEST RESULTS, POINT ALL THE
CROWNS OR BOW TO THE INSIDE OF THE FLAT

You have no doubt noticed by this point that the exact position of the toggles has never been given, but that they seem to be vaguely in the middle. It is common practice not to dimension the exact location of internal bracing, but rather to count on the fact that it is understood that the toggles will be evenly spaced inside the opening. In this case, there are two toggles, but they create three spaces inside the flat. If you had three toggles there would be four spaces, and with four toggles five spaces, and so forth.

It is really the number of spaces that are used to calculate the placement of the toggles. Divide the total distance by the number of spaces to determine the size of each space. In this case you divide 12'- 0" by three and arrive at 4'- 0". Sometimes, the toggles are used to brace something that will be added to the flat later on, perhaps a chair rail, or some other piece of trim. In that case, there may be dimensions that show the toggles are to be installed at a particular height from the bottom of the flat.

Imagine a case where the overall distance is 16'- 0" and the number of toggles is five. This time there you will have six spaces, but it is a bit difficult to divide 16 by 6, so you can convert the feet to inches and try it that way. Doing that, 16 x12= 192, and that number is easily divisible by 6. You can convert the resulting 32 inches back to 2'- 8", or simply continue to work with the inches if that is easier. If you write it down anywhere, be sure to use 2'- 8" because all of the other dimensions have been in feet and inches. If you write 32 instead, it may be misinterpreted as 3'- 2". Those two dimensions are close enough together that a partner may not notice the difference until it is too late.

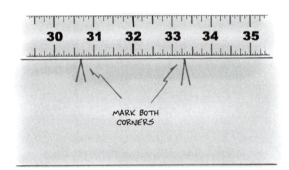

FOR A 1X3, MAKE A MARK 1 5/16" TO EITHER SIDE OF THE TARGET AMOUNT

In the example that goes with our project the two toggles lay at 4'- 0" centers from the end. But that measurement is actually to the center of the toggles, and there is nothing on a 1x3 that marks the center of the board. You could measure 1 $5/16$" to the center of the toggle and place a mark there, but the more accepted method is to measure the stiles at 4'- 0" and 8'- 0" and then to make a mark 1 $5/16$" on either side of that point. That marks the two corners of the end of toggle itself and is a bit more accurate than merely using the center of the toggle. 1 $5/16$" is half of 2 $5/8$". Of course 1 is half of 2, but there is an easy way to find half of any fraction by doubling the denominator. In essence, you are multiplying the fraction by $1/2$. $1/2$ times $a/b = a/2b$.

If toggles are placed every 32", such as in the taller flat we imagined, you can hook the tape measure over the bottom of the flat and make a mark 1 $5/16$" to the side of each

multiple of 32", or 32 - 64 - 96 - 128 -160. Of course it is necessary to mark both stiles since there are two ends to every toggle. Avoid moving the tape for each measurement because that allows placement error to creep in.

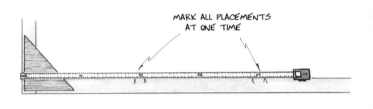

MARKING WHERE TOGGLES GO

After all of the framing for the entire flat has been tacked in place, it is time to attach the corner blocks and keystones. It is a traditional practice to inset the blocks $3/4$" from the outer edge of the flat. This is done in order to allow another flat made from $3/4$" thick stock to fit evenly against the flat when making a 90-degree corner. This is done even if there is no immediate need for that to happen, since flats are often considered to be "stock" scenery, intended to be reused at a later date. I have always gone along with this principle out of a sense of tradition unless there is a reason to deviate from it, and besides, it is easier to tack the framing to the table if there is a space around the edge where the nails can go. It is a fairly simple matter to mark all the corners and toggle locations by using a scrap length of 1x3 held on edge. Putting the blocks closer to the edge will result in a stronger structure, so if there is a concern about strength, you should definitely place the blocks closer to the edge. But if you inset at least a quarter of an inch you will have a much better looking result.

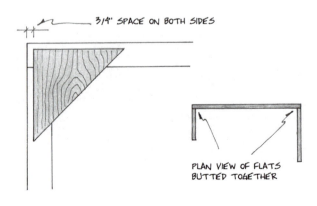

CORNER BLOCKS TRADITIONALLY HAVE A 3/4" INSET TO ALLOW THEM TO FORM A CORNER WITH ANOTHER FLAT

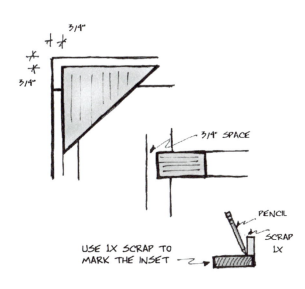

3/4"

3/4" SPACE

PENCIL

SCRAP 1X

USE 1X SCRAP TO
MARK THE INSET

You have four or five minutes to get things set after putting the glue on, as carpenter's glue will start to set after that time. So don't put the glue on until you are ready to staple. Remember that the glue will hold much better than any fastener you could possibly use. For the most part, fasteners really only hold the wooden pieces together while the glue sets up.

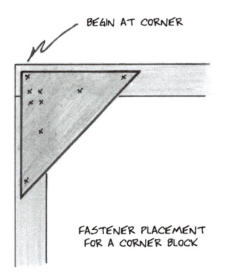

BEGIN AT CORNER

FASTENER PLACEMENT
FOR A CORNER BLOCK

Use a construction stapler with 3/4" long staples in it to attach the 1/4" plywood blocks to their proper positions. Staples are the fastener of choice because the crowns of the staples won't pull all the way through the thin blocks of plywood like finish nails from a nail gun are likely to do. Naturally, any sort of power nailer is much faster than doing the job by hand. Sometimes a shop will use screws for this operation, but that seems like a bit of overkill when glue is used.

There is a traditional pattern used to nail, staple, or screw the blocks in place. It is a good lesson in nailing technique, so you should use it for tradition's sake, even though using glue lessens the need for such exactitude. The pattern is as follows: one in each corner, two on either side of the joint, and one in the inside center on each leg. If you start with the staple that goes in the corner of the flat, it will make it much easier to line up the other two corners. From an engineering standpoint, it makes sense to secure the ends of the block and also the joint break. The center fasteners are added for good measure.

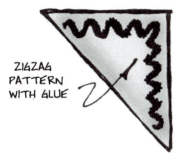

ZIGZAG
PATTERN
WITH GLUE

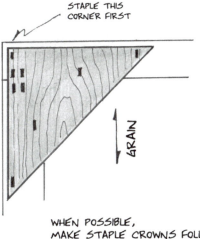

STAPLE THIS
CORNER FIRST

GRAIN

WHEN POSSIBLE,
MAKE STAPLE CROWNS FOLLOW
THE GRAIN DIRECTION

The strongest bond is formed by using a healthy application of aliphatic resin (yellow carpenter's) glue when attaching these blocks. Put the glue on using a kind of zigzag pattern. Put the block in place and then squish it back and forth a couple of times to spread the glue. You can pull one of the blocks back off every once in a while to confirm your gluing technique. The larger the surface area of the glue joint, the stronger the bond will be. Several small dots of glue on the back of the plywood block will just not do.

Keystones are fastened in the same way, but their rectangular shape creates a "double five" of dominoes appearance. Again, there is a staple in each corner, but this time four instead of three. If you are neat and tidy with the nail pattern, your work will have a more professional appearance. There will be less flaking of the top veneer of the plywood if the crown of the staple follows the same direction as the grain of the plywood.

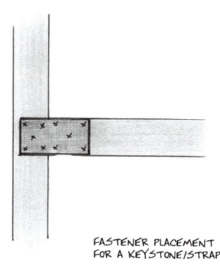

FASTENER PLACEMENT
FOR A KEYSTONE/STRAP

When all of the corner blocks and keystones have been put in place, it is a good idea to wait just a few minutes for the glue to set up somewhat before removing the nails that are holding it in place on the template table. After the flat has been separated from the table, check it over for defects and remove any puckers from the front that were caused by the 6d nails. This will prepare the flat for covering and sizing. When building a show, it is common to generate a large stack of flat frames before going on to the covering stage. Some flats are constructed for use as structural members and may never be covered at all.

Most painted flats are covered with either muslin or canvas. These fabrics are both made from unbleached cotton, with the difference being that the canvas is made from heavier threads and is therefore thicker and more durable. Heavyweight muslin is generally acceptable as a covering because university shows tend to be of fairly short duration and extra strength is not required. Being constantly loaded in and out of theatres takes a heavy toll on scenery.

Some flats are covered with thin plywood rather than fabric. Most of the time that is because the designer has in mind to put something on the surface of the flat that would not work well with a fabric cover. There may be a need to hang lots of artwork on the walls. There may be trim pieces that cannot be accommodated in any other way. Traditionally, flats with a hard cover are made in the "Hollywood" style as described later on, but on occasion traditional flats are used. The main problem encountered in using a hard

cover on this type of flat is that the framing tends to curl up, and it is difficult to get the flat to straighten out when it is assembled. That is because the plywood is placed on the thin edge of the 1x3 rather than on the thicker cord of the 3-inch side.

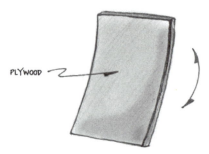

PLYWOOD

PUTTING PLYWOOD ON SOFTCOVERED
STYLE FRAMING CAN MAKE IT BOW

There are many different ways to affix muslin to a flat. The old-style method was to use tacks around the center of the flat, and animal glue (which is something akin to hot glue with a brush) to glue the muslin in place. Tacks are required due to the "instant stick" nature of this adhesive. The use of animal or hide glue has diminished in recent years both for political reasons (like where it comes from), and also because it is very messy to use. Hide glue must be heated in a special pot, and must be kept warm for hours on end. It is not the best thing you have ever smelled (because of where it comes from). Obviously, there is a risk of being burned by the glue. Today this sort of adhesive is mostly reserved for making expensive wooden musical instruments. For centuries luthiers have appreciated the tone that hide gives to stringed instruments. It is also used in antique furniture repair.

FLAKE
TYPE

DOUBLE BOILER

HIDE OR ANIMAL GLUE IS BOUGHT BY
THE POUND AND IS HEATED IN A
GLUE POT

Some people stretch the muslin around the edges of the flat and staple it in the back as with an artist's canvas. That makes it easy to remove (if that is a requirement), but it leaves some unsightly bulges. There is a much cleaner and easier method that requires no fasteners.

THIS FLAT IS USED BY
A PAINTING CLASS, SO THE
COVER IS JUST STAPLED ON

Begin by laying the flat face up on top of some sawhorses. Pull enough muslin off of the roll or bale to hold it to the flat for rough measuring. Leave yourself three or four inches of extra fabric around the outside edges, and rip the muslin to the desired size. Ripping is actually much better than using scissors for this purpose because the muslin will rip much straighter than you can possibly cut it. Scissors are helpful in making a small notch to start the rip. Pull off the excess strings and drape the muslin over the toggles on the inside of the flat.

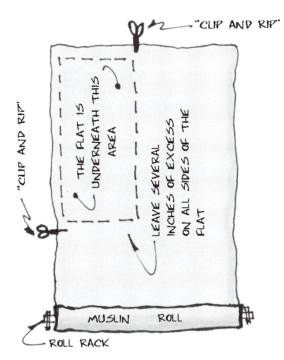

Brush a generous helping of white glue onto the outer perimeter of the flat, spreading the glue over the entire surface of the 1x3. Do not put glue on any of the inside toggles or other framing. The muslin should be attached only on the outside, leaving the inside free. The only exception to this would be for a window flat, or some similar structure where the muslin is to be trimmed on the inside. Pick up the muslin and place it gently on the surface of the flat and into the glue. This will take at least two people, and on a large flat, four.

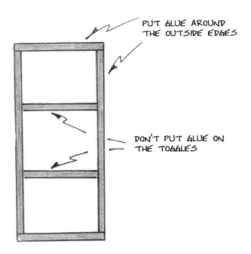

Walk around 90 degrees to the middle of the long sides of the flat and pull opposite one another to lightly stretch the muslin and press it very gently into the glue. Work together toward one end of the flat, straightening and pressing until that one end is finished, and then back to the middle, working toward the opposite end.

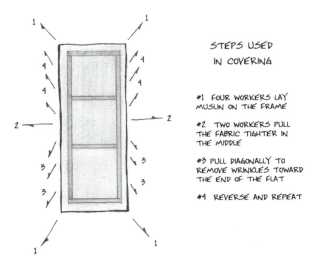

STEPS USED
IN COVERING

#1 FOUR WORKERS LAY
MUSLIN ON THE FRAME

#2 TWO WORKERS PULL
THE FABRIC TIGHTER IN
THE MIDDLE

#3 PULL DIAGONALLY TO
REMOVE WRINKLES TOWARD
THE END OF THE FLAT

#4 REVERSE AND REPEAT

MUSLIN LAYING ON TOP OF FRAMING

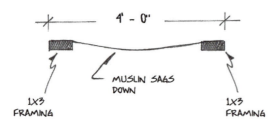

MUSLIN SHOULD SAG ABOUT 1" OVER FOUR FEET

Try not smear the glue around too much when positioning the muslin, because if you wipe it all off, there will be nothing left to adhere the fabric to the wood. It is not necessary to stretch the muslin tightly. It is actually better to leave some sag in the material, but no more than an inch on a four-foot-wide flat. You have used enough glue if you can feel a slight dampness through the fabric, but it is not good to have wet, sticky glue on the surface of the fabric. When it is dry, glue prevents scenic paint from soaking into the cotton fibers. Casein paint will have a noticeably lighter hue in the glue-coated areas.

DRILL A 1/4" HOLE IN THE CAP AND USE THE ENTIRE GALLON JUG AS A GIANT SQUEEZE BOTTLE

USE A 2" POLY BRUSH, OR SOME OTHER CHEAP TYPE TO SPREAD THE GLUE. DO NOT USE EXPENSIVE LINING BRUSH

When the flat has been checked for puckers and bad glue spots, set it aside for at least eight hours to let the glue dry. This gluing technique requires a high degree of finesse during the laying down and straightening out process, but once you have mastered it, it is much faster and easier than any other I have used. See the helpful hints section for some additional advice.

After the glue has had time to cure, it is time to trim and size the muslin. Trimming is best accomplished with a utility knife, or perhaps just the blade from one. Do not use a small Xacto knife blade, because you will not get enough control with such a tiny handle and blade. Stretch the excess fabric off to the side and down just a bit in order to find the corner of the wooden framing. Puncture this spot and hold the blade up against the side of the 1x3. Trim the muslin by running the blade along the edge of the flat. Try to make the edge of the muslin exactly flush with the framing. Use one long motion to slice the muslin rather than hacking at it like a saw.

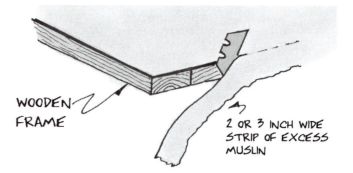

WOODEN FRAME

2 OR 3 INCH WIDE STRIP OF EXCESS MUSLIN

Sizing simply means to shrink the muslin fabric down to its proper size and tension by using a solution of very watery glue and/or paint. The normal ratio is in the neighborhood of 15 parts water to 1 part glue, but the exact amount is not all that crucial. A bit of paint in the mixture will make it easy to tell which part has been treated. Sometimes when speed is of the essence you might use a base color selected by the paint department. You can actually see the covering shrinking and tightening right away. It may be necessary at some point to check the edges of the flat for small sections of loose muslin, and to reglue these with a small bottle of Elmers.

HELPFUL HINTS

Although it is likely that your first flat building experience will be in a class where you will be making only one flat, it is more common to be build a large number of flats all at one time. In our shop, we like to take the individual construction sketches and combine the cut lists into one master list that is used to do all the cutting. In this way, all of the longest pieces are cut first when the lumber selection is at its best. Of course this presupposes that the cut lists are accurate, and it is pretty devastating to learn that there has been some basic misconception after several hundred parts have been cut. So it is best to double check first.

Be sure to cut around knots when it is easy to do so. Often this will mean trimming only an inch or two from the 1x3, and it will result in a much better looking product. It will not be possible to exclude all knots from all parts. Cut away the ones that are easy to do.

If 3/4" construction staples are not an option, try to locate 7/8" wire nails with heads. These nails cannot be used in a pneumatic gun.

If you are using staples, try to shoot them in so that the indentation created by the setting of the crown runs in the same direction as the grain of the plywood. If the mark is perpendicular to the grain, tiny bits of the top ply tend to fly off and leave a messy appearance.

Do not rush the drying of the glue that holds the muslin in place on the flat frame.

Make sure to avoid muslin that has polyester thread in it, because this type will not size. That is normally what is available from a fabric store. They have a different use in mind than covering flats. Wide heavyweight muslin from a theatrical supplier is the best because they purchase goods with a knowledge of what it will be used for and are careful to select an appropriate type.

After flats have been sized or painted and have begun to dry, run your hand between the cover and any toggles that you can. This will ensure that the fabric does not stick to them by accident. If it does, the fabric will size in an odd way, and that will often result in puckering.

If the painting technique is not so heavy as to completely fill the texture of the weave of the muslin, it is possible to remove dents and dings in the surface of the flat. These are often caused by some object (or person) stretching the fabric out of shape and can be removed by resizing with hot water. For a severe case, you might try adding some laundry starch, but be sure to apply it from the back of the flat.

HARDCOVERED FLATS

Hardcovered flats are used when durability is a prime factor. The name comes from the thin sheets of plywood that form the covering. Hardcovers are at their best when smaller flats are required, such as in a TV studio and sometimes a movie set. The weight of the plywood becomes a major problem when the flats are more than 12 feet tall. Most television scenery tends to be in the nine-to ten-foot tall range, and in fact this type of unit is often referred to as a TV or Hollywood flat. The nice thing about the hardcovers is that it is possible to cut holes in them to run cables or fog hoses or the like without destroying the structural integrity of the flat. Pictures can be hung just about anywhere without the need to install additional toggles as is necessary with a traditional muslin covered flat. These factors are especially helpful in television, where many decisions are not made until the very last moment and are difficult to predict. TV flats are often cut up to allow a new camera angle, or entire walls are moved around. The philosophy is that if the camera doesn't see it, it doesn't matter. For television this is true, but in live theatre the audience is free to look wherever they wish, and you must pay a bit more attention to the overall appearance of the setting. Being as neat as possible backstage is important in live theatre because the stage manager cannot call out "cut" if something falls over backstage. The show must go on.

Hardcover construction does have its place in live theatre, especially when smaller parts are required. The techniques used to build hardcover flats are also used to construct similar items.

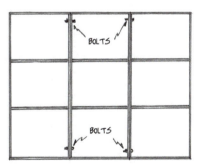

HARDCOVER FLATS CAN BE BOLTED
TOGETHER THROUGH THE FRAMING
ON THE BACKSIDE

TV flats are built with the framing on edge, so that the wall is quite thick by comparison to the standard type. Flats are often bolted or screwed together edge to edge through the framing.

Softcovered flats must be hinged together in back. As mentioned, it is possible to build a traditional softcovered frame and then cover that with plywood. There are occasions where that is the best way to go. This section was written with the "on edge" type of framing in mind.

Since the entire face of the framing is covered with plywood, there is typically no need for corner blocks or keystones, or even corner braces. Hardcover flats are somewhat easier to construct, but not as sturdy as their traditional counterparts. Making a cut list is similar to the earlier process, but the sizes are different because of the way the framing is placed on edge. In the first example, the flat is no larger than four-feet by eight-feet. The reason for this should be clear, being that the plywood covering is available in sheets no larger than that. It is possible to build a hardcover flat larger than 4x8, but special framing techniques must be used.

The overall dimensions are 3'- 6" x 7'- 9". As you would expect, the stiles are the longest framing pieces required, and therefore they should be the first parts to appear on the cut list. The milled thickness of a one-by is actually $3/4$". Just as with the muslin flat cut lists, you must subtract the thickness of the two rails from the overall height of the flat to determine the length of the two stiles.

MATH PROCESS

$$3/4" + 3/4" = 1\ 1/2"$$

$$
\begin{array}{r}
7 - 8\ 2/2" \\
- \ 0' - 1\ 1/2" \\
\hline
7 - 7\ 1/2"
\end{array}
$$

The length of the two rails is the overall width of the flat, 3'- 6". The center toggle is found by again subtracting $1\ 1/2$" from the overall width. Hence our cut list is expressed as:

CUT LIST

2 @ 7'- 7 1/2"

2 @ 3'- 6"

1 @ 3'- 4 1/2"

A window flat can be designed in the same way that a softcover version is, with internal framing forming the window area. Here is an example of that process.

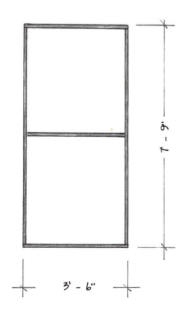

NOTE THE THINNER APPEARANCE
OF THE FRAMING WHEN IT IS
TURNED ON EDGE FOR A
HARDCOVER FLAT

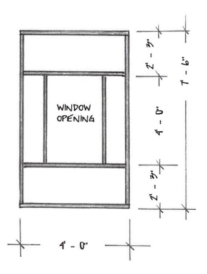

DIMENSIONS OF A HARDCOVER
WINDOW FLAT

The examples so far are flats smaller in size than four feet by eight feet. To go larger than that it is necessary to join the covering plywood together. The normal structural framing can be used to help join the plywood, but you need some extra parts to make that work.

Notice how the facing members are situated so that the plywood covering pieces will be easy to cut and easy to install. The plywood covers are all simple rectangles. This method is much easier than trying to cut the Lauan into a more complex shape, and also ensures that all edges of the covering are connected to the framing.

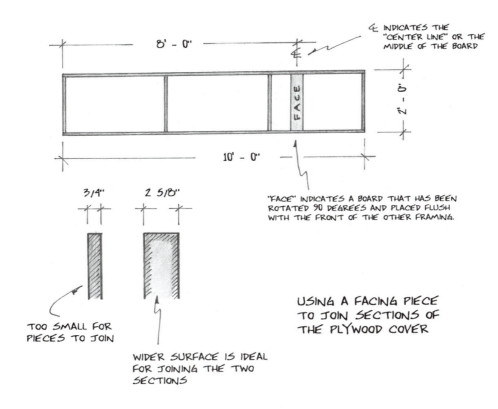

ℓ INDICATES THE "CENTER LINE" OR THE MIDDLE OF THE BOARD

8' - 0"

10' - 0"

2' - 0"

FACE

3/4"

2 5/8"

TOO SMALL FOR PIECES TO JOIN

WIDER SURFACE IS IDEAL FOR JOINING THE TWO SECTIONS

"FACE" INDICATES A BOARD THAT HAS BEEN ROTATED 90 DEGREES AND PLACED FLUSH WITH THE FRONT OF THE OTHER FRAMING.

USING A FACING PIECE TO JOIN SECTIONS OF THE PLYWOOD COVER

The 3/4" wide framing is not wide enough to accommodate the joining process. Each plywood edge would have only 3/8" resting on the framing, and that is not really enough for a reliable connection. A good method of enlarging that surface area is to turn a framing member on its side so that the widest surface is flush with the front of the regular framing. This type of framing member is called a facing piece. The facing pieces do not add much to the structural stability of the flat, but they work well for their intended purpose of attaching the cover. Here is an example of a flat that uses this technique. Notice that the facing piece is used in addition to the normal toggles.

The large surface area provided by the facing piece is excellent for gluing the plywood covering to the frame. You can see in the next drawing to the right how the concept of facing pieces is used to frame a window flat that is larger than four by eight feet.

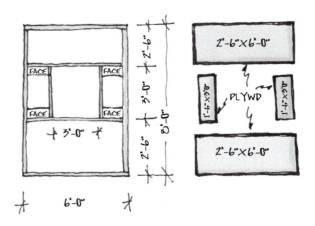

FACE   FACE

FACE   FACE

3'-0"

6'-0"

2'-6"

2'-6"

3'-0"

8'-0"

2'-6"X6'-0"

1'-6"X3'-0"   PLYWD   1'-6"X3'-0"

2'-6"X6'-0"

COVERING A HARDCOVERED FLAT

Sometimes a flat must have a solid covering wider than four feet. In that case, the facing pieces are arranged so that the plywood is applied horizontally. In reality, this would be a very heavy flat, and the excessive weight should be considered when deciding whether or not to use this method. Or perhaps a series of smaller flats can be used. You can see that there is a framing piece running up the middle of the flat that intersects the facing pieces. This internal stile must be notched to allow for passage of the facing pieces.

It is possible to build the unit without this framing member, but great care will need to be exercised in moving the flat, or the two sides of the doorway may easily be torqued to the breaking point. The action of the play may not allow for this member to be used. Sometimes a flat piece of metal, or bar stock may be used in place of the lumber. If so, the "sill iron" should be made from $1/8"$ x 1" stock, and be made to run all the way from side to side, underneath the regular framing. Sill irons are a traditional part of softcover flats used in touring.

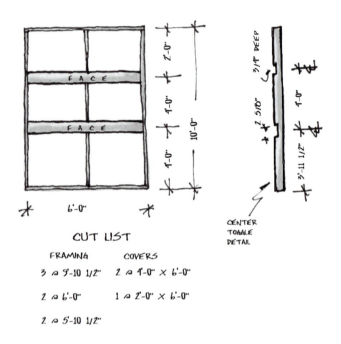

CUT LIST

FRAMING	COVERS
3 @ 9'-10 1/2"	2 @ 4'-0" x 6'-0"
2 @ 6'-0"	1 @ 2'-0" x 6'-0"
2 @ 5'-10 1/2"	

CONSTRUCTION

The joining of the framing of a hardcovered flat is pretty straightforward, although it is necessary to bear in mind that the flat should be put together face up, rather than face down as with a muslin flat. It is not necessary to use the template method because the plywood covering will square up the flat. Be sure to use plenty of glue on the joints, although glue alone will not hold the framing together because of the small surface area involved. The glue does help, however.

The final example is that of a door flat. The bottom rail passes all the way across the bottom of the flat, including the space that is left open for the doorway. This will leave a threshold that an actor must step over in passing through the door, but it greatly enhances the strength of the flat.

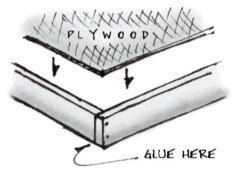

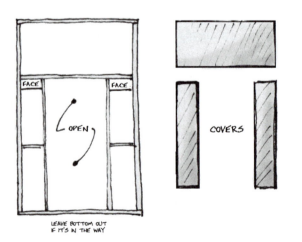

When measuring the placement of internal framing pieces, remember to use the measurement $3/4"$ rather than $2 \, 5/8"$. A speed square is helpful for making sure that the toggles are square to the rest of the framing. After marking a location with two small Vs, use the square to mark a line through one of them and across the board. You can use this mark to line up the toggle when nailing. Often there is a slight discrepancy in the widths of the various framing pieces. Be sure to flush the fronts of the boards with the top of the framing, because that is the front of the flat.

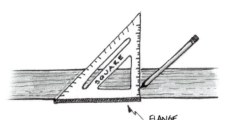

USE A PENCIL AND SQUARE
TO MARK TOGGLE PLACEMENT

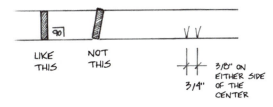

MARKING THE TOGGLE PLACEMENT

The covering for a 4x8 flat does not require any preparation of the plywood prior to attaching it to the frame. Any other size must be cut to fit. Have all the parts cut and ready to go prior to beginning the job of covering. It is often best to cut the covering parts a bit large, say $1/16$" or even $1/8$". That will allow enough extra so that they can hang over the edge a small amount after the cover is stapled on. You can trim this edge flush later. It is difficult to cut out all the framing parts, and the covering parts, and get them to all fit together closely without cheating a bit in this way. If the overall size of the flat is off by even $1/8$", it will most likely go unnoticed, but if the covering falls short by that amount it will most certainly show.

Begin attaching the cover by putting glue on the tops of all framing parts that will be touched by the first section of plywood. Carefully lay the covering in place and adjust it so that one of the outside corners is aligned and flush. The other parts of the cover need not be exactly in place, but just close. Don't worry about them now. Staple the one corner, and then flush up and staple one of the adjacent sides starting from the corner where you began. Use a staple every eight inches or so, aligning and stapling each point in turn. The most common mistake is to try and line up the whole thing at once. It is not really practical, or even necessary to do that.

After the first side is done, return to the corner where you began and staple the opposite adjacent side in the same manner as the first side. This process is used to square up the framing; making one of the corners square should have the same effect on the rest. If the flat is 4x8 or smaller, it is an easy matter to finish up by stapling the remaining two sides. If you have oversized your plywood (sometimes even if you have not), there will be a small overhang on one or both of the two remaining sides. Do not pull the framing outward

and flush the two surfaces in the middle unless it already fits that way at the corner. If you do, you will create a curve on that side of the flat. Try instead to leave the same amount of overhang along the entire length of the side. This is fairly easy to do if you feel the amount overhang at the corner with your finger and then use the same finger to judge the amount of overhang as you work your way around the flat.

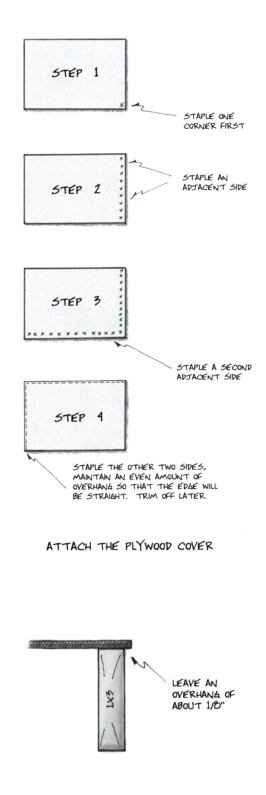

ATTACH THE PLYWOOD COVER

If the flat you are constructing has multiple sections of plywood covering that must be joined with a facing board, it is best not to add any size to the sides that abut each other in the middle, but rather only to the pieces that will overhang the edges. You don't need overhang in the middle, and there is no way to trim it off once it is there.

Be sure to run a line of staples into the internal framing parts as well as the outside edges. Use a straight edge to mark the location of the framing by looking at nail holes on the side. Longer lines can easily be marked using a chalk line. A drywall square can also be helpful.

After the covering has been completed, it is time to trim and fill the flat. Use a router with a laminate trimming bit to shave off the excess covering material. This type of flush trim bit has a large roller bearing on the bottom that makes for a smooth passage along the side. Since the cutters are exactly the same diameter as the bearing that rides on the framing, the cover will be trimmed to exactly the same size as the framing. Before starting, be sure to check for any nails or staples that might be sticking out, as these will permanently damage the bit.

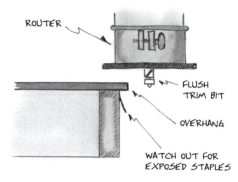

USE A ROUTER TO TRIM THE COVER

You can use joint compound to fill the joints and cracks that are a natural result of the construction process. If there is to be a great deal of movement associated with the piece, then it might be best to use auto body filler, but the joint compound is much easier to use and is incredibly cheap. A five-gallon bucket costs only a few dollars and will last a very long time. Use the thicker variety.

Lots of different types of scenery are made using the same techniques as described for the construction of hard-cover flats. You can extend these methods to many other projects.

It is very common to use plywood strips for the framing parts when the size of the unit is small. You can make the width of the plywood anything required by the plan, wider than would be possible with dimension lumber. If the unit needs extra strength, thicker stock can be used for the covering. If you need to make a profile piece that has a decorative edge, try using $1/2"$ plywood for the cover, because this will hold up better if the profile is complicated. The profile edge can overhang the framing by several inches with no problem.

Fitting together a large number of flats so that the cracks in between don't show is an ongoing struggle. There is really no elegant solution unless the problem has already been solved in the design process. If the design calls for a huge, flat, featureless wall, there is very little the carpenter can do to help the situation. Most designers incorporate breaks into the design that allow the set to be constructed of reasonably sized parts. Quite often there is a column or corner, or some other vertical diversion that will allow two flats to be joined without the edges showing. It is not a good practice to expect to use filler on joints of this sort after the scenery has been erected.

Remember these guidelines when when deciding how to divide a scenery design into buildable units. If you need more than two stagehands to carry a piece, it is big. If four stagehands can't carry it, it is too big and you should either cut it in half, or put wheels on it. If it won't fit through the shop door, it won't make it to the stage.

HELPFUL HINTS

A nail gun will make the process of nailing the framing together much easier to do. The Senco SFN1 gun with the 1 1/2" DA 17 nails or something equivalent is an excellent choice. This is a lightweight gun and is well balanced. The 1 1/2" nails are a good length to use for the framing; 1/4" crown staples are also excellent.

Be careful about where your fingers rest when the nail is fired into the wood. It is fairly easy for the nail to come out the side and into your finger if you leave that digit in the way. The flip side of this is that it is much easier to tell if parts are in line using your finger than by looking at them. Just be careful to move your finger before each shot.

Use a good quality yellow glue on the joints, and remember that this type of adhesive begins to set in just a few minutes. Plan ahead and have all your parts ready in advance.

Lightly sanding the corners of the flat with 100 grit sandpaper will reduce splintering and give the flat a more finished look. Do not round the corners over very much if there are flats that need to fit flush against one another, as this will only make the crack appear larger.

Remember when applying the joint compound that the idea is to fill the holes and not to create a build-up on the surface of the flat. Any amount extra that dries on the surface of the flat will have to be sanded off later, a time consuming and thankless job.

Staples must be used to attach the plywood covers, as nails will zip right through.

The covering material of choice is often 1/4" lauan, a type of plywood from the Pacific Rim. This material has a very tight grain structure, and this grain does not "telegraph" through your paint job. Good quality lauan is sometimes difficult to find. You might have better luck at a lumberyard servicing the cabinet making industry than at a home center. Lauan is also discussed in the chapter on sheet goods. Just be aware that lauan is not terribly sturdy. 1/4" domestic plywood is much stronger, but has a grain pattern that is very easy to spot even after it is painted. Some shops glue muslin or even canvas on the outside of the plywood and framing to achieve a more paintable surface that is extremely durable.

CHAPTER 13

BUILDING STEPS

Actors can't get from one stage level to another without stairs. It is the rare stage setting that does not include them in some way, whether just one step up to a low platform or as a long set of backstage escape stairs. Stairs come in many different types that may be constructed to fit a particular need, but there are some properties held in common by all the various types.

There are three main parts to any set of stairs. The treads are what you step on when going up or down. Risers are the part of the unit that "rise" from one tread to another, and the carriages are the side pieces used to "carry" the weight of the entire unit. Steps vary greatly depending upon the type of materials used, steepness, whether they are left open or boxed in, and stylistic differences.

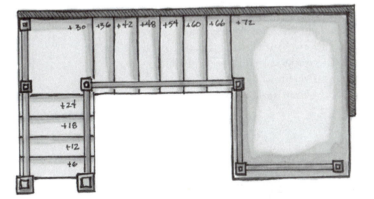

MANY DIFFERENT PARTS WORK TOGETHER
TO CREATE A SET OF STAIRS

STEP BASICS

There are a few general concepts to understand about how steps work. Mostly these have to do with the way the human body controls itself while moving through space. Everyone has tripped over a section of sidewalk that is suddenly higher than the surrounding walk. You have also sat down in a chair that is lower than you think and had a sudden sensation of falling. This happens because the body accustoms itself to certain distances and rhythms and comes to expect them. It is the same principle that makes it possible for me to type these words or for a musician to play the piano without looking at the keys.

When climbing a set of stairs, your body tends to develop a rhythm to its movement, and if one of the steps is of a different height, then it is quite easy to trip on it. For this reason it is important that all risers be of the same height and likewise for all treads to be of the same depth. Without that, a set of stairs can be very dangerous.

It is possible to determine equal risers by dividing the total rise by the number of risers and also equal treads by dividing the total run by the number of treads. Stage stairs are usually easy to plan because stage platforming tends to be in even amounts. If a platform is exactly two feet tall you can determine riser height in even numbers. If you want to have a rise of 6 or 8 inches (commonly used increments), then you can divide that riser height evenly into a platform height of 2 feet, or 24 inches. A 9-inch rise wouldn't work because that height will not divide cleanly into 24 inches. Nine-inch risers will fit neatly, however, with a platform height of 36 inches. Dividing the height of the platform by the individual riser height will produce the number of rises required. That number should be one more than the total number of treads, if the platform itself is used as the top step. The number of treads will equal risers if the top tread is level with the top of the platform. Usually it does not, because that increases the size and expense of the step unit.

In general construction, figuring stairs is more complicated because the height of the second story of a building is rarely so even a measurement, but tends rather to be an amount like 9'- 1 3/4". Even so, the process remains the same.

The height of the rise is usually a design consideration and is determined on the basis of artistic concerns that are beyond the scope of this book, although there are some practical points that should be taken into account. It is best for a technician to understand how choices are made to better interpret the design safely.

It is hard for the average person to ascend a stair that has a rise of over nine inches. It is just too far to raise your foot every time you take a step. Strangely, it is also difficult to negotiate a stair with a very shallow rise, say less than six inches. Perhaps this is because we are just not used to them.

Treads should never be less than nine inches deep if an actor is to come down the stair with any sense of grace. As a general rule, it is much easier to climb a difficult set of steps than to descend. Most people walk with their weight resting on their toes and the balls of their feet. That works well on the way upstairs, even if the tread is quite shallow. But if the front part of your foot is hanging off the tread on the way downstairs, that movement will seem very unnatural and difficult. Normally, it is best not to exceed a slope of 45 degrees with any stair unit. Bearing these limits in mind, a stair with a nine-inch tread and a nine-inch rise is the steepest acceptable unit. If it is necessary to save as much space as possible backstage, then this is the ratio to use for escape stairs. These proportions will require a sturdy handrail and good cliplight.

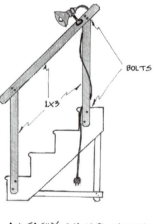

AN EASILY CHANGED HANDRAIL
FOR ESCAPE STAIRS

Sometimes, a stair can have such a shallow slope that this, too, can become a problem. There is a theatre in a western state that has a stair leading up to the lobby with a six-inch rise and a twenty-four inch deep tread. It is not clear whether the builder intended for you to take one step or two on the extra deep tread. One is too far to reach the next step with one stride, and two motions are very awkward. In another example, there are some steps here at the University that run (outdoors) from the Student Union to the ROTC armory. These stairs were also built with very deep treads. They were constructed in the early seventies, a few years after the old armory had mysteriously burned down.

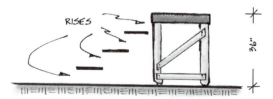

3 TREADS, 4 RISES

Rumor has it that they were intended to be "anti-riot" stairs and very hard to run up, to prevent a reccurrence of the earlier unrest. If you mention this very long stairway to students, they automatically agree that the steps are very difficult to negotiate. The anti-riot theory is appealing as an urban myth, but it seems more likely that the steps were designed to follow the slope of the hill. Whatever the reasoning, they are extremely hard to traverse and make a good illustration of how important it is to have a comfortable rise/run ratio.

TERMINOLOGY

STEP UNIT, OR SET OF STEPS
A number of rises grouped together.

RISER
The vertical connection of two levels or steps.

TREAD
The part you step on.

CARRIAGE
The side framing that keeps the treads and risers together.

NEWEL POST
A large post that anchors the end of, or a bend in, a section of railing. The newel post at the bottom of a stairway is usually the most ornate.

BALUSTER or SPINDLE
An upright piece used to support the handrail. Spindles are rounded and usually turned on a lathe.

LANDING
An area used for a change in a stairway's direction. This is most common when a number of different sections or flights of steps are used.

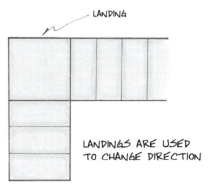

Quite often, a set of drawings for a particular show will indicate that escape stairs should be "pulled from stock" or are otherwise left to the discretion of the carpentry technician. As a result, you may have occasion to determine a common riser height on your own, apart from any plans supplied by the designer.

In order to figure out the common height of each riser, you need to know the overall height that the stairs will ascend, and also the number of steps that will be used. It should be easy to find the overall height, as this is the distance from the floor to the level the stair reaches. The number of steps is a bit trickier as you will need to pick a number that will result in a rise of between six and nine inches. Of course, if you guess the wrong number, you can always try again with no harm done.

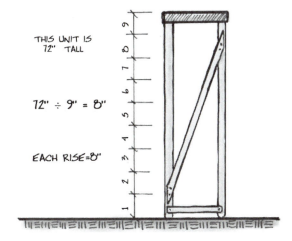

In the previous illustration was a platform with a height of 6'- 0". It is easiest to work this problem using all inches, which for that height is 72". Arbitrarily pick nine for the number of rises, just to see what happens. Seventy-two divided by nine results in a rise of 8" for each step. You can see that one of the 8" rises is actually the space that occurs between the top step and the platform. This is why this stair would have nine rises but only eight treads. You could just as well use eight spaces of nine inches each. Ten spaces would mean an average rise of 7.2 inches, which does not convert easily to a woodworking fraction.

The preceding problem was made quite a bit simpler by virtue of the fact that the first two sets of numbers divided evenly. Unfortunately, this does not always happen, and quite often the process goes a bit more like this: imagine that the platform height is eight feet six inches, which converts to 102". Guessing that eleven rises might work, gives you 9.3 inches per rise. A rise of 9.3" is in excess of the 9" maximum we have set for ourselves. If you subsequently substitute 12 for the number of rises and do the math, you will discover that for 12 risers each individual rise be 8.5 inches. This is lucky because 0.5" is easy to convert to a fractional equivalent of $1/2$". If you need an easier climb, then 13 rises will give you an average of about 7.8 inches each. Again, 7.8 is a decimal number, slightly more than $3/4$".

A decimal expression such as 7.8 may be converted to a woodworking fraction by using a ratio to determine the number of sixteenths that a base ten number equals. Use the equation $z/10 = x/16$. In this equation z represents the number of tenths and x is the number of sixteenths, a fraction that you can find on a tape measure. For the last guess of 13 rises that resulted in 7.8 inches, you can convert to sixteenths in this way:

$$8/10 \ = \ x/16$$
$$x = (8/10)16$$
$$x = 128/10$$
$$x = 12.8$$

which rounds off to about **13/16**

The rounding off will leave a margin of error that is really too small to be of importance. If absolute accuracy is required, try substituting 32 or even 64 as the number under the value x. This will double or quadruple the accuracy of your computations, but that would not normally be required since that tolerance is less than the pencil dot used for marking. As you can see, it is far easier to start out with a more user-friendly decking height, or to choose the 8 $1/2$" riser height to begin with. But some people like math problems!

A STEP BUILDING METHOD

Here is a method of building stairs that uses nothing other than $3/4$-inch plywood. It is presented first because it is an easy and straightforward way to build a small step unit based on very clear engineering principles. It is helpful to limit construction to one material because that streamlines the process, and because that makes it possible to use small scraps that might otherwise be trashed. Also, it produces a neat and clean piece of work that is a major objective of any craftsman.

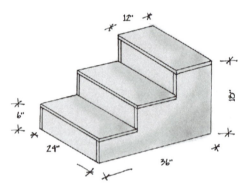

Here is a drawing of a step unit with a 6" tall rise and a 12" deep tread. There are three treads in total, and the width of the steps is 24". Remember that the steps are constructed exclusively of $3/4$" thick plywood. In order to construct this unit, you will first need to develop (wouldn't you know it) a cut list of the parts. Most people find it easier to make the list of parts in order, from the most easily understood to the most difficult to figure out. The easy answers give clues to the difficult ones. A close examination of the drawing reveals that the $3/4$" plywood pieces used for the three treads stretch all the way from the left to the right of the unit. They also extend from the very front to the very back of the 12-inch dimension. There are no other structural members overlapping them that would make the tread pieces smaller than the listed dimensions, so you can determine that there are 3 treads @ 12" x 24". It makes sense that the treads rest on top of the other parts because they are weight bearing. If the treads were nailed on the inside of the other parts, only the nails would be supporting them. The shear strength of a nailed joint like that is not very high.

TREADS

3 @ 12" x 24"

The next part to consider is the bottom riser. Notice in the drawing that this riser piece fits inside the two carriages. The overall dimension of the step is 24", yet to get the width of the riser piece you must subtract $3/4$" and $3/4$" to account for the thicknesses of the two carriages.

$$24" - (3/4" + 3/4") = 22\,1/2".$$

Similarly, you can see that the overall height of the tread from the floor is given as 6", but that this measurement is to the top of the tread while the riser only reaches up to the bottom of it. The tread is $3/4$" thick. List this piece as 1 @ 5 $1/4$" x 22 $1/2$".

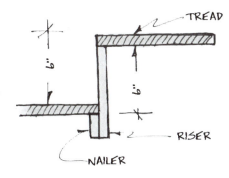

BOTTOM RISER

1 @ 5 $1/4$" x 22 $1/2$"

The remaining two risers require a bit of explanation because they have parts that join in a way that cannot be seen in the original drawing of just the outside of the unit. A section view through the center shows the hidden internal parts.

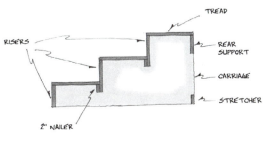

SECTION VIEW OF INTERNAL PARTS

You can see from the exterior drawing that the second and third risers have the same width as the first one did. However, the section view shows that these two risers extend below the underlying tread by a distance of two inches. This allows for a second piece of $3/4$" ply to be connected to the front of the riser. The height of these two risers is not decreased by $3/4$" as the first one was. The reason is clear if you examine the starting and ending points of the rise. The "rise" is a distance, while a "riser" is an actual physical thing.

These risers start $3/4$" below where the dimension places the top of the tread just as the first one did, because that tread rests on top of the riser. However, the risers end up $3/4$" below the dimensioned part of the lower tread, as shown in the drawing, because they extend to the bottom of the tread rather than the top. So even though $3/4$" is lost by subtracting the thickness of the tread on top, it is regained by adding back the thickness of the tread on the bottom. To put it another way, the top of the riser is $3/4$" below the top of the rise, and discounting the 2" nailer, the bottom of the riser is $3/4$" below the bottom of the rise.

When the 2" is added, the total height of the riser is 8". These risers should be listed as 2 @ 8" x 22 $1/2$". The 2" piece of plywood is added in order to give the tread a framing member to rest upon. If this were not done, then the rear of the tread below would be supported only by nails driven horizontally through the bottom of the riser on top of it. Many steps are made in that way, but it proves to be an inherently weak structure. The nails easily bend, and the glue bond breaks. The two-inch nailer prevents that from happening.

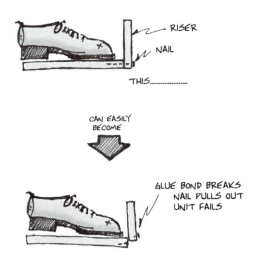

RISERS

2 @ 8" x 22 $1/2$"

NAILERS

2 @ 2" x 22 $1/2$"

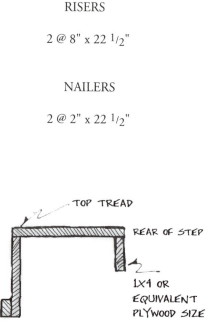

There are some rules with this construction method that make it quite easy to figure a cut list. The first riser piece is always $3/4$" shorter than the overall height of the rise. All other risers, regardless of how many there are, will be 2"taller than the given riser height. The 2" wide nailers we have been discussing are of course only 22 $1/2$" wide because they fit to the inside of the carriages. The horizontal member at the back of the step unit and which supports the top tread will also be 22 $1/2$" wide, with the other dimension varying depending on the width of the step unit. Very wide steps require a beefier member, but a 3 $1/2$" wide strip should prove sufficient for this small unit. The 3 $1/2$" width was selected because it is the same as the milled width of a 1x4. If there is a supply of 1x4 white pine in the shop, you can substitute it for a plywood version of this part.

REAR SUPPORT

1 @ 3 $1/2$" x 22 $1/2$"

The two carriages are the only remaining items for your cut list. These pieces are not rectangles, but rather a more complex shape. Because of that it is not possible to describe them merely by saying they are "so wide by so long." Instead you must make a small sketch and dimension the parts.

The section of the carriage that corresponds to the bottom riser is dimensioned at 5 $1/4$" just as the riser was and for the same reason, that it fits under the tread rather than to the side of it. The next two rises are an even 6" each since they both lose and gain $3/4$" from their respective treads.

The depth of the tread is given at 12 inches. Note that the overall height is 17 $1/4$", $3/4$" smaller than the height of the finished unit.

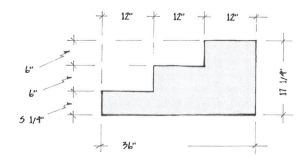

CARRIAGE DIMENSIONS FOR CUT LIST

CONSTRUCTING THE STEPS

When building steps, it is best to use the table saw to rip the $3/4$" plywood into strips of the proper width and then use the radial arm saw to cut the strips to length. The project will be more aesthetically pleasing if the grain of the exterior veneer on the plywood runs the length of the pieces. B/C yellow pine plywood and/or $3/4$" lauan are the best choices of material. C/D is not normally recommended because it is usually too warped and full of voids to fit together well enough to make a good-looking product. Use all of the measuring and marking skills you learned from the chapters on woodworking and flats. This method of construction depends upon a high degree of accuracy from the cutting process, and parts that are not the right size will not fit together well.

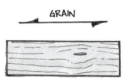

FOR BEST RESULTS, RUN GRAIN THE LENGTH OF YOUR PARTS

Since the carriages are not a simple rectangular shape, they require a bit more work to cut out. If the unit is small with only a couple of steps, then it might be best to cut out a rectangle that is the proper overall size, and then to cut a notch to form the required shape. If the step unit is larger, with a number of steps, this might be too wasteful a process.

If you are making many units at one time, there will probably be some intuitive manner of laying out the parts that will save on materials. At any rate, mark lines for the parts using the sketch you made as a guide, transferring the measurements and connecting the marks with a straight edge. Use either the bandsaw (if the part will fit) or a jigsaw to cut along the lines, remembering to make the kerf fall on the side of the line that will become scrap.

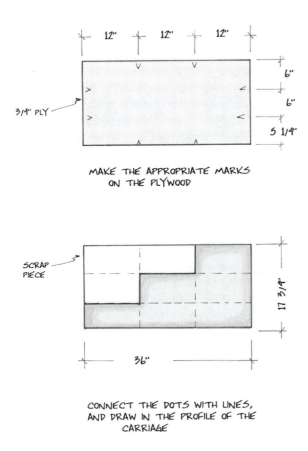

MAKE THE APPROPRIATE MARKS
ON THE PLYWOOD

CONNECT THE DOTS WITH LINES,
AND DRAW IN THE PROFILE OF THE
CARRIAGE

Assembly can be made easier by following a certain order of work. Connect the 2" wide nailer to the eight-inch wide riser first. If you have used a type of plywood that has one side better than the other such as A/C fir or B/C yellow pine, be sure to keep track of the good and bad sides. Of course you want to put the good face of the plywood to what will become the outside when the project is finished. For the two riser parts, this means attaching the 2" wide strip to the good side of the 8" wide riser, taking care to align it with the bottom and the two sides.

Using a nail gun or a construction stapler will greatly speed up assembly. Naturally, there are a variety of other fasteners that will work just as well, but not as quickly.

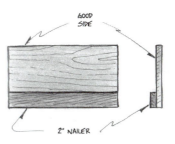

ATTACH THE 2" NAILER TO THE
GOOD SIDE OF THE RISER

When assembling this sort of work, make sure to use plenty of glue to help adhere the two surfaces. Apply enough so that the surfaces are completely coated. You can learn to gauge this amount by putting on the glue (a zigzag pattern is best), and then pulling the two pieces apart to see if that was enough. Pressing the two pieces together and then squishing slightly from side to side will also help to spread the glue. Use any brand of yellow aliphatic resin (carpenter's) glue. It has very fast bonding properties. However, be aware that once this glue is applied, work must proceed apace as there are really only a few minutes at best before the glue begins to set. If you disturb the glue bond after it has begun to set, the strength of the connection will be greatly reduced.

Finishing nails from a gun do not have a great deal of holding power, so the glue really is essential. It is good to make a habit of gluing together more or less every joint on all projects, unless you know from the outset that they will need to be taken apart at some point in the future. When that is the case, screws or bolts are the preferred fasteners.

Finishing nailers of all brands will typically "set" the nail (or staple) an eighth of an inch or so into the surface of the plywood. Be sure to bear this in mind when selecting the length of fastener to use. For a double layer of $3/4$" thick plywood a fastener length of 1 $1/2$" is too long. The "set" of the fastener would cause this length to protrude from the back of the underlying piece of plywood. That can lead to some nasty cuts on anyone handling the scenery and looks just awful. Use a slightly shorter 1 $1/4$" nail instead.

The second phase of assembling the steps is to connect the risers and the carriages. Remember that the carriages will most likely have a good and a bad side, and of course the good side should face outward. It is easiest to stand one of the center risers on end, put glue on the end that is up, and then to lay the carriage on top of the riser. If you nail the center riser first, it is possible to sort of balance the carriage while you go about the business of nailing it. Starting with the end riser will make it very hard to line up the parts. Once a second riser has been attached, the pieces will stand on their own and make it much easier to finish the job. Standing the risers on end will also keep the glue from running off the edge as quickly. Be sure to flush what will become the top of the riser to the top of the carriage, and the face of the riser with the front of the carriage.

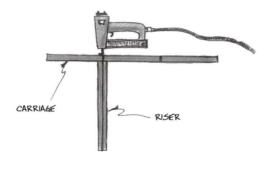

TURN THE RISER ON END TO
ATTACH THE CARRIAGE TO IT

Once you have completed the task of joining the three risers and the support that goes at the back of the top tread, it is time to flip the unit over and attach the second carriage in the same way. Again, remember that gluing is essential! It is this glue that really holds the wood together. You can view the nails as pins that hold the structure together while the glue sets. Nails don't have much strength at all on their own, but staples are more secure. In keeping with this philosophy, remember that it is not necessary to use absolutely all of the nails in your gun, but rather just enough to hold the pieces in place.

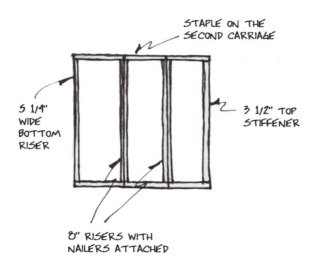

STAPLE ON THE
SECOND CARRIAGE

5 1/4"
WIDE
BOTTOM
RISER

3 1/2" TOP
STIFFENER

8" RISERS WITH
NAILERS ATTACHED

After attaching the second carriage, turn the step unit upright and nail on the treads. Notice that the carriages and risers do not appear to be especially square when you look at them. They most likely are not square at all because we've done nothing so far to make them so. The treads themselves are used to square the unit. Each one should, unless something has gone horribly awry in the cutting process, have four 90-degree angled corners, and two sets of equal sides. This is the ideal shape to use in squaring up a structure.

Put glue on the surfaces that lie underneath the bottom tread, and set the tread into position. Adjust the tread until one of the front corners is perfectly aligned with the corner of the riser and carriage, and put one nail in this corner. Twist the entire step unit until the side of the tread is flush with the carriage, and secure that back corner with a nail. The short side of the tread is connected to the assembly. Now nail the front of the tread, beginning at the first corner you attached and then working your way across to the other side. Aligning two adjacent sides and securing them will automatically square up the entire unit. (Again this presupposes that your cutting was accurate.) This is exactly the same way that a plywood cover is used to square up the framing on a hard cover flat. It is essential to remember to square up the unit as you go along. After the treads are on, it will be too late to affect the squareness of the piece. From here it is a simple matter of nailing the two remaining treads. Remember that a nail every eight inches or so is generally sufficient. Use each one to re-square the unit as you go along.

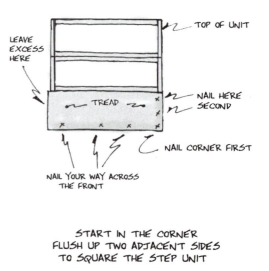

LEAVE
EXCESS
HERE

TOP OF UNIT

TREAD

NAIL HERE
SECOND

NAIL CORNER FIRST

NAIL YOUR WAY ACROSS
THE FRONT

START IN THE CORNER
FLUSH UP TWO ADJACENT SIDES
TO SQUARE THE STEP UNIT

HELPFUL HINTS

It is not necessary to align all parts completely before you begin to nail. It is, however, essential to make sure that the point where you are putting a nail is exactly aligned.

Quite often, the plywood treads will not be an exact fit for the framing structure. There are many reasons for this, with the major one being that plywood is often times slightly thinner than the name would indicate. This is true of most modern plywood and is especially true of sheet goods from the Pacific Rim. They are actually manufactured in metric sizes that are close to the American sizes we use, but not exactly the same. Half-inch is actually 12 mm or approximately 7/16". Three quarters of an inch is actually 16mm or 11/16".

The problem can be addressed by simply allowing the tread to hang over a bit when necessary, and then trimming off the excess with a router and/or belt sander. Leave a space at the back of the tread if it is too small.   Just make sure to maintain the same amount of overhang or underhang all the way around to ensure that the piece will still be squared up properly. It is essential that you flush up the first short side completely in order to make the squaring process work.

Nailing the long sides one step at a time from the first corner to the opposite end will remove any bow or curve from the riser piece. The tread will straighten the riser and help to make the entire project appear more orderly.

A stiffener at the bottom of the step unit in the only remaining free corner will help to prevent the plywood from warping inward.

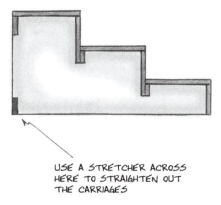

USE A STRETCHER ACROSS HERE TO STRAIGHTEN OUT THE CARRIAGES

The width of the nailer that holds up the back edge of the treads does not have to be 2". That is simply a number I chose because it is easy to add with other numbers. If you are planning to construct a very wide unit of more than 60 inches or so, increase the size of this member to accommodate the longer span. You can build steps up to 96 inches in width using this method and a 3 1/2" wide nailer. The steps require no center carriage and are completely rigid, with no detectable deflection in the center. Methods that require the use of one or more center carriages are much more difficult to assemble.

IF THE TREAD IS TOO SMALL, LEAVE A SPACE BEHIND WHERE IT WILL NOT SHOW

IF THE TREAD IS TOO LARGE, EVENLY DISTRIBUTE THE EXCESS ACROSS THE FRONT WHERE YOU CAN TRIM IT OFF LATER WITH A ROUTER AND/OR A BELT SANDER

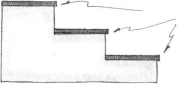

ALTERNATE BUILDING TECHNIQUES

Sometimes the design of a stair makes it necessary to use an alternate method of step building. This is often true when the stair as designed has too many steps, or when an "open riser" look is mandated. Some stairs are curved, or at an angle. Some must be made from metal.

There is a fairly simple method that may be used to construct stairs that are larger/taller than the previous method will accommodate. When the carriage involved is larger than will fit on a 4x8 sheet of plywood, it is almost mandatory that this second method be used. Any step unit that rises more than three feet or so in height will be very heavy when constructed with a solid carriage. In this case the open carriage or "stringer" style is much lighter and is generally preferred.

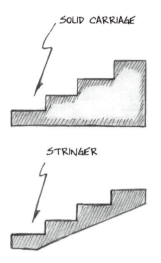

SOLID CARRIAGE

STRINGER

The drawing illustrates the difference between the two types. In reality, the stringer style is constructed in exactly the same manner as the previous demonstration, except for the diagonal nature of the carriage, and the method of marking the notches. This style of carriage is actually somewhat easier to lay out and cut than the closed style. The process is begun by ripping a strip of 3/4" plywood for the stringer. If an eight-foot long section of plywood will not be long enough, it is possible to laminate together thinner stock to make up the stringers.

Be sure to offset the joints in the laminating process to produce a stronger member. For most applications, a 12 inch wide strip of plywood is wide enough for the purpose, although if the stair is to have unusually high rises, deep treads, or a great many steps, it may be necessary to increase the width of the strip to 15 or perhaps 16 inches. It is important that the stringer be large enough to maintain its strength even after the notches have been cut into it.

After the stock for your stringers has been ripped to the proper width, you can mark the location and angle of the notches for the steps. Use a framing square for this job. It is best to use a square that is 16 inches on one side and 24 inches on the other. A speed square will not work. An aluminum square is by far the easiest to use because it is much lighter, and the numbers are easier to read. Remember that with most framing squares, the markings on one side are in twelfths of an inch and in sixteenths of an inch on the other side. The twelfths are used to work on roof pitches and are of little use in scenery building, so you should use the side marked in sixteenths. If you are not sure which is which, count the number of small spaces between the inch marks.

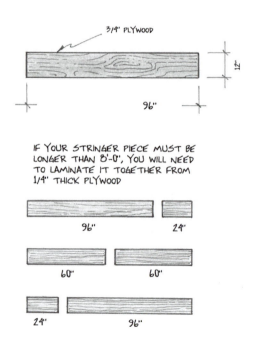

3/4" PLYWOOD

12"

96"

IF YOUR STRINGER PIECE MUST BE LONGER THAN 8'-0', YOU WILL NEED TO LAMINATE IT TOGETHER FROM 1/4" THICK PLYWOOD

96"   24'

60'   60'

24'   96"

WHEN LAMINATING PARTS TOGETHER, OFFSET THE JOINTS AS MUCH AS POSSIBLE. PUT GLUE OVER THE ENTIRE SURFACE OF THE JOINT WITH A PAINT BRUSH OR ROLLER.

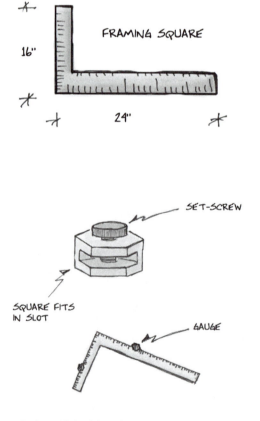

FRAMING SQUARE

16"

24"

SET-SCREW

SQUARE FITS IN SLOT

GAUGE

STAIR GAUGES CLAMP ONTO THE SQUARE SO THAT YOU CAN EASILY RETURN TO THE SAME SETTING

Another helpful tool that is an adjunct to the framing square is the stair gauge. Gauges are essentially small clamps that may be fastened to the edge of the framing square. They make it easy to repeatedly find the same spot on your framing square and function as a jig to increase the accuracy of your layout.

Assume that you wish to lay out a set of stairs with a rise of 6 inches and a tread depth of 10 inches. Take the framing square and lay the corner of it across the plywood so that the 6-inch mark on the short side of the square is even with the near edge of the plywood. Rotate the framing square until the 10-inch mark on the long side of the square lines up with the same edge of the plywood strip. If you have a set of stair gauges, attach them to the square so that it is easy to return to the alignment you set up.

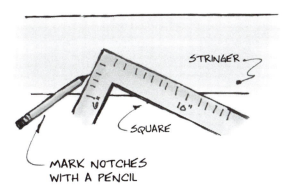

MARK NOTCHES
WITH A PENCIL

Use a pencil to trace around the outside edge of the square to mark one tread depth and one rise. It is best to start at the bottom of the stringer when marking the layout. There is one really tricky part to the process. The bottom riser, as laid out on the stringer, must be shorter in height than the remaining risers by the thickness of the tread, which in our case is $3/4$". Use the framing square and measure down from your tread line $5 1/4$" in two widely divergent places, making sure that you are measuring at a right angle to the tread line.

Use the square as a straightedge to draw a line parallel to the original tread line, and that runs through the $5 1/4$" marks. You have established the very bottom of the stringer, the part that makes contact with the stage floor.

From this point, it is a fairly simple matter of drawing in as many repetitions of the first riser/tread layout as are required to reach the desired height for the stringer. Remember that as you complete the stringer layout you are looking at it upside down. When the top tread line is marked, you will notice that it is not necessary to mark the corresponding riser line that goes with it. Rather, the line should extend downward from the endpoint to finish off the step.

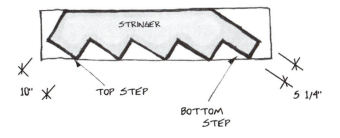

Construction of this type of step unit is basically the same as our first unit, save for the fact that that the carriage is shaped differently. The riser section sub assemblies are built first, and then attached to one of the stringers. Then the opposite stringer is connected, and finally the treads are used to square the unit. You will need help with these stringers because they are so much bigger and heavier than the carriages in the smaller unit discussed earlier.

At this point you may well wonder how this type of stair remains upright since the carriage does not reach all the way to the floor in the back. One way is too leg the stair so that vertical framing members keep the unit erect. You will need two legs in the back and enough bracing to keep the whole thing together.

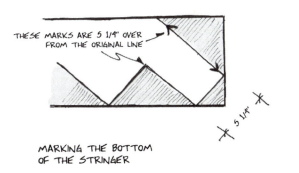

MARKING THE BOTTOM
OF THE STRINGER

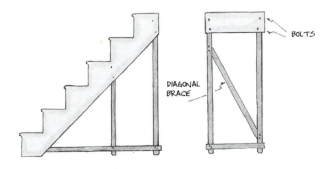

LEGS ON A STRINGER TYPE STAIR

Notice the triangles formed by the bracing in the drawing of the freestanding stair on the last page. You can see one large triangle in the side view created by the horizontal rail, the upright member, and the stair itself. In the rear view you can see two triangles that share a hypotenuse. Triangles are a very strong structural form and are often seen in any kind of bracing.

If the stair connects with a sturdy platform, there is a much more elegant solution to the problem. If the platform level is already supported in its own right, it is easy to use that platform to support the stair. If more than one set of stairs is connected to the platform (a front set and escape, for example), the stairs may actually enhance the stability of the platform by acting as diagonal bracing. An excellent method of attaching this type of stair to a platform is to add a section of plywood at the back of the top step that extends upward to the exact height of the platform. This should be an amount equal to the standard height of one of the unit's risers. The strip of plywood will need to be ripped so that it is wide enough to also extend down to the bottom of the framing member that is supporting the back of the top tread. Bolt through this piece of plywood and through the framing of the platform to very securely join the two units. If you fasten the bottom of the stair to the stage floor with a backflap hinge or two, the stair unit itself becomes a piece of diagonal bracing.

the weight of a person, even when the steps are very narrow, without being joined with a riser. Therefore a thicker and stronger tread material must be used. Most commonly, two-by lumber of some sort is used, probably a 2x12 or a 2x10, as any narrower dimension would be too small for the tread. This type of stair will also have carriages made from a 2x12, and they must be cut out with the stringer method if the overall height of the stair is more than twelve inches.

When 2x12s are used, the thickness of the treads will be 1 1/2" rather than 3/4". As a result, the bottom riser will need to be marked 1 1/2" smaller on the bottom of the stringer rather than 3/4" as noted in the earlier exercise. This type of stair unit may appear to be airier and lighter to the eye, but it is in reality much, much heavier. It lacks the "portability factor" required by most stage scenery. It will also tend to be less precise, and to warp out of shape more easily, so it is not such a good choice from an engineering standpoint.

It is possible to make this unit entirely from laminated plywood by using three layers of 1/2" ply on the stringers. You can use a double lamination of 3/4" ply for the treads instead of dimension lumber, with the advantage being that the resulting material is more stable. If you glue the plywood together so that only the good side is out, its appearance is enhanced, and any natural bow in the plywood will tend to cancel itself out.

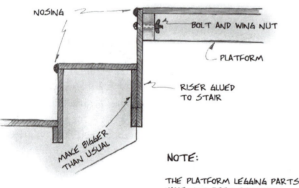

NOTE:

THE PLATFORM LEGGING PARTS HAVE NOT BEEN SHOWN IN ORDER TO MAKE IT EASIER TO SEE THE STEP/PLATFORM JUNCTION

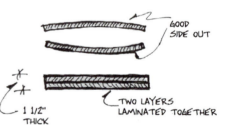

Sometimes the design calls for stairs that have open risers, which is to say that the piece that physically makes up the riser itself is left off. These stairs have a more open appearance to them. In this case, the type of all-plywood construction we have been discussing will not work. The 3/4-inch plywood tread is not nearly strong enough to support

In recent years stair units constructed from steel square tube have become very popular. Indeed, there is much more metal scenery in general because the cost and difficulty of steel or aluminum construction are much less than they once were. One-and-a-half-inch 16ga square tube is a popular choice, but there are many shapes and sizes. Some of these are shown in the chapter on metal working. Steel square tube framing has a very light, open quality that it presents to the audience, which belies the fact that it is in reality far heavier than any other type. However, the unique look of the material has made it a popular choice for designers, especially when the design calls for an industrial look. Although the steel is very heavy, these stairs are not prone to pulling apart from the twisting motion that scenery is often subjected to when it is being moved about.

For steel square tube construction, make a pattern or jig in the shape of a carriage, as discussed earlier. Cut the square tube parts to fit the jig and weld them together. The metal-working chapter goes into detail about how to use wooden blocks to make a temporary jig that will hold the parts in position while they are being welded. After the carriages have been constructed, use straight pieces of tubing to connect the two carriages and form the support for plywood treads.

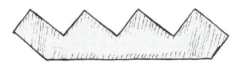

MAKE A PATTERN FROM SCRAP PLYWOOD
AND USE IT TO BUILD A JIG FOR THE
SQUARE TUBE STRUCTURE

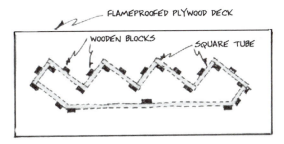

FLAMEPROOFED PLYWOOD DECK

WOODEN BLOCKS   SQUARE TUBE

An alternate method is to form a side runner with a top and bottom chord like a truss. Make the bottom end so that it can mate with the floor at the proper angle. Weld together some rectangular frames that are the proper size for the treads, and connect these in between the two side runners at the proper angle.   It is not necessary to weld together the stringer with notches for the rises and treads, as the rectangular tread forms are welded directly to the side of the stringer truss.

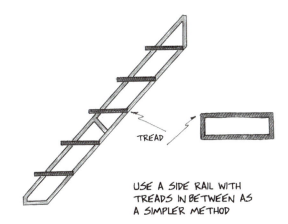

TREAD

USE A SIDE RAIL WITH
TREADS IN BETWEEN AS
A SIMPLER METHOD

CHAPTER 14

DECKING METHODS

Generally speaking, platforming is the most difficult and expensive scenery to build. Platforms are more heavily constructed than most other stage scenery because of the weight they must carry — not only the weight of the setting that is placed upon it, but the combined pounds of all the actors as well. Moving objects create what is known as a live load, which requires a sturdier structure than a static load. Actors who are dancing, or running, or jumping up and down may create a load that is really several times their combined weight. A group of dancers running to one side of the stage will cause a great deal of lateral stress on the structure that elevates the platforming. Care must be taken to assure that any decking system is safe for the type of load that will be placed on it.

The words "platform" and "deck" are often used to mean the same thing. In a subtle way, decking tends to indicate platforms that are part of a system, while saying platform often means a single piece.

You may well notice in this chapter how many of the techniques and processes mentioned earlier in the book are also useful in constructing platforms. Flip back to some of the earlier chapters for more information about tools, woodworking, and especially about working with angles.

COMMERCIALLY MANUFACTURED DECKING

THIS PLATFORMING SYSTEM WAS DESIGNED AS PORTABLE
STAGING FOR CONCERTS IN LARGE ARENAS. IT IS VERY
EASY TO SET UP, BUT IS NOT SUITABLE FOR THEATRE
WORK BECAUSE IT IS TOO HEAVY, AND ISN'T VERY ADAPTABLE.

STOCK DECKING

Most permanent theatre companies use stock decking units to decrease the cost of using platforms. The most common size for a platform is the 4x8, because that is the size of a sheet of plywood. It is often cost effective to have some other stock sizes too, such as 2x8 and/or 4x4. These dimensions are a good fit with a 4x8. You may find that your particular theatre benefits from some other types as well. Some groups like to use a smaller size like 3x4 or 3x6. Unless you have a tiny door to fit through, or some other site-specific problem, it may be best to stick with the 4x8 size and its relatives. A prudent designer will consider the use of standard units in designing a show, so as to reduce the cost of construction. Directors like platforms because they create different levels between actors, and you will have many encounters with decking over a lifetime in show business.

Professional scenery building shops often use either aluminum rectangular tubing or 5/4 clear lumber to frame a platform. That makes for an excellent product but can be a bit pricey for smaller theatres and/or universities. None-the-less, when building stock platforms that you will keep for a very long time it is generally good to splurge on the best materials you can afford. Stock platforms are in constant use for years before they are no longer viable. In view of how long they last the expense seems worthwhile. When constructing oddly-shaped platforms for a particular show, a less extravagant approach may be sufficient.

The projects discussed so far have mostly used one-by lumber or plywood for the framing. Platforms typically need something stronger and more rigid, so 2x4 dimension lumber is often used. It will stand up to years of difficult and/or indifferent use. Sometimes 1x4 framing is enough for a throwaway that doesn't carry much of a load, especially if it sits on the floor. The best covering material is $3/4$" plywood. It is thick enough to make a secure cover with minimal spring to it. Sometimes it is cheaper to use $3/4$" lauan.

A 4x8 platform built with the materials previously mentioned requires a support framing member every 24" in order to keep deflection and vibration to a minimum. A sketch of the framing for a stock platform built with 2x4 lumber and a $3/4$" thick plywood top is shown, with a cut list.

You can see that the end rails are 4'- 0" long and run all the way from side to side, while the toggle rails fit to the inside of the stiles, and as a result are only 3'- 9" in length. Staggering the joints in this way leads to a more secure locking together of the framing. If all of the rails were 3'- 9", it would be remarkably easy to pull the stiles off of the sides of the platform. You can connect the framing together with 16d box nails or 2 $1/2$" drywall screws, but before doing that, be sure to cut notches for the coffin locks.

STILE IS TOO EASY TO PULL OFF
OVERLAP END RAILS THE OPPOSITE WAY

Coffin locks are cam-operated fasteners that are attached to the sides of decking and used to join the platforms together. They negate the use of bolts or C-clamps for that purpose. You can easily make up a set of jigs used to mark coffin lock placement in about an hour or so, and over a period of time the effort will be well rewarded. Coffin locks allow you to lock platforms together quickly and easily, using a $5/16$" hex key. During set up, the decking can be laid out face up and in the position it will eventually occupy. Bolting platforms together can be quite problematic when the height of the decking is too short for a person to crawl under. Bolting together a large number of heavy platforms upside down and then trying to flip them over can be quite a challenge, and it places a lot of stress on the decking.

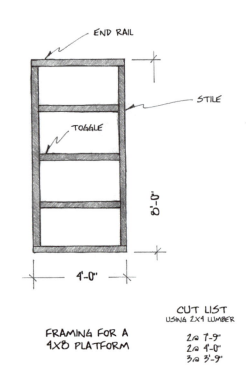

END RAIL

STILE

TOGGLE

8'-0"

4'-0"

FRAMING FOR A
4X8 PLATFORM

CUT LIST
USING 2X4 LUMBER

2 @ 7'-9"
2 @ 4'-0"
3 @ 3'-9"

DRILL KEY HOLE
FOR MALE HALF ONLY

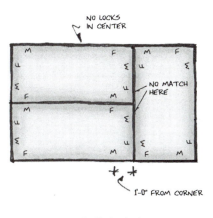

POSITIONING
THE COFFIN LOCKS

There is a way of placing coffin locks in the platforms that will allow the decking to be arranged in a variety of ways. Most often, individual platforms are laid side by side, or end to end when they are used together. Sometimes you need to place one platform across the ends of two others, or to create an L shape.

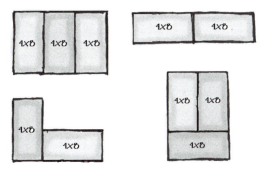

DIFFERENT WAYS OF JOINING
4X8 PLATFORMS

It is possible to accommodate these four possibilities by staggering the male/female halves of the locks, if they are placed at a standard distance from each corner. One way is to center the coffin locks exactly 1'- 0" from each corner of the 4x8 stock platform. In this way, no matter how the platforms are turned, the male/female sides will match up properly. You can see that side to side and end to end the platforms always have two locks touching, which makes for a very strong joint. When the platforms meet from side to end, this is not always the case. If you were to count the middle of the 8'- 0" long side as an end and installed locks accordingly, then the resulting side-to-end joints would have two connections as well. This creates a lot of extra work, and because the decking seems quite secure with the easier method it is not really necessary.

A careful measurement of a casket lock reveals that it is approximately 3 $3/8$" wide and $5/8$" thick (In reality just a bit smaller). This is the size notch you need to cut into the 2x4 framing to allow for installation. The inset distance has been chosen as 1'- 0" from each corner. Because the 2x4 framing members overlap one another, the rails will need the center of the notch to be exactly 1'- 0" from the end, but the stiles, which fit to the inside of the rails, will require an inset of only 0'- 10 $1/2$". In order to easily register the jig on a 2x4, it is designed from a piece of $3/4$" stock that has been ripped to 3 $1/2$" wide. You can make your jig for marking the notch locations to these specifications:

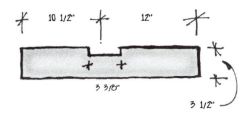

NOTCH MARKING JIG

To use this jig, simply lay it on top of the board, line up the top and bottom with the edges of the 2x4, the end of the jig with the end of the board, and trace around the inside of the notch. Use the 1'- 0" end for marking the rails that run from side to side, and the 0'- 10 $1/2$" end for the 7'- 9" stiles. Use a jigsaw to cut out the notches, or if a large number of platforms are being built, use the radial arm saw with a dado head cutter installed.

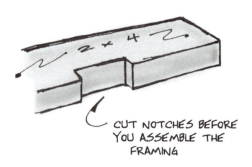

CUT NOTCHES BEFORE
YOU ASSEMBLE THE
FRAMING

The framing is now ready to be nailed together. Begin by connecting the perimeter box. Be sure to accurately measure the placement of the interior framing. It is important for all of the internal parts to be consistent. These are stock platforms, and having exactly interchangeable parts will pay dividends later on in ways that are not apparent now. Sloppy work is just that—sloppy. I know that it sounds like someone's dad speaking, but there really is no way to overstate the importance of having your work be neat and tidy. It is the mark of craftsmen who take pride in their work.

Measuring the internal parts calls for finding the center of the 2x4s, and then the edges. Using a standard tape, follow along the side of the previously connected rectangle until you reach 2'- 0". Count backwards $3/4$", which is half of the thickness of the 2x4. Make a V mark. Count forward $3/4$" to 2'- 0 $3/4$" and make another V mark. Move forward to the 4'- 0" placement and repeat the procedure, and again at the 6'- 0" toggle. Do this on both stiles, taking care to start the measurement from the same end. Now you have marked both sides of both ends of all three toggles. Marking the two corners is a much more accurate method of work, and once it becomes habit it takes no longer than marking just the center. If only the center is marked, there is the problem of determining the center of the end of the 2x4 when putting it in place.

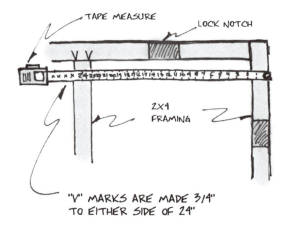

TAPE MEASURE

LOCK NOTCH

2X4
FRAMING

"V" MARKS ARE MADE 3/4"
TO EITHER SIDE OF 24"

Lay the plywood decking in place and attach it. On a permanent unit like this it is best to glue the plywood down, as this is the most secure way to join the parts and will help to prevent squeaking later on. You can use either yellow carpenter's glue, or if the 2x4 stock is a little rough, a construction adhesive like Liquid Nails may work better. The thicker mastic is an excellent gap filler. The aliphatic resin carpenter's glue is not. Following the common practice that you have seen before, begin by aligning one corner of the unit, while leaving the others merely close. Nail or screw this one corner. Work your way along the abutting 4'- 0" side, squaring up and fastening as you go, one step at a time. Go back to the original corner and work your way along the contiguous 8'- 0" length in the same fashion. Since the framing of a platform is very rigid, you many need to use one or more pipe clamps to square the 2x4s to the plywood.

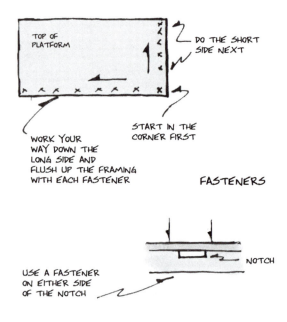

TOP OF
PLATFORM

DO THE SHORT
SIDE NEXT

START IN THE
CORNER FIRST

WORK YOUR
WAY DOWN THE
LONG SIDE AND
FLUSH UP THE FRAMING
WITH EACH FASTENER

FASTENERS

NOTCH

USE A FASTENER
ON EITHER SIDE
OF THE NOTCH

This procedure should ensure that the finished platform is square. Attempting to line up all parts of the platform at one time is a nightmarish procedure and a monumental waste of time. It is far better to begin in one spot and let the procedure take its course. A sheet of $3/4$" A/C or B/C American made plywood is almost sure to be as square as you have any ability to discern. You can place great faith in the ability of plywood to square up your work and will rarely be disappointed.

At this point you are ready to place the holes for attaching the casket locks. It is imperative that you use a jig for this step in order to maintain accuracy. It also speeds up the work by at least an order of magnitude. There is a drawing of this jig that you should refer to while reading the description.

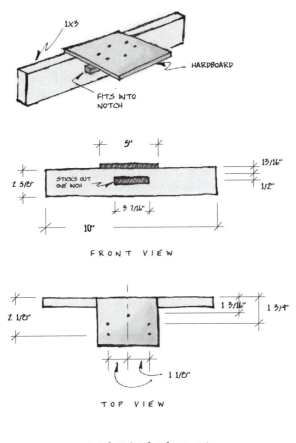

1X3

HARDBOARD

FITS INTO NOTCH

5"

13/16"

2 5/8"

STICKS OUT ONE INCH

1/2"

3 7/16"

10"

F R O N T   V I E W

2 1/8"

1 3/16"   1 3/4"

1 1/8"

T O P   V I E W

HOLE PLACEMENT JIG
FOR COFFIN LOCKS

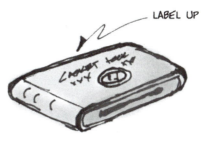

LABEL UP

MALE HALF

The 1/2" by 3 7/16" block is intended to fit inside the notches you cut into the framing earlier. The perforations on top are used to mark the exact placement of the holes to drill for inserting the 5/16" hex key, and for the two screws that hold the coffin lock in place. The notch in the 2x4 that is to your right has been arbitrarily selected to be the male part of the lock. This means that on any side you are looking at, there will be two notches for locks, and that the one on the left will be female, and the one on the right will be male. It really makes no difference which side is selected for which sex, but it is crucial to maintain continuity once a selection has been made.

As you can tell from looking at the jig, different mounting holes are required for each sex. Use the jig to mark placement of the holes, and drill the holes with the appropriate size bit. The keyway requires a 1/2" hole in order to have enough leeway to easily accommodate the 5/16" hex key. If you use 2 1/2" #12 flathead Phillips wood screws to secure the locks, then an 1/8" pilot hole with the appropriate countersink should do the job nicely for those two screws. Make sure to install the male half of the lock with the label up, as this will ensure that the key will turn to the right to lock the device and to the left to unlock.

The screws holding the male side of the lock will fit just to the inside of the 2x4 framing, and do not really penetrate the wood properly. They will still hold just fine. If you would like a neater appearance, glue a small block of one-by material under the notch and the screw will rest between the block and the 2x4 frame. If the platform is framed with 1by material rather than 2x4 stock, you can drill 1/4" holes for flathead bolts rather than using screws. In either case, drill a countersink hole for the head to fit into. You don't want anything to stick up above the surface of the plywood.

Using casket locks greatly lengthens the service life of stock platforms. Drilling bolt holes degrades the framing, and over a period of time it will render the decking unfit for use. The coffin lock system really comes into its own when you are loading the show into the theatre. That process is much, much, easier, and you can connect platforms that are laying directly on the stage floor or have very short legs that you would not normally be able to reach under. Since the decking is laid out right side up, there is no need to turn anything over.

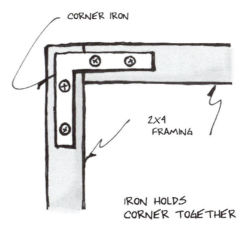

CORNER IRON

2X4
FRAMING

IRON HOLDS
CORNER TOGETHER

Use 1 5/8" #6 drywall screws to secure the plywood tops. This may seem like overkill when used with the glue, but remember that these platforms will be around for a very long time. Another procedure that will increase the life span of a stock platform is to use corner irons to hold together the outside perimeter of the framing. Use the flat irons on the bottom of the platform because they are the easiest to install, and because they do not interfere with the installation of legs. Legs may need to be attached to the inside corner of the framing.

It is best to select a corner iron that is at least four inches long on each side so that there will be enough screw holes for the iron to gain good purchase. The iron will keep the end rail from pulling away from the stile, which it is prone to do. Gluing this joint together is not a viable solution, as there is too much stress, and the bond will not hold. The only drawback is that the platform height is now approximately $3/32$" higher than it once was, but this never seems to create any real problems.

ODDLY SHAPED DECKING

You may often need to construct platforms that are not rectangles. The best method is to cut out the plywood top first and then use this shape as a full-scale pattern in marking the 2x4 framing. This method reduces the amount of information that must be predetermined, and hopefully also reduces the errors that may come from that process. As an example, assume that you need to construct a platform that is half of a 4x8 sheet of plywood, and that is a triangle formed by drawing a line diagonally from corner to corner. Here is a dimensioned drawing of the unit in question:

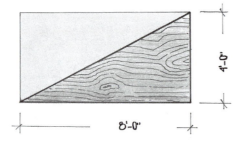

MAKE A PLATFORM
FROM HALF A SHEET

The sketch provides all of the information required to construct this platform, even though you have not been given any information about the number of degrees in any of the angles other than the one corner, which is a right angle. Using the full-scale pattern method, it is not necessary to know these angles, which in any case are rarely given on the designer's plans.

In order to cut out the plywood for the top of the unit, mark the lengths of the two given sides on a sheet of $3/4$" ply and then make a straight line from mark to mark. That works well for any size. This particular example is actually defined by the corners of the sheet of plywood. A chalk line is very handy for this purpose. Make sure that the plywood is good side up when you do the marking, or you may wind up with a piece that is cut out upside down. If you want to mark on the back to reduce the amount of saw tearout on the good side, just be sure to mark everything mirror image. You can use either a jigsaw or a circular saw to make this cut. If you choose the circular (Skil) saw, try using the guide shown in the "How Do You Make…" chapter.

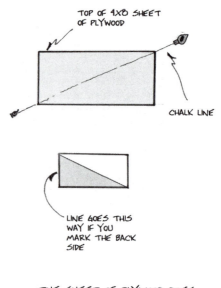

THE SHEET OF PLYWOOD DOES
ALL THE MEASURING FOR YOU

After the top has been cut out, lay it across a pair of sawhorses so that the corners are unobstructed. Trim the end of a piece of 2x4 to make it square and line it up with the 4'- 0" side of the triangle. (You may wish to cut the 2x4 to a length only slightly longer than that side so that it is less cumbersome.) Square up one end with the 90-degree-angle corner, and use a pencil to scribe the length and angle of the plywood onto the 2x4 from underneath. Use the band saw or power miter box to cut the board to length. If you use the power miter box, make a note of the degrees involved, as you will need to know the angle later on in the scenery building process. For the moment, you need only to adjust the saw by eye so that it matches your marked line, and then cut the 2x4.

When using this method, it is best to attach each framing member as you go along because it will simplify the marking process. Otherwise, the piece you just cut will tend to move while the next piece is being marked. For an irregular deck that will not go into stock at the end of the show, you probably won't want to glue the pieces in place. That makes it almost impossible to get anything back apart, and there may be some salvageable pieces. It is enough to screw the top and framing together with 1 5/8" drywall screws. After this first section has been attached, hold another length of 2x4 under the 8-foot long side and scribe the resulting angle from the plywood pattern. You will not be able to cut this angle on most power miter boxes because it is too steep. The saw will not swing around that far. The best way is to use a large band saw if you have one that will accommodate the piece. If not, a circular saw may be used. Cut halfway through on one side, and then turn the 2x4 over to do the same on the second side.

After the piece has been cut, screw it into place and turn the entire platform upside down. The final perimeter framing member may be marked by laying a length of 2x4 stock over the space it will occupy and scribing the two ends. The end of the board with the most obtuse angle can be cut on the power miter box using the same degree setting as before. The opposite angle will be the same as the one previously cut on the band saw. After this last perimeter framing is connected, it is time to mark the interior toggles.

It is not practical to do both sides, as the hypotenuse of the triangle is at an angle. You need a different way of marking that side. Use a drywall square or some other large square to extend your existing marks to the angle side. Square the straightedge up with the known side, and extend the marks outward at a 90-degree angle. It is only necessary to mark the 2x4 framing, not the entire expanse of plywood. Set a length of stock in place flush with the straight side, and scribe the required length and angle from the opposite side. These three toggles can be cut on the power miter box.

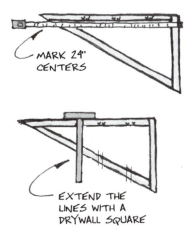

Use 16d box nails or long drywall screws to join the framing where it intersects. A gas or pneumatic framing nailer will greatly speed up the process if available. Be sure to use nails that are equivalent to a 16d box nail. The plywood decking will need to be secured to the toggles with drywall screws. It is probably not necessary to secure the framing of a short-lived platform with corner irons, unless there is some special reason to do so. Sometimes, especially if a show is to be set up a number of times, it is best to put coffin locks on the sides of the platform that will abut a stock platform, or if it is easy to reach under the decking, you can just C-clamp the units together.

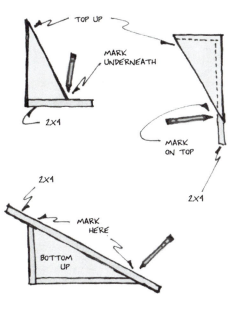

USE THE PLYWOOD TO MARK THE FRAMING

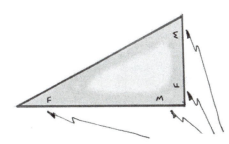

PUT LOCKS ON THE SIDES THAT MATCH WITH THOSE ON STOCK PLATFORMS

Each toggle will be a different length, but each one will have one end that is a 90-degree angle, and another that is the same angle as was earlier cut on the power miter box. Before you can cut the toggles to length, you must first do some layout on the bottom of the platform to determine the toggle locations. Measure along the 8-foot side of the platform, marking both sides of a 2x4 toggle as was described earlier in this chapter in the section about stock platforms.

One way to mark the location of the coffin locks is to lay out the special platform next to some stock units and to mark from one unit to the other. Of course, you can use the same jig as is used for the stock platforms. If you use the notch marking jig you will need to measure the center of the hole nearest the odd angle with a tape measure. The angle end will not work well with the standard jig. Measure the proper distance from the 90-degree angle end.

This same system may be used on more difficult angled pieces. In fact, the more intricate the shape is, the more sense this method makes. Here is a drawing of a more challenging platform:

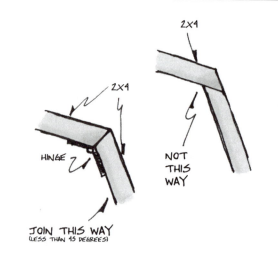

JOIN THIS WAY
(LESS THAN 45 DEGREES)

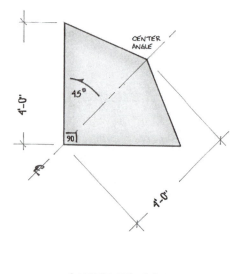

ANGULAR PLATFORM

It is possible for you to determine mathematically the degree size of each angle from the information given in the original drawing. But there is an easier method that requires no math and is reasonably intuitive. You can find the center of the 90-degree angle with a large compass.

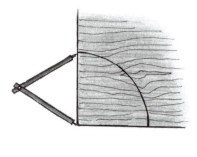

MAKE AN ARC
WITH THE COMPASS

For this platform it is not possible to scribe all of the angles from the deck as was done in the previous example. You do not want to cut the two center angles so that they run all of the way to the edge of the plywood, because the resulting angle would be too steep. For this platform, joining the angle in the center of the outside edge is better accomplished by halving the angle and using a hinge or a corner iron to fasten the two members together. This makes for a much neater and stronger joint.

Open the building compass to a conveniently large angle setting and place its stationary point at the tip of the 90-degree corner of the angle being divided. Mark an arc on the two sides that form the right angle.

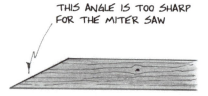

THIS ANGLE IS TOO SHARP
FOR THE MITER SAW

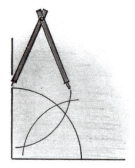

MAKE TWO MORE ARCS
AS SHOWN

Strike an arc from either side of the right angle where your original arc meets the side of the platform top. Draw a line from the beginning corner through the intersection of the two twin arcs. This line should divide the angle exactly in half. The original drawing shows that the center angle on this platform is 4'- 0" from the 90-degree angle corner. Measure 4'- 0" down the center line and make a mark. Use the straightedge to mark lines from the two sides to the center point.

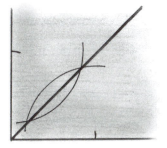

DRAW A LINE THROUGH
THE INTERSECTION TO
FORM A BISECTED ANGLE

Lay a scrap piece of board on the platform top so that it is flush to one side of either of the lines you just marked. Use a straightedge and pencil to transfer the angle to the scrap piece. Put this marked scrap board into the power miter box and adjust the saw until the blade is aligned with the mark. Read the adjustment scale to determine the angle to use when cutting the framing. It just so happens to be 22 $^1/_2$ degrees.

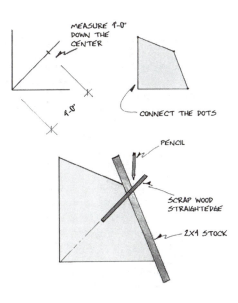

MEASURE 4'-0"
DOWN THE
CENTER

CONNECT THE DOTS

PENCIL

SCRAP WOOD
STRAIGHTEDGE

2X4 STOCK

USE A STRAIGHTEDGE TO
MARK THE ANGLE ON THE 2X4

Cut out the platform lid by following the lines used to make the pattern. Begin the process of framing by cutting two short pieces of 2x4 so that they are 22 $^1/_2$ degrees on one end, and fit to the center angle on the other. Lay each of the pieces on the already cut out platform lid so that they are flush with the edge and meet snugly against one another. Scribe the edges that hang over the side of the plywood, and cut them on the power miter box. Keep the saw set at this angle. Screw the two pieces you have just cut into place on the underside of the platform lid. Trim the end of another length of 2x4 to the same angle that was just used, and match it to the platform for marking. The final perimeter piece will be identical to the one just scribed, except that it will be 1 $^1/_2$" shorter. They will both intersect at a 90-degree angle. Although this particular example wound up with all 22 $^1/_2$ and 90-degree angles, the same process will work with any angles/lengths you choose.

2X4 FRAMING

Notice that the two types of angled corners have been approached in different ways. On the first, the angle was halved, and on the second the framing members were simply overlapped. As a result, the angles in this example could all be cut on the power miter saw (or radial arm saw). If the first angle were scribed directly from the platform lid, it could be too wide to cut on either of these two saws.

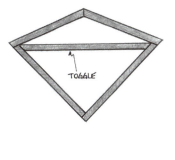

TOGGLE

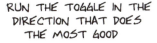

RUN THE TOGGLE IN THE
DIRECTION THAT DOES
THE MOST GOOD

You need only one internal brace for this platform because it is rather small. It should be placed in such a way as to add strength to the span where the two 22 $1/2$-degree angles meet, because that is the weakest part of the structure. It is possible to scribe the angle of this final brace by laying it across the framing already in place. Mathematically computed, the angle for either end is 45 degrees. This is apparent by virtue of the triangle created. It is a right triangle with two equal sides. That description can only belong to a triangle that is 45-45-90.

After the one internal brace has been added, there is no space left greater than two feet by four feet, and hence no need for further bracing.

CURVED PLATFORMS

Quite often, you will find it necessary to build decking with curved edges. In this event, there is generally no way to easily make the framing fit the curved edge of the plywood top. You can build up a curved frame by laminating together thin pieces of plywood. That works well if the edge can be seen from underneath, but most of the time it is not really necessary. The framing can touch in certain spots, and the top can be allowed to overhang in others. If $3/4$" ply is being used, it should be possible to have an overhang of two or three inches without suffering any ill effects. If the curve requires more than this, you may try doubling the thickness of the plywood along the edge.

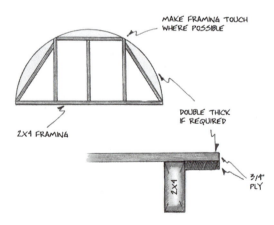

PLATFORM WITH A ROUND EDGE

The previous example of framing for an oddly shaped platform can be repeated as an example of how you may treat a curved surface. A curved surface is really made up of an infinite number of straight sides. Mark the curve of the edge with a set of trammel points if it is part of a circle, or use the grid method shown in the section on full-scale patterns if it is irregular. Trammel points are essentially small clamps that may be attached to a strip of wood to form a very large beam compass. One of the clamps has a steel pin that serves as the stationary point, and the other clamp has a holder for a pencil. You can use strips of white pine left over from ripping down 1x3s as the "beam" part of the compass. It is best to use a lightweight connection because it gives more control over the marking process. A substitute for the trammel points is to use two small strips of wood that are held together with small spring clamps. Put a 4d nail through the end of one of the strips to use as the stationary point, and drill a pencil-size diameter hole through the end of the other. (Make it just a shade small.) Squeeze the pencil into place, and you are ready to go. The size can be adjusted by removing the clamps and sliding the strips of wood back and forth. Do not use a string with a pencil tied to the end of it, because the string will either stretch, break, or get caught on something. The circle will not be true. Sometimes, for a very large arc, you may consider driving a nail into the stationary point and using a steel measuring tape to strike the arc.

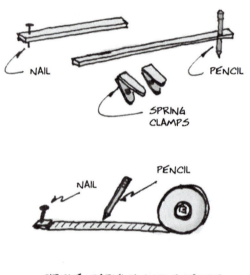

CIRCLE MARKING IMPLEMENTS

After the curve has been established, you can draw in some lines to represent placement of the framing members. It is best to do this in some logical way, but the actual placement is somewhat arbitrary, especially if the curve is irregular. The placement of the framing in the following example is much like the framing in the second oddly shaped platforms example. The same procedures will apply to this project.

The major drawback to this type of framing for a curved platform lies in putting a facing on it. If the curve faces upstage, none is required. Otherwise you will have to bend some kind of plywood around the curve. The problems encountered are: getting the plywood to stay on, and bending the plywood enough to make it match the curve.

Thinner ply is easier to bend but is not as sturdy. Try $1/2$" ply for fairly large curves, and $1/4$" for a tighter radius. Bending plywood is a special type made with the grain in all the plies running in the same direction. It fits around curves easily. It is not very sturdy, but it works quite well if you use two layers laminated together.

Make your framing touch the edge of the curve in as many places as possible in order to give the plywood more support. You can also add small braces that go between the platform top and the facing. Remember when you lay out the curve that anything you add to the outside will make it larger.

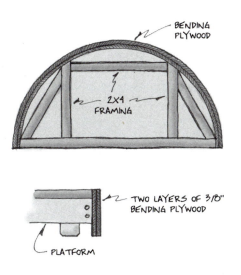

USE BENDING PLYWOOD AROUND THE OUTSIDE EDGE OF THE PLYWOOD TOP
* THIS WILL INCREASE THE SIZE OF THE PLATFORM

LEGGING METHODS

There are many different ways to give height to the kind of platforms we have been discussing, but all of the methods really fall into one of two categories. The first is to put individual legs on each of the platforms, and the second is to build a structure that will support a number of platforms all at once. Choose the type that works best for the given situation. Individual legs are the best solution when the platforms are either very low to the ground, and/or when the platform area is very small. On the other hand, a large expanse of decking several feet off the stage floor definitely calls for some kind of support structure. There is a point in the middle that is not so well defined.

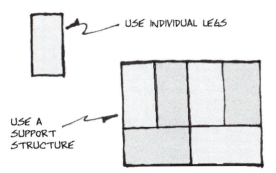

PICK A SUITABLE METHOD

Perhaps the most popular way of legging in small theatre companies is to bolt 2x4 legs into the corners of the platforms. A problem associated with this practice is that drilling the bolt holes tends to degrade the stock platforms. Also, the 2x4s themselves are much heavier and clunkier than necessary to hold up the load. The compression strength of a 2x4 leg is tremendous, and it will hold up a great deal more weight than you are ever likely to place on it. Smaller framing members will support just as well if they are properly constructed.

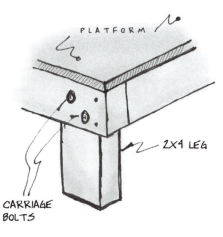

The real problem with legging is to provide lateral strength to keep the structure from twisting out of shape to the side, and/or from "corkscrewing." Care must be taken to keep the legging structure rigid. If all of the parts stay in position, the structure will be safe. If any of the parts bend or twist the structure will fail. The upright parts have the most stress put on them. It is a compression load that pushes straight down the length of the board. Generally, the members that are used to stiffen the structure don't have that much loading. Tensile strength is the ability of a material to withstand a load that may cause it to bend or break. When individual legs are used, the platform framing itself is responsible for that function, and it is not an issue with the legs themselves. It is important to securely fasten the legs to the platform framing.

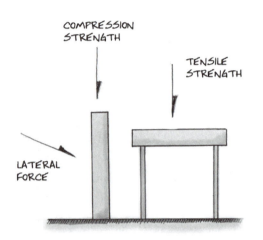

One solution to the problem is to use a "V" leg. They are called this because of the shape of their cross section. It is essentially two pieces of 1x4 that have been glued and stapled together. This is a cost-effective method of manufacture because there are often scraps of this material left over from the construction of other scenery. If this material is not available, you can rip down strips of $3/4$" plywood from whatever scrap is lying around. V legs have two sides forming a corner, and that shape has more ability to withstand twisting in relation to the platform framing. Also, since there are two boards joined at a right angle, the leg is strengthened against bowing out of shape. One single 1x4 would be very dangerous in that regard. It is important to glue the two halves of the leg together so that they remain firmly attached to one another.

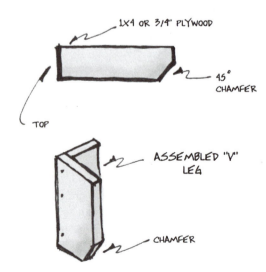

The method of manufacture goes like this:

Determine the length of the leg from the height of the platform less the amount of the thickness of the material covering that platform. If the lid of this platform is $3/4$" ply and the height of the decking overall is 12", then the length of the leg stock will be 11 $1/4$". Put six legs on each 4x8 stock platform. Since each leg has two parts, the total number of pieces required is 12 times the number of platforms involved. If smaller sections of decking are used, figure the number of parts accordingly.

**LEG PLACEMENT
ON A 4X8 PLATFORM**

Cut all of the legs at one time using the radial arm saw and a stop block. It is best to make about 5% extra parts to cover any breakage that may occur during installation. Use the power miter box to put a small bevel, or chamfer, on the outside edges of the leg. This increases the chance that the leg will sit flat on a slightly uneven surface, and besides, it is a very handsome look. It is much easier to do the beveling before the two halves of the leg have been joined.

Connecting the two sides is a simple matter of gluing and then stapling them with a pneumatic gun. Notice that due to the overlap, one of the sides of the completed leg is wider than the other. Sometimes it is helpful to assemble the legs so that half are formatted one way and half the other so that they match on the platform. But structurally, it really doesn't matter.

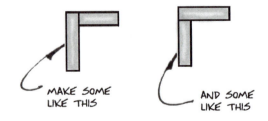

Attach the V legs to the platform from the inside with 1 $5/8$" drywall screws. Put one screw on the skinny side, and two on the wide side. Try not to get too close to the edges or the white pine will split, but the farther apart the fasteners are, the more secure the leg will be. If you are using 3/4" ply for the legs, the danger of splitting is greatly reduced, but the screws are harder to install and may require pilot holes. Using six legs on a 4x8 platform means that there will be no unsupported span of more than 4'- 0". That is compatible with the 2x4 framing and 3/4" plywood top of the platform.

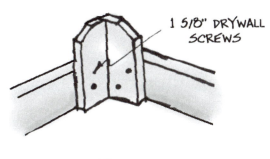

PLYWOOD TOP
UPSIDE DOWN

1 5/8" DRYWALL SCREWS

There is some concern that the screws may not have enough holding power to make a safe connection. It is important to use screws that are long enough, and to make sure that they are tightly installed. There should be no gap of any kind between the leg and the framing. Make sure to use the proper number of legs in your system. Six legs per 4x8 platform is slightly redundant and will provide extra protection. Do not use less. If the plywood top of the platform has been "glued and screwed," it will provide some measure of protection from the leg from pressing upward (or the framing downward) and creating a structural failure. If the load on your platforming is high, you can add a safety feature by gluing bocks on the outside of the leg structure so that the load from the platform frame is transferred to the leg by more than just the screws holding the leg to the frame.

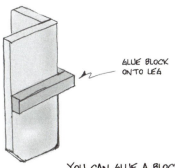

GLUE BLOCK ONTO LEG

YOU CAN GLUE A BLOCK OF WOOD ONTO THE FACE OF THE LEG TO IMPROVE ITS LOAD CARRYING CAPACITY

A far more likely failure would come from lateral stress on the leg. There are ways of managing that problem as well.

As a rule of thumb, you can consider that a platform legged as described needs no lateral support if it is 12" or less in height. The width of the leg is large enough, and the distance of the platform from the floor low enough that the structure has little danger of breaking loose under normal conditions. Only 7 3/4" of each leg is exposed below the bottom of the framing. It is imperative though, that the platforms and legs be properly constructed and assembled. For heights over 12" bracing is required. Sometimes it is enough to simply band the bottom of the legs with a 2" wide strip of 3/4" thick material that will keep the legs from being twisted outward. If the height warrants it, diagonal bracing should be used. Note how the bracing runs in different directions for added strength. You should use similar bracing even when bolted-on 2x4 legs are used. They are prone to failure from the same kinds of lateral forces.

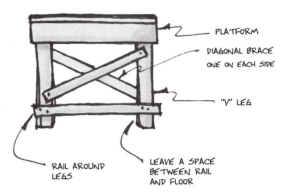

PLATFORM

DIAGONAL BRACE
ONE ON EACH SIDE

"V" LEG

RAIL AROUND LEGS

LEAVE A SPACE BETWEEN RAIL AND FLOOR

Putting individual legs on a large number of platforms can become quite expensive in both labor and materials. There is considerable unnecessary duplication of the upright members and also the added problem of how cumbersome the units can become. It is quite easy for one or more of the decking units to become out of square, especially if they are very tall. The more of them there are, the less likely they will all fit together properly. Individual legs are fine when the decking area is very small and/or low to the stage floor, but larger and taller decks require a different approach.

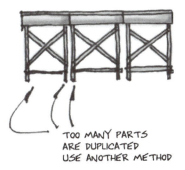

TOO MANY PARTS ARE DUPLICATED USE ANOTHER METHOD

CARRIERS

"Carriers" are so called because they carry the weight of the decking. They are intended to hold several platforms at once, and the effectiveness of this method increases with the number of platforms involved. It does not work particularly well with just one or two. It is best to make the taller carriers as welded steel frames, and there is a discussion of that process in the section on steel frame construction. Here I will concentrate on the wooden type, but the principles of one type carry over to the other.

Carriers are essentially short stud walls, like those in a house but made from different materials. Most of the time 1x4 lumber can be used. Alternatively, $^3/_4$" plywood is a good choice if the carriers are 8 feet or less in length or if for some reason you need the extra support of a wider member. I have used this method many times, and there have been no problems with it. However, using lightweight framing requires stringent quality control to make sure that all of the joints are properly glued. If that is problematic in your particular situation, consider 2x4 construction instead. But it does make for a much more cumbersome product. Adjust the cut list numbers to reflect the thicker material.

The size and shape of the decking area is of great importance in designing the carrier system. For the purposes of this discussion assume that the deck being constructed is twenty feet by twenty-four feet in size, and that it should be 18" tall. Here are two possible ways to get this size using standard 4x8 platforms.

Support the deck so that there is no span greater than 4'-0". You can accomplish this by running the carriers at four-foot centers. If the carriers are made from 1x4 material, then the 3 $^1/_2$" wide lumber is easily wide enough to support the 2x4 framing of two platforms at once. It is crucial that platforms not be left hanging by their casket locks alone and that the platform framing rests firmly on the carrier. In laying out the placement of the carriers it is important to make choices that will make the job of setting up the decking easier. Sections of carrier that are too large or too small will make the job harder to accomplish. Here is one possible solution to the carrier layout problem. Note that all of the units are the same size. That will make it easier to manufacture them.

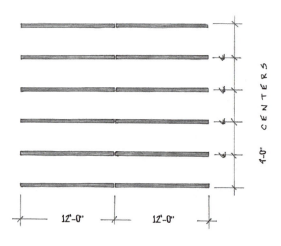

PLAN VIEW OF CARRIER LAYOUT

The next step in developing a plan for this project is to determine the overall height of the carriers. For the V legs, you subtracted only the thickness of the platform covering material, but for this type of support it is necessary to account for the thickness of the entire platform, framing and all, because all of the platform will be resting on the carrier. In this demonstration the thickness of the platform is 4 $^1/_4$". Hence the overall height of the carrier is 13 $^3/_4$". It is now possible to derive a cut list for this project. Notice that there are quite a few pieces involved, but by using interchangeable parts that can be cut out all at once, the time saved is considerable. Remember to rank the cut list from the longest pieces to the shortest because this is the order in which they should be cut. It will be easy to find the material suitable for the short sections after the long ones have been cut.

One really advantageous aspect of using the carrier method is that resting the framing of the platform on the carrier increases the stability of the platform. The load on top of the platform is assumed by the entire structure and the full width of the chord of the framing members rather than just the portion connected by the legging screws.

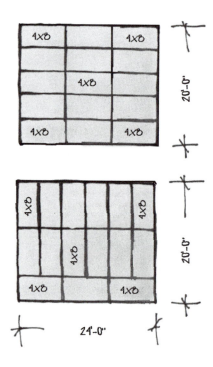

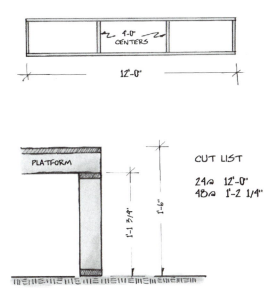

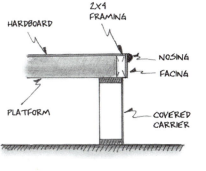

MAKE SURE THAT THE PLATFORM
FRAMING STAYS ON THE CARRIER

The carriers are glued and nailed together in the normal way, but they also need some kind of lateral bracing. Without it, they will tend to rack out of shape into a parallelogram, and the entire deck might fall. The importance of keeping the upright members vertical is paramount. The 1×4 uprights have enough compression strength to hold up a reasonable load, but compression assumes a downward force. If the uprights are allowed to tilt, failure is imminent. You can avoid this by bracing the uprights diagonally.

If the carriers are reasonably short, and the size of the decked area is large, then the carriers may be screwed to the floor and to the undersides of the platform framing. Do the layout by measuring the placement of the decking area, and then setting the carriers on four-foot centers. The carriers on the outside edge should be flush with the edges of the platforms. Make sure that the interior carriers are placed where the platforms join, and that both decks are supported. If the decking is higher and more support is required, use triangular rack braces.

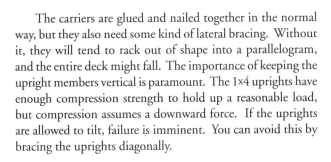

THESE BLOCKS ARE ESSENTIAL

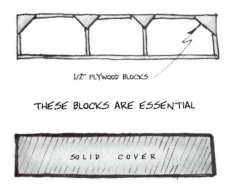

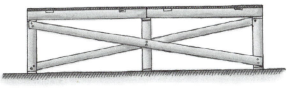

USE TRIANGLE FORMING RACK BRACES
AS REQUIRED

RAKED DECKING

Many productions require a full stage rake. Attempting this type of staging using individually legged platforms can be a complete nightmare. The legs wind up at an angle, and determining the length of each separate leg is a major undertaking. The carrier method is far superior, and once the rake has been built, it can be set up or struck within an hour or two. The carrier units themselves are easy to store for future use. Building a large rake is expensive, so you might well consider designing one that works well for multiple productions.

The rack bracing is applied using 1/2" plywood corner blocks similar to those used to put together standard softcover flats, only thicker. Glue and staple them into place. If your load is very heavy, consider using thicker materials or metal framing. Sometimes it works out well to cover the entire surface of the carrier so that it is really a hardcover flat. This type may be used to form its own facing material, especially if the platform is allowed to hang over a bit.

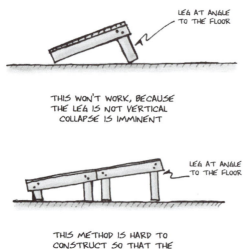

LEG AT ANGLE
TO THE FLOOR

THIS WON'T WORK, BECAUSE
THE LEG IS NOT VERTICAL
COLLAPSE IS IMMINENT

LEG AT ANGLE
TO THE FLOOR

THIS METHOD IS HARD TO
CONSTRUCT SO THAT THE
DECK IS EVEN AND STABLE

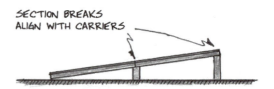

SECTION BREAKS
ALIGN WITH CARRIERS

CARRIERS EVERY 4'-0" ON CENTER

The first step in designing a raked stage decking system is to determine what the angle itself is to be. This angle is not normally expressed in degrees, but rather as an amount of rise over a given amount of run, or as a size that has a certain height in the back. Normally it is determined by the stage designer, however, anything over a few inches per foot is very steep and difficult to walk on without injury. If you are unsure of what is reasonable, lay out a platform at an angle and have the production team in to discuss the matter. If there is a desire to have the rake fade gracefully into the flat stage floor, special sections of decking will required, but standard 4x8 platforms may be used for the balance of the staging.

Once the amount of slant has been determined, a full-scale pattern of a section view of the rake should be marked out on a clean part of the shop floor. Begin by snapping a chalk line on the floor and then inking this mark in with a Sharpie and a long straightedge. Over-marking the line will make sure that it is plainly visible. The chalk mark will tend to become smudged and obscured after a short while. This first line represents the top of the decking. Let us say that the rake is 30" tall in the rear, that the part made from stock 4x8 platforms is approximately 20 feet deep from front to back, and that it is 32 feet wide.

Make a mark on the base line somewhere near the right hand end, and another mark 20 feet to the left. (See Figure 1 on page 207.) Measure down the thickness of a standard platform, 4 1/4", and mark a parallel line. Using a square, connect the two parallel lines with right angle marks on the two ends. The resulting rectangle represents the space that is occupied by the 4x8 platforms. Mark in the divisions between the decks at 4'-0" increments.

The next step is to draw in the line that represents the stage floor. (See figures 2 and 3.) Use a compass to strike an arc that is 30" in radius from the top right-hand corner of the drawing. Snap a line through the bottom left corner of the drawing and the outside edge of the arc.

A seen in Figure 4, use a framing square to extend a right angle between the floor line and the rectangle that represents the platforming. When the carriers are constructed, they will rise straight up from the floor and intersect the bottom of the decking at an angle.

Our staging is twenty-something feet deep and thirty-two feet wide. The "something" measurement will be occupied by the part of the staging that is custom made to blend the rake into the stage floor. The remainder of the decking can be put together out of 4x8 platforms in the following way.

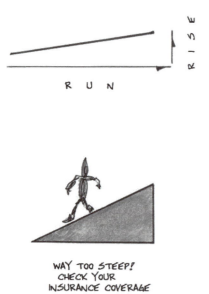

RISE

RUN

RUN

WAY TOO STEEP!
CHECK YOUR
INSURANCE COVERAGE

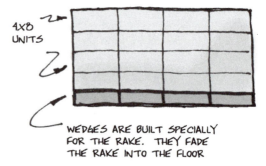

4X8
UNITS

WEDGES ARE BUILT SPECIALLY
FOR THE RAKE. THEY FADE
THE RAKE INTO THE FLOOR

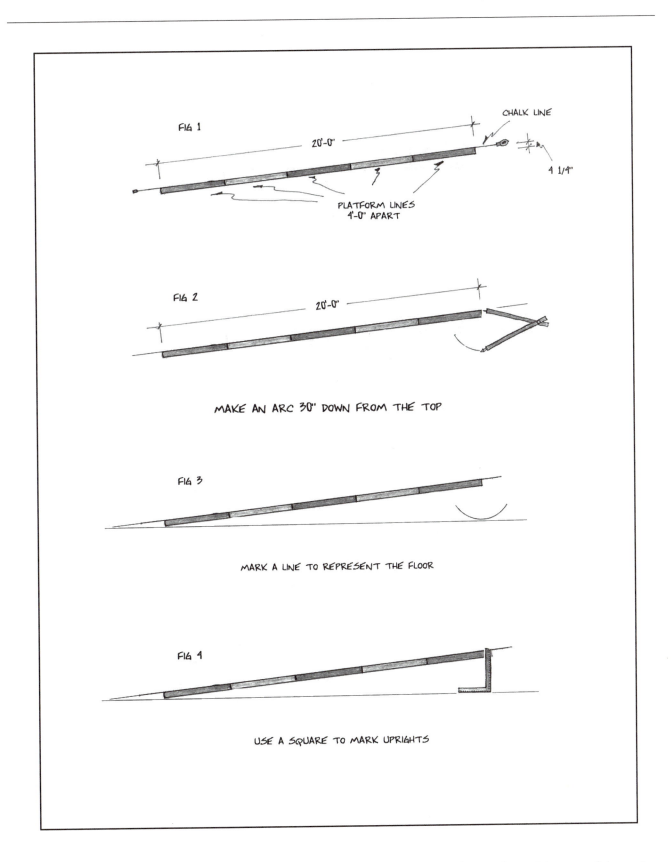

FIG 1

20'-0"

CHALK LINE

4 1/4"

PLATFORM LINES
4'-0" APART

FIG 2

20'-0"

MAKE AN ARC 30' DOWN FROM THE TOP

FIG 3

MARK A LINE TO REPRESENT THE FLOOR

FIG 4

USE A SQUARE TO MARK UPRIGHTS

The platforms are laid out so that the eight-foot direction runs from side to side and so that there will be a joint break every four feet running up- and downstage. You will need a carrier every four feet.

You can now draw in the upright parts of the carriers. Extend a line from the floor line to the bottom of the decking at each break point. Use a square to ensure that this line is at a right angle to the floor line and runs to the centers of the break lines between the platforms. The downstage end of the rake meets the floor and does not need a carrier. On the upstage end, the back of the carrier should be flush with the back of the platform.

If the carriers are to be framed with 3 ¹/₂" wide stock, make a parallel line 1 ³/₄" to either side of the original center line. That will mark the outer edges of the carrier stock. A deck about 30" tall is about as high as the 1x4 can be expected to secure. A large area of decking is actually more stable than a small one. If the area of your actual deck is small, or the load on it is high, use a larger framing member. Remember that the critical factor is keeping the upright members vertical and rigid.

Use a piece of 1x4 stock to transfer the size and angle of the uprights of these carriers. Trim one end so that it is square, and lay that end on the floor so that it is flush with the line marking the top of the bottom plate. This should be ³/₄" up from the baseline representing the stage floor.

Use a straightedge to mark the angle on the top of the upright, transferring this from the line marking the bottom of the top plate. Repeat this procedure for each size of upright. The resulting pieces will become the patterns used to create all of the upright members.

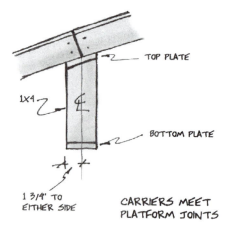

CARRIERS MEET PLATFORM JOINTS

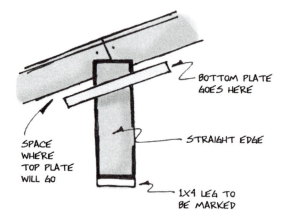

Draw a ³/₄" thick line on the top and bottom of each carrier shape. These lines represent the top and bottom plate of each carrier. Draw a ³/₄" mark to the bottom of the line that represents the top of the special downstage platform, the one that must be specially built at an angle. Draw another line ³/₄" from the downstage edge of the row of stock platforms, the ones that have a corner touching the stage floor. These lines will be used in the marking of parts to make the wedge-shaped platforms.

Use the same technique to transfer the size and shape of the ribs used in building the downstage wedges. It is a good practice to lay the pattern pieces back down on your drawing after they have been cut out. This will give you a chance to double-check your work.

FIG 5

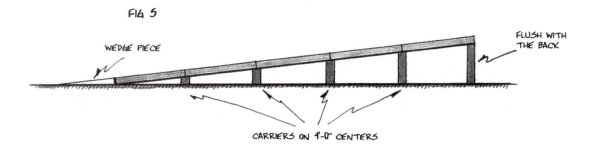

COMPLETED LAYOUT

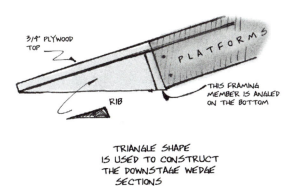

TRIANGLE SHAPE
IS USED TO CONSTRUCT
THE DOWNSTAGE WEDGE
SECTIONS

The top and bottom plates of the carriers and the back edge of the wedge platforms are left to describe. The bottom plate on each carrier is merely standard 1x4, but the top plate must be bevel cut to fit the tops of the uprights. The angle for ripping will be the same angle as the top of the upright pattern, and you can use one of these pieces to set the angle of the table saw. The width of the finished angle-cut plate can be measured off of the full-scale pattern.

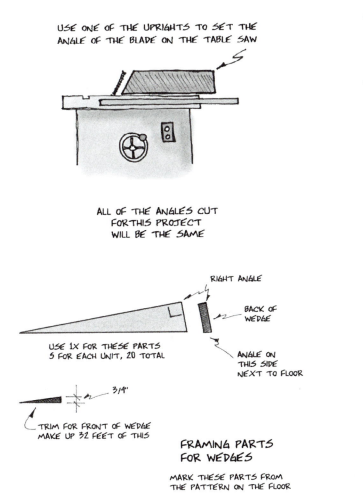

USE ONE OF THE UPRIGHTS TO SET THE
ANGLE OF THE BLADE ON THE TABLE SAW

ALL OF THE ANGLES CUT
FOR THIS PROJECT
WILL BE THE SAME

RIGHT ANGLE

BACK OF
WEDGE

ANGLE ON
THIS SIDE
NEXT TO FLOOR

USE 1X FOR THESE PARTS
5 FOR EACH UNIT, 20 TOTAL

3/4"

TRIM FOR FRONT OF WEDGE
MAKE UP 32 FEET OF THIS

FRAMING PARTS
FOR WEDGES

MARK THESE PARTS FROM
THE PATTERN ON THE FLOOR

The specifications of the back framing member of the wedge platforms can be determined in the same way. Because they rest squarely on the floor at all points, it is fine to frame these platforms entirely of 3/4" stock. That will easily carry the load.

Before a cut list can be compiled, you must use the width of the rake to determine how many of each kind of carrier will be needed. This influences how many copies of each piece to make. Since this rake is 32'- 0" wide, it will be possible to span the distance with two carriers that are 16 feet long. You will recall that 16 feet is the longest commonly found length for dimension lumber.

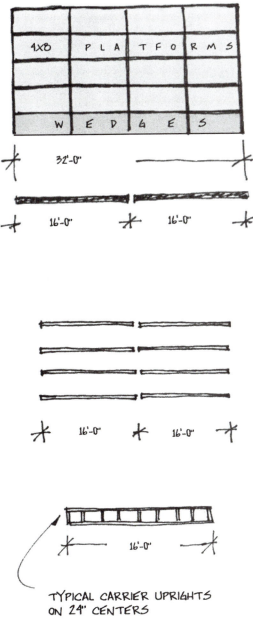

TYPICAL CARRIER UPRIGHTS
ON 24" CENTERS

Finally, you arrive at the cut list of the carrier parts. The uprights are described by the patterns made from the drawing. They are spaced at 2'- 0" intervals. The top and bottom plates are also listed.

CUT 18 OF EACH TYPE FROM THE PATTERN YOU MADE

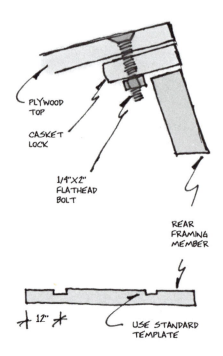

PLYWOOD TOP

CASKET LOCK

1/4"X2" FLATHEAD BOLT

REAR FRAMING MEMBER

12"

USE STANDARD TEMPLATE

The wedge platform parts are also placed on 2'- 0" centers, so you will need five of them for each eight-foot-long platform. It is easiest to make the tops of these ramps blunt on the downstage end. The sharp angle is very hard to cut and has a tendency to break off unexpectedly. If a smooth transition is required, a triangle-shaped piece can be made separately and tacked to the floor after the rake is in place. This small piece is much easier to cut and can be made from solid hardwood for durability. The upstage framing member can be computed by using the angle and size of the wedge shape.

There is not a good way of connecting the wedges to the 4x8s without using coffin locks, unless they can be held in place by sheets of sound-deadening material, and that would greatly lessen the structural integrity. The corner where the locks are installed is square, and the wedge is 8'- 0" long so the process is much the same as for a standard platform. The only change involves the method of fastening the coffin locks to the platforms. The one-by framing is too narrow for the screws to get a bite, so use $1/4$" flathead bolts instead.

When the ramp is set up, begin by placing the wedge pieces in their proper location on the stage floor. Measure 4'- 0" up from the upstage side of the wedges. This will be the center of the lowest set of carriers. In reality, the actual distance is a fraction of an inch smaller, because the 4'- 0" dimension is the top of the rake rather than the line along the floor. Most of the time the difference is negligible. If the rake is really huge or really steep, it might be best to measure the true amount from your full-scale pattern. Screw the carriers into position using $1\,5/8$" drywall screws. The center of the next set of carriers will be 4'- 0" upstage of the first. It is important to remember that the measurement is to the center of the carrier. So you really need to mark $1\,3/4$" to either side of the center, or just put the tape down and move the carrier itself around until it fits.

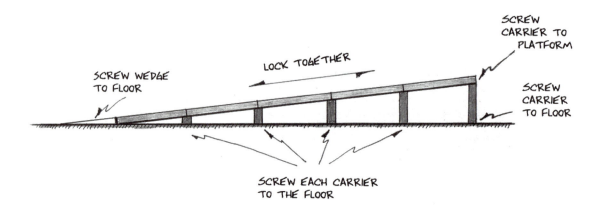

SCREW WEDGE TO FLOOR

LOCK TOGETHER

SCREW CARRIER TO PLATFORM

SCREW CARRIER TO FLOOR

SCREW EACH CARRIER TO THE FLOOR

After the first carrier is in place, it is possible to measure from downstage edge to downstage edge, as this will in effect be the same as measuring from center to center. Keep measuring from the downstage carrier in four-foot multiples rather than moving the tape each time, because this will reduce error. The last carrier will need to be 4'- 0" from center to back to keep it from sticking out upstage. Screw through the bottom plate into the floor and through the top plate of the carrier into the platform framing. Consider the effect of firmly securing the front edge of the rake to the stage floor with screws. This will create a very large diagonal brace where the platforms become one side of the triangle, the floor another, and the carriers the third leg. This makes a very strong structure. You can see the importance of being able to make a secure connection between:

1) the floor and the deck
2) the sections of the deck itself
   (the individual platforms)
3) the carriers and the decking
4) the carriers and the stage floor

If you cannot make all these structural connections, this system will not be safe. If you are concerned about a high lateral load or just an excessive live load, use larger framing members and/or extra diagonal bracing. Again, a very large rake is more stable than a small one. The example shown is of a medium-size rake.

SOUND DEADENING

Hard shoes pounding against the $3/4$" plywood top of a platform can make a most distracting noise. The clomping and thudding of feet in a blackout remove much of the magic of the moment. The easiest way to deaden this type of unwanted sound is to carpet the platforming. Unfortunately, the carpet approach is not always feasible due to design factors. Here is a method of deadening sound with insulation and hardboard that works quite well and has the added bonus of also improving the appearance of the deck.

Use one of several different types of thin insulating material. You can use Homosote, or there are other products that work just as well, such as extruded foam insulation with a foil cover. The loosely compacted material is intended to insulate a house from cold, but it will insulate sound vibrations just as well. Foam insulation is a bit less likely to fall apart, and it is not as flammable or possibly toxic as the asphalt impregnated type of homosote. The material chosen should be relatively thin (about $1/2$"), and should come in 4x8 sheets. It is crucial that all of the sound-deadening substrate be the same thickness. This method is at its best on large areas, and it can become problematic on small sections of oddly shaped decking.

Refer to the sketch of a decking layout comprised of stock, 4x8 platforms. The deck measures 20'- 0" x 20'- 0". The most straightforward method of joining the decks together is shown. The second layout describes a way of putting down the insulation so that the joining cracks of the insulation do not fall in line with the joints of the 4x8 platforms. This will prevent the "telegraphing" of uneven joints upward toward the finished surface.

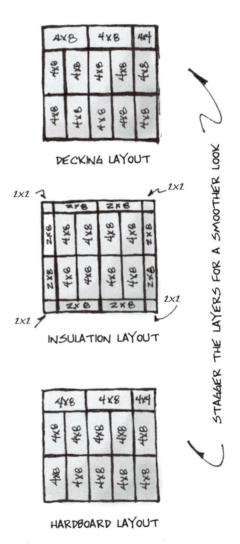

DECKING LAYOUT

INSULATION LAYOUT

STAGGER THE LAYERS FOR A SMOOTHER LOOK

HARDBOARD LAYOUT

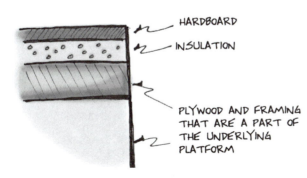

HARDBOARD

INSULATION

PLYWOOD AND FRAMING THAT ARE A PART OF THE UNDERLYING PLATFORM

The final step in the process is to lay down sheets of $1/4$" hardboard to use as a paintable surface. The finished product will appear much flatter and more solid than just using the tops of the platforms themselves. The foam itself is too flimsy to be the top layer. You can use a layer of just hardboard with no foam at all, but of course that provides only minimal insulating results, although it does greatly improve the physical appearance of the deck.

It is not necessary to attach the insulating material to the platforms. It will lie there just fine on its own, and in the end will be securely bound by the hardboard. Anything over a $1/2$" thickness of insulation is troublesome to manipulate when putting down the deck. It is important to use a material that will hold together well if you intend to reuse the panels consistently. You can see from the diagram that there are some stock parts that are required. Other than 4x8 sheets, it is helpful to keep pieces which are 2x8, 2x6, and 2x2. These sizes can be used to cover a deck made from 4x8, 2x8, and 4x4 platforms. If the deck you are building has odd angles and shapes, it will be necessary to cut some pieces to fit. There can be cracks of $1/2$" or so between the sheets of insulation with the finished product suffering no ill effects.

Tempered hardboard that is $1/4$" thick makes the best cover. It is possible to use the untempered board, but it will not last as long, and it will tend to curl up in spots. Some hardboard has two good sides and if you choose it, the reusable surface is doubled. Of course that type is more expensive. The hardboard is installed with the same orientation as the original platforms. It is not necessary that you follow the exact same plan, but that is often the most expedient thing to do.

Make small countersink holes in the surface of the hardboard about every foot around the outside perimeter of the sheet. Use 1 $1/4$" drywall screws to fasten the hardboard to the deck. It is not generally necessary to put any screws in the centers of the sheets.

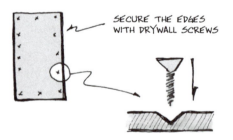

SECURE THE EDGES WITH DRYWALL SCREWS

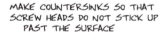

MAKE COUNTERSINKS SO THAT SCREW HEADS DO NOT STICK UP PAST THE SURFACE

The hardboard can be painted either before or after it is put in place. Painting beforehand can improve the logistics of the load in. The sheets can be laid out in advance and painted before load in occurs. Standing around waiting for the floor to dry can be problematic during tech week. The timing can be tailored to fit your production schedule.

STRESSED-SKIN PLATFORMS

There are times a special type of platform is required for which the standard construction methods are simply inappropriate. Sometimes a platform must cover an unusually large span, and/or must have a clean and streamlined appearance. There are special problems when the bottom of the platform will be seen. Stressed-skin platforms have both a top and a bottom cover, so the bottom looks just as good as the top. The way they are constructed makes them much more rigid, and more supportive than the traditional platforming method, even though they may be thinner than a platform made with 2x4s.

FRAMING

$1/2$" PLY

$1/4$" PLY

STRESS SKIN PLATFORMS HAVE A PLYWOOD COVER ON BOTH THE TOP AND BOTTOM

The secret to stressed-skin manufacture lies in the way the bottom cover or "skin" keeps the platform from bending. These platforms have exceptional tensile strength. In order for any framing member to bend, two things must occur. The top of the member must compress, and the bottom must stretch. Bending of this sort will eventually cause the lumber to break when the force applied is enough to stretch the material so far that the fibers that hold it together are ripped apart.

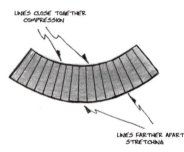

LINES CLOSE TOGETHER COMPRESSION

LINES FARTHER APART STRETCHING

THIS DRAWING MIMICS THE EFFECTS OF BENDING. NOTICE HOW THE LINES ON THE CURVE ARE FARTHER APART ON THE BOTTOM AND CLOSER TOGETHER ON THE TOP. THE BOTTOM STRETCHES, WHILE THE TOP COMPRESSES.

The bottom skin in a stressed-skin platform prevents the bottom of the structure from stretching because it spreads the stress of the load over the entire platform rather than letting it concentrate on one framing member. All of the materials used in a stressed-skin structure are intended to work in concert, and they must be securely joined together, or the structure will fail. All of the joints in a wooden platform must be properly glued together in order for the system to work. This concept cannot be over-emphasized.

You can build this type of platform using $1/2$" plywood for the tops and $1/4$" ply for the bottoms. Make sure to use a good grade of plywood that is very strong, lightweight, and has a paintable surface. It is possible to use $1/2$" ply rather than the normal $3/4$" for the top surface because the framing members of the platform are much closer together and will reduce the amount of flex created by footfalls. If the load you must support is excessive, then increase the thickness of the top deck, and/or the thickness of the framing. In general, it is a good policy to keep the weight of this type of platform down. Stress skin platforms tend to be rather large, and any reduction in weight is greatly appreciated by the stagehands. This type of decking is not intended to be covered with the sound-deadening materials described previously.

After the framing has been glued and nailed together, the top of the platform may be attached. The plywood should be used to square up the framing in the usual way, by starting at one corner and working the two adjacent sides. The framing used in this platform will be prone to bowing, but because it is more limber, it will be easier to work into place than framing on a 2x4 deck. Be sure to use sufficient yellow aliphatic resin glue to ensure that the plywood is completely adhered to all of the lumber framing over the entire surface of the one-by. It is very important to glue every inch of every joint on a stressed-skin platform. If there is a problem keeping the internal framing in place during this process, cut a number of spacers to keep the framing from wandering. Staple the top plywood to all of the framing, not just the perimeter, so that it will be held together firmly while the glue sets up. A pneumatic gun really makes this job easier.

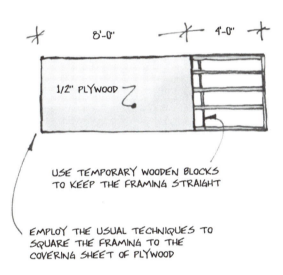

USE TEMPORARY WOODEN BLOCKS TO KEEP THE FRAMING STRAIGHT

EMPLOY THE USUAL TECHNIQUES TO SQUARE THE FRAMING TO THE COVERING SHEET OF PLYWOOD

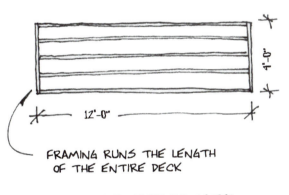

FRAMING RUNS THE LENGTH OF THE ENTIRE DECK

WIDTH OF THE FRAMING MEMBER DEPENDS ON THE LENGTH OF THE SPAN, WEIGHT, AND TYPE OF LOAD.

Use $3/4$" thick dimension lumber for the framing of stressed-skin platforms. Care should be taken to avoid knots that seriously impair the structural integrity of the lumber, but a few small, hard knots are unlikely to create any problems. Framing members should be designed to run across the open span, even if this is the entire length of the platform. Space the members at no more than 12" apart, on center. This will provide sufficient support for the $1/2$" plywood top.

If the size of the top requires more than one sheet of plywood, the two adjoining sheets should be scabbed together securely. This is very important, and the structure will fail if it is not done properly. Glue and nail a 4" wide slat of $1/2$" plywood to the underside of one of the plywood sheets, half on and half off. The protruding half will be used to connect the second sheet. Do not cut notches in the framing to let in the connecting slat, but rather use several small pieces. Notches may well remove too much of the white pine framing for it to support properly in the weakened condition. Do extend the connecting slat so that it covers as much space as possible between framing members. Again, it is very important that all wooden surfaces that touch each other have a proper glue bond. Nails alone will not hold.

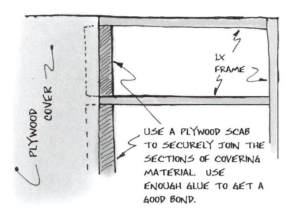

USE A PLYWOOD SCAB TO SECURELY JOIN THE SECTIONS OF COVERING MATERIAL. USE ENOUGH GLUE TO GET A GOOD BOND.

After the glue has cured overnight, use a flush trim router to clean up the edges. Stressed-skin platforms must use some kind of carrier-type structure to elevate them, because there is no place to attach any sort of individual leg. If steel frame legging is used, the decking can usually be held in place by virtue of its own weight when blocks are attached to the underside of the platform to keep it from sliding. You can also use hinges or other angular fasteners.

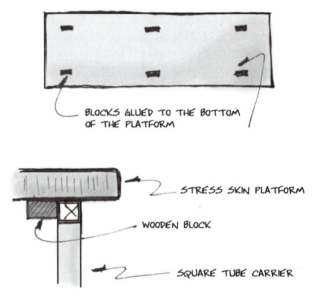

BLOCKS GLUED TO THE BOTTOM OF THE PLATFORM

STRESS SKIN PLATFORM

WOODEN BLOCK

SQUARE TUBE CARRIER

After you have let the glue set up a bit, turn the platform upside down so that the framing is visible. This is a good time to work on sound deadening the interior, if that is necessary. Insulating the platform is not a very fun job. Unfortunately, stress skin platforms often sound like a drum unless they receive some help. The least expensive method is to use fiberglass roll insulation. It is cut and inserted into the "bays" just like in the walls of a house. Unfortunately, each piece will need to be cut laterally, because the bays are not the normal 14 $1/2$" found in the studwalls of a house. Faced insulation will cut down on the fiberglass wool that gets onto the tops of the framing. Care must be taken that insulation on the framing is not allowed to interfere with the glue joint on the bottom skin. You can use foam insulation instead. It is easier to work with but is more expensive.

The $1/4$" bottom ply should be attached in the same manner as the top was, including the use of the connecting scabs. Make sure that the plywood joint on the bottom falls in a different place than the top did.

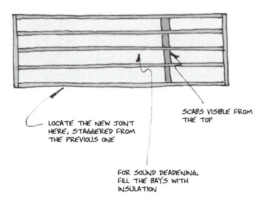

LOCATE THE NEW JOINT HERE, STAGGERED FROM THE PREVIOUS ONE

SCABS VISIBLE FROM THE TOP

FOR SOUND DEADENING, FILL THE BAYS WITH INSULATION

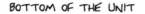

BOTTOM OF THE UNIT

CHAPTER 15

METAL FRAME
CONSTRUCTION

In recent years metal framing has become increasingly popular as a medium for scenic construction. The use of welded steel or aluminum tubing allows scenery to be constructed from material that is smaller in cross section, more securely joined, and in some cases lighter than traditional wood framing. This method has the added advantage of being very quick to assemble using easily constructed jigs. Furthermore, there is actually more salvageable material left from steel framing than from the wooden type. There are some quite large scenic units for which metal framing is the only logical alternative.

MATERIALS

So far, the phrase "metal framing" has been meant to include either aluminum or steel. There are advantages and disadvantages to either product. Aluminum is much lighter than the steel, but steel is considerably stronger than aluminum. Welded steel square tube is about one-fifth the price of its extruded aluminum counterpart. Aluminum is more difficult to weld than steel is, and requires special techniques.

Square tube gets its name from the shape of the cross section, which is, of course, square. It is quite often the most useful shape, although tubing is also manufactured in round or rectangular cross sections. Steel tube is bent from bars of flat stock, and one side has a seam where the edges of the bar have been welded together. This seam generally appears as a slightly darker, sometimes bluish stripe. Aluminum is extruded through a die in order to get whatever particular shape is required. Cutting and grinding steel framing requires the use of special metalworking equipment, whereas the much softer aluminum can usually be cut and shaped with ordinary woodworking tools. Welding aluminum requires a TIG or MIG welder, whereas steel may be worked with an ordinary arc welder, or even oxyacetylene.

This chapter is written with steel tubing in mind because it is much less expensive, but there is not that much difference in the types of structures you can build with one or the other. There are certain health risks associated with inhaling the dust produced while working with aluminum that are not so much of a concern with steel.

Building the structural parts of a set from steel square tube can be less expensive than using wooden parts. The difference in price is due to the way steel joints are welded together. The resulting connections are much stronger than any kind of wooden joinery, and you can easily make angular shapes that are much more difficult with wooden scenery. Less bracing is required, so fewer running feet of material are required for steel structures than for traditional wooden methods.

Steel tubing is available in many sizes and cross sections. A reasonably well stocked supplier should have square tube in a variety of sizes from half-inch to four-inch. Rectangular tubing is available in sizes like 1x2 inches, 1x3 inches, $1^1/_2 \times 3$ inches, and so forth. Some shapes/sizes can be special ordered. The wall thickness of the tubing is described with a gauge system. The smaller the gauge number, the thicker the tubing wall. As in the case of wire gauges, this is the exact opposite of what would seem logical. As a point of reference, 10ga tubing is approximately $^1/_8$" thick, while 16ga tubing is about $^1/_{16}$" thick. (16ga, $^1/_{16}$" is easy to remember.) From a structural standpoint, it is the outside dimension of the tubing has the most impact on the rigidity of something you make from it. For lightweight structures it is generally best to use the thinnest wall available. 20-gauge tubing is an excellent lightweight material, but it can be some-

what difficult to find because it is not very popular for general construction. The 16-gauge is much more common. Unless you are building something that must withstand extreme forces (perhaps you should consult a professional engineer), it is best to steer clear of really thick tubing like 10ga. It is just too heavy for most theatrical use. You can spot thick wall tubing by looking at the corners. Thicker wall tubing has rounder corners. This makes sense when you think about how square tubing is made by bending a flat piece of steel into a square shape and welding the sides together. It is sometimes important to be able to spot the welded side of the tubing because the steel on that side is often harder than the steel on the other three sides.

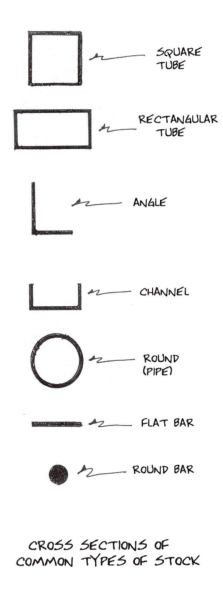

CROSS SECTIONS OF
COMMON TYPES OF STOCK

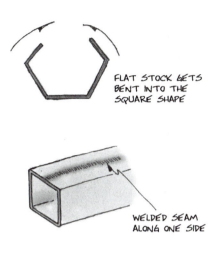

FLAT STOCK GETS BENT INTO THE SQUARE SHAPE

WELDED SEAM ALONG ONE SIDE

WELDING EQUIPMENT

There are two very common types of welders used to join steel. One is the generic arc welder and the other is the Metal Inert Gas type, which is abbreviated as MIG. A MIG welder is by far the easiest kind of welder to use for welding steel and is far and away the most popular. A MIG welder is somewhat more expensive to purchase than a standard arc welder because its mechanism is much more complicated.

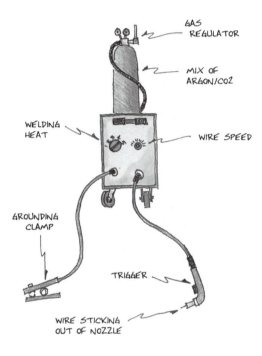

GAS REGULATOR

MIX OF ARGON/CO2

WELDING HEAT

WIRE SPEED

GROUNDING CLAMP

TRIGGER

WIRE STICKING OUT OF NOZZLE

BASIC PARTS OF A MIG WELDER

Most square tubing comes in 24-foot lengths, which is an excellent thing if you need long pieces. It is not so good when looking for a place to store the material. Many construction projects are centered around 8- or 12-foot lengths, so the 24 foot size is even more appealing in that regard, since those numbers divide into 24 evenly. Some smaller size tubing comes in 20-foot lengths, while black steel pipe is a standard 21-foot size. Black steel pipe can be found at plumbing supply houses. It is very heavy in relation to square tube, and the round shape is problematic when cutting and fitting parts together. It is common to find 1 1/2" black steel pipe used for battens in stage rigging. Pipe sizes refer to the inside diameter, while tubing sizes describe the outer dimension. Pipes are really meant to hold water on the inside, while square tube is not.

The 1 1/2" size square tube is very popular for several reasons. First of all, 1 1/2" is the same thickness as any wooden two-by. It is also the same thickness as two pieces of one-by stacked on top of one another. It is often handy to work with materials that are the same thickness, because the parts line up better. Second, it is difficult to obtain thinner gauges in larger tubing that is really intended for heavy construction purposes, and in theatre we are always concerned about the weight of portable scenery. Last of all, and perhaps the most important, the cross-section of 1 1/2" square tube is large enough to have a fair amount of rigidity all on its own, without being doubled, or made into a truss. Some small units are better constructed from 1" or even 3/4" stock when that rigidity is not required. *Structural Design for the Stage*, by Holden and Sammler, is an excellent resource for anyone interested in studying the structural properties of specific materials.

An arc welder is essentially a very large rectifier unit that changes AC power into DC power. Two long cables are attached to the output of the machine. The ground has a clamp on the end that gets connected to the steel you are welding. The other cable has a smaller clamp to hold an electrode, which is a replaceable wire stick coated with flux. The flux is a catalyst that aids in the welding process. When the electrode is brought into close contact with the steel, a circuit is completed between the positive output of the welder, the electrode, the steel being welded, the ground clamp, and the negative terminal of the welder. Since the electrode is only tangentially in contact with the steel, the electricity must jump across that small gap in order to complete the circuit. When that happens a small spark or "arc" is created. The arc is very hot and melts the steel. The electrode gets hot and the tip of it melts as well. Molten steel from the electrode mixes with the molten steel on the edges of the joint being welded. Three pieces of steel are being melted and joined, the two pieces being connected, and the electrode from the welder itself. When the molten steel cools and hardens, all three should be joined at the molecular level, so that theoretically they are all one homogenous piece. (In reality, the heating and cooling make a slight difference in the composition of the welded area.)

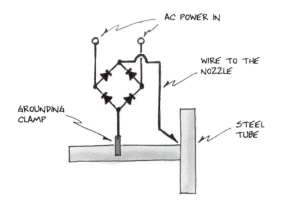

VERY BASIC SCHEMATIC
OF A MIG OR ARC WELDER

CIRCUIT MUST BE COMPLETE FOR WELDER TO WORK

There are several fairly problematic consequences of arc welding. Of course the light produced is extremely bright and will cause serious injury to your eyes if you look at it from a close distance. (The distance from the arc while you are welding is very small.) Special equipment must be worn to protect your eyes while welding, and the glass is so dark that you cannot see anything through the glass when it is in place. The electrode will complete the circuit the instant it is in close proximity to the steel. So it is difficult to coordinate your movements to get the electrode in position, get the helmet in place, and then strike the arc.

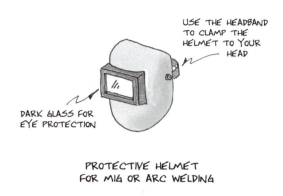

PROTECTIVE HELMET
FOR MIG OR ARC WELDING

The electrode is consumed by the welding process and must be frequently changed. The flux, the very hot steel, and oxygen from the air combine to form slag on the surface of the steel while you are welding. The slag is messy and can get in the way of welding.

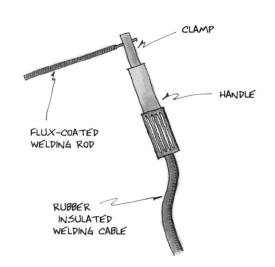

The MIG welder addresses some of the difficulties of using an arc welder. The MIG welder also uses a large rectifier to change AC power into DC power. It also has two cables that carry electric current and complete a circuit. One of them has a grounding clamp, but the other has a nozzle in place of the electrode. The nozzle emits an inert gas that surrounds the joint while welding is taking place. The inert gas, most often an argon/CO_2 mix, protects the molten steel from oxygen in the air, and as a result no slag is formed on the weld.

A MIG welder is sometimes called a "wire welder" because it uses a spool of wire in place of the electrode that is found on a standard arc welder. The wire is fed through the nozzle from a spool that contains enough of the wire to last for a very long time in even a very busy shop, so it does not need changing very often. The arc on a MIG welder is not struck until you pull a trigger on the nozzle. This makes coordinating the welding process much easier to do. You can rest the wire in the nozzle on the joint to be welded, cover your eyes with the hood, and then pull the trigger to start the welding process.

SPOOL OF WIRE IN A MIG WELDER

Remember that welding requires you to melt both of the parts forming the joint, and to allow the resulting metals to flow together so that they become indistinguishable from one another. A good weld should have a "puddled" appearance. You should be able to see that both parts melted and that the resulting joint line shows evidence of it. If the weld looks like many globs of steel stuck on the surface, the metal did not really flow together. There has been no penetration of the heat.

NOTE THE EVEN PUDDLING ALONG
THE LENGTH OF THE WELD

LOTS OF BLOBS AND SKIPS

If the metal you are welding is really thick, it may be necessary to prepare the joint by grinding so that the heat from the arc can melt the steel all the way through its thickness. If you are welding 16ga tubing, that will not be necessary because the wall is so thin.

Make the weld by slowly moving the electrode or wire back and forth across the joint line. Make sure that heat from the arc is applied to both surfaces. If you move too quickly, there will not be enough heat to properly melt the two parts. If you move too slowly, there will be too much heat and the steel will completely melt and drop out, creating a hole. Some people describe the movement across the joint as a zigzag pattern, and others as making small circles with the nozzle. On a MIG welder, pulling the nozzle back from the joint will reduce the amount of heat present at the

weld. Moving closer will make the weld hotter. If you pull back too far, the gas will not be able to completely encase the welding area, and also the wire may melt before it gets close enough to the steel to complete the circuit. This can cause a popping sound while you are welding. It will also happen if the wire speed is too high, and the wire is intermittently forced against the steel in a way that causes the spark to stop for an instant. Different diameters of wire are available, and of course the heavier gauges are meant for thicker welds. 035 is a good size for 16ga tubing.

There are two variable settings on a MIG welder that can be used to get a good flow to the metal. One has numbers like 1 through 5 and is used to adjust the current flow. The more power used, the more heat will be concentrated on the weld. Use a higher setting for thick materials and a lower setting for thin materials. The other variable is the speed of the wire coming out of the nozzle. Generally, the wire speed should be higher if you are welding at a high temperature, but this is somewhat variable, so you will need to experiment to discover the best setting. You can also adjust the gas flow, but it is generally not necessary to change that once the welder has been set up originally.

It is not really the aim of this chapter to teach you to be an expert at using either an arc or MIG welder. It takes more time than that, and you need to have personal instruction. The few preceding paragraphs were meant as an overview of the process. The rest of this chapter is concerned with how to prepare, cut, and assemble parts for welded steel scenery. That is actually the most difficult and time consuming part of the job.

Welding can be very dangerous if safety rules are not followed, so study the craft carefully before you begin. This book describes some special methods developed over the years to enhance accuracy and speed up production. The processes are intended for a shop with a MIG welder, which can be purchased for around $2,500. It is an excellent investment for a shop. Some people describe a MIG welding set-up as "the hot glue gun of metalworking" because of how easy it is to use. If you have experience in other forms of welding, it should be possible for you to do fairly good work with only a few minutes practice.

Looking at the light produced by any type of welding without protection will cause extensive retina damage, especially if you are very close at hand, i.e., when you are the person welding. The welds are very hot, and you will receive a severe burn if you touch the steel shortly after welding it. You can get a nasty sunburn on exposed skin if you weld for a long period. Use all protective gear that is required for your particular equipment. This includes at the very least: safety glasses, a hood, special gloves, and screens to mask other workers from your welding. Be sure to read, understand, and follow all of the safety instructions that come with your welder.

CUTTING AND FITTING THE PARTS

The most difficult part of metal construction is the cutting of the pieces and "jigging" them together so that they will stay put while you are welding them. After the parts are joined, grinding the welds flat can be another lengthy chore. Of course, any cut job necessitates the development of a cut list. Here is an example of a cut list for a simple project:

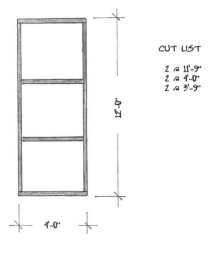

CUT LIST

2 @ 11'-9"
2 @ 4'-0"
2 @ 3'-9"

MAKE FROM 1 1/2"
STEEL SQUARE TUBE

The process of making a cut list for this welding project is exactly the same as the process of making a cut list for a flat, or a step unit, or a platform. Overall dimensions are given on the drawing, and it is your task to determine which framing members overlap the other members. This drawing indicates that the top and bottom rails overlap the upright members in the same way they would on a hardcover flat. The directions say to construct the unit from 1 $1/2$" 16ga square tube. Consequently, the length of the upright stiles will be 3 inches shorter than the overall dimension, while the rails run the full length of the stated size.

Now that you have a cut list, you must cut the steel. Aluminum can be cut with woodworking equipment, but steel requires special techniques.

The most practical tool for cutting small sections of steel is a chop saw, sometimes known as a cut-off saw. This is really sort of a misnomer, as a chop saw is really a type of grinder and not a saw at all. Rather than using the teeth of a blade to cut, this tool grinds the metal away with an abrasive blade. The blades must be changed frequently, as the abrasive material is also worn away during the cutting process. Small chop saws are relatively inexpensive, around $300, and are a very expedient and forgiving way to cut steel. They function in much the same way as a power miter box, with a

hinge in the back that lets the user press the grinding blade down onto the work. This allows gravity to work for you when cutting. There should be a metal plate or fence on the table of the saw that allows the user to cut angles. This is done by loosening a pair of machine screws and rotating the plate to the desired angle. There are marks on the plate to indicate angles, but they are often not very accurate. Perhaps the manufacturer of your particular chop saw will have improved on the design, but if not, you might try using a speed square to set the saw to either 90 or 45 degrees. For other angles, use the power miter box to cut a three or four inch wide board to the desired angle, and then use this pattern to set the angle on the chop saw. Hold the length of the board against the fence, and then lower the blade. Adjust the fence so that the angle of the pattern board matches the blade, and tighten the fence into place.

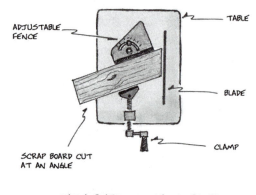

ADJUSTABLE FENCE

TABLE

BLADE

SCRAP BOARD CUT AT AN ANGLE

CLAMP

CUT A BOARD ON THE MITER SAW
AND USE IT TO SET THE ANGLE

The saw should have a clamp of some sort in the front so that the steel can be securely held in the saw while cutting. A chop saw sprays out a shower of sparks while it cuts the steel, and you should take care to protect yourself and others. Be sure to follow all the safety rules listed on the tool. Be especially mindful of the fire danger from this tool. If you've never used a chop saw, you will most likely be surprised by the abundance of sparks that the tool will create. These sparks can get into sawdust and smolder for a very long time before a fire is noticed.

THE CHOP SAW MAKES

LOTS O' SPARKS

If you have the room, and will be cutting a lot of steel, it might be worth your while to set up a radial-arm-saw-type bench for your chop saw. If no wall space is available, you can work on a nonflammable concrete floor instead. Make up a number of wooden blocks that are the same height as the top of the saw table from the floor. They can be used to hold the tubing up off the floor and level with the saw. This creates a flexible method of supporting the tubing while cutting, because you can move the blocks around as required.

Each piece must be marked and cut in turn, in much the same manner as working on a radial arm saw. Don't try to rush the cut; let the chop saw work at its own pace. The speed used to cut any material is called the "feed rate." If the motor on the chop saw, or any other cutting equipment, begins to slow down and bind excessively, you are moving too fast. It is also possible to move too slowly, causing the work to heat up unnecessarily from excess friction.

Usually it is best to mark the piece to the right as the keeper, and then draw a new section to be cut through the saw. (Sorry to all you left-handed folks, but that's the way the saws are made!) It is easier to slide the pieces over the blocks if you rotate the tube so that only one corner is facing down while you are moving it. This way there is less friction and the steel will slide easily over the blocks rather than knocking them out of position.

After the steel is cut you will need to dress the ends a bit to remove burrs left by the chop saw. It is pretty easy to do this with a few strokes of a large, rough file. A grinder can also be used, and it is really a matter of personal preference. Some of the pieces will have an open end exposed in the finished product, and may need to have the interior burr removed as well. A file will fit inside easily. It is not necessary to spend a great deal of time in treating the ends of pieces that will be welded together. However, it is sometime difficult to jig up the parts if there is a large burr on the end of the tubing. If the defect is small it will most likely melt away during the welding process. Most burrs on the inside will not show.

Steel tubing is often coated with a layer of oil. The steel mill does this to keep the product from rusting while it is at the supplier. It is generally a nasty, grimy sort of oil and for years I have suspected that it is one way of recycling used motor oil.

THINGS ARE EASIER TO SLIDE
WHEN ON A CORNER

Sometimes there's a little, and sometimes there's a lot. It is best to take care of the oil problem shortly after the stock arrives by wiping it down with a spray cleaner like 409 or Simple Green and paper towels. It's a dirty job, but someone has to do it. It is important to get at least the major portion of the oil off the tubing, so that it is not there when you are welding. It seems problematic that the suspect oil will otherwise be vaporized into an inhalable gas by the welding process. Besides, it is very messy.

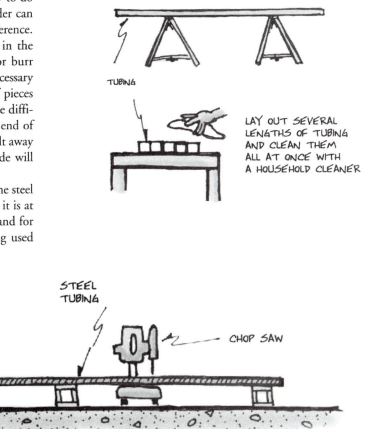

LAY OUT SEVERAL LENGTHS OF TUBING AND CLEAN THEM ALL AT ONCE WITH A HOUSEHOLD CLEANER

ASSEMBLY

After the square tube has been cleaned, cut, and filed, it is time to join it together with the welder. If the frames are very large, you can tape out a sizable right-angle pattern on the concrete floor of the shop, and use it in much the same way as a template table is used to square up flats. Several sheets of plywood can be laid down and used to mark the angle. Run a length of white gaff tape ripped in half down the edge of the plywood to make the mark. It is very easy to see. Using several sheets of plywood to mark the right angle will ensure that it is proportionally large enough to enhance accuracy in the layout.

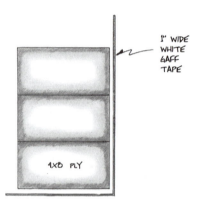

USE SHEETS OF PLYWOOD AND
WHITE TAPE TO MARK OUT A
REALLY LARGE RIGHT ANGLE

Start with the bottom rail, and then add a stile. Stage counterweights may be used to hold the ends of the square tube in place. They are quite heavy and, of course, will not burn. If your theatre uses the old style lead weights it would probably not be a good idea to use them for this purpose, as they might easily melt and/or become toxic.

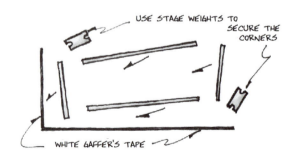

SQUARING THE FRAME

Concrete floors are often times quite unlevel. It is a good idea to make up a supply of small wooden wedges to use in leveling the joints. You can make these from short sections of 1x12 which are cut diagonally on the radial arm saw or power miter box. It is important to use something to arrange the faces of the square tube so that they are on the same plane with one another before welding.

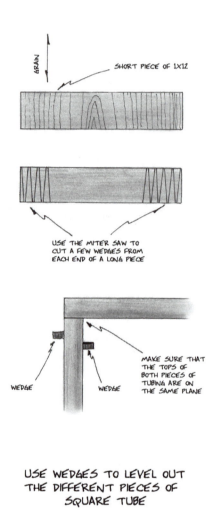

USE WEDGES TO LEVEL OUT
THE DIFFERENT PIECES OF
SQUARE TUBE

If you will be tech screwing some other material to the square tube, avoid having the welded seam side up when laying out the unit. Because the heating and cooling of the welding process tempers the metal, the seam is oftentimes much harder steel than the regular mild steel of the body of the tube, and it will be more difficult to get the tech screws to start there.

Most of the units you build need to have only the faces welded together, and there is no need to weld fillets into the corners. If the scenery is to be used in a rough way, you should determine if the extra welds are warranted.

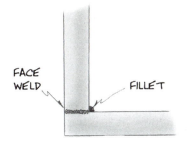

FACE WELD

FILLET

Quite often you will need to produce multiple sections of the same or quite similar units. If these units are small enough, lock together several flameproofed platforms and use them as a template to easily fit together the individual pieces of steel. The advantage of this method is that the units are then automatically arranged into the proper shape and alignment. After a unit is welded on one side, it can be removed, and another one put in its place. This sort of jig is at its best when a large number of multiples are required, and the piece is very complicated. There is a certain point at which the time required to set up the jig is too long to make the process practical, but generally, the method works really well. Use small (2"x 2" or so) 3/4" thick wooden scraps and a pneumatic finish nailer to speed up the procedure. In this case, a nail gun is better than a stapler because it makes the blocks easier to remove when you no longer need them. Quite often it is possible to organize your work so that all the units requiring a set group of blocks are done first, then switch to a new group that is similar, and so forth. That keeps block changing to a minimum.

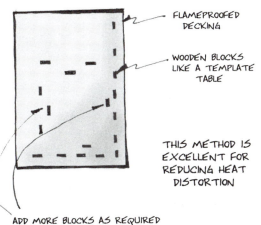

FLAMEPROOFED DECKING

WOODEN BLOCKS LIKE A TEMPLATE TABLE

THIS METHOD IS EXCELLENT FOR REDUCING HEAT DISTORTION

ADD MORE BLOCKS AS REQUIRED TO LOCK THE TUBING INTO PLACE. THE SAME SET-UP CAN BE USED FOR MANY COPIES OF THE SAME PIECE.

It is a good practice to weld all the frames on one side first, and then stack them with the unwelded side up. That makes it easy to weld all of the reverse sides at one time. You can attach the ground to the bottom frame, and it will not need to be moved until the entire stack of frames has been completed. Contact will be preserved through the entire group of frames. This sort of labor-saving technique is small on its own, but if you use enough of them, they will greatly speed up your work. As a practical concern it is best to do all of the metal work for a show first, and as quickly as possible to get it out of the way. Welding tends to clog up the shop because it is dangerous for other people to work in close proximity. I avoid doing metal work and woodwork in the shop at the same time because of the fire hazard it creates. Some shops have separate facilities for the two types of work.

The final phase in the manufacture of metal frames is grinding the welds. There are lots of inexpensive grinders in the 3" to 4" size. This is a very common tool that is easy to find, and a large number of manufacturers keeps the price low. Look for one that has a grinding disk that is easy to change, as the disks tend to wear out frequently. There are also much larger grinders used in auto body work. They create a much flatter surface, but the larger size is heavier and more difficult for many people to use.

You do not need to grind all of the welds, but rather only the ones that will come into contact with some other material, such as a plywood cover or another steel frame. Also grind any area that is left bare and is visible to the audience. Remember when grinding the welds that it is only necessary to make the area flat, or nearly so. Most novices tend to go too far and create a depression at the site of the weld, which requires more work than necessary and also tends to weaken the joint. Grinding is a noisy, smelly, and somewhat unpleasant chore, and it is best to keep it to a minimum whenever possible. Remember to consider where the sparks are going. Always wear eye and hearing protection when using any type of grinder.

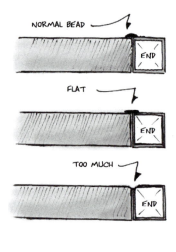

NORMAL BEAD

END

FLAT

END

TOO MUCH

END

DON'T GRIND OFF SO MUCH
AS TO WEAKEN THE WELD!

Laying out metal frames can be made easier if you follow certain guidelines. Proper planning will also reduce the amount of materials that are required. The following concept of how to arrange steel square tube supports for decking is based on using standard 4x8 platforms that are joined together with casket locks. Start with these units as a base, and then add other specially built decking to form whatever shape is required. As you no doubt realize, this is due to the expensive nature of constructing platforming. If your group will exist long after any one particular production is over, it is in your best interest economically to retain certain elements for reuse. One 4x8 platform is pretty much like another in this regard. If you are building a set that will be used again and again over a long period of time, it might be for the best to use another approach, one that exactly matches the specific requirements of that show.

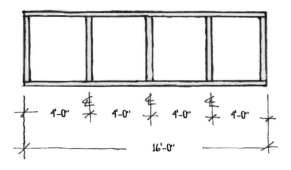

4'-0"   4'-0"   4'-0"   4'-0"

16'-0"

This scheme of designing decking frames requires an upright member about every four feet when using 1 1/2" 16ga steel square tube. That spacing is enough to hold the weight of the decking and a reasonable amount of live load as well (live load indicating movement, as with people). If you know that there is to be an inordinate amount of stress that will be

placed on the decking structure, calculate more exactly the support required. It is critical to keep the upright members vertical. The compression strength of a 1 1/2" section of steel square tube is tremendous, but if the support structure is allowed to warp out of shape, disaster is imminent. Generally speaking, the greater surface area a decking unit has, the more stable the structure will be. No matter what type of legging system you use, ten 4x8 platforms linked together will have much, much more stability than one alone.

When designing a decking system with square tube, it is best to think of the platforms as a group, rather than as separate pieces. Here is a drawing to use as an example.

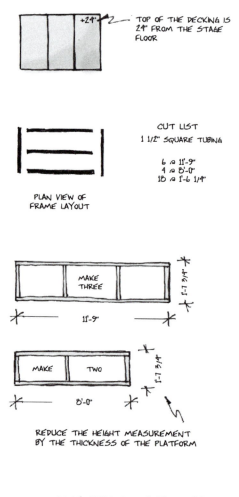

+24"   TOP OF THE DECKING IS
24" FROM THE STAGE
FLOOR

CUT LIST
1 1/2" SQUARE TUBING

6 @ 11'-9"
4 @ 8'-0"
18 @ 1'-6 1/4"

PLAN VIEW OF
FRAME LAYOUT

MAKE THREE

11'-9"

1'-7 3/4"

MAKE TWO

8'-0"

1'-7 3/4"

REDUCE THE HEIGHT MEASUREMENT
BY THE THICKNESS OF THE PLATFORM

CONSTRUCTION SKETCHES
AND CUT LIST

Rather than legging three separate 4x8 platforms, one system is used for all of them. The 11'- 9" frames stretch all the way from one side of the deck to the other, and therefore tie the three platforms together for more stability. Notice that these longer sections are designed to fit inside the shorter, 8'- 0" frames. This is done in order to reduce the number of different-sized units to be constructed and feeds into the wooden block jig philosophy of construction.

You may recall that the end rails of a standard 4x8 platform were made to run the opposite direction of the internal toggles so that the joint could be interlocked and made stronger. With these legging frames the opposite is true. The welded frames will be bolted together, so there is no concern that the joints will accidentally pull apart. Bolting through is a very secure method of joining two pieces.

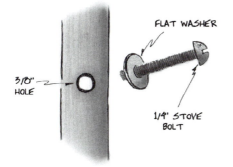

If the two outer frames were made 12'- 0", the center frame would be a smaller size and would not easily fit in the jig. Notice that the interior toggles are placed on approximately 4'- 0" centers, meaning that the centers of the uprights are four feet apart. On the 8'- 0" frames it is essential to locate the uprights at precisely the center in order to facilitate the connection of the middle frame. But placement of uprights on the longer frames is not as critical, as they don't connect with anything else. Even so, you should make them all the same since they will be done on a jig anyway, and you might wind up using them differently later on. You could measure them as exact thirds, or perhaps just put each one in a convenient amount from either side. It is often the case that a bit of time spent now to make everything neat and tidy will pay great dividends later on when some change is required. Also, precise work is an essential part of craftsmanship.

Connect the metal frames together using $1/4$" round headed bolts and wing nuts. Washers are a good idea, especially if you oversize the holes at $3/8$". A $1/4$" hole is barely large enough for a bolt to fit through one hole. It is difficult to get the bolt through such a tight opening when at least four holes are presented, such as is the case when drilling through the four walls of two sections of square tube,. A larger $3/8$" opening allows for easy alignment and bolting of what are often times awkwardly large frames.

Sometimes non-rectangular platform shapes are required. These frames do not fit together in the tidy manner of our earlier example. Care must be taken to keep the frames located under the decking in such a way that the wooden framing of the platform and the steel frame of the legging system will work in concert. It is imperative that these two mem-

bers come into contact with one another at least every four feet, although the steel framing of the leg frames and the wooden framing of the platforms do not need to be exactly the same shape. Here is an example of how this can be accomplished:

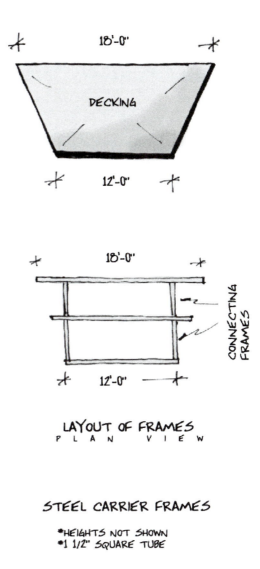

As seen in this example, the steel support frames are still used in a rectilinear way, and the normal bolting method may be used. The joining of the steel undercarriage and the wooden decking are not necessarily continuous with one another, but the rule of maintaining contact at least every four feet is preserved. This type of set-up is easily constructed because the parts are easy to measure and they fit into the jig well, but the process is best suited to a situation where the platform will not need to be faced. It will work well with a fabric skirt that is attached to the wooden frame. This type of underpinning is functional, but not really something you would like for the audience to see.

Here are some sketches for the individual parts.

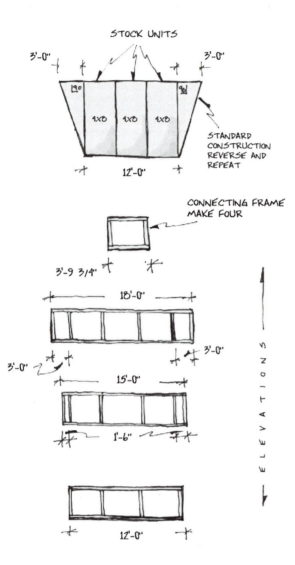

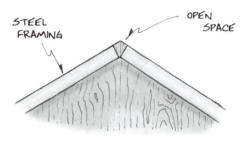

STEEL FRAMING STOPS SHORT OF THE CORNER

the layout. Of course it is possible to do this on the drawing board, and then scale off the resulting drawing with a rule. Quite often designers do that and then list a dimension for the length in question. Either way will work. In this case, the angle measurement is likely the most accurate description to work from. It can be problematic to scale measurements off a drawing because of the relative sizes involved. Be careful doing that, because measurements taken from a small-scale pattern are generally less accurate than measurements taken from a large-scale pattern.

The steel framing sections must meet at an angle, but cutting miters on all of the frames is too difficult a process, and even if you did manage it, the angles on the horizontal parts would not fit the sides of the uprights well. It is better to hinge the frames so that they only touch corner to corner. This means that the frames will need to be shorter that the overall dimensions of the platform faces. A method of computing the actual size must be developed. Using either a framing square or a 1 1/2" strip of plywood, mark a line along the edge of the decking to simulate the placement of the square tube framing. Make a line at a 90-degree angle from this line wherever the lines cross in the corners. This reveals the true sizes of the frames.

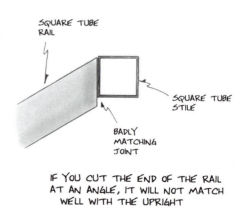

IF YOU CUT THE END OF THE RAIL AT AN ANGLE, IT WILL NOT MATCH WELL WITH THE UPRIGHT

In the example on the next page, the metal frames are made to match the shape and angles of the decking. Unlike the earlier example, you can cover these frames with plywood or some other material so that they mask the underside of the platforms. In order to determine the exact sizes of the metal frames, lay out a full-scale replica of the unit to use as a pattern. Since you are copying a decking piece, build the platform first, and use it with standard 4x8 platforms as a pattern.

Take note that only one angled piece of decking must be built from scratch, as the other two sections are managed by using standard 4x8 platforms. The back side of the unit is not dimensioned, since it is possible to determine that dimension by marking the angle, 60-degrees, and then measuring four feet along the adjacent sides. This is the opposite approach of an earlier project. Marking a tangent toward the center of the piece at 90-degrees from either side completes

It is difficult to bolt or screw hinges in place on a metal frame, but it is easy to simply weld them on during the construction of the frames. Use 3" butt hinges for this purpose. They are inexpensive, especially when purchased in bulk. It is best to use the square cornered type, and make sure that they are steel, not brass.

Most hinges are brass plated, and that is fine. Brass plating or a primer coat of paint will not really make any difference to the welding process. Loose pin backflap hinges are not well suited to this project because they are too flimsy, and the same could be said about any other hinge smaller than the 3" butt. Sometimes a strap hinge will work, but they are generally the wrong shape.

Weld the hinges on after the frames have been constructed and trial fitted on top of the pattern. Setting up on the pattern ensures that the angles are properly adjusted. Vise grip clamps are excellent for holding the hinges in place while they are being welded. If the hinges are located to the inside of the unit, they will not be in the way of any covering that might be attached to the frame, but that is not always possible. Loose pins made from bent 30 or 40-penny nails will make it easy to connect the hinges together.

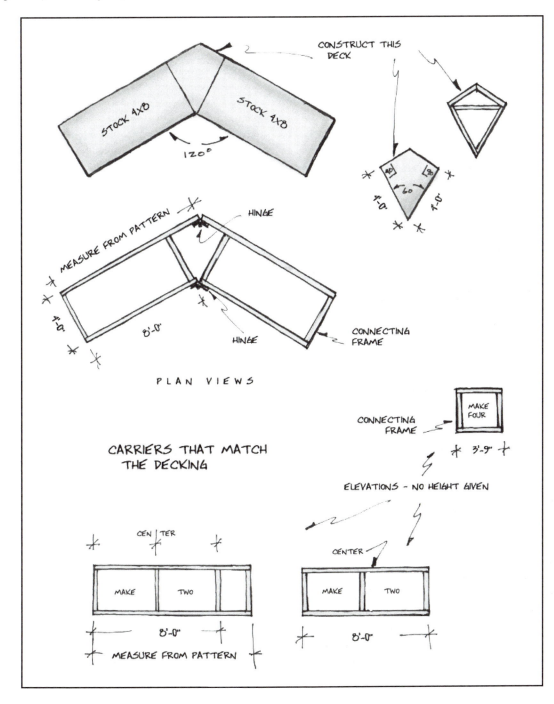

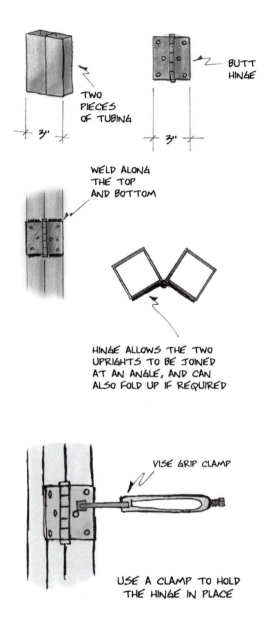

WELD ALONG
THE TOP
AND BOTTOM

HINGE ALLOWS THE TWO
UPRIGHTS TO BE JOINED
AT AN ANGLE, AND CAN
ALSO FOLD UP IF REQUIRED

VISE GRIP CLAMP

USE A CLAMP TO HOLD
THE HINGE IN PLACE

CONNECTING THE PLATFORMS

Connecting the wooden platform sections to the steel frame undercarriage may be done by one of several different methods. The method you choose is dependent upon how many platforms there are, the way they will be used, and/or the materials that are on hand and easily available.

Perhaps the easiest method is to drill $3/16$" holes through the top member of the steel frames and use 2 $1/2$" drywall screws to connect the wooden framing of the decking to the square tube. These holes are easier to drill from above, before the platforms are set down on the frames. The weight of the platform will keep it pressed against the metal frame; the screws are just to prevent the platform from slipping off the side.

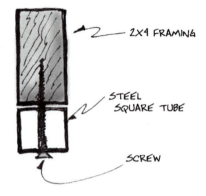

If the decking system must be struck and reassembled repeatedly, it might be best to weld flanges onto the tubing instead. If the flanges are placed to the inside of the 2x4 platform framing, they will be out of sight, but will still prevent the platforms from sliding off the undercarriage. The set-up can occur by simply laying the decking into place after the steel framing has been erected. Similarly, your load out will not held up by waiting for screws to be removed. It is often helpful to bend the flanges in slightly in order to make the parts fit together more easily. Sometimes a thin metal spacer between the flange and the tubing will have the same result. Be sure to put enough flanges in the proper locations, not only to keep the platform on the frames, but to keep the frames from racking out of shape.

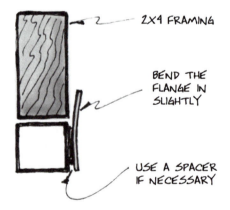

A similar result can be achieved by attaching wooden blocks to the inside of a platform's 2x4s. If the wooden blocks project past the bottom of the framing for an inch or so, the platform can be held in place with no fasteners. Uniform blocks of $3/4$" plywood may be used for this purpose, and if properly installed will still allow the platforms to be stacked up squarely.

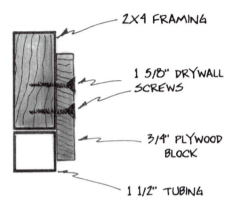

2X4 FRAMING

1 5/8" DRYWALL SCREWS

3/4" PLYWOOD BLOCK

1 1/2" TUBING

Sometimes the decking system is so large, heavy, and solid that there is no need to attach it to the floor. This will especially be true of wide and low decks that have no tendency to tip over. When the square footage of the platforming is small, and the height is substantial, it is clearly best to lag bolt the bottoms of the frames to the floor. A $3/8$" x 3" lag bolt is a good size. Drill $1/2$" holes in the steel frames while they are still in the shop. A $1/4$" pilot hole into the wooden floor will make it easier to screw in the bolt. This method may be used to secure spot towers, lighting towers, and other such metal frames with no fear that the unit will fall over. Just be sure to use enough lag bolts of a proper size, and be sure that the flooring is solid enough to hold the threads of the lag bolts.

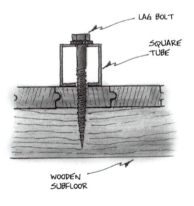

LAG BOLT

SQUARE TUBE

WOODEN SUBFLOOR

MAKE SURE THAT THE BOLTS GO FAR ENOUGH INTO THE FLOOR

The kind of steel framing discussed so far can be dismantled and stacked against the wall when not in use. It is very easy to move about (except for the weight) and can be fitted into a truck without using up too much space. The flat nature of all of the pieces makes them easy to assemble with the types of jigs already discussed. Sometimes it is preferable to put the frames together into cubes. This method

will avoid the doubling of vertical support elements in the corner of an assembled frame and hence will require less material. It also creates an airier, more open look if the framing is to be visible to the audience. This approach is often the best when the size of the decking piece involved is quite small. If the object is to construct a platform that is three feet square and six feet off the ground, and which does not need to break down, then making one solid tubing structure is a good idea. The process of constructing a unit of this type calls for creating two side frames in the normal manner. These frames are connected directly by horizontals rather than by using additional frames. You don't need a framed platform to finish off the top. Tech screw $3/4$" plywood to the top instead.

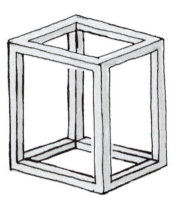

MAKING ONE SOLID PIECE HAS A NEATER APPEARANCE, BUT IT IS MUCH MORE DIFFICULT TO CONSTRUCT

The concept is simple, but the execution is somewhat more complicated. The problem lies in arranging all the parts so that they are square to one another in a three-dimensional rather than two-dimensional setting. Arranging two dimensions on the floor is easy, but branching off from this into the air requires some new techniques. The most expeditious way is to use some of the frames themselves as braces. As shown in the diagram, the frames are easy to clamp to one another, and if all has gone well they should be a perfect right angle. Sometimes it is helpful to lay a stage weight on the bottom of the frame in order to keep it firmly on the floor. It may well be necessary to use several of the squaring-up frames at one time in order to keep the structure in line.

There is generally no shortage of old frames from past shows or new pieces under construction that may be used in this way. It is best to tack weld this sort of work and get all of the parts in position before completing the welding. Heat distortion can be a real problem and will warp the entire structure out of alignment unless kept to a minimum. When a piece of tubing is welded on one side, it will tend to draw up toward that side as it cools. Tack welding parts, and making sure that they are firmly braced during welding, will reduce that effect.

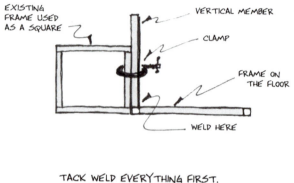

EXISTING FRAME USED AS A SQUARE

VERTICAL MEMBER

CLAMP

FRAME ON THE FLOOR

WELD HERE

RACK BRACE

TACK WELD EVERYTHING FIRST. THIS ALLOWS FOR SOME ADJUSTING AND REDUCES THE EFFECTS OF HEAT DISTORTION.

Welding supply shops carry right angle magnets that work in the same way as the larger squaring up frames. They are much easier to put on, but their small size can be a drawback. Use whichever method seems the best at the time.

Sometimes you may need to ensure that a structure can be leveled out very exactly over a slightly uneven surface. In this case, leveling devices may be easily manufactured from $1/2$" carriage bolts and hex nuts. The nuts are welded to the bottom of the tubing where it touches the floor. Drill a $5/8$" hole in the tubing to allow the bolt to pass through. Screw the bolt into the nut and set the frame in place. Height adjustment is accomplished by wrenching the bolt in or out. A wrench will work with the flat spots intended for a torque washer. The addition of the nut and bolt should be figured into the design of the height of the platforming.

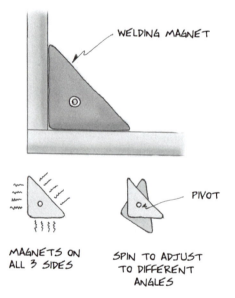

WELDING MAGNET

MAGNETS ON ALL 3 SIDES

SPIN TO ADJUST TO DIFFERENT ANGLES

PIVOT

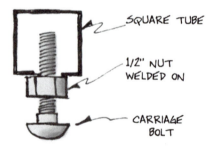

SQUARE TUBE

1/2" NUT WELDED ON

CARRIAGE BOLT

I have found that this type of frame construction is generally quite sturdy enough when the face welds are properly executed. On occasion, I feel the need to weld the corners of a unit when it will receive a high degree of lateral stress. On rare occasions, there are some structures that require the addition of some type of rack bracing, which can be accomplished by the addition of a 45-degree brace across the corner of one or more of the frames. This is more often required for scenery built with small gauge tubing. It does not often happen with the 1 $1/2$" 16ga stock, but you should consider the implications of a structural failure and plan accordingly.

CHAPTER 16

FULL-SCALE PATTERNS

    Full-scale patterns are used to produce work that does not lend itself to an ordinary cut list. Some units of scenery are so oddly shaped that the normal methods are simply not possible. This frequently occurs when lots of angles are used, or if the shapes are curved. The full-scale pattern technique allows you to mark framing parts directly from the patterns, or in some cases the pattern is marked on plywood that becomes a part of the unit. Most of these techniques have been touched on in other chapters, but it seems best to organize them all in one place. Theatre scenery tends to have very fanciful shapes and profiles that require the builder to be more inventive than carpenters engaged in general construction.

    Throughout history, painters have used a gridding technique to reproduce scale drawings into full size. If a drawing has been rendered in a $1/2$" scale, each $1/2$" on the drawing is equal to 1'- 0" in full size. You can use this method by dividing the drawing into $1/2$" squares, and the surface you would like to transfer the design to in 1'- 0" squares. It is possible to transfer the drawing to the larger scale one square at a time with a high degree of accuracy. Scenic artists use this method daily in their work. If a profile piece of scenery is to be constructed, the same technique will serve the stage carpenter well.

THERE ARE SOME THINGS
YOU CAN'T JUST MEASURE,
AND MARK WITH A CHALK LINE

USING A GRID

Gridding off a profile quite often requires the input of a scenic artist. Most often the carpenters will lay out plywood, grid it off into one-foot squares, and then request that the scenic artist or designer mark the profile. Depending on the personalities involved, you might wind up marking the outlines inside the squares and then just getting them checked by a more artistic member of the team. (Unless, of course, YOU are that person.)

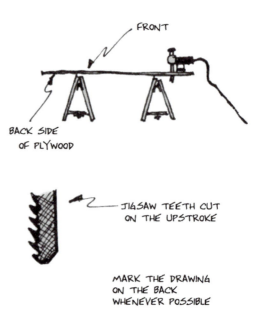

FRONT

BACK SIDE
OF PLYWOOD

JIGSAW TEETH CUT
ON THE UPSTROKE

MARK THE DRAWING
ON THE BACK
WHENEVER POSSIBLE

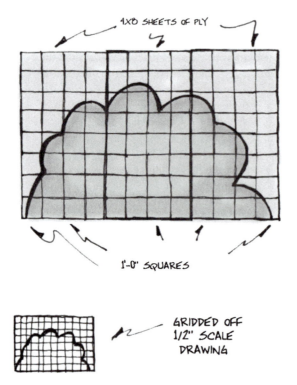

1X8 SHEETS OF PLY

1'-0" SQUARES

GRIDDED OFF
1/2" SCALE
DRAWING

You can also reduce tearout by cutting with the grain. You may recall how ripping creates less tearout than cross cutting. You may be able to line the plywood up in such a way as to keep as many lines as possible running with the grain of the wood. Obviously, this is problematic when cutting curves. But tearout is also less if you cut at an angle that pulls on the wood fibers rather than pushing them. If you are cutting at an angle to the grain, one side of the kerf will be pushing, and the other side will be pulling. Make sure that the keeper piece is on the pulling side of the kerf. If you have a large curve it is possible to reverse the angle of your cut where the grain direction changes and make the entire curve smoother.

Once the outline of the piece has been marked in charcoal, it is a good practice to retrace it with a Sharpie marker so that the line is clearer. Charcoal tends to vibrate off the plywood during the cutting process, and having a clear and indelible mark makes the job of cutting much easier. The more complicated the work is, the more important it is to retrace. One word of caution: laquer-based pens can be difficult to paint over. This is especially true if the paint is a light color.

After the design has been laid out, you will need to cut the profile edges with a jigsaw. The teeth on a jigsaw blade cut on the up stroke so that the saw is pulled against the work. That keeps the saw from bouncing around so much. Unfortunately that means that most of the tearout tends to occur on the top of the plywood. You can mark the pieces on the backside so that the front will have a cleaner edge. If the design is really complicated, this can be more trouble than it is worth, and it may not be necessary.

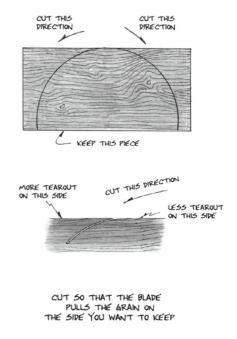

CUT THIS
DIRECTION

CUT THIS
DIRECTION

KEEP THIS PIECE

MORE TEAROUT
ON THIS SIDE

CUT THIS DIRECTION

LESS TEAROUT
ON THIS SIDE

CUT SO THAT THE BLADE
PULLS THE GRAIN ON
THE SIDE YOU WANT TO KEEP

Very often, the profile you are working with will be on several sheets of plywood that must be joined together later. It is difficult to get the cut on one sheet to line up exactly with the cut on the next one. This is especially true of marks that were made with charcoal and markers. It is often better to leave extra material at the joints and to trim that excess off after the panels have been joined together.

LAYOUT PATTERNS

A related method uses a full-scale pattern to mark angled pieces where dimensions are known, but not angles. This often occurs when building scenery. It is generally more accurate to use this method, which does not include determining the angles from a scale drawing. "Scaling" from the drawing can lead to some fairly large errors, as the drawing is so small in relation to the true size of the scenery that a pencil dot can be as much as an inch. If you make a large pattern from dimensions on the plan, you are using the best information to build the piece.

The drawing shows a hard framed portal that must be constructed from steel square tube. The offstage edge is square, with lengths of steel meeting at 90-degree angles. The inside profile is full of odd angles, and we don't know what they are. You are given the dimensions of the scenery and the locations of the angled intersections. That is all the information that is required to do a layout of the portal.

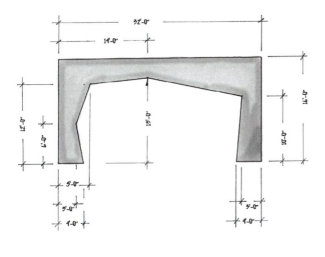

CONSTRUCT THIS HARD PORTAL FROM 1 1/2" SQUARE TUBING AND 1/4" PLYWOOD

The first step is to mark the outside and inside profiles of the shape on the floor. The floor is a good place for this procedure because it requires no preparation other than sweeping. The floor is always there and doesn't cost anything. Sometimes it makes more sense to do the layout on plywood, and other times you may want to use paper if the size is really small.

SNAP A BASELINE ON A CLEAN FLOOR

You will be marking the framing pieces by laying them on top of the drawing, and there is no need to move the drawing around. This particular unit is made from welded steel, so a concrete floor is an obvious choice for fire safety reasons. It is fairly large, and it would be difficult to lay out enough platforms to do a wooden block jig. The jig seems less necessary since only one copy will be built. Heat distortion is less of a problem on a large flat piece that has relatively few parts for its size. These are all factors to consider when deciding how to go about your work. Start the layout procedure by snapping a chalk line on the floor in a convenient location.

Form a 90-degree angle line perpendicular to the original by using one of the following methods.

Use a sheet (or several sheets) of plywood to form the angle. Lay one edge of the sheet on the line, and draw along the adjacent side to form the 90-degree angle. This is much more accurate than using a framing square because the plywood is so much larger, and the proportional amount of error that can creep in is much smaller.

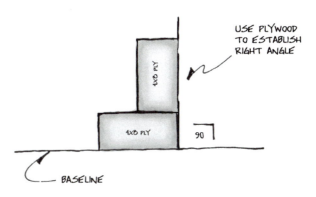

USE PLYWOOD TO ESTABLISH RIGHT ANGLE

BASELINE

As an alternative you can use the "3–4–5" method of creating a right angle. It is stated that for any triangle with sides that are 3, 4, and 5-units long, the corner formed by the intersection of the 3-unit and 4-unit sides will be a right triangle. This holds true for triangles that are multiples of these numbers such as 6–8–10, or 9–12–15.

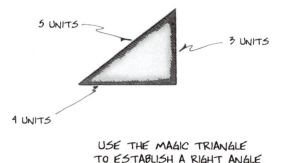

USE THE MAGIC TRIANGLE
TO ESTABLISH A RIGHT ANGLE

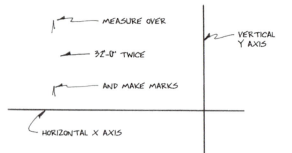

MEASURE OVER TWICE AND SNAP
A NEW LINE TO MARK THE OTHER SIDE

Measure along your base line 12'- 0", and establish two points of reference. Then use two tape measures, one to measure up 9'- 0", and the other to triangulate the 15'- 0" between the 9'- 0" mark on the tape, and the 12'- 0" mark on the floor. That will establish a right angle. This technique is easiest to do with three people, one to hold the end of each tape measure on its respective mark, and the third to move the tapes back and forth until the 12'- 0" and the 15'- 0" marks are aligned with one another. Make sure that you are consistent about which side of the tape measure you are using. Drawing a line through this point and the original corner mark will establish a line perpendicular to the base line.

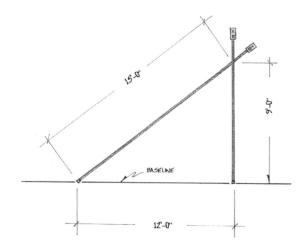

USE LARGER MULTIPLES OF 3, 4, 5
FOR GREATER ACCURACY

Once the base line and the 90-degree tangent have been established, you can plot the remaining points. Measure along the x axis to determine the width of the unit. It is possible to establish another 90-degree angle for this line, but it is much easier to simply measure twice, one toward the top and once at the bottom, and connect the dots.

The same method may be used to establish the top line of the unit. The remaining points are plotted according to their measurements from a known position by following the dimensions shown on the sketch. Often it is helpful to think of the layout as a graph with an x and a y axis, and the layout of the remaining points is a process of measuring from these axes. The widths of the two leg bottoms can be measured directly from either side of the portal. The remainder of the points that establish the diagonal lines can be plotted up from the bottom and over from one of the sides. The lines between the points can be drawn in with a straight edge, or if the distance is too great, use a chalk line. Whatever the method, it is best to finish by darkening in the line with a Sharpie so that they will be easy to see and less likely to be accidentally swept away.

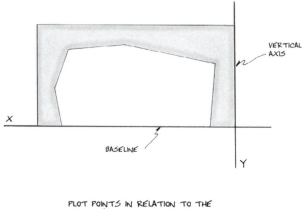

PLOT POINTS IN RELATION TO THE
X AND Y AXES. THEN CONNECT
THE POINTS WITH STRAIGHT LINES

The next drawing shows how the portal is divided into several different parts, or units, and how the framing is to be placed. The decisions about where the break lines fall are made in accordance with the realities of what size materials are available, and what it is reasonable to expect humans to carry and assemble. Generally speaking, fewer parts equal less expense, but they can be much more difficult to assemble and transport. Try to make units that can be carried by no more than four stagehands. If it takes more than that the piece is probably too large.

Also look for natural break lines in the design of the scenery itself. Quite often there is already a difference in paint color, or a piece of trim running along the scenery. It is clear that your break lines will show much less if you follow the same path.

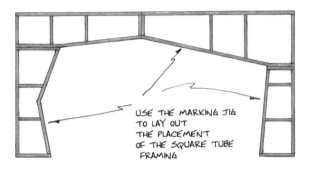

USE THE MARKING JIG
TO LAY OUT
THE PLACEMENT
OF THE SQUARE TUBE
FRAMING

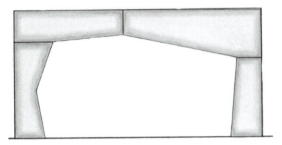

DIVIDE THE PORTAL INTO BUILDABLE PORTIONS
ALONG REASONABLE BREAK LINES

Marking the pieces is a matter of laying a section of the square tube on the pattern, and then using a straight edge to transfer the angle and the length to the tube. Make certain the piece of tube is flush with all the edges of the pattern except the one you are about to mark. Close one eye as you adjust the straightedge so that it is lined up with the mark on the floor. The tricky part is to hold the marker so that it is directly above the line on the floor. There is a tendency to mark the piece with the correct angle, but too long or too short. It takes a bit of practice to get this technique.

The method of marking the separate sections should be intuitive, and it must be decided on a case-by-case basis. Experience will teach you the best ways to do that, by observing where the shape changes direction. There is a trick that makes marking the actual framing members a bit easier.

The steel square tube that was specified to frame this portal is 1 1/2" wide. Rip a scrap piece of plywood to that width and use it to mark the placement of the framing members. Lay the jig along the outside edges of the pattern and use it to make a mark 1 1/2" to the inside. Take care to properly mark the overlapping of the framing, accurately mapping out which sections extend all the way to the side and which ones stop short. Measure the proper placement of all the required toggles using the same method as described in earlier construction chapters. Use the "measure 3/4" to either side of the center" approach.

This portal will be covered with sheets of plywood, so take that into consideration when deciding where the toggles should go. The 1 1/2" square tube is wide enough to join the seams of adjacent plywood panels using tech screws. Your 1 1/2" wide marking tool should make it easy to mark the actual sides of the toggles. When all of these steps are complete, and you have established your pattern, it is time to begin marking the actual pieces to be cut. Notice that you have not formed a cut list, and that we do not yet know any of the angles involved.

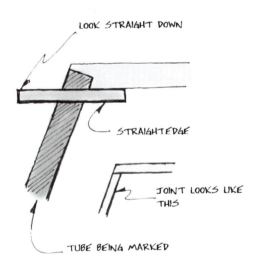

LOOK STRAIGHT DOWN

STRAIGHTEDGE

JOINT LOOKS LIKE
THIS

TUBE BEING MARKED

Lay the square tube in the chop saw, and adjust the saw until it is set at the proper angle. Lower the blade and sight down the side of it to check for proper alignment. This is rather like looking down the length of a board to see if it is bowed or warped. If you are using this technique on a wooden structure, substitute "power miter box" for "chop saw."

After the angle has been cut, lay the resulting piece back down on the pattern to check it for the proper size. You may want to refer back to the discussion of angles in Chapter 11 that talks about the relationship that angles have to one another in the same shape. Many of the angles in this project are the same. It is, of course, easiest to cut all of one angle and then all of another. If you are ever uncertain which other angles are the same as one you have just cut, put that first piece down on the pattern in various places to look and see. After all of the pieces of square tube have been cut and laid in place, the full-scale pattern they are laying on makes a wonderful layout jig for welding.

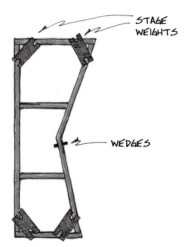

STAGE
WEIGHTS

WEDGES

USE THE STANDARD
METAL FRAME TECHNIQUES

CHAPTER 17

BUILDING DOORS
AND WINDOWS

Doors and windows are perhaps the most commonly requested scenic element after flats, platforms, and steps. Doors have as many different looks as there are designers drawing them, but they do tend to have some properties in common.

Doors and windows may be built either as an integral part of a wall structure, or they may be constructed as separate units. There are occasions when you are best off building a window as part of the structure of a design. If the show must break down either to tour or because it has multiple scenes, having a separate door unit can be quite cumbersome. It is probably easier to move the wall with the door in it. If the wall is double sided, it would be very difficult to build a door and frame that can be inserted.

Much of the time, independent units are more cost effective—especially for a show with a single box set. Doors (or windows) can be removed from one wall and reused in another. Eventually a stock is built up that can be recycled and will cut costs in the long run. If your theatre has a main season and a lower budget "studio season," the lower budget shows can definitely benefit from being able to pull scenery from stock. Of course, you will need ample storage space if you plan on keeping everything you build.

Even if the frame is built as part of the wall structure, you will still need facings, trims, and stops. You can use many of the same techniques shown in this chapter to build the frame as a part of the wall. The sections on hanging a door will work with any type of construction.

There are a lot of variables here, so pick the method that seems most appropriate at the time. The real difference is in the frame rather than the door itself. This chapter presents a method of building door and window frames that are strong and easy to put together. There is also information about constructing and altering the doors themselves.

THE DOOR ON THE LEFT WAS MADE BY ADDING PARTS TO A STANDARD HOLLOW-CORE DOOR. THE DOOR TO THE RIGHT IS A FACTORY-MADE, HARDBOARD TYPE. THE FRAME WAS MADE USING THE METHODS IN THIS CHAPTER.

DOORS

There are two main parts to a door, the slab, or shutter, and the frame. The first thing to determine in designing a door system is the size of the slab and the type of motion the door will have. Doors can be hinged for a variety of motions, using standard butt hinges, double action hinges like a kitchen door, folding doors, or as a sliding door. A majority of doors wind up being plain old butt-hinge doors.

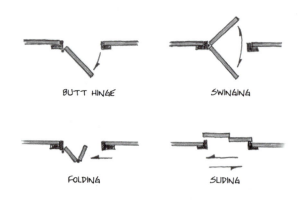

TYPES OF DOOR MOTION

It is quite common to buy or recycle a door, and then build the frame that surrounds it. Most factory-made doors are either 7'-0" tall or 6'-8" tall. The standard modern size for a residential door is the smaller 6'-8" height. Exterior doors, commercial doors, and antique doors may all be the taller 7'-0" size. Some doors that were originally constructed for a special project may be considerably larger, but the two heights mentioned account for the vast majority of shutters available.

STANDARD SIZE
OF A MODERN DOOR

The width of a door is given in feet and inches. The narrowest you usually find are about 1'-6", and the widest commonly manufactured are in the neighborhood of 3'-6" or so. Doors generally come in even inch widths like 2'-4", 2'-6", 2'-8", etc. Do not be surprised if you run across an old used door that is a strikingly odd measurement, for it may well have been cut down at some point in its life, or it could have been originally manufactured to fit an odd-sized hole. Back in the day, building a house was a much less scientific endeavor than it is today, and it is quite common to find salvaged Victorian architectural details with unique measurements.

A slab door is flat on both sides. Frame and panel doors are made by constructing a frame of stiles and rails, with panels inserted to make the door solid. French doors are built with window panes for a light, airy look. Louver doors have an interior made up of slats so that air is allowed to pass through. Z doors are made of vertical planks and are held together by braces that form a Z.

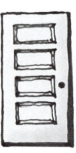

SLAB

PANEL

PANEL

FRENCH

LOUVER

"Z" DOOR

The names of the parts of a flat that we use in the theatre were adapted from the names of the parts used to construct a panel door. It is not possible to build a door that is one solid piece of wood. Of course trees don't grow that big, but even if they did, the resulting structure would be very unstable. You have seen how an ordinary 1x12 tends to cup out of shape because of the width of the board and the way that the growth rings dry out. Imagine how much cupping would occur if the board were 36 inches wide. Also, you recall how wood tends to swell across the grain when the weather is humid. If the door were really one solid piece of wood with the grain running vertically, it would tend to shrink or swell a tremendous amount depending on the humidity. So the proportionally slender rails and stiles are used to form the outer structure of a door, and the much wider interior panels are loosely joined inside a mortise, so that they can change in size without affecting the rest of the door.

RAISED PANEL

THE PANELS IN A DOOR ARE HELD
IN THE STILES BY A "TONGUE AND GROOVE"
TYPE OF JOINT. THE PANELS ARE NOT
PERMANENTLY ATTACHED

MAKING DOOR FRAMES

Although you may often buy or salvage the actual door, it is very rare to find a door frame suitable for stage use. They must almost always be constructed from scratch. Doors are removed from the building during demolition, but the door frame is an integral part of the structure of the building. New doors are often sold pre-hung, so that the jamb or frame comes with it. Unfortunately, these factory made jambs are really not suitable for stage work because they are entirely too flimsy and rarely have the sort of style that the design calls for.

The method of building a frame that is presented in this chapter presupposes that the door frame is independent of the wall it fits into. This method is based on laminating together strips of plywood in a way that creates a very strong structure. It works equally well with either soft- or hardcovered flats. If you are building a frame that is permanently connected to a hardcovered wall flat, you can use many of the same techniques, but you will not need to laminate the facing trim, because the flat already provides a rigid frame structure.

The narrative used to describe this construction method is quite detailed. Many drawings are included to illustrate the laminating method. Laminating plywood parts is a great way to construct all sorts of things, so part of the aim of the chapter is to get you acquainted with that style of construction. Laminated plywood is very strong and quite stable. It does not work well as wooden trim that will be stained, because the grain pattern is all wrong. Scenery is mostly painted, so that is not such a problem in the theatre.

Assume that the door used in the demonstration is 2'- 8" wide and 6'- 8" tall. One of the first things to do is to determine the size of the rough opening. This is the hole that must be left in the wall flats where the door will be placed. An independent frame requires that the rough opening be at least 2" wider and 2" taller than the shutter used in the frame. Add the numbers to get a rough opening size of 6'- 10" in height, and 2'- 10" in width. These dimensions should be used when working up a cut list for the wall flats. It does not matter whether hardcovered or softcovered flats will be used. The rough opening can actually be several inches larger and still work if the frame facing is wide enough.

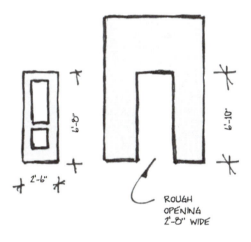

ROUGH
OPENING
2'-8' WIDE

The door facing is constructed of overlapping strips of 1/2" thick plywood. The best type for this purpose is lauan, because of its very tight grain pattern, and also because of the fact that it is lightweight and inexpensive. Failing this, I would suggest 1/2" A2 cabinet grade plywood because it has an easily painted surface as well. B/C yellow pine is sound structurally, but the grain tends to telegraph through, and finishing can be a problem. If you are willing to sand the base coat, it will work just fine. The door jamb is built of 1x4 white pine, although you can use plywood for this also if it is on hand. Be sure to use 3/4" because the 1/2" used for the facing is not strong enough. The facing is usually accented with trim selected by the designer, but the basic structural parts involved are the facing, the jamb, the stop, and a threshold piece across the bottom that will help the door keep its shape.

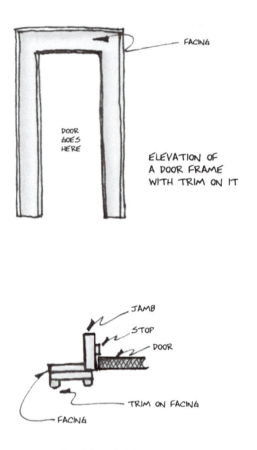

ELEVATION OF
A DOOR FRAME
WITH TRIM ON IT

PLAN VIEW OF SECTION
THROUGH DOOR AND FRAME

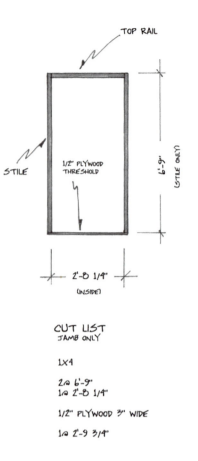

CUT LIST
JAMB ONLY

1X4

2@ 6'-9"
1@ 2'-8 1/4"

1/2" PLYWOOD 3" WIDE

1@ 2'-9 3/4"

Begin your door frame cut list with the jamb. The two uprights need to be an inch longer than the door itself is tall. The added inch will accommodate the $3/4$" thickness of the top rail, with an extra $1/4$" space left over to give the door room to operate. That is really a minimum. If you think that the shutter part of the door may have problems opening, give yourself a bit of extra room. A house door needs to fit closely so that the insulation will be effective, but that is not a problem on a stage door. The top rail should be the width of the door plus $1/4$".

Again, the extra quarter inch provides enough leeway for the door to swing without having to worry about the thickness of paint and other such hidden dangers. It will also make it unnecessary to mortise a space in the jamb for the hinge, which can be a very time consuming process. The section of $1/2$" plywood that forms the threshold extends all the way from the outside of one of the stiles to the outside of the other. Hence it should be 1 $1/2$" longer than the top rail. The width of the stock you should use varies depending upon the style of the scenic design, but 3 $1/2$" (a 1x4) is generally a good starting point. It is best to assemble the jamb before going on to the facing.

Sometimes, having a threshold across the door opening can be a hazard to actors, or a problem if something like a wheelchair must be rolled through the doorway. You can omit the threshold and still use this method, but the resulting structure will not be as strong. Most of the time the $1/2$" height of the threshold is not enough to cause major problems unless you are using it in conjunction with a hardcovered flat that already has a framing member across the bottom.

Once the jamb has been constructed, you can move on to the facing. This method requires that the facing be made of two distinct layers. The first is connected to the front of the jamb. The width of this facing is determined by the style of the trim involved. Modern doors may have a casing less than 3" wide, but most period doors require something considerably larger. This example is of a large period molding trim that will be 5" wide, so the width of the facing piece is 5". Insetting the facing $1/4$" from the inside of the jamb will give the barrel of the butt hinge someplace to go. Mounting the door hinges is covered later in the chapter. Leaving a space also creates an additional reveal around the perimeter of the door. Generally speaking, the more reveals (or shadow lines) that are on the trim, the more complex it will appear to be.

Measure the width of the inside of the door jamb and add 10" inches, 5" for either side. Now add $1/2$" to this total which will account for the $1/4$" reveal that will be left all around the door jamb.

Once again, it is best to attach these parts before going on to the next batch, at least until you are familiar with the process. After that you can save time by cutting all of the parts for all of the doors and windows at one time. Remember to inset these pieces $1/4$" from the inside of the door jamb. Gluing is essential!

The next series of parts are used to strengthen the door frame, which as you can no doubt tell is very wobbly at the moment. The second layer of $1/2$" ply gets laminated to the backside of the facing pieces that were just installed.

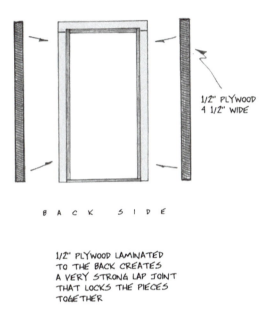

EXTENDS 5" PAST
REVEAL LINE ON JAMB

A

1/4" REVEAL

2'-8 1/4"

F R O N T   S I D E

1/4" WIDE REVEAL

A

FACING

JAMB

SECTION THRU
DOOR FRAME

1/2" PLYWOOD
4 1/2" WIDE

B A C K   S I D E

1/2" PLYWOOD LAMINATED
TO THE BACK CREATES
A VERY STRONG LAP JOINT
THAT LOCKS THE PIECES
TOGETHER

Overlap the joints at the top corners to reinforce them. It is amazing how strong the frame becomes when these parts are added. If you measure the back of the facing piece you discover that it is 4 $1/2$" wide, since $1/2$" of the original 5" width was used to connect the facing to the jamb. Measure the length of the facing from top to bottom to get the length of these two side pieces. Not only do they do a great job of stiffening the corner, they also make the facing an inch thick, so it appears more dimensional. Square the frame before laminating the parts.

Measure the inside height of the jamb and add $3/4$" to that measurement to get the total length of the two upright facing pieces. Again, $1/4$" is for the reveal, but the remaining $1/2$" is for the thickness of the threshold. Cut the pieces from $1/2$" plywood.

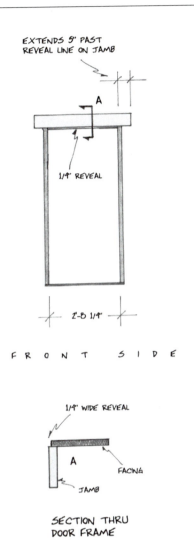

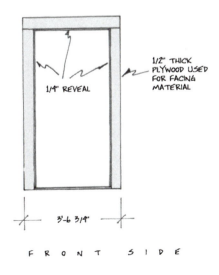

1/2" THICK
PLYWOOD USED
FOR FACING
MATERIAL

1/4" REVEAL

3'-6 3/4"

F R O N T   S I D E

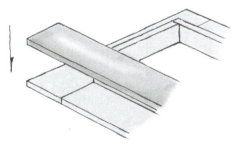

LAMINATING THE REAR LAYER
CREATES A VERY STRONG JOINT

If the audience will not be able to see the top of the door, it is not really necessary to fill the gap across the top. This top section does not cross any joints, so it has no structural function. You may wish to fill in that space if it will make it easier to get the trim on the front.

YOU CAN LEAVE
THIS SPACE OPEN

4 1/2" WIDE
REAR LAYER

Now you are ready to work on trim for the door frame. The trim is what will give the door its style. Until this point, there is not much difference in the construction method used for one type or another, excepting the basic width of the facing, which is generally larger for an ornate style. From this point forward the process is dictated by the design provided by the scenic designer. Here are some approaches to producing a few of the most common styles. Quite often, the clarity (or lack thereof) of a design will leave some decisions about the exact nature of the trim to the discretion of the technician.

A SKETCH LIKE THIS
IS OPEN TO
INTERPRETATION

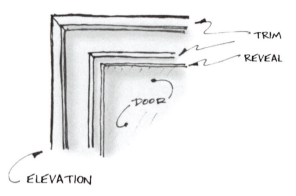

TRIM

REVEAL

DOOR

ELEVATION

The most straightforward approach is simply to band the edges of the facing with some variety of small trim. It is amazing what even the most easily produced stock will add to the appearance of a door. I think what is important is that there be something there to catch the light and reveal a shadow, but the exact nature of the trim is not so important. It is generally better to use something fairly large and rectangular around the outside edge, and a smaller, softer-edged trim toward the inside. The outside trim should be attached flush with the edge to create a thick slab to cover the intersection of any baseboards or chair rails. You can locate the inner trim a small distance away from the edge to create an extra reveal.

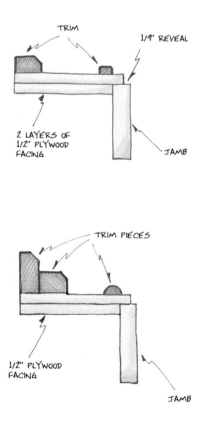

TRIM

1/4" REVEAL

2 LAYERS OF
1/2" PLYWOOD
FACING

JAMB

TRIM PIECES

1/2" PLYWOOD
FACING

JAMB

These trims will need to be measured and cut to fit. If they are just rectangular in cross section, they can be left with 90-degree angles. If they have any other profile, it will be necessary to miter cut the corners. It is easiest to cut a 45-degree end first and then to cut the 90-degree to length. The 90 is easier to line up in the saw. Naturally, the trim on the header has a 45 at both ends. It is best to cut a piece, put it on, cut a piece, put it on, and so forth because it is less confusing and gives you a solid, physical position to mark from. Marking the pieces by holding them up to the door frame is more accurate than measuring and is less prone to mistakes. If you are right-handed and work your way around the door clockwise, the "keeper" piece will always be to your left. That is the most natural position for using the right-handed power miter saw.

The outer edge of the door facing is now made up of a number of layers of different materials that are probably not exactly flush with one another. Use the belt sander to even things up a bit. After a rough sanding, fill any large holes with joint compound, and finish by hand sanding when the mud is dry. You will be surprised how much two or three minutes with a piece of 100 grit sandpaper can do. Easing the corners of your woodworking even a small amount will greatly improve the overall look of the work.

The Victorian target mold style is quite popular, especially if your theatre produces classic American dramas. There are several ways of approaching it. The most obvious visible difference about this style is that the corners are not mitered, but rather blocks are used to cover the change in direction. All of the trim sections end with a 90-degree angle. There is a target mold block in both of the top corners, and a plinth block at the bottom of each side of the facing. The corner blocks are used to change the direction that the trim is running. This style makes technical sense when you consider that the trim pieces were all cut to size with a handsaw. It must have been quite difficult to cut such large trim entirely by hand.

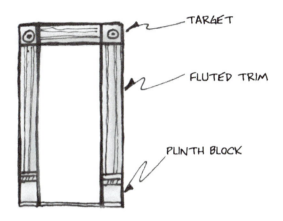

Making the target molds and plinth blocks is, as you would imagine, the challenging part of this assignment. Sometimes it is possible to purchase them from a salvage yard. The target molds were originally turned on a lathe, and you can make exact copies that way from a pattern. But it is a time consuming task. If you have even one example of a target you can use it to make a mold and then replicate the target using Bondo, which is auto body filler. You can make a block that has rectilinear relief cut with a saw. Or you can use a router to simulate the carving that was formerly done on a lathe. There is another very easy way to fake a similar item that looks good on stage.

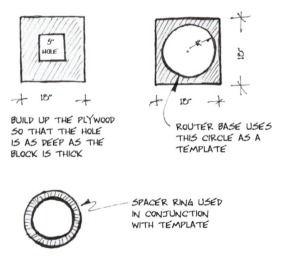

Using a router to create a target mold is not terribly difficult if a jig is used to control the movement of the router. The jig really consists of two parts, a frame that holds the block in place, and a circular guide for the router. The standard size for a target mold is 5" square, and the thickness should be about 1" thick. You can plane this down from a section of two-by material, or if necessary you can just use the two-by with its full thickness. The frame to hold the block in place can be made from plywood, and its thickness should be the same as the block. Use whatever thicknesses of plywood are required to build up to that amount, and make the plywood square large enough to accommodate the router plate, or about 18" square. The exact amount depends on the size of the block, the diameter of your router's face plate, and the design of the profile being cut into the block.

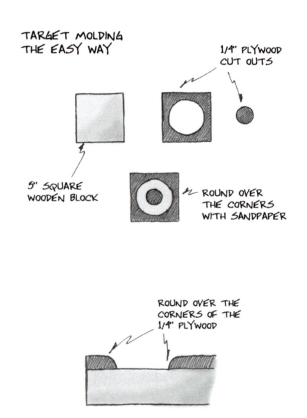

TARGET MOLDING THE EASY WAY

1/4" PLYWOOD CUT OUTS

5" SQUARE WOODEN BLOCK

ROUND OVER THE CORNERS WITH SANDPAPER

ROUND OVER THE CORNERS OF THE 1/4" PLYWOOD

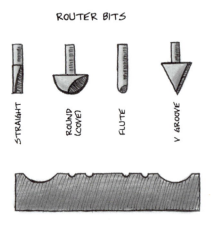

ROUTER BITS

STRAIGHT   ROUND (COVE)   FLUTE   V GROOVE

SECTION THRU TARGET

The block and the guide must be perfectly aligned if the profile is to be properly centered in the block. The precision of the profile is dependent upon the smoothness of the circular guide. The distance of the router cut from the center of the block is a function of the diameter of this guide, and the round wooden bushing is used to change that distance in order to increase the complexity of the profile through the use of multiple passes. Again, the exact sizes will need to be worked out on the basis of the design involved, and the tools and materials used. The router bits you select must be plunged into the work and cannot have a guide pin or bearing on the bottom. This process requires a considerable amount of work to assemble the jigs, but the advantages are that the finished product looks very "real," and that an infinite number of corner blocks can be made from the same jig. It will take all afternoon to make the first one, but only a couple of minutes to make the second. If you use multiple passes, make sure to do all of the blocks with each set up before changing bits.

There is a simpler method that looks almost as good and is much easier to put together. It uses thin layers of $1/4$" plywood to simulate the carving detail. This is a "build up" rather than a "carve into" process. Cut out two plates as are described in the drawing. Mount them on a block of one-by that has been cut down to a 5" square. Careful sanding of the edges of the plywood will round it over and help to create the illusion that the block is one solid piece.

The plinth blocks are much simpler to produce. Originally, they were made by running a long piece of stock through a shaper to get the correct profile. That length of trim was then cut into five-inch wide pieces to match the width of the rest of the trim. The basic profile of a typical block calls for a trim strip at the top that sticks out somewhat, and it is easily simulated with some half-round.

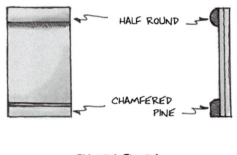

HALF ROUND

CHAMFERED PINE

PLINTH BLOCK

To vary the style a bit, you can use more than one strip of half-round, or some other trim to increase the number of reveals. The beginning block should be the same width and thickness as the target mold and about twice the height.

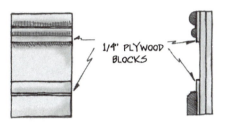

ANOTHER APPROACH

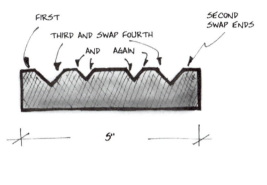

CUT ALL THESE ANGLES WITH THE SAME
DEGREE SETTING BY REVERSING THE BOARD

FIRST

SECOND
SWAP ENDS

THIRD AND SWAP FOURTH

AND   AGAIN

5"

YOU CAN MAKE THIS TRIM ON THE TABLE SAW
USING A REGULAR CIRCULAR BLADE. SET THE
ANGLE AT 45 DEGREES AND SWAP THE ENDS
BACK AND FORTH. READJUST FENCE AS REQ'D

The basic run of trim between the blocks can be made either as a solid piece, or as a series of different strips. It is best not to make this too terribly complicated. The trim should be symmetrical from the center line. A round nose bit on a shaper table is an excellent way to create the rounded channels. The table saw can be used to make the V grooves, and if a shaper is available, it can be used to create beaded effects. It is easier to get the trim sections through the saw if you keep them reasonably short. Sixteen-foot lengths are difficult. Give each piece a bit extra length so that the ends may be trimmed later. Mistakes almost always occur at the end of the board. Since the trim is symmetrical from the center, it is possible to make two passes with each setting of the saw or router table. Just turn the board 180 degrees, and make the second pass. Be sure to do all of the pieces of trim before readjusting the tool. Make all of the trim you will need at one time so that all of the pieces will match. It never hurts to make a few extras just in case.

The build-up method can also be used with these long sections of trim. Cut small strips of trim and apply them to the facing you've already assembled. If you are using this method, just be creative, but look for shapes that are in keeping with the feel of the original. The outside edges should have a larger, squarer profile than those in the center, and again, all the pieces will require a mirror image double.

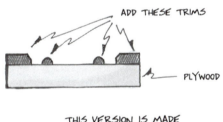

ADD THESE TRIMS

PLYWOOD

THIS VERSION IS MADE
BY BUILDING UP TRIMS

THERE ARE
SEVERAL WAYS
TO MAKE THE
LONG SECTIONS
OF TRIM

Another popular type of doorway design uses a cornice molding at the top of the opening. The basic unit can be made in the same way as previously described. A section of one-by is used across the top as stop for the top of the cornice molding. If you let this stick out a bit, and finish it with some half round or other trim, it will become just another part of the molding. You can use one strip of trim at the bottom of the cornice and another one at the top of the door opening. If you would like for the cornice to be very large and grand, it is possible to build up the thickness of the top of the facing to increase its scale.

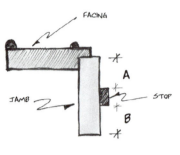

IF THE DOOR SWINGS ONSTAGE, MAKE "A"
THE THICKNESS OF THE DOOR SLAB.

IF THE DOOR SWINGS OFFSTAGE, MAKE "B"
THE THICKNESS OF THE DOOR SLAB.

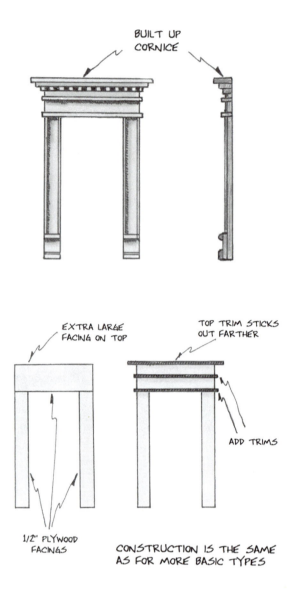

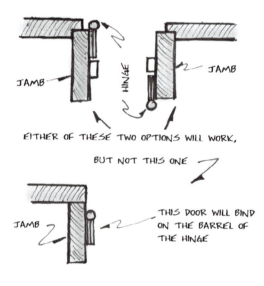

If the door is to open offstage, place the stop by using the same method from the rear of the jamb. The back has only one logical corner to mark from. At this early stage it does not matter whether the door swings left or right, because the stop will need to run on both sides and the top of the jamb anyway. I do not mortise a hole for the hinge into the jamb because it is too hard to do, and stage doors do not really need to fit that tightly anyway. You accounted for the thickness of one leaf of the hinge when you figured the size of the jamb on the original cut list.

If your door frame will be used to hold a door hung with butt hinges, it will need to have a stop strip installed. This strip is generically $5/8$" x 1 $1/4$", but it often varies, for aesthetic reasons. The stop is intended to keep the door from swinging too far into the jamb, so the name fits. A butt hinged door will not operate properly without one. If the door is to swing onstage, the stop should be placed with its onstage edge the same distance from the front of the jamb as the door is thick. Rip a scrap strip of plywood to the same width as the thickness of the door you are hanging. Use this plywood as a guide jig to mark the placement of the stop. If you left a $1/4$" reveal at the junction of the jamb and the facing, the corner of the jamb is the point to measure from. If not, measure from the corner of the facing. A butt hinge will not operate properly if the barrel of the hinge does not extend past the jamb. It is not possible to hang this type of door in the middle of the jamb without a great deal of rather unattractive gouging of the wood.

If a rounded top is required for the door, the frame design must be modified a bit, but the basic concept remains the same. This style is easier to build if you begin by cutting out the facing first. Suppose that the width of the facing is to be 4", and the door itself is to be 2'- 6" wide. It is of standard height, and the arch is Romanesque. Here is a drawing for the face frame showing how the parts fit together. The inside of the frame should be 2'- 7", which is large enough to accommodate a bent plywood reveal around the inside edge of the frame, with $1/4$" added to ease door installation. You can mark the pattern on a sheet of plywood. If the size of the door is very large, it might make more sense to divide the arc into smaller pieces. This will save on materials.

Cut out all the parts, and then glue and staple them into position. At this point the curve of the top will be stiffened and squared, just like the rectilinear unit shown earlier. The pieces are different shapes, but the process is just the same.

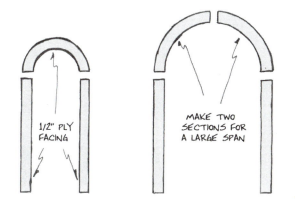

CURVED FACINGS FOR AN ARCHWAY

The straight part of the jamb can be cut to length from $3/4$" x 3 $1/2$" stock. Measure the length from the bottom of the facing to the point where the curve begins. Subtract $1/2$" for the thickness of the threshold. The jamb and side facings can be glued and nailed together, along with the threshold. The second layer of facing should be cut so that the joints fall at a different place in order to create a solid, laminated structure. Make the width of the back layer $3/4$" smaller than the first one where the jamb is in place, but make it run all the way side to side along the curve where you don't yet have a jamb.

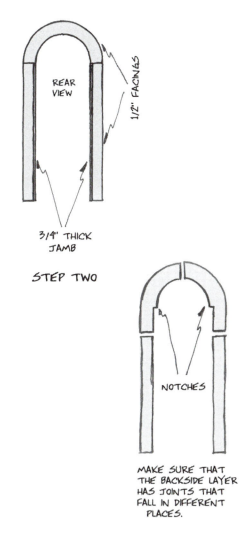

STEP TWO

STEP THREE

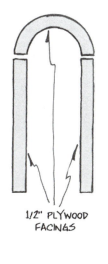

STEP ONE

Now you need to fill in the curved section of the jamb. As you will recall, the opening was made 1" wider than the actual size of the door. This was to accommodate the wood used to fill in the curved section. The best material to use for this purpose is a type of bending plywood that is commonly made from either birch or lauan. Bending plywood is made so that all of the grains in all of the plies are oriented in the same direction. As a result, it is not nearly as strong as regular plywood, but it is extremely flexible. This type of plywood is available in two basic types. One has the grain running the length of the sheet and can be used to bend around tall, thin objects like a column. The other has the grain running across the 4'- 0" direction. This latter type is used to bend around larger, shorter objects like a barrel. Bending plywood is generally $3/8$" thick and is an excellent choice for lining the inside of the doorway arch. The "barrel" type of bending lauan will give you the longest strips to work with and is the best choice. If bending plywood is not available, $1/4$" thick regular lauan or fir plywood will do the job if the arc to be covered is large enough in diameter. It is much harder to put on.

This completes the basic frame. If you feel that the unit needs to be stronger, add another layer of bending lauan to the outside of the curve, or use some small blocks to beef it up. If you use support blocks on the back side, you will need to leave space for them in the rough opening you have in the wall.

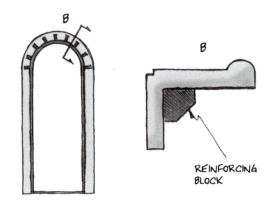

GLUE ON SMALL BLOCKS OF WOOD
TO REINFORCE THE JOINT
IF NECESSARY.

RUN A STRIP OF
BENDING LAUAN
AROUND THE
INSIDE OF THE
DOORWAY TO
FINISH IT OFF.

STEP FOUR

1/4" REVEAL

1/2" PLY
FACING

3/4" JAMB

BENDING
PLYWOOD

Rip several strips of $3/8$" thick bending lauan to $3\,3/4$" wide. Glue and nail a length around the top of the opening first. It would be nice if the center of the strip is at the top of the door, but exact placement is not crucial. However, it is important that the ends of the strips extend past the point where the curved and straight sections join each other. This will impart extra rigidity to the structure. Be sure to use glue. The width of this strip is $1/4$" shy of the actual thickness of the jamb in order to provide a reveal for the barrel of the hinge. Accordingly, make sure to flush it up with the back of the 1x4 jamb and then leave an even $1/4$" space around the curved part. Cut two pieces of bending lauan to fit into the remaining gaps. Glue and nail them into place.

If a door stop is required, rip down a couple of $1\,1/4$" wide strips of the bending lauan and attach them in the normal way. Using the bending lauan will make it possible to match the curve.

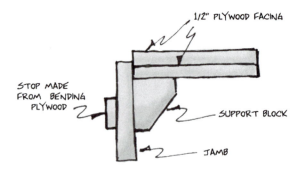

1/2" PLYWOOD FACING

STOP MADE
FROM BENDING
PLYWOOD

SUPPORT BLOCK

JAMB

If trim is required around the outside edge of the face frame it can be made from Ethafoam rod ripped in half on the band saw. The Ethafoam can easily be bent to any possible door diameter. If the door width is reasonably large, it may be possible to bend a piece of white pine around the outside of the frame. The chances are improved if the length of pine is kerfed prior to bending. This is done by cutting a series of slots into the board. Kerfing effectively reduces the thickness of the trim piece. With a thinner piece the outside edge will need to stretch less, and the inside curve will need less compression. This type of work requires considerable filling and sanding. If you have a curved top door that is not round, it is possible to cut out a narrow band of 3/4" plywood that matches whatever shape is required.

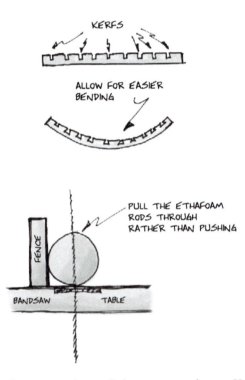

KERFS

ALLOW FOR EASIER BENDING

PULL THE ETHAFOAM RODS THROUGH RATHER THAN PUSHING

FENCE

BANDSAW   TABLE

Perhaps your plans call for a stone archway. You can create that effect by covering the facing with a thin layer of polystyrene foam. Mark divisions on the foam to represent the stone segments and carve out the blocks.

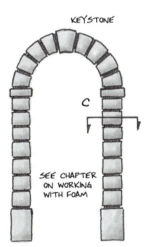

KEYSTONE

C

SEE CHAPTER ON WORKING WITH FOAM

COVER AN ARCH WITH FOAM TO MAKE IT INTO STONE

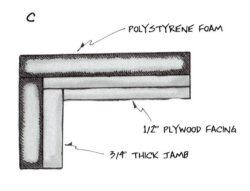

C

POLYSTYRENE FOAM

1/2" PLYWOOD FACING

3/4" THICK JAMB

SECTION THRU FOAM COVER

I like to use the expanded foam for this because it is easily carved into rounded shapes, but really, any kind will do. Add cheesecloth to form a protective coating over the tender foam. More information on working with foam can be found in the chapter on that topic. For a really sturdy piece, plywood can take the place of the foam, but it is of course, more difficult to round over the corners.

Here are some diagrams on how to add a transom light to a door frame. A transom is basically a small window on top of the door that allows for ventilation when the door is shut. You will need to build one of these if you do a play like *The Front Page*, or perhaps *Kiss Me Kate*. The resulting frame is considerably taller than a normal opening.

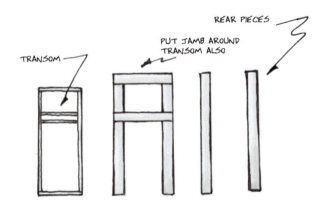

REAR PIECES

PUT JAMB AROUND TRANSOM ALSO

TRANSOM

Here is a plan for construction of a door that must fit under a stairway and that is consequently slanted on the top. This door has a slant of 45 degrees, but the angle can be easily altered to fit a specific stairway. The construction method is the same as the previous types in that the face frame is two layers and overlaps in the corner. This is really the key to the method used for all of these examples. The shape and size of the doorway may change, but the basic construction style remains the same.

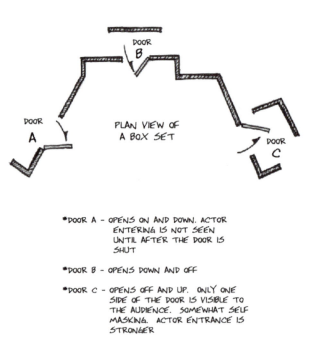

THIS DOOR IS
DESIGNED TO FIT
UNDER A STAIRCASE

1/2" PLYWOOD
FACING

CAN LEAVE OPEN

FROM
THE
FRONT

FROM
THE
BACK

ATTACH LAYER FROM
THE BACK

1/2" PLYWOOD FACING

CONSTRUCTION DETAILS

MAKING THE DOORS

Most of the time it is easier and less expensive to purchase doors than to make them yourself. There are many replications of panel doors available that are made from shaped hardboard and have a hollow core. They are reasonably lightweight and inexpensive. Stage doors are generally meant to be painted, even if that means painting on a wood grain effect, so the fact that the doors are made of hardboard is not a problem. Architectural salvage yards are generally full of doors that have been removed from razed structures. There are times, however, when specific types of doors must be made in the shop, because the design calls for something unique.

First a word about door placement. The direction a door swings is an important factor in the movement of actors. A door that opens the wrong direction makes it difficult for the action of a scene to take place. A home entry door almost always opens to the inside, so that a chain and/or certain types of locks may be used. The entrance door to a business almost always opens out to make sure that the exit will remain clear in case of a fire. Doors that open onstage can make entrances quite awkward, especially if they open "on and down." Doors that open "off and up" will help to mask the area behind the door and will reduce the need for offstage masking. Planning the movement of a door is a design responsibility, but you should have a basic understanding of how those decisions are made.

DOOR
B

DOOR
A

PLAN VIEW OF
A BOX SET

DOOR
C

*DOOR A - OPENS ON AND DOWN. ACTOR
ENTERING IS NOT SEEN
UNTIL AFTER THE DOOR IS
SHUT

*DOOR B - OPENS DOWN AND OFF

*DOOR C - OPENS OFF AND UP. ONLY ONE
SIDE OF THE DOOR IS VISIBLE TO
THE AUDIENCE. SOMEWHAT SELF
MASKING. ACTOR ENTRANCE IS
STRONGER

You may often find it necessary to make some kind of French door, which is really a window you can walk through. In fact, some people refer to these doors as French windows. French doors that open offstage only show on one side, and thus only one side of a real door will need to be reproduced. If it is possible to buy a "real" door, that is absolutely the best thing to do. Unfortunately, scenery designs often call for a door of a specific size that may not be commercially available, or a door with a unique size or style of window panes.

Another reason to include this method of door building is because it is a good example of a laminated construction. Laminating means to glue together a number of different layers in order to make an object that cannot easily be cut from one single piece. It has been discussed repeatedly throughout the book in such diverse structures as stress skin platforms and flat building. The method just covered of constructing door frames is another example of laminating.

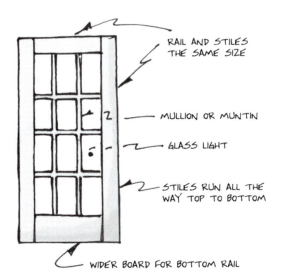

RAIL AND STILES THE SAME SIZE

MULLION OR MUNTIN

GLASS LIGHT

STILES RUN ALL THE WAY TOP TO BOTTOM

WIDER BOARD FOR BOTTOM RAIL

Start designing the structure of the door with a frame that defines the perimeter. The width of the stiles and rails is dependent upon the size of the door. A wide door can support the visual weight of broader stiles than a narrow door can. Double French doors will benefit from reducing the size of the two stiles that touch each other in the middle. The bottom rail of any door should be wider than the top rail.

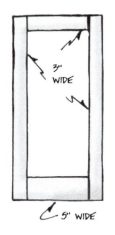

3" WIDE

5" WIDE

1/2" PLYWOOD PARTS

Begin by ripping down some $1/2$" plywood so that it is 3" wide. The best material to use is either $1/2$" lauan or cabinet grade plywood. It is important to use some good stock for this project, as the door will need to stay flat and true on its own, with no help from the surrounding structure. Plywood of any type almost always has at least a small amount of bow to it. The door is made of two layers glued together, and it is important to alternate the bow so that the two layers are in opposition to one another. The finished product will be very flat and stable if you do, but it will be warped and unusable if you do not.

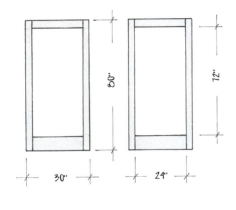

OUTER AND INNER SIZES

You will need one section of plywood that is 5" wide to use as the bottom rail. Note that the stiles run all the way up and down, while the rails fit to the inside. This is the exact opposite of most theatrical construction, but it is the standard method for doors because of the way that hinges are installed on a door. Rip some $1/2$" plywood to cover the joints in the back in the same way you made the facings of the door frames. The rails of the $1/2$" plywood in back run all the way from side to side, opposite to the way the front layer was used, so that the joints are reinforced. Do not put these sections together yet because the mullions will need to be cut and installed first.

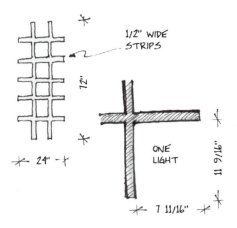

1/2" WIDE STRIPS

12"

24"

ONE LIGHT

11 9/16"

7 11/16"

All of the window sections or "lights" should be the same size. Normally, these lights are taller than they are wide to give the door a slimmer, more elegant appearance. It is best to use a proportion in the neighborhood of 8" wide by 11" tall, but these measurements are intended for reference only. The exact amount will be determined by the size of your door. The outside dimensions of the example door are 30" wide by 80" tall. Use all inch measurements in order to streamline the math. The inside dimensions are 24" wide by 72" tall. Using the rule of thumb about the proper proportions of a light, it is apparent that this opening is capable of holding three lights across and six lights vertically.

The width of the mullions varies from window to window, but it is generally best to make them as narrow as is practical in order to avoid having the window appear too clumsy and homemade. $3/8$" is a good size visually, especially if you plan on adding anything to the sides later on. That is very narrow structurally and you might be better off using $1/2$" wide stock instead. This example uses $1/2$" because the math is easier to follow.

If you need make a door with three lights across, you will have two mullions to account for over the width of the opening. Adding these together gives you one inch; 24" minus 1" is 23". To get the width of each individual light, you must divide the total distance by the number of lights. Twenty-three divided by three is 7 $2/3$. Unfortunately, there isn't a $2/3$" mark on a tape measure, so you must convert this fraction into something useable.

(Strangely, $2/3$ just happens to be a fraction that can be marked with a framing square. One side of the square is divided into 12ths, and $2/3$ can easily be converted to $8/12$. However...)

You can infer something from a higher fraction that is closer to the given amount. The smallest fraction of an inch that can be reliably interpreted from a tape measure is $1/32$". If you multiply $2/3$ by $11/11$ (which is really 1) you get $22/33$, which is remarkably close to $22/32$. This number is most likely close enough, and the discrepancy will work itself out. The fraction $22/32$ can be reduced to $11/16$, and so the total width of every light is 7 $11/16$".

A similar process may be used to determine the heights of the individual lights. The number of spaces is six, and the number of mullions is five. Five times $1/2$" is equal to 2 $1/2$". Subtract this amount from the total height of 72", and you get 69 $1/2$". Divide that amount by six (the number of spaces), and the answer for the height of each of the lights is approximately 11 $6/10$". Using our previous method, the fraction $6/10$ is equal to $18/30$, which is reasonably close to $18/32$ or $9/16$. Hence our measurement for the height of each light is 11 $9/16$". I'm sure that just reading about this technique, it seems so horribly complicated, but after you have done it a few times you realize that it is all just fifth-grade arithmetic in a very complicated word problem.

Now that you have measurements for the lights, your next step is to put the basic frame together. It is necessary for the backing strips of the mullions to extend onto the back of the perimeter framing so that the parts can be firmly attached. The pieces you cut as backing strips for the frame pieces must accommodate the mullion backing strips.

The perimeter frame backing strips for the rails should be cut to a length of 3" + 7 $11/16$", which is 10 $11/16$". This will leave a space in the center for the vertical mullions. You will need two of these pieces at 3" wide for the top of the door, and another two at 5" wide for the bottom. Assemble the frame using a template table to square it and securing the joint with glue and construction staples. There will be a wide gap in the center that will get filled in later by the vertical backing strips.

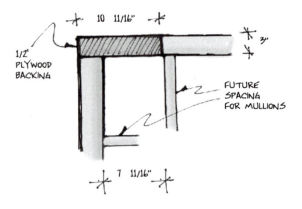

Now turn your attention to the mullions. The first thing you need is some stock that is $1/2$" wide by $1/2$" thick. Rip enough to make all of the mullions and the backing strips. It is best to make the vertical members continuous, and to cut the horizontal mullions to fit around them. The total length of the upright mullions is 72". You will need two of them.

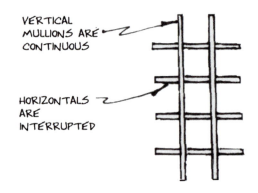

The horizontal mullion pieces for the center are 7 $11/16$" in length, and 15 of these are required. You will also need to cut the backing strips that allow the mullions to be attached to the frame. If the vertical slats run continuously from top to bottom, then it is the horizontal slats that must have a backing strip that is continuous from side to side. The horizontal backing strips should be 30" in length, and 5 are required. The vertical backing pieces will be 11 $9/16$" in length. That is the same as the vertical height of each one of the lights. You will need only 8 of these pieces, as the ones that cover the top and bottom will need to be longer in order to reach across the width of the top and bottom rails. The top two should be 11 $9/16$" + 3", or 14 $9/16$". The bottom two should be 11 $9/16$" + 5", or 16 $9/16$". Wow. That's a lot of fractions, but hopefully you can understand the logical progression of the process. Understanding the process used to get the numbers is much more important than the actual fractions themselves.

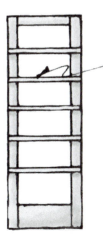

THESE BACKING STRIPS OF 1/2" PLYWOOD RUN ALL THE WAY FROM SIDE TO SIDE

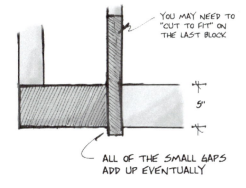

YOU MAY NEED TO "CUT TO FIT" ON THE LAST BLOCK

5"

ALL OF THE SMALL GAPS ADD UP EVENTUALLY

Now you have a large group of small pieces and a perimeter frame. I would suggest that you use a stop block on the radial arm saw in order to increase precision in the cutting process. Be sure to double check the measurements. If you have cut your pieces to the proper length, it should be relatively easy to assemble them. Sometimes it is best to "dry fit" all of the pieces together before gluing them in order to double check your work at the saw. You can avoid a lot of tedious measuring by using your already cut blocks to do it for you. The previously installed corner backing pieces locate the placement of your vertical mullions. Use the four $1/2$"-wide backing pieces you have already cut to attach the two vertical slats.

When all is ready, glue and staple all of the horizontal backing pieces into place. This completes the joining of all of the front parts of the door, but it is still necessary to fill in the gaps on the back so that it is flat, stable, and able to accept the clear acrylic sheet that is substituted for glass. Some of the parts are already cut and ready for placement. Cut the remainder to fit from the $1/2$" plywood that has already been ripped down to 3" or 5".

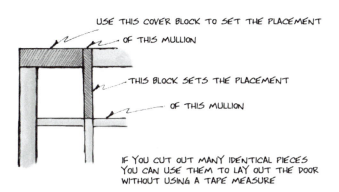

USE THIS COVER BLOCK TO SET THE PLACEMENT OF THIS MULLION

THIS BLOCK SETS THE PLACEMENT

OF THIS MULLION

IF YOU CUT OUT MANY IDENTICAL PIECES YOU CAN USE THEM TO LAY OUT THE DOOR WITHOUT USING A TAPE MEASURE

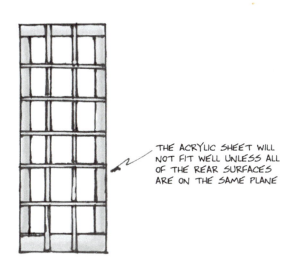

THE ACRYLIC SHEET WILL NOT FIT WELL UNLESS ALL OF THE REAR SURFACES ARE ON THE SAME PLANE

Use the eight 11 $9/16$" vertical backing pieces to set the gaps between the horizontal mullions by placing them temporarily in the spaces between the slats. If there is a difference between the pieces you have cut and the area they must fill, try to work it out by dividing the discrepancy between the pieces. If the amount is too great, you may wish to cut one or more of the members a bit differently. If things are way off, then there is most likely an arithmetic error somewhere.

I realize that this all seems so horribly over-complicated, but using the laminating technique is a great way to build large and/or complicated shapes. I have used it for all kinds of things from really long stiffeners to wagon wheels to trees. Cutting the parts for a project like this is made easier by the fact that sizes keep repeating themselves.

A few years ago, I used this method to build several sets of Art Deco-style doors that it would not have been possible to purchase commercially. Those doors were made from three layers of half-inch lauan and had lights with unusual shapes.

The third layer gave me a thicker door that was extremely stable. Of course it was a bit time consuming, but the end product was very pleasing to the designer and to myself. Hopefully the patrons liked them as well.

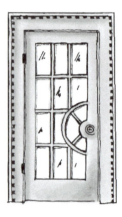

IF YOU CAN'T BUY IT
YOU'LL HAVE TO MAKE IT

Acrylic sheet, also known as Plexiglas, can be cut and drilled with ordinary woodworking tools as long as you take care not to overstress the material. It can be quite brittle, especially when working with very thin sheets. Cut a sheet of $1/8$" thick acrylic to 30" x 80", the size of the outer dimensions of our door. Drill an $1/8$" diameter hole every foot or so around the outside edge of the plastic, about an inch in from the edge. Use these holes to screw the sheet into place. Be careful not to overtighten the screws, or the plastic will break.

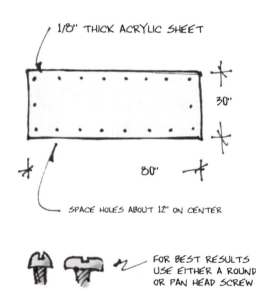

1/8" THICK ACRYLIC SHEET

30"

80"

SPACE HOLES ABOUT 12" ON CENTER

FOR BEST RESULTS
USE EITHER A ROUND
OR PAN HEAD SCREW

The only thing really wrong with this method is that the mullions lack a sense of complexity. Real mullions have a profile edge rather than just a square corner. You can dress these up a bit by adding some trim around the inside edges of each of the lights. Rip some stock to about $1/8$" x $1/2$" in size. You will need enough to do the entire job and some extra for mistakes. If you have been successful in making your lights a uniform size, it should be easy to cut these insert pieces to length. There are 27 lights in this door. Cut at least 54 pieces that are 11 $9/16$" long. Cut a similar amount of horizontal sections to 7 $7/16$" long. This is $1/4$" shorter than the original members that will account for the two $1/8$" thick trim pieces, which will be put into place first. If these trim pieces are reasonably snug, it should be possible just to glue them in place without fasteners. After the glue is dry, sand the entire door to finish it off. Sand your project before the acrylic sheet is attached to avoid scratching it. Sometimes it is best to put off installing the glass until after the door has been painted.

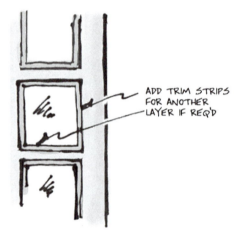

ADD TRIM STRIPS
FOR ANOTHER
LAYER IF REQ'D

An alternate and easier method of adding to the trim, is to build up something on top of the mullions. Rip down some white pine into $1/4$" x $1/4$" strips. Mount these strips in the center of the mullion faces, and around the perimeter of the frame. Leave a space around the perimeter that matches the space between the edge of the trim and the edge of the mullion. This will help to create an extra reveal line. A larger piece of trim used around the outside edge of the door will give it a heavier, more realistic look.

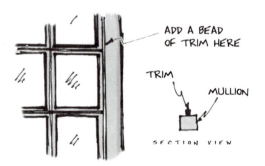

ADD A BEAD
OF TRIM HERE

TRIM

MULLION

SECTION VIEW

"Real" doors of this sort are made using cutters on a shaper. A shaper is like a really large stationary type of router, where the cutters are sticking up rather than down. Two sets of cutters are used to form positive and negative profiles. The cutters have been very precisely manufactured so that the wooden parts they cut will have a snug fit that is suitable to join with carpenter's glue.

SHAPER AND RAISED PANEL DOOR
YOU CAN SEE A FINGER BOARD USED TO HOLD THE WORK FLAT TO THE TABLE, AND A SET OF CUTTER HEADS IN THE CENTER.

You can make a door by cutting the sides of the stiles so they have a positive profile, and the ends of the rails so that they have a negative profile. Glue and clamp all of the joints together. Most passage-type doors are somewhere between 1 1/4" and 1 3/4" thick, and you need to use cutters that will accommodate that thickness. They tend to be quite expensive, but you can use them many times. Cabinet door cutters are much more common and are meant for stock that is about 3/4" thick. The smaller doors are much easier to construct.

HOLLOW-CORE DOORS

Sometimes you may wish to alter a lauan hollow-core door into another shape, or to put a window in it, or make some other modification. Hollow-core doors are an excellent choice for this sort of thing because they are lightweight and inexpensive. These doors are engineered using the same principles as a stress-skin platform. There are two thin sides that are glued onto a lightweight framing. There are small lumber or composite strips around the outside to provide hard points for attaching hardware and for keeping the profile rigid. The inside of the door is braced with corrugated cardboard bent into a zigzag pattern. This makes for an amazingly strong structure, considering that the outer skins are only 1/8" or less thick. Such lightweight materials make it easy to cut the door to some other shape, but care must be taken to ensure that the edges of any modified area be resealed to preserve the rigidity of the structure.

These doors are available in a wide range of sizes. Some are prehung in a jamb and are not suitable for our purposes. You can modify a hollow core door for much less than it costs to make an equivalent structure yourself from scratch. It is a lot less trouble too, but remember that 6'- 8" is the tallest they come.

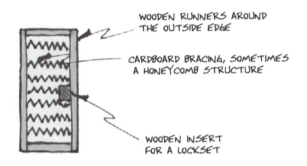

WOODEN RUNNERS AROUND THE OUTSIDE EDGE

CARDBOARD BRACING, SOMETIMES A HONEYCOMB STRUCTURE

WOODEN INSERT FOR A LOCKSET

INTERIOR OF A HOLLOW-CORE DOOR

Changing the top of a hollow-core door is a common way of remaking one. For this example suppose that the design calls for the top of the door to have a rounded profile. Before cutting the door, check to see if there is a marking for the top, and/or a marking for the bevel side. On some doors, the block of solid wood that makes it possible to install a lockset is of such a size and shape that the door can only be used one way. This type should have "top" marked on one end. The bevel edge is the one that will hold the lockset, and the opposite edge is the hinge side. The bevel is provided to make the door seal more tightly, and also to close without striking the jamb. If the profile of your door is such that it will make a difference which side is which, then you must determine which end/side you should work from before beginning. These doors come in left- and right-handed versions, so you have a 50-50 chance of the bevel being correct. If necessary, you can run the door through the table saw to change the direction of the bevel and only lose about an eighth inch or so of material. The door will probably still fit OK, and you can make sure by not mortising for the hinge. That would get your eighth inch back when the door is hung.

DOOR BEVEL

JAMB

To lay out the circle that forms the top of the door, use either a large bow compass or trammel points. (That shop-made compass just keeps coming up, doesn't it?) Use a jig saw to cut away the unused portion of the top. Be aware that the surface of a lauan door is easily splintered, so take whatever precautions are available. The grain of the door runs up and down. If you cut from one side to the top, and then start over on the other side to the top, most of the tearout will occur on the scrap part of the door.

Note that the inside of the door is filled with cardboard spacers, and that some of them extend all the way to the edge you have just cut. It will be necessary to peel back the cardboard a bit to install the new edging. This can be done with a sharp chisel or a utility knife. Don't tear away more than is necessary, as the cardboard is in large part what really what holds the door together. The resulting space between skins will be somewhere in the neighborhood of 1 1/8". Measure your door exactly and trim down a length of 2x4 so that it is the same thickness. This can be done on a thickness planer if you have one, or on the table saw by making a cut from one side, turning the piece over, and making another pass from the other side, or on the bandsaw if yours is large enough to cut through the 3 1/2". Lay the resulting 1 1/8" x 3 1/2" stock on top of the door. Use the center point to mark the ends of the boards so that they will fit together end to end. Depending on the radius of the curve, it may take several sections of wood to fill the void. Use a straight edge to mark the end angles from the center point of the original curve. This will ensure that they fit together properly. You need only about an inch or so of material inside the door.

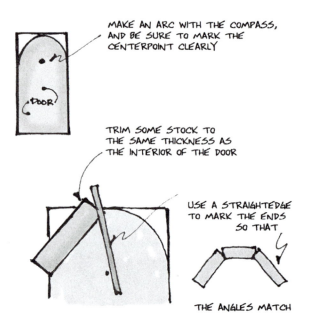

MAKE AN ARC WITH THE COMPASS, AND BE SURE TO MARK THE CENTERPOINT CLEARLY

DOOR

TRIM SOME STOCK TO THE SAME THICKNESS AS THE INTERIOR OF THE DOOR

USE A STRAIGHTEDGE TO MARK THE ENDS SO THAT

THE ANGLES MATCH

It is best to join these filler pieces to the door using only glue because the lauan skins are so thin that any type of nail or screw or staple will do more harm than good. Use plenty of glue, and clamp the two sides together using some extra boards to spread out the holding power of the clamps. The boards will also keep the clamps from making round marks in the soft lauan skin.

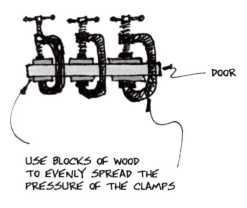

DOOR

USE BLOCKS OF WOOD TO EVENLY SPREAD THE PRESSURE OF THE CLAMPS

Don't worry about cutting a curve on the filler boards until after the glue has set up. It is more important to get a good glue bond so that the door will stay together well. If you cut the curve first, it will be much harder to line everything up.

Another common modification to a lauan door is to make an insert, such as a window, in the center of the door. The process is much the same as with the top of the door, but this time you will need to put some glass in the hole. Cut out the center of the door, so that the hole is larger than the glass area needs to be. Fill in the edges with small strips of wood glued into place. These will need to be the same thickness as the inside of the door, and the process is much like that used for the curved top door, except that the pieces are straight instead of curved.

Rip some stock to perhaps $1/2$" x 1 $1/2$" in size, and use it to line the inside of the hole where the window will go. These pieces form the base for mounting the glass and also cover up the rough edges left over from installing the spacers inside the door. Let these pieces stick out just a bit to make a line of trim around the window. Allowing the trim to stick out from the surface will give the insert a cleaner look than trying to match everything up flush. Cut some small trim pieces to $3/8$" x $1/2$" (or get some small quarter round) and use this as a stop to hold the window in place. Notice how the trims are sized to create a number of reveals that enhance the appearance of the window. Of course "glass" refers to acrylic sheet. Real glass on stage is quite dangerous.

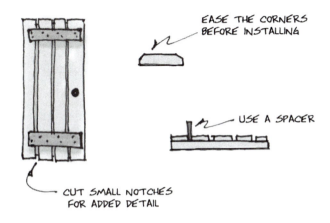

CUT SMALL NOTCHES FOR ADDED DETAIL

EASE THE CORNERS BEFORE INSTALLING

USE A SPACER

These have been only a few of the possibilities of altering/making doors, but the methods shown here can be adapted to fit many more needs.

HANGING DOORS

The process of attaching a door to a jamb is known as hanging the door. Whether it is a door that you have bought, made, or found on the street, the process of hanging a door is basically the same. The door must be checked for the proper size to fit into the jamb, hinges must be put on, and the lockset installed. The procedure must occur in that sequence in order to avoid repeating a step.

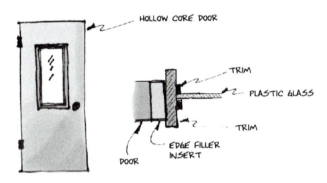

HOLLOW CORE DOOR

TRIM

PLASTIC GLASS

TRIM

EDGE FILLER INSERT

DOOR

PUTTING AN INSERT IN A HOLLOW CORE DOOR

Occasionally, it is necessary to make a door look as though it is made of strips of wood, rather than one solid slab. This can easily be done by adding some strips to the front of a hollow core door. It is tempting to simply use the table saw to plow some grooves into the surface of the door, but the veneer is so thin that it cannot accept such treatment. Cut some strips of $1/4$" lauan to the desired widths. Use a sander to ease the corners of these strips before they are put into place. Glue and staple them to the door using spacers made of an appropriately thick material. The spacers are a quick way to ensure uniformity when laying down the individual slats. Just be aware that the spacers tend to let the slats creep out of alignment after a while. Every so often (once or twice on something as narrow as a door), use a tape measure to check if the slats are parallel to the side. Fudge them back into position if there is a problem. Remember that this process will make the door thicker than it was. It will therefore require more room in the jamb, and the door stop must be laid out accordingly.

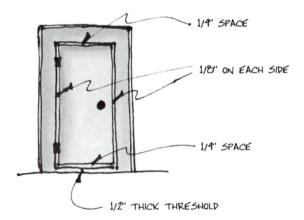

1/4" SPACE

1/8" ON EACH SIDE

1/4" SPACE

1/2" THICK THRESHOLD

Any door you are hanging must be slightly smaller that the hole it will fit into. This would seem to be obvious, but the real problem is how much smaller. The amount varies from one situation to another, but in general, stage doors do not need to fit as tightly as "real" doors do. The front door to your home must keep out rain and cold drafts, so a tight fit is mandatory. These factors are not usually a problem on the stage. It is much more important in the theatre that the door operate smoothly and dependably. If the door is too tight, it may swell from humidity and stick. Faux finish painting tends to be quite thick, and may cause the door to bind. Keeping in mind that the door should have some extra play, I like to leave $1/4$" space at the top, $1/4$" from the threshold, and $1/4$" from side to side. Thus, if the opening is 30" x 80 $1/4$", the door slab should be 29 $3/4$" x 79 $3/4$", so trim it down accordingly. In a perfect world, the frame would have been constructed to exactly the right size, but in reality this rarely happens. The designer may often not find "just the right look" until long after the frame has been built. It is always good to use methods that are flexible enough to make reasonable changes. Of course, there is just no way to cut down a 36" wide door to fit into a 30" wide frame.

Note that the bottom of the door is already spaced $1/2$" from the floor because of the thickness of the threshold. This means that the swinging door actually has $3/4$" clearance from the stage floor, which is just about right. This will allow the door to pass over irregularities on the surface, and/or things like rugs that may not appear on the groundplan. Also, if the wall is not exactly plumb, you may have a problem with door clearance as it swings open wide. If the wall is tilted slightly toward the door side, this is almost sure to happen. Leaving extra clearance space is a good idea. The audience won't see it and it is good insurance.

THE 3/4" SPACE WILL ALLOW THE DOOR TO SWING EASILY OVER OBSTRUCTIONS ON THE FLOOR WITHOUT GETTING JAMMED

As shown before, the side of the door that holds the lockset is traditionally beveled a few degrees to ease the process of closing the door. If you need to trim one side to make the door fit, that is generally the side to trim. If you must trim more than a quarter of an inch or so, you may need to consider what effect this will have on the solid wood inserts on the inside of the door that form the stable base for the lockset. Sometimes it is best to trim just a bit off both sides of the door. If the door is solid wood the question is how much can be lost before the proportions get screwy. There are limits to how much may be removed without ruining the door. Any trimming of the vertical size is best done from the bottom. Remember to ease the corners just a bit with sandpaper once the trimming is done.

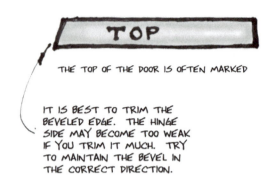

THE TOP OF THE DOOR IS OFTEN MARKED

IT IS BEST TO TRIM THE BEVELED EDGE. THE HINGE SIDE MAY BECOME TOO WEAK IF YOU TRIM IT MUCH. TRY TO MAINTAIN THE BEVEL IN THE CORRECT DIRECTION.

The next step is to install the hinges. The butt hinges you use will need to be of a proper size for the thickness of the door. All of the barrel of the hinge must extend past the face of the door, or it will bind when operating. If the hinge is extremely large, it may cause the lockset side of the door to bind on the jamb when closing.

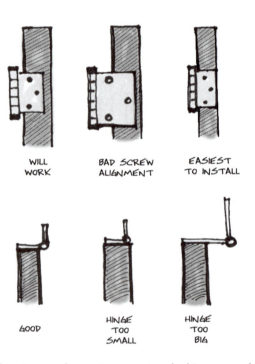

WILL WORK

BAD SCREW ALIGNMENT

EASIEST TO INSTALL

GOOD

HINGE TOO SMALL

HINGE TOO BIG

There is some leeway in mounting the hinges as to how far they extend onto the edge of the door. It is possible to install the hinge so that it is more to one side than the other, but care must be taken to ensure that the screw holes not get too close to the edge. All of the hinges must be of the same size and type, and must be mounted in the exact same way, or they will bind. Binding is indicated by creaking and groaning noises, and by an increasing difficulty in swinging the door. Binding will eventually cause the door to fail by causing the screws to pop out. Binding is a result of the hinge pins being out of alignment with one another, so that some part of the structure must warp out of shape when the door swings.

Most lightweight stage doors will work just fine with two hinges. Sometimes, when an unusually heavy or peculiar door is required, it may be necessary to use three hinges. Study the door to determine which side of the door the barrels should be on (the side the door swings to), and which end will be the top of the door. Lay the door down so that the hinge edge is up in the air. It is customary to center the top hinge 7" from the top, and the bottom hinge 12" from the bottom. Make the marks accordingly. It is fine just to mark the center of the placement, as the hinge will most likely have a screw hole in the middle that can be used to align the hinge. Open the hinge to a 90-degree angle and place it on the door edge, centered on the mark you just made. Snug the hinge up to the corner so that it is square and the two lines you mark on either side will be also. Mark the top and bottom of the hinge. Repeat the procedure on any other hinges.

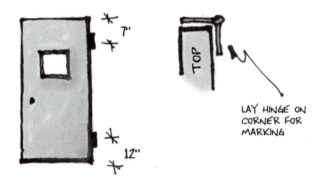

7"

12"

TOP

LAY HINGE ON
CORNER FOR
MARKING

Use the marks you made as a guide in mortising the wood to accept the hinges. A mortise is a depression created in wood so that the face of the hardware will be flush with the surface. There are jigs that you can buy for your router that act as a guide in making the mortise, and if you have one, then follow the directions on the box. If not, you can make the mortise free hand with the router, and/or use a hammer and chisel.

Using a chisel takes a bit of skill, and the chisel must be very sharp to work well. Begin by marking the outline of the mortise using the hinge itself. Make sure that the flat side of the chisel is facing away from the mortise. The bevel side is toward the mortise. Use the hammer to strike the chisel and cut in along the outside lines. Once the perimeter has been established, use the chisel to score the inside of the mortise area, every $1/4$" or so. This scoring must be done at a right angle to the direction of the grain of the wood. Try to hit the chisel with the same amount of force on every blow so that it will cut into the wood the same amount each time. Notice that these actions result in some quasi-loose $1/4$" wide chunks inside the mortise area. These can be removed by raking the area with the chisel. Use the chisel with the flat side down to pare away small slivers of wood. Do not use the hammer

when the chisel is in the flat position, because there is too much danger of splitting the wood and/or removing too much material. Repeat the process until the mortise is smooth and clean. The hinge should fit in so that it is square, snug, and flush with the surface of the door edge. The chisel must be very sharp in order to work well.

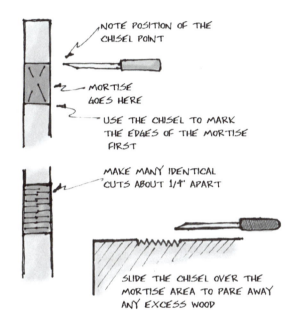

NOTE POSITION OF THE
CHISEL POINT

MORTISE
GOES HERE

USE THE CHISEL TO MARK
THE EDGES OF THE MORTISE
FIRST

MAKE MANY IDENTICAL
CUTS ABOUT 1/4" APART

SLIDE THE CHISEL OVER THE
MORTISE AREA TO PARE AWAY
ANY EXCESS WOOD

A router will speed up the job, but it is still better to finish off with the chisel. After the area has been marked, set up your router with a straight cutting bit. The bit should extend past the face plate an amount equal to the thickness of one leaf of the hinge. Use the router to clear away the interior of the mortise, leaving just a bit at the edges. The router is hard to control without a jig, and it is difficult to get the edges just right. It is easier to just get close, and then use the chisel to finish off the job.

BIT SHOULD EXTEND BELOW
THE PLATE AN AMOUNT
EQUAL TO THE THICKNESS
OF ONE LEAF OF THE HINGE.

FINISH EDGES WITH A CHISEL
WHEN NECESSARY

Once the mortises are complete, attach the hinges to the door. Use the screws that came with the hinge. Drill pilot holes if necessary. Make sure that the hinges go on straight, and that they hang on or off the door the same amount. Otherwise the door will not swing straight and/or will bind. Be certain to attach the hinges so that they are top up, so that the pins are removable going up. If the hinge is upside down, it is sometimes possible for the pin to slip out inadvertently. If the door is really small in the jamb you may not need to mortise at all, but there will be a fairly large gap as a result.

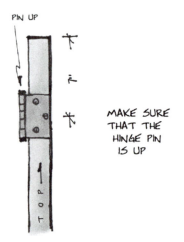

MAKE SURE THAT THE HINGE PIN IS UP

PIN UP

I think that it is easiest to install the lockset before the door is hung, but it is certainly possible to do it after. There are a number of different types of locksets, but only a couple of them are in common use today. Old-style sets may require a huge square mortise in the edge of the door and are extremely difficult to install. I try to avoid these. If you must use one, my advice is to study the lock and use the methods shown for simpler sets first.

SIDE VIEW OF AN OLD STYLE LATCH THAT REQUIRES A LARGE MORTISE

APPX 3 1/2"

The two main divisions of locksets are those known as locking, and the simpler, passage type. Some dummy sets are sold for closet doors that are really just for show. Dum-

mies consist of just the knob with no latch, and will not hold the door shut at all. Passage knobs are intended for interior rooms where there is no need to restrict access by locking the door. Locking sets are those that include a lock. Passage knobs are the most useful in the theatre, as there is generally no need to lock any door on a set unless the action of the play calls for it. Even then it is best not to really lock the door because it may be difficult to unlock later on. Dummy knobs work well if some other catch is used to hold the door shut.

NO SPINDLE REQUIRED

GETS SCREWED DIRECTLY TO THE DOOR

DUMMY KNOB

Newer locksets have three main parts, the knob with the spindle attached, the knob that the spindle fits into, and the latch. The spindle is a shaft that fits through the latch. The latch operates when the spindle rotates, and is what holds the door to the jamb. The strike plate fits on the jamb and defines a hole for the latch to fit into. Note that the spindle is permanently attached to one of the knobs. In older locksets, the spindle is a separate part.

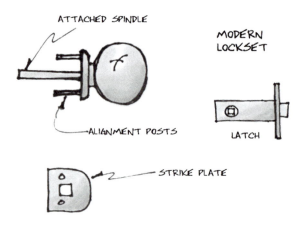

ATTACHED SPINDLE

MODERN LOCKSET

ALIGNMENT POSTS

LATCH

STRIKE PLATE

Installation of the new-style locksets is rather straightforward. If the set has just been purchased, then there should be some instructions in the package. What they basically say is that two holes will need to be drilled into the door, a large one on the face for the knob/spindle assembly, and a smaller one on the edge for the latch. These sizes vary a bit depending on the manufacturer, but the large hole will be somewhere in the neighborhood of 1 $3/4$" to 2" in size and the small one either $7/8$" or 1". The center of the knob, and therefore the large hole, should be 36" from the bottom of the door, or for a panel door, centered on the toggle closest to that amount.

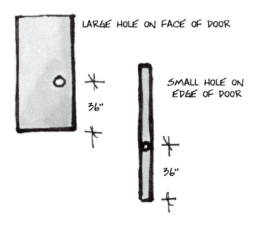

LARGE HOLE ON FACE OF DOOR

SMALL HOLE ON EDGE OF DOOR

36"

36"

A new lockset will have a template in the package that shows how far to mark the hole from the edge of the door. If the template is missing, measure the latch from the outside part to the center of the spindle hole. This is the distance in from the edge of the door to the center of the large hole. This hole should be drilled all the way through the door slab. If you are using a hole saw, cut through one side far enough for the pilot hole to get established on the other. Turn the door over and center the hole saw on the pilot hole. Then drill the second side. This will prevent tearout on the backside of the door from drilling all the way through. The tearout will be confined to the inside of the door.

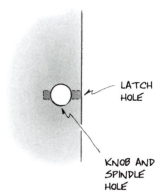

LATCH HOLE

KNOB AND SPINDLE HOLE

The $7/8$" latch hole is centered the same measurement from the bottom of the door, and it should also be centered front to back on the edge. This hole will be drilled all the

way through to the large hole. Sometimes it is necessary to drill past the large hole, when the latch needs to extend further into the door. To determine the depth of the $7/8$" hole, hold the latch up to the door and see what is required.

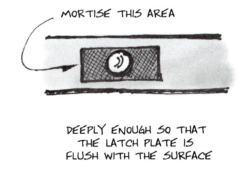

MORTISE THIS AREA

DEEPLY ENOUGH SO THAT THE LATCH PLATE IS FLUSH WITH THE SURFACE

Once these holes have been drilled, a mortise must be created in the door edge so that the latch plate will fit flush to the edge of the door. If the latch plate is not mortised into the door, it will catch on the jamb when the door is shut. Feed the latch into the door as far as it will go, and square it up with the edges. Mark around the perimeter of the plate and remove the latch. The mortise can be made with a chisel in the same way that the hinge mortises were made. Slide the latch back into place and secure it with the two screws provided.

SELECT THE PROPER ORIENTATION FOR THE LATCH BY FLIPPING IT OVER

Make sure that the latch is pointing in the right direction for it to work. The bevel side should be on the side of the door that fits into the frame. Feed the knob with the spindle through the latch. There are most likely two screw posts on the knob that line up with holes in the latch. It should be intuitive how the other knob fits on and how the screws are used to connect the two knobs. A screwdriver on angle will usually fit well enough to tighten the screws, but sometimes an offset screwdriver is required. The door is now ready to hang in the jamb.

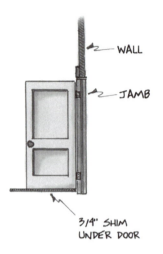

WALL

JAMB

3/4" SHIM
UNDER DOOR

You have made no mortise in the jamb to accept the hinge halves that must fit against it. "Real" doors are mortised into the jamb, but I can find no reason to do it for the stage. The door will fit just fine if you have accounted for the discrepancy by making the door a tad smaller as discussed earlier. You will recall that the door was left $1/4$" narrow for the hole. Half of this amount is used up by not mortising the jamb, and the remaining $1/8$" is to allow a bit of slack for the door to close easily. Mortising the jamb is a time consuming chore.

The door must be fitted into the jamb. Either install the frame in its wall with drywall screws, or clamp the door frame to something to keep it vertical. Lay a $3/4$" thick shim on the floor at a right angle to the hinge side of the opening. Set the door in place with the hinges in a position to be screwed onto the jamb. The shim will automatically adjust the height of the door in the frame, but it is important that the entire assembly be plumb, or the shim will not work properly, and the centering will be off.

STOP

LEAVE A SMALL SPACE
TO KEEP THE DOOR
FROM BINDING

When screwing the hinges in place, make sure that there is about a $1/16$" to $3/32$" gap between the face of the door and the door stop. If the door is hung too far into the jamb, it will hit the stop and not close properly. If the hinge has been installed so that the far edge of the hinge (opposite the barrel) is flush with the edge of the door, it will be easy to gauge the alignment. Put only one screw in each hinge, and shut the door to see if it fits well. If it does not close properly, take note of where it is binding, and fix the problem. If there is a good fit, finish putting in the rest of the screws.

1" HOLE FOR
LATCH

YOU CAN BEND
THE STRIKE
PLATE TO GET
A BETTER FIT

The final step is to install the strike plate. Close the door and mark the center of the latch. This should be 36" from the bottom, of course, but it is easier and more accurate to mark the placement from the latch. With the vertical placement taken care of, measure the thickness of the door, and divide the amount in two. This is the distance of the center of the strike plate hole from the edge of the door stop. Drill a 1" diameter hole about $1/2$" deep on this mark. Put the strike plate into position, and screw it down. There is a bit of trial and error involved in finding the correct front-to-back placement for the strike plate. Opening and closing the door a few times after the hole has been drilled will make it easier to judge the exact placement. It is usually not necessary to mortise the strike plate unless there is some compelling reason to do so (Like the door won't shut without it!).

There are other types of knobs, spindles, and latches. The other main type of system uses an old-style spindle that is separate from the two knobs. This spindle is square, and it has machine screw threads on the corners to make it possible to screw the spindle into the knob. The spindle is square so that a set-screw through the knobs can be used to keep them from rotating on the spindle after the screws are tightened.

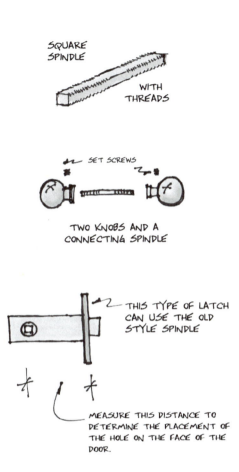

SQUARE SPINDLE

WITH THREADS

SET SCREWS

TWO KNOBS AND A CONNECTING SPINDLE

THIS TYPE OF LATCH CAN USE THE OLD STYLE SPINDLE

MEASURE THIS DISTANCE TO DETERMINE THE PLACEMENT OF THE HOLE ON THE FACE OF THE DOOR.

use a set screw to secure it. Feed the spindle through the hole to the opposite side of the door. You will most likely want to use some kind of rosette or plate to cover the $^3/_4$" hole drilled in the door. The knobs won't turn efficiently without them. Screw in the other knob so that it fits snugly, but with sufficient room to turn very easily, and use the second set screw. The return spring on the latch is not very strong, so if there is any binding of the mechanism, the latch may not pop open and keep the door shut.

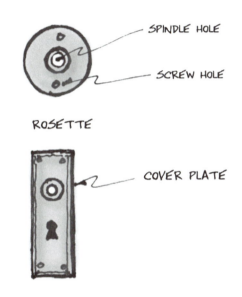

SPINDLE HOLE

SCREW HOLE

ROSETTE

COVER PLATE

There are some kinds of oddball spindles that have no threads, and these will not work with the kind I am describing. Some spindles have threaded holes in them so that the set screw is actually screwed into the spindle, rather than being held in place by threads on the knob. Most of the time, the different types will not work interchangeably. The square spindle with threads but no holes in it is the most commonly found. It is meant to work with most old glass knobs and other "antique" types. These locksets were originally intended to work with the large square latches that require considerable expertise to mortise. This type of lock most often uses a "skeleton" type of key. You can still buy these, but they are rather difficult to install. An alternative is a new type of latch that is being made to fit the old style of spindle. It looks like a regular modern latch, but the spindle hole is made to fit the older, square spindle. They are excellent for hanging antique-style knobs that are very popular with designers.

Installation is quite simple. Scribe a line that is 36" from the bottom of the door. Use the latch to determine the distance of the center of the spindle from the edge of the door and drill a $^3/_4$" diameter hole. Mark, drill, and mortise the latch hole in the regular way. Install the latch with its two screws, again making sure that the latch is pointing the correct way. Screw the spindle into one of the knobs, and

There are many different types of doorknobs, latches, locks, plates, etc., and more are invented every day. The two types presented here are the easiest to work with, but you will no doubt run into many more. The basic principles of measuring, mortising, and mechanics should remain mostly the same.

WINDOWS

Window techniques are very similar to those used in the construction of doors. The basic idea is to put together a frame that will fit into a rough opening in a wall made of flats. The rough opening should be enough larger than the insert so that the window will fit in easily. The facing trim is quite a bit larger than the part of the window that fits through the opening, so you can have considerable space between the opening and the window itself. If the space is too small, however, you won't be able to get it to fit in the opening.

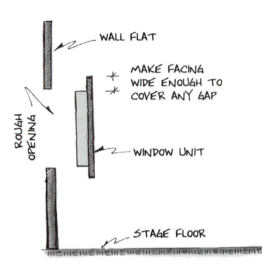

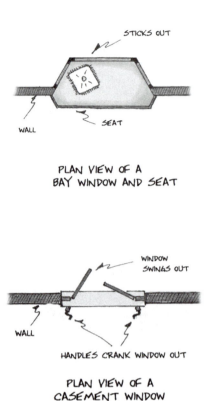

PLAN VIEW OF A
BAY WINDOW AND SEAT

PLAN VIEW OF A
CASEMENT WINDOW

Window jambs are made in the same way as door jambs, but since the facings do not normally extend all the way to the floor, an apron is placed across the bottom of the unit. The differences are mainly cosmetic, with the structural methods of joining the parts together remaining the same.

The movable portion of a window is called the sash, and each window pane or section of glass is known as a light. The bottom part of the window where you could rest an object is the sill. Trim that fits on the wall under the sill is the apron. Windows having two sashes, one hung over the other rigged to slide up and down are called double hung windows and are the most popular type. A window that cranks outward when a handle is turned is a casement widow. A series of three or more windows that project out the side of a wall is a bay window. Old style windows use a pulley system with ropes and weights to balance the weight of the window and keep it from falling down. This is where "sash cord" gets its name, because it was originally used to connect the sash with an iron weight hidden inside the wall.

The first step in making a window is to determine the size of the jamb as it relates to the rough opening and the size of the sash. You can let the dimensions of the sash determine everything else. If the opening occupied by the sash is 24" wide by 36" tall, then the inside of the jamb will be 24" x 36". The outside measurement will be 25 $\frac{1}{2}$" x 37 $\frac{1}{2}$" when framed with one-by material. You should make the rough opening in the flats somewhat larger than this. Just to make things even and to give a little extra room to insert the window, you should make the rough opening $\frac{1}{2}$" larger in each direction. For this example, the rough opening would be 26" x 38". As a rule of thumb, the rough should be 2" larger in each direction than the sash opening.

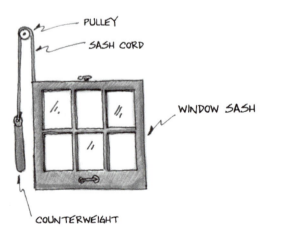

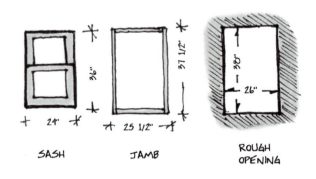

The next step is to build the jamb, and this is done in the same way as a door jamb. The width of the material used is somewhat dependent upon the style of window, and the method of constructing it. Sash that must actually move up and down will require an extra amount of room to fit in all of the working parts. As in door construction, the stiles run all the way from top to bottom, and the two rails fit inside.

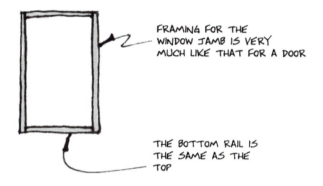

FRAMING FOR THE
WINDOW JAMB IS VERY
MUCH LIKE THAT FOR A DOOR

THE BOTTOM RAIL IS
THE SAME AS THE
TOP

The width of the stock used to create the facing is dependent upon the design of the trim, but for our purposes say that the facing itself will be 5" wide. You would normally want the window trim to match the door trim. As you will recall, the door trim had a $1/4$" reveal between the jamb and the facing so that the barrel of the hinge had a place to go. This particular window will have an extra piece added to the jamb later on that will take the place of this reveal, so you do not need to account for it now.

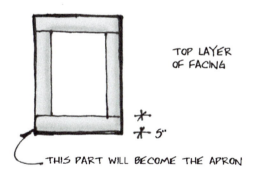

TOP LAYER
OF FACING

← 5"

THIS PART WILL BECOME THE APRON

The rear piece of plywood for the facing must be ripped narrower than the front section to allow for the space taken up by the jamb. In this case, since there is no reveal, the $1/2$" plywood should be 4 $1/4$" wide. Naturally, you will want to arrange the corner so that the two layers of plywood overlap one another and give the joint a great deal of strength.

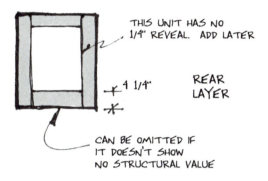

THIS UNIT HAS NO
1/4" REVEAL. ADD LATER

← 4 1/4"

REAR
LAYER

CAN BE OMITTED IF
IT DOESN'T SHOW
NO STRUCTURAL VALUE

So far, no parts have been included that would represent a window sill. In an old-style real-world window, the sill, or stool, was put in first. The facing trim around the window and the apron were attached last. This is still the way to go when you are nailing everything directly to a solid wall, but since we are making a removable independent unit, it makes more sense to create a strong box shape first and add the trim later. There is no concern about how well the window will keep out wind and rain, so there is no need to add an angle to the sill. The sill is formed by cutting a strip of white pine that protrudes from the facing about 1 $1/4$". The exact size and shape will depend upon the design, but generally it works well to use stock 1" thick and to extend the sill past the edges of the facing by one or two inches. Glue and nail the sill in place. Cut some small blocks of pine that will fit on the ends of the sill between it and the wall. These parts are to fill the small gap that exists there. Glue these parts in place and use clamps to hold them until the glue sets. It is best to do any shaping of this piece now, before any other trim is in the way. White pine is rather soft, and it is quite easy to get a rounded over profile with just a sander. Finish trimming the face frame with whatever trim style is appropriate to your design.

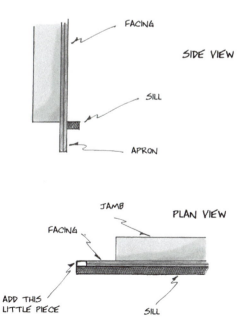

FACING

SIDE VIEW

SILL

APRON

JAMB

PLAN VIEW

FACING

ADD THIS
LITTLE PIECE

SILL

Building the sash can be the most difficult part of the job, and certainly the most time consuming. It can be done in the same way as the French door shown earlier, using slats and backing pieces, and this probably is the most realistic method other than using a shaper and a set of mullion cutters. An easier method is to use a solid section of plywood and cut out the lights. Lay out the sash so that it is the right size, bearing in mind that the outside edge of the frame will need to be larger in scale than the mullions are. Of course there are always windows at the architectural salvage yard.

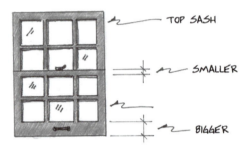

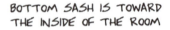

BOTTOM SASH IS TOWARD
THE INSIDE OF THE ROOM

Also, the bottom rail of the lower sash is generally sized a bit more generously to allow for a handle to be installed. The bottom rail of the top sash is intended to line up with the top rail of the bottom sash, which allows for the installation of a sash lock. The bottom sash fits toward the inside of the room and passes on that side of the top sash. This is to prevent rainwater from collecting on the top of the bottom sash.

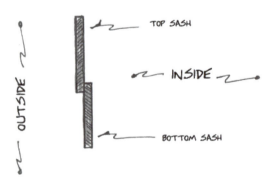

Drill a $3/8"$ hole inside every light and use a jigsaw to cut out each individual opening. Somewhere in the process you will decide that this method cannot be the easiest way, but it truly is. It will speed up your work to have a standardized way of cutting the squares out. If the hole is drilled near the corner of the light, then it is easier to cut along the one

side, back up a bit, then turn and cut along a contiguous side. Make the same cuts on all of the lights, then turn the sash around and repeat the process. This saves you from having to twist the saw around too far. Marking the back is no harder than marking the front, and it will save you a lot of tearout on the good side.

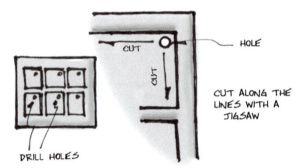

If you must make a large number of sashes, then it is oftentimes helpful to make a pattern that may be used in conjunction with a router to make any number of multiples. The advantage is that all of the parts will be exactly alike, but this also means that great care must be taken to make a pattern that is straight and true. You can use this same technique on other construction projects that require many multiples of a complex shape like grills and other wrought iron work.

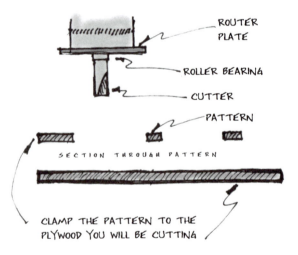

The router bit you should use is called a flush trim pattern bit. It differs from a standard flush trim bit in that the roller bearing is on the top of the cutter rather than on the bottom. This allows the pattern to be secured on the top of the piece being cut out. The router is then run around the profile with the roller bearing running along the edge of the pattern. The cutter extends through the piece being cut and trims it off to the exact size and shape of the pattern. This works best with a $1/2$" shaft router and bit, and you should get one if you will be doing a lot of this type of work. A $1/2$" router is much steadier with less vibration and chatter. It is much more time effective if you can cut through the $1/2$" lauan used for the sash in one pass. It is possible to do the job in a number of passes (each one a bit deeper), but, of course, that takes up a lot of time. If the window sections you are replicating are large, it may be best to make the pattern from a rigid material like $3/4$" plywood. The thinner lauan is easier to work with, but the narrow mullion shapes may bend excessively during the routing process.

The best tool of all is a CNC robot router. This machine uses a robot arm to make very precise cuts with a pin router. They are quite expensive, starting in the $50,000 range, but it is incredible to watch them work. If you have one of those, congratulations!

If a router is used, then the resulting lights will have slightly rounded corners. This will make it impossible to use any sort of trim insert, which would most likely be too time consuming anyway. A small rounding-over bit may be used to ease the corners of the mullions. This is not terribly realistic looking, but it does add a little something to the work.

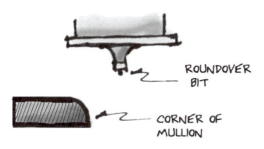

ROUNDOVER
BIT

CORNER OF
MULLION

In some cases, the sash can be simply nailed into the frame as is, or Plexiglas may be screwed to the back. You might wish to just glue it on with Liquid Nails or some other mastic. If the window must move up and down, or if you would like to make it a bit more realistic, some thickness must be added to the sash. Usually, it is only the bottom sash that will need to be padded, as it is not really possible to see the thickness of the top sash from the inside of a room. The Plexiglas will still need to adhere directly to the back of the $1/2$" lauan to prevent a space from showing. The buildup is to make a greater distance between the face of the top sash and the face of the bottom sash.

Rip some $3/4$" white pine so that it is an inch or so wide. Glue and nail it to the perimeter of the rear of the bottom sash. Trim and sand as required. The glass for this window will need to be cut to fit to the inside of these edge pieces. It will probably be easier to put a small bead of Liquid Nails along the edges and over the mullions than to use screws in such thin material. Lay some scrap muslin on the glass to protect it, and then set several stage weights on top to keep the assembly pressed together for a few minutes until the mastic sets up a bit.

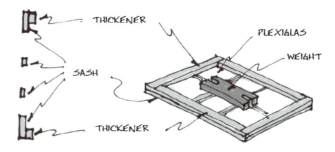

THICKENER

PLEXIGLAS

WEIGHT

SASH

THICKENER

The top sash can be inserted into the frame and secured. The back of the glass should be flush with the back of the jamb, and the whole thing snug to the top of the frame. Lay the bottom sash inside the window directly in front of the top sash, and measure the distance from the front of it to the front of the face frame. Subtract $1/4$" to determine the width of the trim that will hold the bottom sash in place. The $1/4$" is to make up for the reveal that was included in the door frame but left out of the window frame. The main purpose of this trim strip is to keep the sash from falling forward out of the frame. If the sash is too snug to move easily, now is a good time to trim it down.

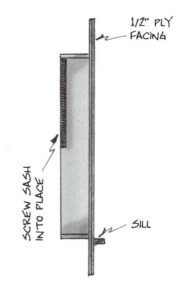

1/2" PLY
FACING

SCREW SASH
INTO PLACE

SILL

Cut some $1/2$" lauan so that it is the proper width to fit the space you measured earlier. Obviously, there must be some type of coordination between this process and the decision of how wide to rip the framing for the jamb. If the jamb is too narrow, the sash will not fit properly. Hopefully, you will know what sort of window you are building before you start, and some of these decisions can be made from the outset. Screw or nail this strip into position on the jamb using the bottom sash as a guide to exact placement. Do not glue it, because you might have to get it back out if there is a problem with the sash. The final section of trim to make the window operate is a section of $1/2$" lauan that is ripped to the same width as the thickness of the top sash. This piece will keep the sash from falling out the back of the window when it is at the bottom of its travel.

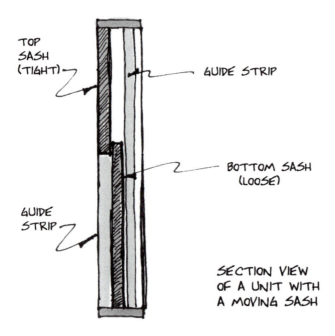

TOP SASH (TIGHT)

GUIDE STRIP

BOTTOM SASH (LOOSE)

GUIDE STRIP

SECTION VIEW OF A UNIT WITH A MOVING SASH

CHAPTER 18

WORKING WITH POLYSTYRENE FOAM

The trade name Styrofoam is used in the vernacular to indicate a number of different plastic products. These foam products are useful in building scenery because they are so lightweight and easy to shape. One of the drawbacks of foam construction is that the foam is also easily torn up. There are ways of coating the foam to give it a tougher exterior, hence making it more useful to us. Foam is at its best when used to construct large, oddly-shaped structures like rocks, geometric forms, or perhaps cornice pieces. It is fairly easy to create very textural surfaces with foam.

In recent years a method of coating foam with a super-strong epoxy material has made it possible to use it on the outsides of commercial buildings. In construction work, foam is often used as a cheaper substitute for large cornices and other exterior trim. Foam has been used to build scenery like that for many years, and for the same reasons. The foam adds a lot of bulk, cheaply, and without making the unit too heavy.

CORNICE MADE FROM EXTRUDED POLYSTYRENE

FOAM PRODUCTS

Styrofoam is a polystyrene product made by the Dow Chemical Company. Like Kleenex, or Masonite, or Plexiglas, there is a tendency to call any similar foam product by the same name. Actual Styrofoam is an extruded polystyrene product that is bluish in color. "Extruded" means that the polystyrene material is forced through a die, and the shape of the die determines the shape of the sheet of foam. A cutter slices off the sheet after eight feet of it has been extruded through the die. Styrofoam is an open-cell foam, and it has a spongy texture on the inside. Usually it is sold in 4x8 sheets of varying thickness, most often $3/4$", 1", and 2". In construction, it is used for insulation purposes.

Most Styrofoam is sold as "Score Board," meaning that there are score marks at certain intervals that make it possible to break the foam into 16"- or 24"-wide strips without using a saw. Sometimes this scoring is problematic when cutting the foam to other sizes. This type of polystyrene has a fairly smooth texture when cut, and tends to retain sharp corners. It is easy to cut with a saw, but not as easy to carve as other types of foam. It is at its best when a smooth texture is required.

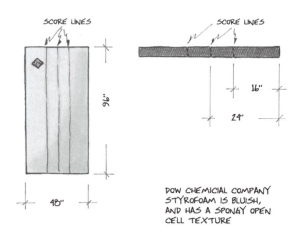

SCORE LINES

SCORE LINES

96"

16"

24"

48"

DOW CHEMICIAL COMPANY STYROFOAM IS BLUISH, AND HAS A SPONGY OPEN CELL TEXTURE

Expanded polystyrene is a similar yet different product. Expanded foam is manufactured by putting tiny polystyrene pellets into a cooker. The pellets are exposed to steam heat, swell in size, and stick together. The size of the vat determines the size of the foam blank that is produced. Many different local companies produce expanded polystyrene through this process. The ones in my area make an original blank of foam that is two feet thick, four feet wide, and sixteen feet long, much larger than the extruded product. If you go directly to a factory (which may well be a more approachable operation than you think), it is possible to purchase these large chunks and/or smaller sections that have

already been cut up. Sometimes this type of foam is sold in fairly large pieces for use as flotation units for docks or houseboats. Large blocks can be easier to use for sculptural projects, but most often, thinner sheets are more practical.

At the factory, the large sections of foam are sliced into a more usable size with a hot wire machine. A hot wire is just that, a special type of wire with enough direct current passing through it to make it hot enough to slice the foam by melting its way through it. Quite often it is possible to see the slightly curved striations from the cutting process on the face of a sheet of foam.

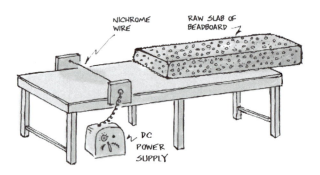

NICHROME WIRE

RAW SLAB OF BEADBOARD

DC POWER SUPPLY

HOT WIRE FOAM CUTTER

Expanded polystyrene is easily recognized by its white color and pebble-like texture. As the explanation of its manufacture indicates, it is comprised of small, $1/8$" diameter beads of foam that are stuck together. When carving this type of foam, the beads separate from one another, and this makes expanded foam quite easy to carve, especially for large, rounded shapes. The residue from the carving process looks like the stuffing used for beanbag chairs.

BEADBOARD IS EASIER TO CARVE INTO LARGE ROUNDED SHAPES

WHEN WORKED, IT FLAKES OFF IN TINY WHITE BEADS

Carved polystyrene is a great way to simulate stone work for arches, columns, and cornices. These structures normally have a somewhat rough texture in the real world, so the naturally nubby texture of the foam is not a distraction. It is generally better to build a framing support structure and to cover that with a thin layer of polystyrene than to make the entire unit from solid foam. But it is certainly possible to use foam in a structural way, especially if a coating material is used to reinforce the structure. Sometimes foam can be used to make very nice stucco when a really rough textural quality is required. The same foam techniques are very successful when used to make tombstones and other funereal monuments, which for some reason tend to be required in a large number of plays.

Foam is easily cut with a variety of woodworking saws and can be shaped with conventional carving and smoothing tools. You may wish to avoid cutting the foam with a "hot wire" technique, using a torch or chemicals to melt the surface, or any other method that causes the foam to deteriorate chemically. Although there is not any well-known serious discussion of extraordinary danger involved in working with the material in this way, burning plastic of any kind releases fumes that may at best be described as unhealthy. If it gives you a headache, it cannot be good for you. You can avoid the issue by avoiding the process.

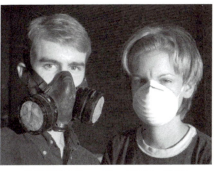

RESPIRATOR   OR   DUST MASK

CHOOSE THE RIGHT PROTECTION

Most safety in the shop is really just a matter of common sense. Although there is no obvious danger in working with foam, it only makes sense to take at least minimal precautions. If you must break down the foam chemically, be sure to wear an approved respirator, not just a dust mask. Do it outside, or in an area with good exhaust fans.

PORTAL PROJECT EXAMPLE

Let us say that you will be building a large portal that must frame the entire stage. The design calls for an arched opening bordered with a stone trim. The portal should be constructed in small segments that can be bolted together and hung from a batten. You must then develop a manner of adhering the stone relief shape to the inside, curved edge of the portal. Of course, the stone work should be very light, as the entire portal is meant to fly on a batten. Since the bottom of the arch is well within reach of actors and stagehands, it is best to give the stone a protective coating that is strong enough to withstand the occasional bump and scratch.

CHEMICALS

AVOID RELEASING TOXIC GASES FROM FOAM AND OTHER PLASTIC PRODUCTS

BURNING

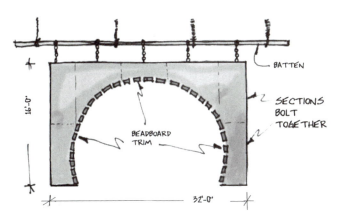

BATTEN

SECTIONS BOLT TOGETHER

BEADBOARD TRIM

16'-0"

32'-0"

Use a respirator when cutting the foam on a table saw, because the heat of the blade rubbing against the foam tends to make it melt just a bit. You should always wear at least a dust mask to screen out the ever-present bits of foam that are in the air, even when carving by hand. The particles are very large, so an ordinary dust mask will work for them.

Of course the portal must be designed around transportable panels. You should construct the stone work so that the transitions between panels do not show any more than absolutely necessary. Proportion the stones in the arch so that a mortar joint line appears wherever there are two panels joined together. This is fairly easy to do since the stones are of somewhat random size anyway.

In this example, the wooden parts of the portal are made as hardcovered flats, and are easiest to build in 4x8 chunks. Softcovered flats would work just as well, or even something framed with metal tubing. This particular design was for a rather small proscenium opening, so the hardcovered flat approach was the most appealing.

Once the framing structure is completed, rip expanded polystyrene strips to the proper size. This width is, of course, dependent upon the design and the size of the finished product. Keep in mind that the larger the pieces, the harder they will be to bend. For our project, the diameter of the curve is large enough, and the width of the facing strip of foam narrow enough, that there should be no problem in bending the foam around the curve. If the foam cannot be bent without breaking, it is possible to make it bend by kerfing it, or you could simply cut the curve into the foam by marking it against the wooden portal structure and cutting the arc with a jigsaw. It is not necessary to be incredibly accurate in cutting the parts since they will be carved into a rounded profile and covered with cheesecloth. Even so, this does not mean that you can have inch-wide cracks everywhere.

TRANSFER THE CURVE FROM THE WOODEN PORTAL PIECES TO A SHEET OF FOAM

USE A JIGSAW TO CUT THE CURVE. SAVE A PIECE OF THE SCRAP FOR THE NEXT STEP

ADD A CHUNK OF FOAM TO THE ROUNDED SCRAP TO MAKE THE MARKING JIG

SCRAP

MARK THE SHEET WITH THE PROPER WIDTH

If it is necessary to kerf the foam, lay several of the sections together side by side and cut notches about halfway through the foam at regular intervals. The notches will make the foam bend much more easily. It is important that the

spaces between cuts be even, or the foam will not bend evenly and will tend to break at the irregular spot. The spacing of the cuts, and their depth, are both a function of how flexible the foam slat will need to be when completed. It is best not to go overboard in cutting the notches, or they may be visible in the finished product.

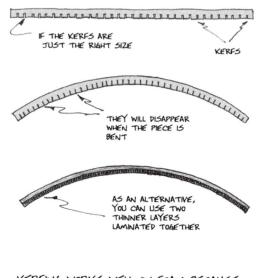

IF THE KERFS ARE JUST THE RIGHT SIZE

KERFS

THEY WILL DISAPPEAR WHEN THE PIECE IS BENT

AS AN ALTERNATIVE, YOU CAN USE TWO THINNER LAYERS LAMINATED TOGETHER

KERFING WORKS WELL ON FOAM BECAUSE IT IS SO EASILY STRETCHED AND COMPRESSED

It would seem that the path of least resistance might be to just bend the foam with no cutting at all. Sometimes it is best to use two thin layers of foam rather than one thicker layer, because the thin pieces are more easily bent. Not all expanded polystyrene is of the same quality. Some manufacturers grind up old trimmings and mix them back into the mixture for new foam. This is fine up to a point, but if too much is used, the foam becomes brittle and will not bend very far without breaking.

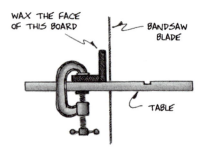

WAX THE FACE OF THIS BOARD

BANDSAW BLADE

TABLE

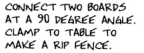

CONNECT TWO BOARDS AT A 90 DEGREE ANGLE. CLAMP TO TABLE TO MAKE A RIP FENCE.

You will need to rip a large number of relatively narrow strips of foam material. The foam is very light in comparison to plywood, so it is easy to handle when you carry it around the shop and feed it into the table saw. This free way of manipulating the sheet foam will make you think that it will be easy to rip on the table saw. Just the opposite is true. You should use extreme caution when using the table saw with foam products. It will tend to jump around in the saw, and get kickbacks. It is much easier to rip the foam on a bandsaw that has a rip fence. If your bandsaw does not have a fence, it may be possible to clamp a board on the table so that it produces the same effect.

Attach the foam using Liquid Nails and pins. The pins (usually largish nails) will be removed after the adhesive has had time to set up. Liquid Nails is a mastic, or highly viscous liquid adhesive, which has been around for decades. It is commonly used as a construction adhesive for gluing panels to floor joists and walls. It comes in a tube and is applied using a standard caulking gun. It works well for foam work because its thick, gooey texture tends to make the foam want to stick together from the moment the pieces touch. Yellow carpenter's glue and/or white polyvinyl glue will stick foam to wood, but the drying time is greatly extended because the foam prevents ventilation of the joint. Woodworking glues don't work well when joining foam with foam. Water-based contact cement is also a possibility, but the drying time required and the "instant stick" nature of that adhesive are definitely negative qualities for this project.

recently come out with a new line of special formulas, and one of them purports to be designed especially for use on foam. It takes much longer to set up and does not stick nearly as well as the original formula, although it is less detrimental to the foam. Other companies make similar products that may work just as well. Mastics are also available in bucket containers, so that you can apply them with a knife. It is generally easier just to stick with the caulking tube approach. Use this product in a well-ventilated area.

You need not be too particular when applying the foam to the wooden structure. Most of the time it is better for the foam to over run the joint a bit. Any tiny amount of extra foam is easily removed with a carving tool. Do not try to trim the ends of the slats until after they are attached to the wood and the adhesive has had time to set up. They can be quite easily trimmed with an ordinary handsaw after the unit is stable. The pins may be pushed through two different layers of foam or may be driven through a slat of foam and then slightly into the wooden structure. Do not drive the nail in any further than is absolutely required, or it will be difficult to remove later on.

As indicated earlier, the ends of the foam pieces may be cut off with a handsaw. There are few occasions in the modern world when a hand tool is actually better than a power tool, but working with expanded polystyrene is one of them.

Expanded polystyrene is often called "bead board" because of the way the particles flake off when you cut it with a saw or carve it with other tools.

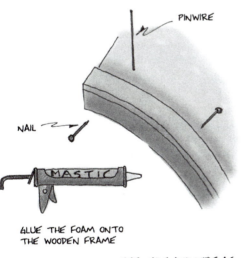

GLUE THE FOAM ONTO THE WOODEN FRAME

USE NAILS AND WIRE AS PINS TO HOLD IT IN PLACE

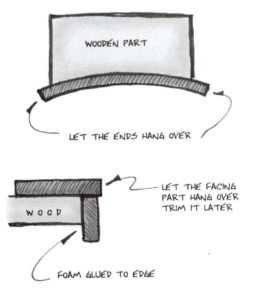

The major problem involved in using any petroleum-based adhesive on foam is that the adhesive tends to melt the foam on contact. Liquid Nails is no exception, but usually the melting effect is not enough to prevent the foam from bonding. The company that manufactures Liquid Nails has

Use the handsaw to rough out sections of a carving. You will get much better control with a handsaw because it cuts more slowly than a power tool. A loose hacksaw blade with gaffer's tape on one end is also good for smaller cuts. Use the fastest cutting tool that you can without endangering yourself or the foam. It is hard to make really small cuts with a full-sized handsaw.

The all-time champion bead board carving tool is the Surform. It greatly resembles a cheese grater. Surforms are made by the Stanley Tool Company in a variety of types. Some are long and flat, some long and curved, and some are short and either flat or curved.

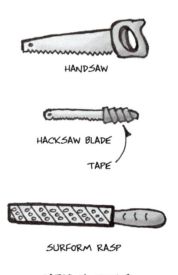

HANDSAW

HACKSAW BLADE

TAPE

SURFORM RASP

CARVING TOOLS

The Surform you select for a particular job is largely a matter of personal taste, but the longer ones seem to work the best. Like its relative the file and/or the wood rasp, there is a handle part and a cutter part. This tool was originally intended to shape wood by peeling it away just like a cheese grater grates cheese. It is highly effective at pulling apart the small beads that make up the foam, and with a little practice you will easily be able to round over the edges of the foam.

Sandpaper is another useful tool for carving foam. In this case rougher is better, and 80 grit is about the smallest that is aggressive enough to work efficiently. You can use it to finish off the project after the carving is complete. If you can locate some 30 or 40 grit paper, it is rough enough to actually be used for carving. A sanding block is good for the rough carving paper. Sanding blocks can be made in a variety of shapes, and the foam will assume the negative shape of the block.

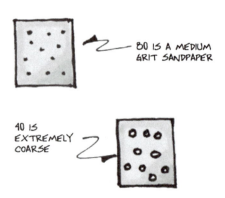

80 IS A MEDIUM GRIT SANDPAPER

40 IS EXTREMELY COARSE

Begin carving the stone archway by laying out the joint lines. A regular Sharpie marker is the best tool for writing on foam. Mark the joints an appropriate distance apart, making sure that one falls at each junction between two panels. Use the Surform or a rounded-over sheet of sandpaper to carve away the indentation.

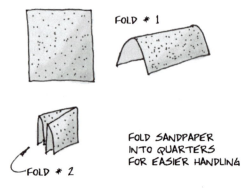

FOLD # 1

FOLD # 2

FOLD SANDPAPER INTO QUARTERS FOR EASIER HANDLING

When using sandpaper by hand, never tear the sheet. Fold it into fourths and use it that way. This will give you a semi-stiff pad to work with. When one quarter of the paper is exhausted, turn or refold the pad so that a new surface is exposed. This makes the sandpaper much easier to hold and to use. Sometimes folding the already quartered paper one more time can make the perfect tool for carving the joint lines.

Rounding the edges of the foam is best done with the Surform. Begin by trimming off any excess foam where a facing piece overlaps a side piece. Work on the project with the unit lying face up. Hold the tool so that the grater is cutting on the downstroke. This will prevent the facing foam from being accidentally being pulled away from the face of the flat. Keep the Surform at a slight angle and lightly work the entire surface. Hold it flat against the edge. Move the tool around to different areas in an even pattern. A little here, a little there. Don't try to take too much off in any one pass with the Surform. It is much better to use a light touch, because the carving will go really fast anyway. If you go too fast you will not be able to tell when you are getting a nicely smoothed profile.

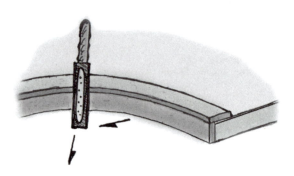

MOVE THE TOOL DOWN AND TO THE SIDE. HOLDING THE SURFORM TIGHT TO THE BOTTOM PIECE OF FOAM WILL TRIM THE OVERHANGING PIECE TO THE SAME SIZE

To shape the outside corner of the foam, hold the Surform so that the length of it is running the same direction as the corner to be rounded over. Lightly run it up and down the length of the corner. Begin by chamfering off a 45-degree bevel and then slowly alternate the angle of the Surform between 90 and 0 degrees. Do not press too hard with the tool, but rather just skim the surface, rotating back and forth until the desired curvature is obtained. The inside corner is shaped in a similar manner, but the Surform must be held at a slight angle in order for it to fit into the curve. Use some 80-grit to finish smoothing the curve and any touching up that must be done. Sometimes it is helpful to lay the various pieces of the portal together so that there is a means of judging that the same amount of curvature is maintained throughout. Once you have the hang of it, this is really an easy and fun process. The actual carving of a portal like this should take no more than half an hour to complete. The cutting and fitting of the parts would take several times that.

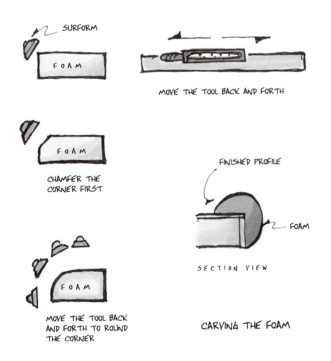

SURFORM

FOAM

MOVE THE TOOL BACK AND FORTH

CHAMFER THE CORNER FIRST

FOAM

MOVE THE TOOL BACK AND FORTH TO ROUND THE CORNER

FOAM

FINISHED PROFILE

FOAM

SECTION VIEW

CARVING THE FOAM

Since this foam is well within reach of the stage, the surface should be coated with something to toughen it up and prevent damage. The most effective method is to coat the foam with a layer or two of cheesecloth. When sealed in place with paint, the cheesecloth forms a tough "skin" that is both flexible and resistant to abrasion. It will not offer much protection from sharp punctures or being repeatedly stepped on.

The flexible nature of the cheesecloth coating makes it work well with the compressible and resilient polystyrene. On occasion, when a smoother texture is required, it is pos-

sible to substitute muslin for the cheesecloth, but the muslin is much harder to apply. Cheesecloth is a gauze-like material that was at one time used in draining cheese. (And it still is as far as I know, which isn't far at all.) It has a very loosely woven appearance much like a very fine net. The variety required for this technique is 100% cotton. Synthetic fibers will not work, as the sealer will not adhere properly to them.

Cotton cheesecloth is commonly available from large fabric stores in boxes of 100 yards. Buying the cheesecloth by the box is a good idea because it is cheaper that way, and it often takes more of the fabric for any given project than you would think. Theatrical fabric suppliers sell a gauze material that they often refer to as cheesecloth. It comes in wider widths and has a finer weave. It is much more difficult to work with than the fabric store variety and is not recommended unless you need a fine texture.

The sealer used in sticking the cheesecloth to the foam is usually leftover paint, but just about any waterbased liquid with glue in it will work. You can gather all the remaining paint that is still usable from recent projects and mix it together in one or more five-gallon buckets. Avoid spoiled casein paint and runny washes. Thick paint is a better gap filler, and no one will want to work in the shop if you use really stinky old rotten casein. It is imperative to use water-based paints. A gallon or two of flat black latex and the proper ratio of flame retardant additive will produce an excellent all-around gray basecoat, backpaint, and cheesecloth sealer all in one. The mixture should be left slightly thick for use with the cheesecloth, several steps more viscous than is normal for backpaint. If you don't have any paint that you would like to get rid of, or would like to use a specific color, you can use straight latex out of the can. It takes quite a bit of paint to get the cheesecloth to stick properly.

Begin with the foam unit on sawhorses at a comfortable height. When pulled from the box, cheesecloth is about 9" wide and is folded over so that it is four layers thick. Sometimes it is appropriate to use the cloth with that many layers, but it is usually easier to work with one or two. One layer is fine for some projects, but generally the more layers, the more protection the coating will provide.

The key to making the application job run smoothly is to start by properly draping the cheesecloth. It is helpful to put down a coat of paint first, then to lay the cheesecloth down onto the paint while it is still wet. This will keep the cloth in place while you are draping it. Lay the cloth so that it extends onto the surface of the plywood at least an inch or so, and leave enough hanging down to wrap around to the wood on the back of the flat. This will ensure that the foam remains securely fixed to the flat.

Leave a fold of the cheesecloth at each joint depression so that there will be enough slack in the material for it to be forced down into the crack with a wet paintbrush. You needn't be too picky about this procedure. By the end of it, paint will be all over your hands and arms up to the elbow, so get used to it. If the cheesecloth is not positioned exactly, pick it up and move it around. It is far better to leave a bit of extra slack in the cloth than to have it wind up stretched tight over a joint line. That would effectively wipe out the carved detail. For a project like this, it matters little if the cloth is overlapped or folded over itself in places; indeed this can sometimes create a desired amount of extra texture.

100 % COTTON CHEESECLOTH

CHEESECLOTH COMES FOLDED INTO FOUR LAYERS

IN A BOX

END OF FLAT DISGUISED BY A JOINT LINE

DRAPE THE CHEESECLOTH SO THAT THERE IS PLENTY OF SLACK TO PROJECT DOWN INTO THE JOINTS. IT IS BETTER TO HAVE TOO MUCH THAN TOO LITTLE.

Don't be too stingy with the paint. The gauze should be completely saturated with paint in order to adhere properly to the foam. When dry, the foam/cheesecloth combination is incredibly tough, much like a hide, and the extension of the cloth onto the surrounding wood makes it very difficult for the foam to become dislodged from the wooden structure.

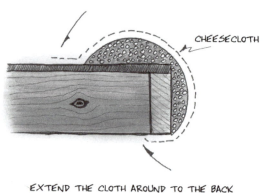

CHEESECLOTH

EXTEND THE CLOTH AROUND TO THE BACK FAR ENOUGH TO MAKE A GOOD CONNECTION TO THE WOODEN STRUCTURE SO THAT THE FOAM WILL NOT PULL OFF EASILY

MAKING A CORNICE

Another common use for foam is to make large, built-up cornices. A cornice is used at the top of a wall and is theoretically less likely to be damaged. It is better not to use cheesecloth on a cornice because of the rough texture the cloth creates. A cornice is usually a smoother piece of work. It is problematic to use foam for trims that are within reach of the stage floor because it is just too fragile. The relative seclusion of the cornice and its bulky form make it a natural for foam construction. Quite often the blue Dow Styrofoam or some other extruded polystyrene type is the best material for this job because it is so much smoother than bead board.

The design for a cornice of this type must take into consideration the materials that are used to construct it. Put the cornice together from strips of foam that have been ripped down on the band saw or table saw. It is fairly easy to glue together a number of 8-foot or longer sections and then cut these to the proper length and angle. That makes cutting the angles less problematic than trying to miter each piece individually. Instead, put together stock parts that are long enough to cut the needed pieces. Avoid having a butt joint between two pieces on the same wall by laminating together sections long enough to reach from corner to corner.

Here is an example of a cornice that is designed for polystyrene construction.

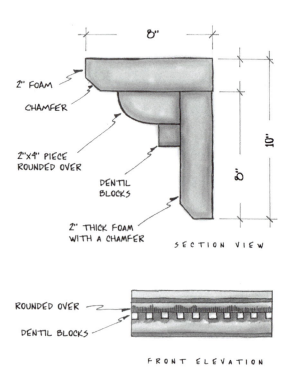

8"

2" FOAM

CHAMFER

2"x4" PIECE ROUNDED OVER

DENTIL BLOCKS

2" THICK FOAM WITH A CHAMFER

10"

8"

SECTION VIEW

ROUNDED OVER

DENTIL BLOCKS

FRONT ELEVATION

The section view reveals the size and shape of each trim member. You also need to know the total length of trim required for all of the wall sections. Estimate the lengths from your ground plan. Some of the walls may be longer than eight feet in length and thus will require the construction of an extra-long section of trim. It is possible to connect the foam pieces with offsetting joints so that the finished product extends to virtually any length, but at some point the length of the cornice will make it simply too cumbersome to deal with effectively. Remember that outside corners require an extra amount of material, and that cutting miters in general tends to use up the trim faster than expected. It is much easier to make a few extra lengths of cornice from the outset than to be forced to replicate a section of trim at the last moment. This particular molding includes a dentil type of detail, which is essentially a series of blocks glued on with a space between each one.

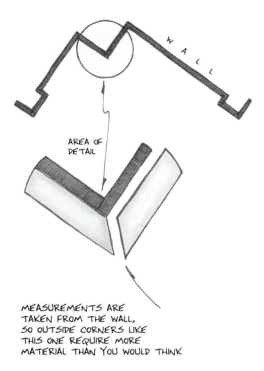

AREA OF DETAIL

W A L L

MEASUREMENTS ARE TAKEN FROM THE WALL, SO OUTSIDE CORNERS LIKE THIS ONE REQUIRE MORE MATERIAL THAN YOU WOULD THINK

The first task is to determine the widths of all the parts and the number of strips required of each size. It is best to rip down all of the foam parts on the bandsaw. You can use a table saw, but the foam is so light it tends to jump around in the saw and get kicked back. Be cautious if you do decide to use a table saw.

If you are clever, you can cut out the parts so that the scoring indentations are either hidden inside the cornice or wind up as scrap on the shop floor.

Sometimes there are 45-degree angle chamfers that must be ripped along one or more of the pieces. It is best to cut the strips to size first, reset the saw, and then cut all of the chamfers at the same time. Use a hold down or finger board to keep the foam in place. Start the foam through the saw by pushing, and then have an assistant pull the strip through

the rest of the way. This will greatly reduce the tendency of the foam to kick back. The same techniques work well on the bandsaw, even though there isn't much danger of a kick-back on that saw.

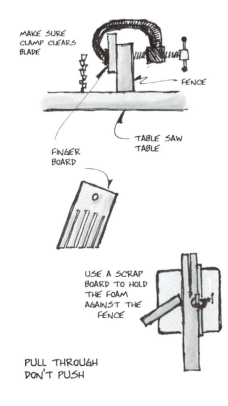

MAKE SURE CLAMP CLEARS BLADE

FENCE

TABLE SAW TABLE

FINGER BOARD

USE A SCRAP BOARD TO HOLD THE FOAM AGAINST THE FENCE

PULL THROUGH DON'T PUSH

Once the foam has been ripped into strips, it is time to cut the sections to length. If you are making nothing but 8-foot long units, the job is already done. A 10-foot section requires 8-foot and 2-foot lengths. You may need to also use 4 and 6 or 5 and 5 if the molding needs extra stiffening. When making longer sections, remember to stagger the location of the joints.

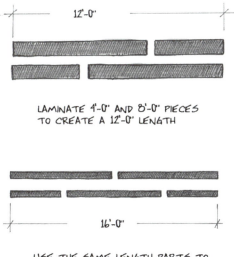

12'-0"

LAMINATE 4'-0" AND 8'-0" PIECES TO CREATE A 12'-0" LENGTH

16'-0"

USE THE SAME LENGTH PARTS TO CREATE A 16'-0" SECTION OF TRIM

Connect the strips of foam together to form the cornice. Apply a zigzag pattern of Liquid Nails to the edge of the back section and attach this piece to the top section. Use the adhesive on any surfaces that are to be glued together.

A zigzag pattern spreads the adhesive out over a larger area, increasing the holding power of the glue. Bring the parts together and squish them back and forth a few times to further spread the glue. This will also have the advantage of using suction power to hold the parts together while they bond. Use nails, pin wire, stage weights, or whatever is necessary to hold the parts together as they dry. When all of the trims are together, go back and check the connections several times, as they may tend to pull apart. Use stage weights or template blocks to make sure that the assemblies remain straight and true while they dry. If there is enough wall space, a straight wall is excellent for this purpose.

Now comes the task of cutting the cornice parts to length and mitering the ends to fit around the wall angles. You can compute the sizes on paper with measurements taken from the actual walls. If the walls are straight, plumb, and the angles involved are true, then it is a fairly straightforward process. Measure along each of the walls to verify the length of each. Sometimes there is a discrepancy (gasp) between the plans and the actual construction. Since you are cutting the cornice to fit on the wall and not on the printed plan, it is best to go right to the source for your measurements.

Make a small sketch of each piece of trim as you include it on your cut list. Show the angle that must be cut and the direction that it runs. Dimension the sketch with the size you measure from the wall. Indicate which part of the angle the dimension relates to. This will reduce confusion when you begin cutting.

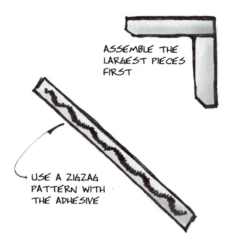

ASSEMBLE THE LARGEST PIECES FIRST

USE A ZIGZAG PATTERN WITH THE ADHESIVE

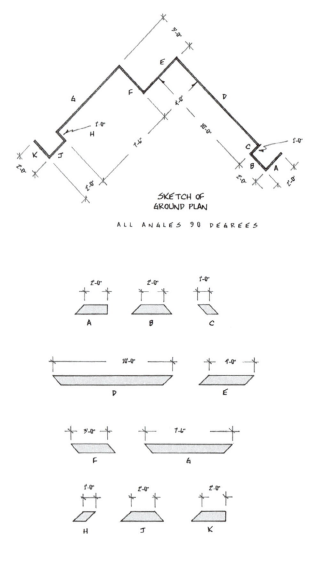

SKETCH OF GROUND PLAN

ALL ANGLES 90 DEGREES

Once all of the parts have bonded along a curved line, no amount of tugging and pulling can straighten them out again. Do not hurry the curing period. It is best to assemble these parts in the late afternoon and come back to them the next morning.

Save the dentil molding until last. Use the radial arm saw to cut a strip of foam into the necessary cubes. It would be really time consuming to measure the placement of each cube, so consider using the cubes themselves to do the spacing. It is common for the space in between the blocks to be the same distance as the size of the blocks themselves. You can use unattached blocks to set the spaces between the cubes you are gluing on.

The dentil mold does not have to fit with any other parts, so it is only necessary to make sure that the measurements are close enough to look good. It is common to have to pull some of them off and re-space them to accommodate the miter joints. Since the blocks are very small, air can get around the edges, and it is much easier to use regular carpenter's glue to attach the dentil mold than to use a mastic.

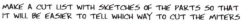

MAKE A CUT LIST WITH SKETCHES OF THE PARTS SO THAT IT WILL BE EASIER TO TELL WHICH WAY TO CUT THE MITERS

If there is an unknown angle, use a scrap board and the power miter saw to determine the angle by trial and error. Cut the board and hold both halves in the corner. If the joint is open, reduce the number of degrees. If the points do not meet, make the angle more acute. After all of the sizes and degree angles are known, it is time to cut the cornice pieces.

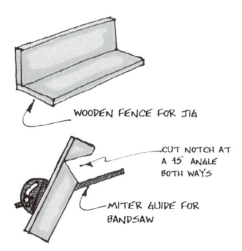

There are two ways of cutting the mitered angles. One method is to use a very large bandsaw. It must have a guard that you can raise high enough to accommodate the 8" height of the trim. That can be a problem. The other is to construct an old-style wooden miter box large enough to house the 8" depth of the cornice. I have tried several times to cut the foam trim one segment at a time first and then glue the cornice together, but it takes too much time and does not fit together well. It is much more expedient to cut the entire cornice at once.

WOODEN FENCE FOR JIG

CUT NOTCH AT A 45° ANGLE BOTH WAYS

MITER GUIDE FOR BANDSAW

A bandsaw that is large enough to accommodate an 8" tall item will most likely have a miter guide. The stock miter guide is a bit small to handle such a large piece. Instead, you can add a wooden jig to the guide. The jig is merely two pieces of plywood glued and nailed together and then bolted to the miter guide. Make it as large as will comfortably fit on your bandsaw. The wooden section will be easier to use if there is an equal amount of wood, and hence weight, on either side of the miter guide. If you put the jig together and use the bandsaw itself to cut the 45-degree angle notch out of the base, the resulting V will be usable as a reference point in lining up the cornice on the jig. Most of your cuts will be either 45 or 90 degrees. This jig will not cut angles greater than 45 degrees.

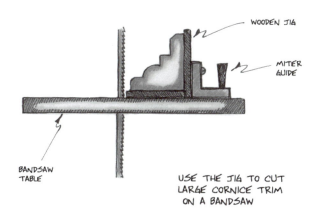

WOODEN JIG

MITER GUIDE

BANDSAW TABLE

USE THE JIG TO CUT LARGE CORNICE TRIM ON A BANDSAW

Cutting the foam is somewhat of a balancing act, but the cornice is very light and, of course, there is almost no resistance to the blade cutting through the piece. A second person may be required to aid in holding up the far end. Make sure there are no pins left in the foam that can damage the saw. It is advisable to begin by cutting the longest pieces first. The cut list was made so that there is a diagram of each section to better define the angle directions. All of the measurements are from the wall surface, and so must be marked to the backside of the cornice. It takes a bit of practice to learn to visualize the placement of the pieces and the direction that the angles run. Making the cut list with diagrams of this sort will help.

Begin by trimming off one end to the proper angle. Use the same (left or right) end first for each section of the cornice so that they stay in order. Turn this first section of cornice right side up and measure the proper length across the backside. Use a speed square to mark the angle all the way across the top if the angle is either 45 or 90 degrees. If the angle is an intermediate number of degrees, use the scrap boards you cut earlier on the power miter box to define that angle. Once the top of the cornice has been laid out, extend the marking around the sides. On the front of the cornice, the mark can only carry on an inch or so before it hits the profile of the individual sections. On the back, the mark can be scribed all the way to the bottom of the cornice. It is advisable to extend the marking around as much of the foam as possible because that will help you visualize how to angle the cut through the cornice when you get to the saw. The more time you spend marking, the less likely you will be to make a mistake at the saw.

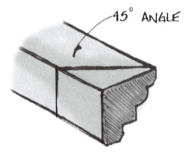

If it is not possible to cut the trim on a bandsaw, a large miter box will work just as well, perhaps better. The miter box is definitely more accurate, and the only downside is the time required to put it together. The box will be easier to use if it is the same size as the trim you are cutting. A tight fit will prevent the piece from moving around while you are cutting it. The cornice in the example is 8" across the top, and 10" tall, so these are the dimensions of the inside of the jig.

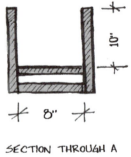

SECTION THROUGH A
MITER BOX

You could make a box from just three boards, but the structure would be really weak to cut such large and cumbersome trim. It is better to have more strength in the bottom of the jig, which you can easily get by using two pieces across the bottom span. Leave a small space in between them. Make the side boards wide enough so that they will stick up 10" even after the bottom part is taken into consideration.

The length doesn't matter so much, but it is nice if the box is at least 3' long so that it is stable enough to work well. Glue and staple the boards together so that you have a U-shaped box that is 8" wide and 10" high on the inside. Slots cut into the sides of the box are used to guide the handsaw that will cut the actual cornice. The slots must be cut so that they accurately represent the angles you need. The table saw can be used to begin the cuts by using its miter guide and running the box through the saw upside-down. The saw will not be able to cut all of the way through the sides of the box, so use a circular saw or a jigsaw to complete the cut. For this project, you would need a 90-degree cut and two 45-degree cuts, one going in each direction. In real life, you would also need some other odd angles if required for your project. The directions for marking the individual pieces of cornice are the same as for the method that used the bandsaw. Making the miter box is time consuming, but it is much easier to cut a cornice in a miter box than it is on the bandsaw.

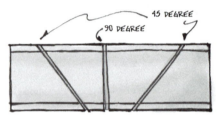

PLAN VIEW OF A MITER BOX

YOU CAN USE THE TABLE SAW TO ACCURATELY START THE SLOTS

Cut all of the sections of cornice in turn and check each against the wall flats to verify that all is well. Use some 80-grit sandpaper to finish off any rough spots on the foam. If there are dentil blocks, it may be necessary to remove a few of them and fudge the spacing a bit to make them look right. Sometimes it is easier to wait until now to put the dentil blocks on the trim. Use latex caulk on the rough spots. It is pliable enough to work well with the bendable foam.

There is an easy way to attach the cornice to the wall using some 1/4" plywood strips adhered to the top of the cornice with Liquid Nails. If the tops of the walls will show from a balcony, it may be worth your time to miter all of these plywood pieces so that they fit very tightly, but if not, just make sure that the strips run to within a few inches of the end so that they provide enough support. The strips need to extend off the rear of the cornice molding far enough so that they can be screwed to the tops of the flats. For a softcovered flat this might be only 3/4", while for hardcovered flats you may wish to leave as much as 3". There should be enough extension onto the top of the foam so that the adhesive can get good purchase. The exact amount depends on the amount of stress placed on the joint. The only thing holding the cornice is the glue, so make sure the bond is good. Of course the foam is very light, and about 6" of coverage would seem plenty for this project. Just make sure to test the grip before hanging the cornice.

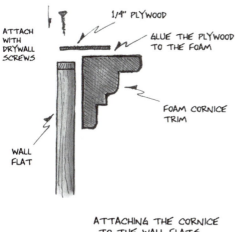

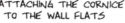

ATTACHING THE CORNICE
TO THE WALL FLATS

The cornice will be hung at a height that should be well out of the way of stage action so there is generally no need to go so far as to coat it with cheesecloth. It is nice to give the surface a coating of some kind of heavy sealer for protection as well as to give it a slicker looking finish. Products like Bin or Sculpt or Coat are excellent for this purpose. It is imperative that you determine that any sealer used is compatible with the chemical nature of the foam. Oil-base-paint or fiberglass resin will reduce the polystyrene to a heap of mush.

TOMBSTONE PROJECT

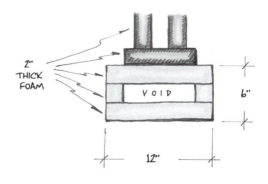

TOMBSTONE PROJECT

Creating a tombstone is a really fun student project. Perhaps I've built too many versions of *Tom Sawyer* and *Christmas Carol*, but it seems that the theatrical demand for tombstones is quite high. At any rate, this graveyard monument uses all of the skills you've learned so far. Here are some construction sketches for the piece:

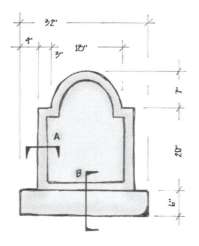

DIMENSIONS FOR THE PROJECT

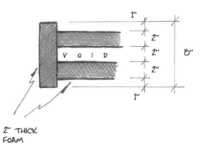

2" THICK
FOAM

SECTION THRU A

SECTION THRU B

It would be possible to carve this piece from one solid chunk of foam, but it makes more sense to use readily available sheet goods instead. The exterior of this unit will give the appearance of being massive and sturdy, but inside the tombstone is hollow. This reduces the amount of product used, and hence the cost. Start by cutting out the front and back pieces of the vertical slab. The layout consists of a rectangle and half a circle, which are easily laid out using a drywall square, a compass, and a Sharpie marker. Cut the pieces out with a jigsaw, and use the first one as a pattern for the second.

Set the radial arm saw so that the blade is $3/4$" above the table. Make a mark on the wooden guide that is 1" to the right of the kerf where the blade passes through the fence. Each time the blade passes through the foam, move the stock 1" to the right as indicated by the mark on the fence. When you have prepared a long enough section to cover the distance around the semicircle, reset the blade $1/2$" higher than it was. Repeat the kerfing operation, but this time cut away foam just to the side of the previous pass. Repeat again with a shallower cut if necessary. This will form a kind of "digital" looking dart or V shape in the foam that will close up as the foam is bent around its circle.

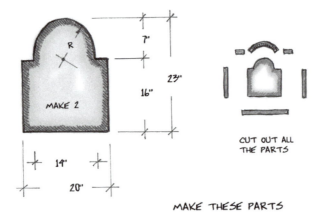

MAKE THESE PARTS

CUT OUT ALL THE PARTS

ATTACH THE KERFED PART FIRST

USE SCRAP PIECES AS SPACERS

The edging around the vertical portion of the tombstone is made of the same 2" thick foam. Rip an 8 foot long section of this foam to use as stock. The straight sections are easily cut to length, and it matters little which way the joints overlap. The edging for the rounded top will need to be kerfed in order for it to bend enough to fit the diameter of this curve. The radius is small, so the kerfing must be quite severe and will require an extra technique.

You are now ready to assemble the top section. Use two or three pieces of scrap foam as spacers and join the vertical slab sections (which were the first parts you cut out) using Liquid Nails. The spacers are used to keep the sections 2" apart, and to give the total thickness of 6". Glue on the 8" wide top strip you kerfed earlier, leaving about an inch of overhang on either side. It will be difficult to gauge the exact length of this piece because it fits on a circle. Just remember that it is easier to trim a bit more off the kerfed section than it will be to make a new one. Glue on the two flanking pieces to help keep the curve in place while the Liquid Nails sets up. Attach the remaining trim pieces and set the entire assembly aside until the mastic has bonded sufficiently to hold while you work on rounding over the corners.

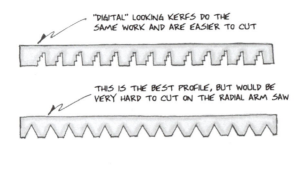

"DIGITAL" LOOKING KERFS DO THE SAME WORK AND ARE EASIER TO CUT

THIS IS THE BEST PROFILE, BUT WOULD BE VERY HARD TO CUT ON THE RADIAL ARM SAW

USE THE RADIAL ARM SAW TO KERF THE FOAM

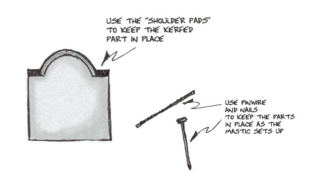

USE THE "SHOULDER PADS" TO KEEP THE KERFED PART IN PLACE

USE PINWIRE AND NAILS TO KEEP THE PARTS IN PLACE AS THE MASTIC SETS UP

Cut out pieces for the top and bottom of the base. Rip enough of the 2"x 2" stock to fit around the perimeter of the hollow structure. Cut the 2x2 strips to length, and glue all of the parts together. Set this section aside to dry.

BASE

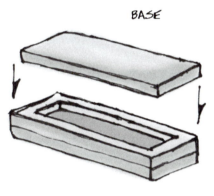

It is easiest to work on carving and finishing these two subassemblies while they are apart, and then to join them before the cheesecloth is put on. Use the Surform to even any parts that are sticking out, and round over all the corners. Most builders agree that the more you round over, the older and more weathered the finished product will appear. You may wish to add a few cracks and some lettering. Use a Sharpie to mark the lettering and a pointy X-acto Knife to cut them out. Normally a large handled utility knife is better for any type of cutting, but in this instance a long and thin blade is the best. Cut straight in around the outside edges and rake out the center like a chiseled mortise. Smooth all surfaces with a piece of 80-grit sandpaper.

The final step before painting is to cover with cheese-cloth. This project is a bit more challenging to cover than the stonework was. It is best to cut the cloth into 12" or 18" squares of single thickness before beginning, because large sections are too hard to control. Bunch up the cloth where it must fit down into crevices like the letter carving. If the cheesecloth does not go down into the cracks properly, your hard work creating texture will tend to disappear.

A very quick, but messy way to carve any kind of polystyrene foam is to use a drill and a wire wheel. Some wire wheels are intended to be used to remove rust and old paint from wrought iron railings and the like. These wheels are perfect for carving because they are mounted on a shaft and can easily be inserted into a drill.

There are two main types. One of these is two or three inches in diameter with a brush of wire around its outside edge. The other has what looks like short lengths of wire rope sticking straight ahead out of a central hub. Both of these types of wire wheels are used to carve by inserting them in a variable speed drill and simply gouging and shredding the foam from the surface of the block. This technique can be used to create a number of really rough textures like stucco, bark, or rock. The hub with the wire rope sticking straight out is the easiest to control, while the other wheel is more aggressive about removing the foam. They both spew out an unbelievable amount of foam chips. Safety glasses and a respirator are a must, and you can expect to be completely covered from head to toe with small bits of foam. A good shop vac is essential for clean up. I have found that anytime foam is involved in a project it is best to sweep and vacuum up the leavings right away so that they are not tracked all over the theatre.

CUT AROUND THE EDGES FIRST. SCORE THE INSIDE AS THOUGH MORTISING WITH A CHISEL. RAKE OUT THE EXCESS FOAM WITH A SCREWDRIVER.

USE LONG, THIN, BLADE

GOES IN DRILL CHUCK

WIRES STICK OUT FROM THE SIDE

GOES TO DRILL CHUCK

THESE WIRES RESEMBLE AIRCRAFT CABLE

CHAPTER 19

HOW DO YOU MAKE...

This chapter is devoted to explaining the construction of some specific devices that are very commonly encountered in theatrical work. They did not fit into the flow of the other chapters but are important "how to" topics. The projects are not listed in any order and are intended for use as a reference work. Perhaps they will give you ideas for problem-solving devices of your own.

SHOP-BUILT CHAIN MOTOR BOX

CUE LIGHTS

Construction sites often need temporary lighting fixtures that can be tied up around the job. To accommodate this need, manufacturers offer a rubberized, standard screw base socket attached to a basket that is used to protect the bulb in a harsh environment. In years past the baskets were made of metal, but now the yellow plastic type predominates. You can find this product marketed under a names such as "String-O-Lites," which is actually a quite descriptive title. There is a 50-foot or so run of wire with the sockets spaced along its length. You are really only interested in the sockets, and the roll of wire will not be needed. It is most likely a solid type rather than stranded, and as such is not suited to the requirement of a flexible, portable, cable. You may be able to locate the same rubberized sockets and baskets as separate items, and that will work just fine, too.

The wire leads from the socket are connected to the coil of wire with wire nuts or some other kind of mechanical splicer, and you will just have to live with whatever length of lead is provided. If it is less than three inches, you won't be able to connect two of them together, and the usefulness is limited.

Gang two sockets together to make one cue light. Doubling up may prevent some horrible mistake during a performance, for if one of the bulbs should happen to burn out or become disconnected in some way, there will be a second to carry on the fight. That happens much more frequently than you would think and is standard procedure for a commercial touring company. In that profession, the cue lights are sent out as a part of the electrics rental package.

Strip both of the white wires and connect them to the neutral terminal in your connector. Strip both black wires and connect both of them to the hot terminal in your connector. Use a terminal end (spade or ring) when appropriate.

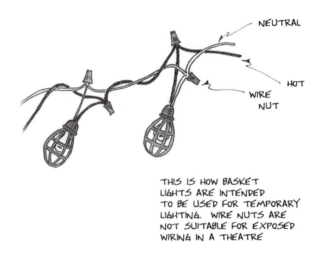

THIS IS HOW BASKET LIGHTS ARE INTENDED TO BE USED FOR TEMPORARY LIGHTING. WIRE NUTS ARE NOT SUITABLE FOR EXPOSED WIRING IN A THEATRE

Cut the sockets loose from the wire, leaving at least two or three inches of tail. Since the entire socket assembly is nonconductive, there will most likely be no ground wire, just a hot and a neutral, color-coded black and white respectively.

TWIST-LOCK CONNECTOR

Naturally, different types of connectors are hooked up differently, and you should refer to the manufacturer's instructions for details. In general, however, you will find that most wiring devices use a silver, nickle-plated screw for the neutral terminal and a plain brass screw for the hot terminal.

It is important to keep this procedure straight. The neutral wire should connect with the large metal screw base inside, which is easy to touch by accident. The hot wire should connect to a small conducting plate in the bottom of the fixture, where it is much less likely to cause harm. If you reverse the leads, the opposite will be true, and the risk of electrical shock will be greatly increased.

The 20-amp pin connector is the most common sort of cable end used in the theatre. As far as I know, they are not used by any other field, and are only available from a theatrical supplier. On a grounded pin connector, the pin in the middle is the ground (which you may not need for this project). It is not exactly centered, but rather is a bit to one side. Of the remaining two pins, the one that is the closest to the ground is the neutral. The one that is farthest from the ground is the hot. This selection method works the same for either male or female ends. You need a male end.

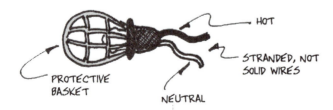

PROTECTIVE BASKET   HOT

STRANDED, NOT SOLID WIRES

NEUTRAL

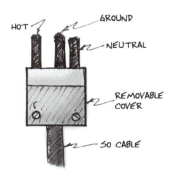

PIN CONNECTOR

It is curious to note that before the grounded pin connector was developed, there was no way to ensure that the hot/neutral dedication was preserved. The connector could be turned either way. This was also true of the standard household Edison, or parallel blade plug, before that type was polarized by making the neutral blade wider than the hot blade. Now the off-center placement of the grounding pin makes sure that the hot and neutral wires are connected to the appropriate terminals.

Remember not to strip off too much insulation from the wires. This is probably the most common cause for a short-circuit. Most devices have a chart that tells how much to strip, but a general rule of thumb is to limit this amount to that which will just fit into the terminal or attachment point. Be sure to use whatever strain relief the manufacturer has provided. Some additional wiring tips are available in the chapter on lighting.

It is common practice to use small, round, colored, 7 $1/2$-watt bulbs in a cue light. Failing this, try using a 15-watt pear shape. Do not use higher wattage bulbs because they will light up the entire backstage, and possibly start a fire when someone carelessly hangs a costume next to the light. Colors become important when more than one cue light is used in the same location (for different cues happening at nearly the same time). If you use these lights often, and move them around a lot (like on a tour), it is often helpful to color code the light and any cable used with it so that it is easier to hook up. Use the same colored tape to mark the switches at the stage manager's desk. Cue lights make excellent circuit test lights, and can also be used as a dancer's spotting light.

STAGE MANAGER'S DESK

On a touring show (and on Broadway), the stage manager's desk is most often the personal property of the production stage manager rather than either the production company or a rental house associated with the show. It might

be built by that same stage manager (hmm...), or by some local stagehand, or even a friend. As a result the quality varies greatly, and so does the style. There are, however, some common features that are always found.

STAGE MANAGER'S
DESK

The desk is quite literally just that, a desk where the stage manager can sit to call cues. Since many prefer to stand much of the time, it is common to see the desk as a tallish structure using a stool rather than a chair. The top is almost always slanted, and this gives it the appearance of something old Bob Cratchit might have used. There are doors for storage underneath, and it is helpful if this storage area can be secured with a lock. The desk will get moved around a lot, and a nice cabinet lock will be hard to secure if the case gets racked out of shape. They are also much easier to break into. It is common to use a resettable padlock like a Sesame Lock. This way, there are no keys to lose, and the number can be set to an easily recalled combination like your birthday or some historical date. A combination lock can provide access to a larger group of people when necessary. Then you can reset it to a new number when too many people know the old one.

There are some electronic devices that are very often a part of the stage manager's desk. The main station for the headset intercom system is often located here so that the stage manager can easily change channels, volume, etc.

PAGE MIC

There should be some sort of paging microphone to reach the dressing room monitors for actor's calls. Quite often, you will find a video monitor on top of the desk that gives the cue caller a view of the stage and sometimes a separate view of the conductor in the pit.

On a tour, these electronics are often supplied by one or more of the rental companies that have been contracted to provide equipment for the show, and they may ride in a separate container, which is then stacked on top of the desk.

One thing that is definitely a part of the desk itself is the bank of cue light switches. It is advisable to have at least five or six of them in order not to run short. They are usually located in a strip above the table surface, below any shelves used for the intercom and/or video/audio monitors.

STAGE MANAGER'S DESK
WITH CUE LIGHT SWITCHES
THE FEMALE TWIST LOCKS ARE OUTPUTS

If the switches are mounted on a removable plate, installation and servicing will be made easier. Outputs should be located on the rear of the desk and can be either panel mount or the pigtail type. Putting the entire desk on casters will make it easy to move around when necessary.

CYC STRETCHING CLAMPS

A sky cyclorama is a 30-foot tall piece of fabric that is as wide as the rigging system will allow. It is difficult to keep this curtain from becoming wrinkled, especially if it has been folded for storage (which is not recommended). A cyc is usually washed with very bright lights in order to create a sky effect. These lights are almost always at a rather oblique angle, one that causes any wrinkles or folds to create unsightly shadows. As a result, it is often necessary to stretch the cyc out in order to remove the wrinkles. A bottom pipe will stretch out the bottom of the cyc, but something more is required for lateral stretching left and right.

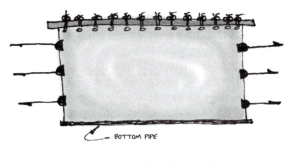

BOTTOM PIPE

USE THE STRETCHERS TO PULL OUT
THE VERITICAL WRINKLES

A series of clamps that can be attached to the sides of the cyc are used with pull lines leading offstage. The clamps should be designed to minimize any damage to the cyc from tearing.

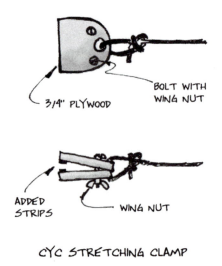

3/4" PLYWOOD

BOLT WITH
WING NUT

ADDED
STRIPS

WING NUT

CYC STRETCHING CLAMP

Two, 8"-wide, 3/4"-thick plywood blocks can be used for the two sides of the clamp. They will have a better appearance if you dress them up a bit with some chamfering, and it is absolutely necessary to sand all corners and edges in order to avoid ripping the cyc fabric. Two 1/8" thick strips on the clamping side of the jaws will make it easier for the device to get a good bite on the cloth. Drill oversized holes for the quarter-inch bolts that hold the two sides together. The clamp halves will sit at an angle, and the bolt needs extra room to fit loosely. A larger hole on the offstage side provides a point to attach the tying off line.

Use a trucker's hitch to get a nice tight pull on the lines. If you leave a short line with a bowline at the end of it tied to the clamp, you can use the two-line method of the trucker's hitch, and then the clamps can just stay on the cyc even when it is not in use. It will take several clamps on each side to get all of the wrinkles out of the drop.

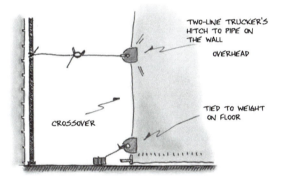

AVOID BLOCKING THE CROSSOVER

Sometimes it is difficult to find anything to tie off to in the theatre, especially when a crossover is required. On these occasions, tie the bottom clamp off to stage weights on the floor, and the next one over head height. This will allow actors to pass by the ropes. Another method is to lag a lighting tower to the stage at either end of the cyc, and use them as tying off points.

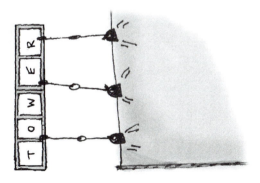

YOU CAN TIE THE LINES TO A TOWER

Lately there is a trend toward using a rear projection screen (RP) and a bounce drop to do the same sort of effect as a sky cyc. It is not advisable to use these stretchers on an RP screen because the material is too delicate. It is generally not necessary anyway.

LIGHTING TOWERS

Lighting towers are the modern equivalent of booms and/ or ladders. They use space much more efficiently and are easier to travel, easier to set up, and much safer to use.

The problem with booms is that they tend to be tippy when over a certain height. Hanging an equal number of lights yoked out to either side will help, but the resultant effect is to use up a large amount of valuable wing space. The lights can be hung going onstage and on one side in order to conserve space, but this exacerbates the tipping problem. Most boom bases have no means to lag them to the floor for security, although it is possible to pile on a few sandbags to increase the weight of the base.

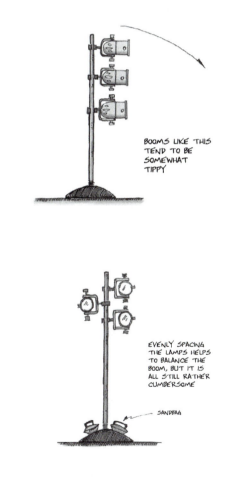

BOOMS LIKE THIS TEND TO BE SOMEWHAT TIPPY

EVENLY SPACING THE LAMPS HELPS TO BALANCE THE BOOM, BUT IT IS ALL STILL RATHER CUMBERSOME

SANDBAG

Ladders are used on the ends of electrics hanging over the stage. They allow electricians to hang lights downward off the batten, effectively increasing the length of the pipe that is used for side light. Ladders are nice in that the floor under them is kept entirely clear of obstructions, and if your show has a lot of rolling units they may be the best option. Even so, there are some real problems associated with hanging them.

LADDERS ARE A GOOD SOLUTION FOR THE "TIPPY" PROBLEM, BUT MAY CAUSE PROBLEMS IN WEIGHTING THE ARBOR.

LADDERS KEEP THE STAGE FLOOR CLEAR

C CLAMP

Many times ladders are several feet taller than the distance from the batten to the floor when it is at its lowest trim. This makes loading the weights a bit of a problem. Either you load the weights with the arbor somewhat low, which may not be possible (and is certainly not safe without taking extra precautions), or you must hang the ladder on the pipe at an angle and somehow straighten everything out as the pipe goes up. Possible, but cumbersome. There really is no elegant solution to that problem other than making sure that the ladders are not too tall for the system. But then they will probably be too short to work effectively.

If your booms are not too tall and there is minimal movement backstage, they will work just fine. If your ladders fit between the pipe and the floor when the batten is all the way in, then they are an excellent means of keeping the floor clear, and it only makes sense to use them.

Towers approach the problem from another direction. They are modular units connected together to form a taller structure. Lights fit inside the tower and are thus protected from actors and moving scenery. On a tour, the lights stay inside the towers for the move, just like a rock-and-roll truss. This saves a good deal of time remounting them for each city and reduces time spent focusing. Of course, this approach appeals to anyone's sense of what is neat and tidy, but I also like the way that the towers can be lagged to the floor. When properly done, bolting them to the floor is so secure that there should be no concern that they will tip over. You can never say that about a boom. It is important to use lag bolts that go all the way down into the sub floor so that they get a really good "bite."

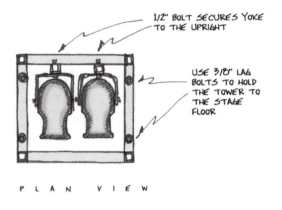

1/2" BOLT SECURES YOKE TO THE UPRIGHT

USE 3/8" LAG BOLTS TO HOLD THE TOWER TO THE STAGE FLOOR

P L A N   V I E W

Six feet tall is a good size for a tower section because it is not too hard to move around, and multiples of six just happen to fall at convenient heights. Anything lower than six feet tall is a good height for floor mounts or "shin busters." Twelve feet is enough overall height much of the time, while eighteen feet is about maximum. Most shows in most houses will trim at somewhere between eighteen and twenty-four feet and it should not be necessary for a lighting tower to go any higher than that. The taller the tower, the more difficult it is to stand up, and the more inherently unstable it will be. You might find that two eight-foot sections are more suitable to your needs. Anything smaller than a six-foot height would seem problematic from the standpoint of being overly complicated to construct.

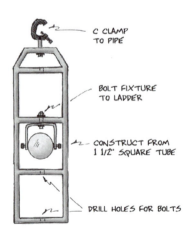

C CLAMP TO PIPE

BOLT FIXTURE TO LADDER

CONSTRUCT FROM 1 1/2" SQUARE TUBE

DRILL HOLES FOR BOLTS

LADDER FOR 4 LIGHTS

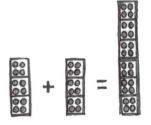

STACK THE TOWER UNITS TO MAKE A TALLER ONE

This design for a tower creates a unit that is wide enough for two lights to fit side by side. That will allow you to hang more units right at the top and/or bottom where they are most needed. Provide enough space for the lights to fit in and for the shutters to operate, but keep in mind that it is best to make the tower as thin as possible in order to save on deck space. One saving grace is that given the location of the tower offstage, the focus of the lights is almost always straight ahead and down a bit, so there is no need to leave space for them to turn much to the side. A two-foot square tower is about the right size. You can see how neatly all of these measurements add up for storage.

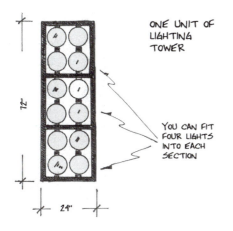

ONE UNIT OF
LIGHTING
TOWER

12"

24"

YOU CAN FIT
FOUR LIGHTS
INTO EACH
SECTION

You can also see that this design allows for twelve lights on one-foot centers in each section of tower. On an eighteen-foot tall tower, that means a capacity of thirty-six units per side, for each pair of towers. This should be enough for just about any lighting designer. Of course, most of the time the spaces in the middle are not really used for lighting and can be an excellent location for a sound or video monitor, a fog machine, or some other piece of equipment. All of this and each tower takes up only four square feet of deck space!

Use square tube to construct the tower. (See the chapter on metal frame construction.) It is really just a box with some vertical members connected by horizontals. Make the towers as one solid piece rather than as a series of bolt-together frames. In addition, there are two vertical square tubes that run up the inside back of the tower that are used to connect the lights themselves. It is not necessary to use any C-clamps, just drill a hole in the upright and use $1/2$" bolts that are $2 1/2$" long through the square tube and the light yoke. Use washers throughout to make it easier to turn the light when focusing. If you intend to leave the lights in the towers for an extended period, it might be worthwhile to invest in some nylon lock nuts that will keep just the right tension on the bolt and lessen the chance that the nut might vibrate off.

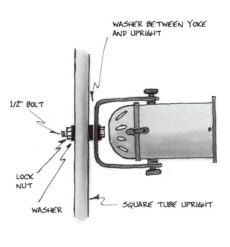

WASHER BETWEEN YOKE
AND UPRIGHT

1/2" BOLT

LOCK
NUT

WASHER

SQUARE TUBE UPRIGHT

**LIGHT BOLTED TO UPRIGHT
ON A LIGHTING TOWER**

Be sure to provide four holes in the top and bottom of each tower section so that it can be bolted to another section or to the floor. Make the placement of all the holes exactly the same so that each of the sections can fit together interchangeably. This will make assembly easier.

When setting up the show, hang all of the lights in the various tower sections before standing them up. Lay the sections out on the floor, bolt in the lights, and also bolt the sections together in the order they will work. Place the tower so that the bottom section is close to where the tower will eventually live. Use two people to foot the tower, and everyone else in the theatre to walk it up. If there is any doubt about the ability of the hands to control the tower on its way up, use a safety line on the top of the tower. You can use a regular bull line coming down from the grid, rail, or electrics jump. Jockey the tower into final position, and lag it to the floor right away. Make sure that you use bolts which are large enough to hold the tower securely, at *least* $3/8$"x 4".

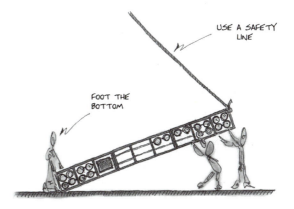

USE A SAFETY
LINE

FOOT THE
BOTTOM

PUT THE BOTTOM IN PLACE,
AND WALK THE TOWER UP

L -JACKS

Jacks are typically used to hold a piece of scenery in an upright position. Most often, they are connected to the back of a column or flat with hinges so that they can be either removed or folded against the unit when not in use.

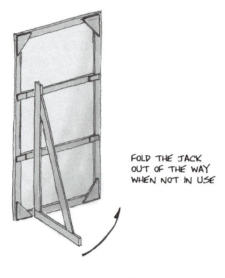

FOLD THE JACK
OUT OF THE WAY
WHEN NOT IN USE

L-JACK ON A FLAT

You must add weight to the jack in order to stabilize it. A twenty-five pound counterweight placed diagonally between the framing members is great for this purpose. In a TV studio, sandbags are often used.

USE A STAGE
WEIGHT TO HOLD
THE JACK AND
FLAT IN PLACE

Another method of stabilizing the jack is to hinge it to the floor. This method has the advantage of being considerably more secure, but it is much more difficult to adjust when necessary, requiring the movement of the hinge. If your scenery must be struck during the show, the simple weight method is probably your best bet unless it is possible to loose pin hinge the jack to a section of decking.

There are two similar styles of wooden L-jacks, and the difference is created mostly by the size of the units involved. The traditional type is characterized by a tall vertical, a shorter horizontal (hence the name), and a connecting diagonal. This works fine in a jack that is ten feet or less in height, but eventually an increasing size dictates a slight change in design.

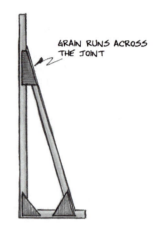

GRAIN RUNS ACROSS
THE JOINT

TRADITIONAL L-JACK

The taller type is truncated at the top, with a number of internal braces, and the resulting structure is somewhat stronger and more rigid. Construction methods are generally the same.

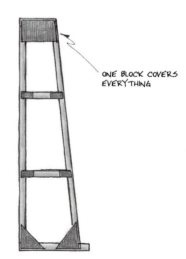

ONE BLOCK COVERS
EVERYTHING

NEW AND IMPROVED L-JACK

It is more efficient to make a number of jacks all at one time. Laying out the diagonal and the cover blocks takes a bit of time, but it is easy to cut out multiples of those pieces. It may take 20 minutes to lay out and build one jack, but only 30 minutes to build two. If you make extra jacks of a commonly used size, you will have some stock units to pull from.

It is easiest to build jacks on a wooden squaring up template table such as was described in the chapter on flat construction. This allows you to quickly form the L corner, and to tack the parts in down on the table, so they are held in place while the blocks are glued and stapled.

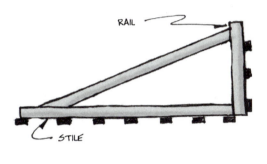

USE A TEMPLATE TABLE
TO SQUARE THE JACK

A cut list is easily derived. The bottom rail of the jack extends under the stile and the diagonal brace. It is usually in the neighborhood of two and one-half feet in length. Use whatever size base is appropriate to fit in backstage. There is no top rail. The jack should be tall enough to connect with a convenient and logical point on the unit being braced. On a flat, this could mean either the top toggle rail, or perhaps about two thirds of the way up one of the stiles. For a 12'- 0" flat, an eight foot tall brace would need about a two foot rail. When using 1x3 stock that gives you a cut list per unit of 1 @ 7' - 9 $\frac{3}{8}$" and 1 @ 2'- 0".

The diagonal brace must be scribed from these two members like the method used in full-scale patterns.

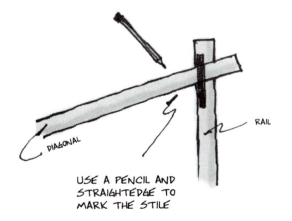

USE A PENCIL AND
STRAIGHTEDGE TO
MARK THE STILE

Tack the rail and stile into the square corner of the flat frame. Measure down a few inches from the top of the stile, and a few inches in from the end of the rail. Usually, I like to leave a bit more space at the top than at the bottom. This shortens the diagonal a bit, but the real purpose is mostly aesthetic. The jacks just look better that way. Lay a section of stock over the marks and then scribe cut lines on to it. After you have cut the first one and checked it for a proper fit, it can be used as a pattern to cut the rest. This will save a considerable amount of time.

When all of the 1x3 stock has been cut to length, tack down the diagonal for the first jack. A regular corner block can be used for the 90-degree-angle corner. If the other bottom angle is reasonably acute, a regular corner block turned with the hypotenuse down can be marked and trimmed to fit. The grain of the plywood will be at less than a right angle to the joint, but will still be satisfactory. The top intersection of the pine framing is generally too acute to use any stock parts, so plan on cutting these blocks from scratch using scrap $\frac{1}{4}$" plywood. Run the grain of the plywood horizontally. There is no need to inset these blocks $\frac{3}{4}$" from the edge of the framing as in a regular softcovered flat, but a $\frac{1}{4}$" inset will give the unit a nicer appearance.

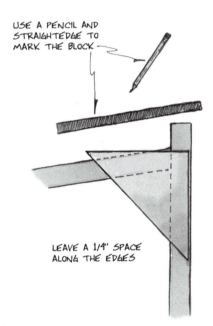

USE A PENCIL AND
STRAIGHTEDGE TO
MARK THE BLOCK

LEAVE A 1/4" SPACE
ALONG THE EDGES

This jack has been pictured with the 90-degree-angle corner to the left because that is the most natural way for it to fit on the template. Sometimes, a jack will hinge better if the blocks are on the other side of the unit, especially if the jack is expected to fold back tightly against the flat. It is smart to make some left-handed and some right-handed jacks. The parts are all the same except for the oddly shaped blocks that need to be a mirror image. (Reverse and repeat.) On occasion, you may want to put blocks on both sides when a super heavy-duty jack is required.

STIFFENERS

Stiffeners are often used in conjunction with L jacks to provide a wall bracing "system." The function of a stiffener is to improve rigidity in general and to keep various sections of scenery on the same plane. Stiffeners are not just for walls made of flats, but this type of construction does provide a good example of the principles involved. Information about stiffeners is also available in the section on flats.

Stiffeners are most often wooden and can be as simple as a single length of 1x3 or 1x4. Sometimes, a long wooden stiffener is laminated together from several layers of plywood. This creates a very stable structure. As with any laminated product, be sure to offset the joints and use enough glue to ensure the necessary strength.

When hinging a stiffener to a group of flats, placement of the hinges is very important. There should be a hinge at the extreme ends and at every joint between the flats. On a softcovered flat, the framing allows for easy connection to the stiles. On a hardcovered flat, that won't work, and it is better to hinge to the tops of the toggles, or perhaps the top rail.

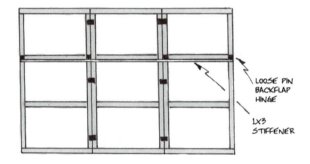

SOFTCOVERED FLAT STIFFENER

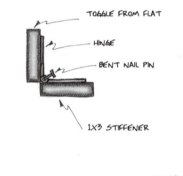

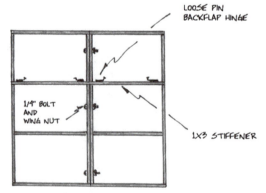

HARDCOVERED FLAT STIFFENER

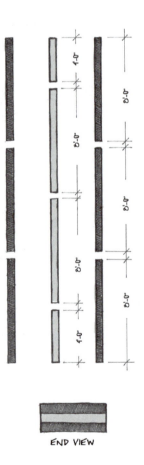

END VIEW

STIFFENER PARTS

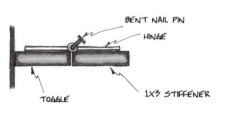

Stiffeners can also be made from a length of square tube with the hinges welded on. The advantage is that the tubing comes in 24-foot lengths and is considerably tougher than wood.

Always locate the hinges on the top of the stiffener so that it does not tend to "flop down" when the scenery is elevated. Maintaining a methodical approach to the framing of the flats during construction makes installation of a stiffener much easier. Perhaps all of the discussion in the chapter on flats about how to properly locate the toggles makes more sense now.

Stiffeners can be used to align flats on more than one plane. Here are a couple of examples of how they can be used to form corners. In this case, more than a simple bar is required. Essentially, a softcovered type of flat is built, but not covered. It is used only for its framing value.

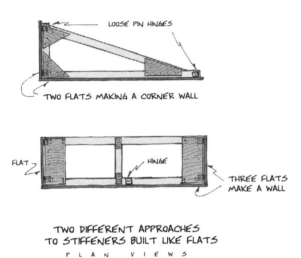

TWO DIFFERENT APPROACHES
TO STIFFENERS BUILT LIKE FLATS
P L A N   V I E W S

Sometimes a stiffener is used to connect oddly shaped profile pieces. Here a tree is used as an example. The central trunk is constructed as one piece, but it would be quite difficult to transport this unit with all of the other limbs attached.

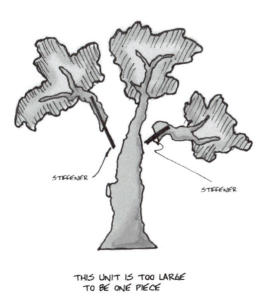

THIS UNIT IS TOO LARGE
TO BE ONE PIECE

In this case a stiffener is permanently affixed to the small sections, and loose pin hinges are used to fasten the other end to the main trunk. It is often useful to put at least two hinges on one side and one on the other to "trap" the stiffener in place. In addition, small scabs on the back of the added unit are helpful in keeping the pieces from twisting and telegraphing the joint.

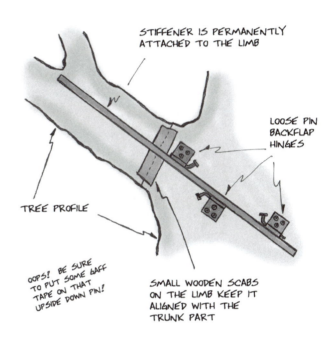

CANE BOLTS

Cane bolts are used to position and secure rolling units to the floor when the action of the play is such that the unit would lurch unpleasantly without them. When viewed from the side, it is easy to see where this item got its name. There are really two parts to a cane bolt, the bolt itself and the sleeve that is used to connect it to the decking unit. The latter is a section of pipe for the bolt to run through, and a welded-on flange with screw holes in it. Cane bolts are commercially available, but in keeping with Murphy's Law, I have found that the flange is almost always the wrong size to fit on my platform, or the bolt is just not quite long enough to reach the stage floor. Making the hardware yourself is not too difficult and ensures a great fit.

It is best to use at least $1/2$" stock for the bolt. This size is hard to bend into the cane shape, but it is also less likely to bend when pressure is applied during the show. If necessary, weld a handle onto the shaft instead of bending. The $3/8$" size of bolt may be OK for some lightweight applications, but I have been disappointed by how easily it can be bent. It is always disquieting to sit at a rehearsal and see two actors run across the stage and fling themselves on a bed being held into place by bolts that are too small. Of course in the production meeting the director said it just had to sit there!

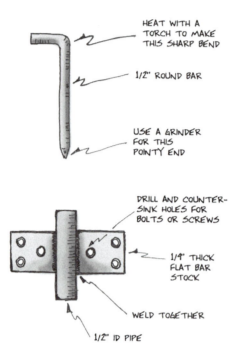

SHOP MADE CANE BOLT

If you would like for the bolt to remain with the unit while it rolls, a chain link cut in half and welded into place on one of the flanges can be used for this purpose. Make sure that the bolt is retained high enough to keep from dragging.

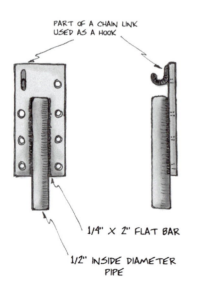

CANE BOLT BODY

Sometimes it is possible to just drill through a unit and use that hole as a means of pinning the unit to the floor. This won't work if there is a large gap between the bottom of the unit and the floor because there will be too much play in the assembly.

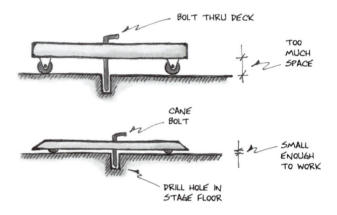

Grinding the end of the pin so that it is slightly pointy will make it easier to insert it into the deck. Never use more than two bolts, because it will be far too hard to line the piece up, and besides, it is just not necessary. If you concentrate on getting one pin into its hole, it is fairly easy to rotate the unit so that the other simply drops in on its own.

Notes on Mounting Casters

There are two main types of casters: swivel and rigid. As the names imply, the swivel casters rotate around a vertical axis and can line up with any direction of travel. Rigid casters are fixed, and once bolted to a platform they will allow it to move only back and forth along the same line. Stagehands sometimes call these smart and dumb casters.

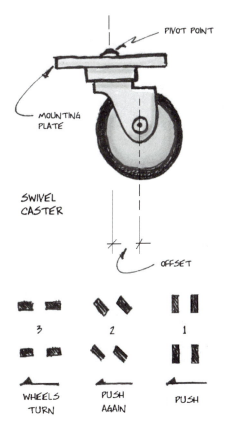

SWIVEL CASTER

RIGID CASTER

MOVES BACK AND FORTH ONLY

At first glance, it would seem that swivel casters would always be more useful than rigid because of their ability to change direction, but this is not necessarily so. The center of the wheel of a swivel caster is offset somewhat from its pivot point on the mounting plate. When in motion, the wheel of the caster follows behind this pivot point, and it is this "drag" principle that causes the caster to rotate in the first place. If the wheel were directly under the pivot point, it would have no reason to turn and align itself with the direction the scenery is moving.

Having said this, it is necessary to apply extra force to the unit to get it to begin moving not only because of the inherent inertia problem, but also because of the necessity of forcing all of the casters to turn and line up with one another. The unit will invariably lurch to the side a bit when this happens, and it is difficult to get it to track straight under some circumstances. This problem can be overcome by lining the unit up offstage, pushing onstage a bit to align the casters, and then leaving it alone until time for the cue. This works fine when going onstage, but there is no way to repeat the process going off. Also, if a unit has four swivel casters, it will often tend to drift to one side or the other, especially if one of the casters becomes hung on something.

If you are sure that a platform will need to move on only one track, all rigid casters can be used. It is important to align the casters with one another and with the unit so that the wheels will turn smoothly without chattering. Use a straightedge to keep the caster plates parallel to one another. Rigid casters are often used with a pallet, especially one meant to be operated with a push stick. (See next section.)

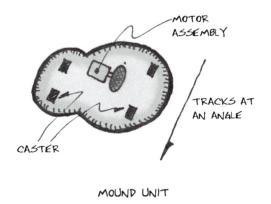

MOUND UNIT

I was once on a tour of *Camelot* designed to use a large mound unit, on rigid casters, which had to track up-and-downstage at an angle. There was no deck used in the show, and hence no way to use any sort of winch or tracking system. The unit was animated by a large DC motor and a soft rubber tire for traction. After a few trips back and forth, the mound would creep out of alignment. The entire crew would gather around and wrestle it back into place every few performances. Although there were some obvious engineering problems, it worked well enough for the purpose.

One excellent technique is to mix rigid and swivel casters on the same piece. If you put two rigid casters on the front of the unit, and two swivel casters on the rear, it will steer more or less like a car in reverse. Steering your end to the left will cause the unit to move right, and steering right induces a leftward turn. The advantage is that there is no tendency for the scenery to drift in the wrong direction and one person can easily steer it. The bad side is that just like parallel parking, if you don't hit the mark, you'll just have to back up and try again because there is no way to scoot it over sideways.

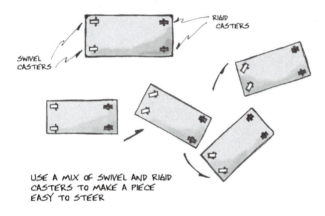

USE A MIX OF SWIVEL AND RIGID
CASTERS TO MAKE A PIECE
EASY TO STEER

Another solution for some units is to use just two rigid casters, placed so that the scenery can be tipped on one side where the wheels are, and then maneuvered like a two-wheeled dolly. Obviously this will only work when the size and weight of the piece are reasonable. One advantage is that there is no need to lock the unit in position. This method works best if the piece in question is between chest high and head high. It is often used on large theatre speakers.

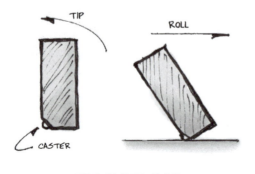

TIP AND ROLL UNIT

It seems appropriate to spend a moment discussing some of the parts and qualities of casters. Casters used in the theatre almost always have a mounting plate. In contrast, many furniture casters use a spindle that is intended to fit inside a socket, like you would find on a chair leg. These are not very helpful in theatre, because the spindle method of mounting is not really strong enough to hold much weight, although I have on occasion used casters with a bolt or threaded stud connector when joining the caster to a piece of steel square tube.

In general, the larger the wheel on a caster, the easier it is to roll and the less likely it is to hang up on a rough floor surface. On the other hand, large wheels are harder to get to swivel and change direction. Softer wheels are more difficult to roll than harder ones, but they make less noise. Steel wheels are way too noisy unless you are at a Rolling Stones concert. A high-quality caster rated to carry a lot of weight has a nice set of ball bearings that should be evident when you handle it. If a caster makes a horrible squealing noise when it rolls, then the load is too heavy. Good casters have a load rating that tells you how much weight you can put on them. You should probably order these from a supply house rather than get them at the local hardware store. Good casters are expensive but will pay for themselves over time, especially at a resident company or school.

Always mount casters on the bottom of the framing. If you mount them on the underside of the lid, the framing will become disconnected and fail. If you must caster to the lid on a lightweight piece, take extra steps to ensure that the plywood holds. Use bolts, screws, steel plates, or whatever seems appropriate to beef up the joinery. One good practice when using stock platforms is to run a plate under several of the framing members and then attach the caster to that plate. This method works well when there are several small sections to be ganged together. Just remember that fewer casters will make a sweeter rolling unit, but there must be enough wheels to properly support the structure.

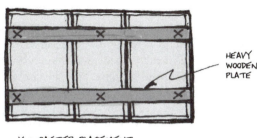

X = CASTER PLACEMENT

BOTTOM OF A ROLLING UNIT
MADE FROM THREE 4X8 PLATFORMS

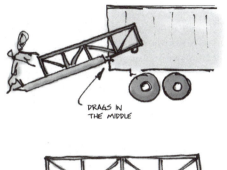

DRAGS IN
THE MIDDLE

SMALL RIGID CASTER

A SMALL CASTER IN THE CENTER
OF THE TRUSS MAKES IT EASIER
TO GET THE PIECE UP A RAMP

Sometimes it is possible to use a starter section that has enough casters to stand on its own, and then add on more sections that are supported half by the original section, and half by their own casters. This will drastically reduce the number of casters that must be used. This method works well when the unit must be disassembled for transport.

PALLETS

In the theatre, pallets are very low platforms that are used to move scenery on and off stage. Most often, there are one or two pallets on either side of the stage, and they are operated with a push stick to move on and off. When the pallet is pulled offstage, the scenery on top of it (most often furniture or some other prop) can be changed so that a new batch is pushed back onstage the next time. Sometimes the pieces are just laid on top of the pallet, and sometimes it is necessary to fasten them with loose pin hinges. This is a really old-style practice that has been around for a very long time. You can use the same idea for more dimension types of scenery.

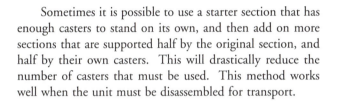

HALF THE CASTERS
ON THESE UNITS

PINCH CLEAT
LOCKS DECKS
TOGETHER

THIS PART IS SELF-
SUPPORTING

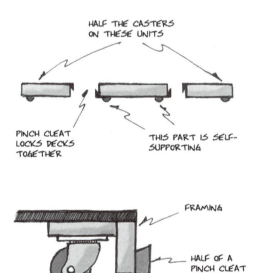

FRAMING

HALF OF A
PINCH CLEAT

If you have a large and/or long piece that must move from one level to another (like up a ramp into a truck) it is often helpful to install two rigid casters in the center of the unit to help it over the hump. If these casters are smaller than the regular ones, they will only touch the ground when necessary.

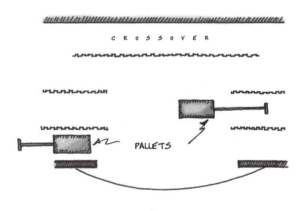

CROSSOVER

PALLETS

TWO PALLETS WITH T HANDLES

The push stick is pinned to the offstage side of the pallet to roll it back and forth. A stick is used so that the stagehand doing the actual work will not be seen. Steel square tube is excellent for this purpose because it is very strong for its size. It is best to paint the stick either black or the color of the deck in order to make it as unobtrusive as possible. A spike mark is set up so that it matches with the end of the handle when the pallet is in place.

WAITING ON
A CUE

If a stagehand rolls the pallet onstage to the spike mark, sets the push stick handle on the floor, and then stands on top of it while the scene is played, then the pallet will be in its proper location and stay there. If done properly, the stagehand will be behind a leg and thus hidden from view. It is difficult to complete a cue like this trailing a headset wire, so it is a good example of a time to use cue lights. A T-handle makes it easier to pull on the pallet and get it to roll back off stage.

Here is an excellent method of making a pallet that I saw once on a touring Broadway show. The unit is built much like a stress skin platform with a top and bottom layer of plywood. Rollers are used rather than casters, because of their lower profile. It is necessary to use quite a few of the rollers in order to disperse the weight of the pallet and its load.

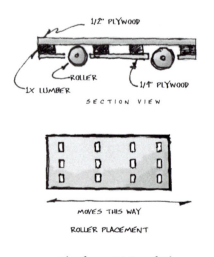

1/2" PLYWOOD

ROLLER

1X LUMBER

1/4" PLYWOOD

SECTION VIEW

MOVES THIS WAY

ROLLER PLACEMENT

PALLET WITH ROLLERS

BOXES

Rolling boxes are used extensively in touring where supplies and equipment must be loaded and unloaded frequently. They are also quite handy to have around a resident theatre to store cable, props, and so forth. They are also great as a work box. Some touring boxes are covered with carpet, or laminate, or have metal edges and complicated latching systems. These are fine boxes, and especially well suited for electronics. They are, however, somewhat difficult to manufacture without investing in a specific technology, and that is not cost effective for small production numbers. There is an older style of wooden box that works just as well and is very easy to build with standard materials in even a very modest shop. This type of box has plywood sides and corners reinforced with 1x4 lumber.

You will need to start by knowing the interior dimensions required by the equipment you will be storing. Cable crates should be no more than waist high, and about 30" square for 20-amp jumpers and somewhat larger for multicable. That stiff, large-diameter cable is harder to coil into a small space. The lid should be hinged to open up and then flop all the way around to the back, out of the way.

CABLE CRATE

TYPICAL PROP BOX

A good size for a prop box is 48" wide by 72" tall and 20" to 24" deep. It is easy to run a show out of this kind of box if it has double doors in the front and a number of shelves inside. After the show, the doors can be locked for security. Casters will allow you to roll the box around as needed.

On a touring production, the studio that builds the scenery and props often constructs this type of wooden case for pieces that are too delicate to travel loose in the truck. These boxes come in all shapes and sizes and often have interior partitions to hold specific items. There is an entire industry devoted to making quite similar crates for trade shows.

Construction is pretty straightforward. Cut slabs of plywood to size for the bottom sides and top. Use $3/4$" ply for the bottom, and $1/2$" for everything else. Make sure to adjust your cut list to account for the thickness of the plywood where it overlaps. (See the chapters on construction.) Don't worry about lids or doors yet; it will be easier to figure them out after the body, or case, is done. Glue and nail/staple the plywood body parts together. Make sure that the sides sit on top of the $3/4$" plywood bottom. This will make for a stronger structure when the strapping goes on and casters are attached.

The 1x4 strips will reinforce all of the edges and corners. Wherever possible, the overlap of the lumber should be the opposite of the overlap of the plywood. This will give the strapping a better purchase on the plywood. Use plenty of glue, and staple from the inside, through the plywood and into the 1x4 whenever possible. Use fasteners on the outside to join the corners of the lumber.

In order to make a door or lid fit properly, extend the 1x4 lumber $1/2$" past the edge of the plywood edge where the lid will fit. Cut the plywood for the lid so that it fits loosely inside the strapping but on the plywood edges of the case. Align the edges of the strapping for the lid with the outside edges of the case strapping. In this way, the lid is interlocked in position when closed, but the outside of the case will be smooth.

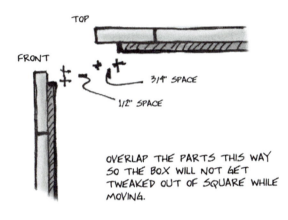

Use a router with a $1/4$" rounding over bit to ease all of the corners of the box, inside the strapping and out. Not only will this prevent your hands from getting splinters later on, it will also make the box last longer by preventing large cracks from developing in the strapping.

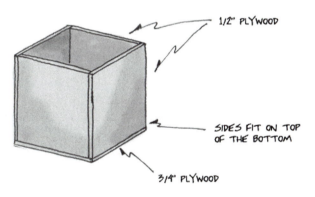

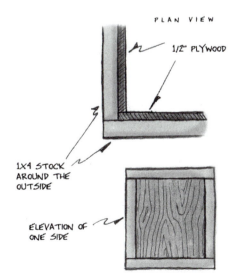

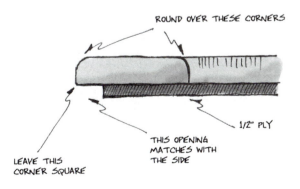

Interior dividers and shelves can be held in place with cleats, glued and screwed to the inside walls. It is generally not a good idea to set the shelf into a dado groove because there is too much movement in the casework, and the shelf will tend to pop out.

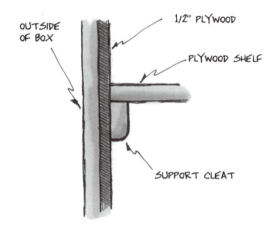

Be sure to bolt the casters on the bottom to ensure that they will stay attached. T-nuts are useful for this, because they keep the bolt end from sticking out and catching on things. A cable crate may weigh hundreds of pounds when fully loaded, so bear this in mind when selecting casters. Use large strap hinges for the doors, and bolt these on also. A hasp should be provided to secure the lid, and if necessary, a padlock for security. If security is not a problem, a short length of sash cord can be stapled to the box, and the end run through the hasp to keep it shut.

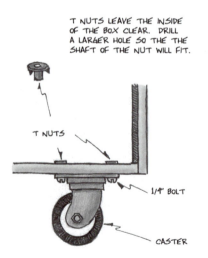

Metal corners can be screwed on to beef up the strength of the wooden corners of the box. There are many types of these; just pick something big enough to really do some good. Finally, a good coat of waterproof paint will help to protect the box from rain and from scraping up against other objects.

LAMP RACKS

Lamp racks are used to store lights and other equipment when it is not in use. A touring rig uses lamp racks specifically designed to:

A) hold lamp bars made of unistrut with several fixtures on it, and

B) fit into a tractor trailer truck.

This makes for some fairly specific requirements, and the racks tend to be quite large. In a resident theatre, a lamp rack will probably hold only single instruments with C-clamps. The overall size may be dictated by what will fit in an elevator or through a door, and you should investigate these parameters for your particular venue. I have found that a rack that is 72" long, 60" tall (excluding casters), and 18" wide will hold most kinds of fixtures and will fit almost anywhere.

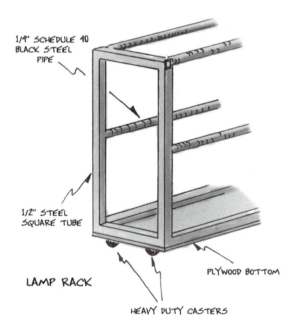

Lighting C-clamps are intended to fit on a round pipe. Pipe is somewhat difficult to weld together at an angle and is very heavy. Square tube is much easier to work with, but the C-clamps will not fit on it, so a compromise is in order. An excellent rack can be made by using square tubing for the end frames and black steel pipe for the connecting pipes. Either 1 1/4" or 1 1/2" pipe will work. If you select the same size used in your theatre for the electric hanging positions, it will make it easier to run the C-clamp bolt when moving the lights back and forth.

The basic principle involved is to lock together two boards cut at an angle. The piece will be hung securely from the top, as long as no one pushes up on it and disengages the cleat. When hanging, the bottom of the cabinet will press hard against the wall, which is why the hanging surface must be sturdy and rigid. There are lots of fun ways to use this technique on different types of scenery. It is great for quick assemblies.

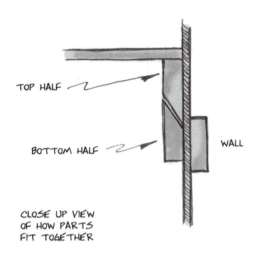

TOP HALF

BOTTOM HALF

WALL

CLOSE UP VIEW
OF HOW PARTS
FIT TOGETHER

It is a good idea to provide a plywood bottom to the rack for gel frames and barn doors and the like. You may wish to use two swivel and two rigid casters if the racks must travel long distances with one person pushing them. If they must be maneuvered through tight spaces, four swivel casters will probably work better.

PINCH CLEATS

Pinch cleats are used to easily attach a cabinet or awning or similar object to a wall surface. The wall must be rigid for this technique to work. For instance, a softcovered flat is generally not acceptable unless it has been specially framed to accommodate the cleat.

CIRCULAR SAW GUIDE

Most of the time you can free-hand with a circular saw, but on occasion it is nice to be able to work with more precision. In that case, you can use this shop-made guide to ensure a straight cut. Make exact cuts by lining up the edge of the guide with the line you would like to cut.

The jig is very simple to make from a couple of strips of plywood. After assembly, run the saw down the channel and trim off the edge of the guide so that it is exactly the width of the saw table.

FRONT ELEVATION   SECTION

HANG THE CABINET ON THE WALL
USING A PINCH CLEAT, SO THAT
IT IS EASILY REMOVED.

THE OPPOSING ANGLES DRAW THE
TWO HALVES OF THE CLEAT TOGETHER.

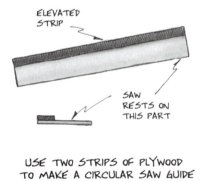

ELEVATED
STRIP

SAW
RESTS ON
THIS PART

USE TWO STRIPS OF PLYWOOD
TO MAKE A CIRCULAR SAW GUIDE

The kerf will fall to the outside of the guide, so it is generally best to line the jig up so that it is on top of the piece you will be keeping.

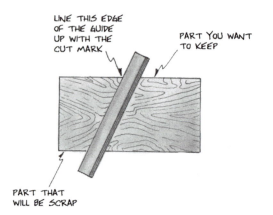

The guide must be firmly secured to the work. You can do this by clamping it down or by using drywall screws. The clamps are sometimes problematic when the saw motor doesn't have enough clearance to move over the tops of the clamps.

Make sure that the left side of the saw table stays securely against the thick part of the guide in order to make a straight cut. With a little practice, you can "plunge" the blade into the work in the middle of the plywood rather than starting from the edge. This will allow you to cut square holes in the center of a sheet of plywood or other shapes that do not continue all the way to the side of the sheet.

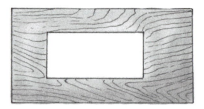

USE THE SAW GUIDE TO CUT INSIDE CORNERS BY "PLUNGING" THE SAW BLADE INTO THE WORK

You will need to have a different guide for each saw if the distance from the blade to the side of the table is not the same. Rotating the saw to an angle will make the guide just a bit smaller when you go to use it on a ninety-degree cut. You can make similar guides to use with a router. That will allow you to make really straight dado cuts with a straight-edged trimming bit.

Backstage Handrails

Here is an easy way to make traditional-style handrails for escape stairs and other elevated structures. The uprights and the actual rails (notice that the horizontal part is called a rail) are both made from 1x4 stock, something that is commonly found in most shops. This particular style is designed to be removable and reusable. That is convenient if the scenery must be struck and reassembled, and/or if you would like a stock of parts to use with different shows.

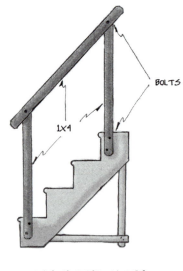

THIS HANDRAIL CAN BE EASILY REMOVED

It is important to ease the corners of the 1x4 to prevent splintering. The ends have also been chamfered to make them easier to use and to improve their appearance.

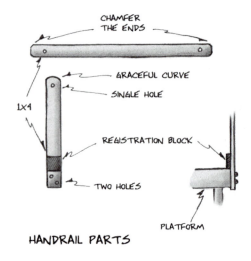

HANDRAIL PARTS

Bolts are used to attach the stiles to platforming and stairs, but you can also use drywall screws for the same purpose. If the stairs are to be struck and reassembled frequently, it makes much more sense to use bolts, but if there will be only one setup, it might be kinder to other stock units just to screw the parts on. Be aware that screws do not hold nearly as well as the bolts. If you have any doubts about the soundness of the structure, use the bolts.

Note that two bolts are used to secure the stile to the steps or platform. This will keep the uprights rigidly plumb. A block of wood is also attached to the upright stile to keep it rigid, and that makes it easy to make it just the right height as well.

At the same time, only one bolt is used in the top of the stile. That will allow the rail to be attached at an angle. If you are striking the show with the intention of putting it back up, you can leave the stiles and rail bolted together in one piece. Take out the bottom bolts, and fold up the rest of the hand rail into one convenient unit.

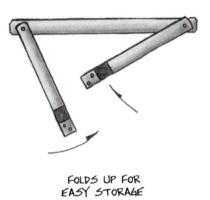

FOLDS UP FOR
EASY STORAGE

CURVED STAIRS

True circular or spiral stairs have a center post or column. In a steel or cast iron example, the treads are cantilevered out from the center pipe and are kept in place with a spiral handrail. It is certainly possible to weld together that sort of structure from steel pipe and plate, but you would most likely be better off with a factory made version or something from architectural salvage. Curved stairs are something else. They are quite often much wider than a spiral stair, and the bottom carriages are boxed in. Actually, this method will work with any odd shape, not just a circular curve.

This method of constructing curved stairs is similar to the one shown for rectilinear stairs in Chapter 13. It features all plywood construction and uses nailing strips on the risers. It uses many of the techniques associated with full-scale patterns. You may wish to refer back to those topics if you are unsure of the techniques shown here.

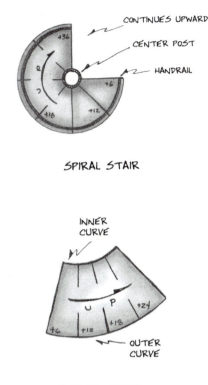

SPIRAL STAIR

CURVED STAIR

Begin by laying out a full-scale pattern of the stairs you wish to make. You can do this on paper and transfer the pattern to wood, or just lay out the whole assembly on 3/4" plywood from the outset. Use trammel points to mark the inner and outer diameters. The treads may not be dimensioned on the plans. Even if they, are it is generally more accurate to mark the outside profile of the unit and then divide the space up into the correct number of treads. Be sure to clearly mark the center point of the two arcs you made in originally laying out the curves. That is the convergence point of all the lines you will be marking for the treads, although the treads do not extend that far.

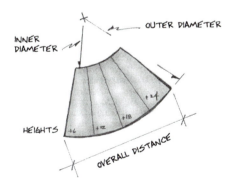

YOU WILL NEED THESE DIMENSIONS

You can use a bow compass and the trial-and-error method to divide the outer arc into the desired number of parts. Set the compass to a trial size and divide the arc into segments. There will be some amount of error at the end of the process. "Guesstimate" your correction by dividing the error amount by the number of segments. You should be able to determine a reasonably accurate layout within three or four tries.

USE A COMPASS TO DIVIDE THE
STAIR INTO EQUAL SEGMENTS

Mark straight lines across the arcs as shown in the diagram. These two lines delineate the locations of the two carriages. The exact placement is somewhat arbitrary, but pick a spot reasonably close to the edge of the stair. The carriages must be parallel to one another. Mark another pair of lines $3/4$" to the inside of the original ones. This space represents the location of the $3/4$" ply used to form the carriages.

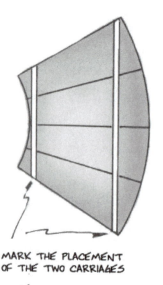

MARK THE PLACEMENT
OF THE TWO CARRIAGES

THEY SHOULD BE PARALLEL
TO ONE ANOTHER

Use this pattern to lay out the size and shape of the two carriages. They will not be the same, since they intersect the diverging rays at different distances from the center point. You will be making straight carriages to fit against round steps. You will need to cut angles for each place where the carriage and riser intersect. The angles will be different from step to step, but the same angles will transfer to the second carriage if the carriages are parallel to one another.

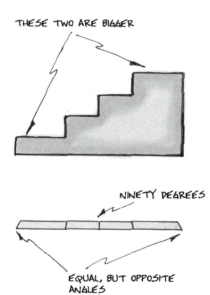

THESE TWO ARE BIGGER

NINETY DEGREES

EQUAL, BUT OPPOSITE
ANGLES

Tread depths will vary because of the way the lines run across the steps, so you will have to measure each one separately. This is the difficult part about this method, measuring and transferring all of the angles and sizes. It will take the most time, but it is important to get a good fit. Use an adjustable jigsaw or circular saw to cut the angles needed for the vertical cuts. All of the horizontal cuts will be ninety degree angles.

Cut out the treads from the pattern. This would be a great time to use the saw guide jig shown a few pages back. Notice that there will be some loss of tread size, because of the kerf created by the saw blade, if you cut directly from a $3/4$" plywood pattern. You can do that if the unit is very small, but a large one will not fit on the 4x8 sheets very well. Cutting directly from the pattern will cause the treads to be a tiny bit too small, but the discrepancy will not usually be a problem. If you you are making a very large number of these units, it might be worthwhile to mark paper patterns and get the sizes exactly right. Most of the time you can simply hide the loss as a small gap to the rear of the tread.

CUT OUT THE FIRST TREAD
AND USE IT AS A PATTERN
TO AVOID HAVING TREADS IN
TWO PARTS

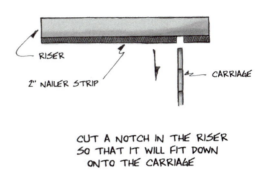

CUT A NOTCH IN THE RISER
SO THAT IT WILL FIT DOWN
ONTO THE CARRIAGE

Measure the distance from the inner arc to the outer arc to get the length of the riser parts. This is also the same as the length of the treads. The risers will go all the way from side to side because there are no carriages to fit inside of. Instead, the risers will be trimmed to fit on top of the carriages. The ends of the risers are 90-degree angles. Make the bottom of the carriages ³/₄" short on the first tread to allow the bottom riser to fit to the front of the carriage.

When all of the notches are cut, assemble the treads and risers into 90-degree angle units. It is very different from the technique used with rectilinear stairs. This is due to the fact that it is difficult to line up the risers and carriages in the same way as a normal stair since there are odd angles and shapes involved. It is more accurate to line up the riser of one step with the tread of the next to get the closest fit. If you have a pattern marked on paper, or on the floor, you can use that to help judge the best alignment. In any case, be sure to lay all the pieces out together and check the fit before you begin to assemble.

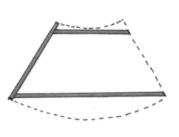

THE BOTTOM RISER INTERSECTS
IN THIS MANNER

ASSEMBLE THE TREADS
AND RISERS FIRST, THEN
ADD THEM TO THE CARRIAGES

Connect a 2" nailer to the front of each riser. Place each riser on top of the pattern and mark where it hits the carriage. You will need to cut a notch through the 2" nailer and bottom of the riser so that the riser will set on the carriage with the nailer sticking down and the top of the riser even with the top of the carriage. You can cut this slot at an angle if that is easy for you to do, but really it is only necessary to cut the slot wide enough to account for the thickness of the material at an angle.

There is one other piece to take into consideration before you begin the assembly. This is a curved piece used at the bottom to help in putting a facing on the unit. You may need one for each of the curved sides, or if one faces upstage, just the side that faces the audience. The facings do not have much of a structural function and are really just decorative.

It is best to mark these pieces at the same time as you are laying out the original pattern. Lay a section of plywood so that one edge is against the outer mark of the carriage. Use the compass to mark the same curve as will be to the outside of the stair. Cut out this piece so that one side is the arc, and the other a straight line.

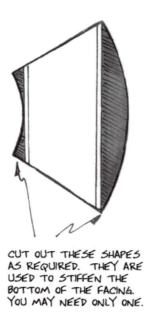

CUT OUT THESE SHAPES AS REQUIRED. THEY ARE USED TO STIFFEN THE BOTTOM OF THE FACING. YOU MAY NEED ONLY ONE.

Attach this section to the bottom of the carriage, the bottom of the lowest riser, and any support pieces to the rear of the unit. If the stair is large, you may wish to add some uprights between some of the treads and the bottom curve in order to have more support for the sides. Use $3/8$" bending plywood to cover the curved sides. It is easier to cut the shape of the risers/treads somewhat big and to trim to the exact size with a flush trim router after the facing has been put on.

If you need a unit with more than five or six treads, consider making it in more than one piece. The curve of the treads on anything larger will probably be too tight for the straight line carriage, and/or the unit will be very heavy.

FOAM RUBBER BRICKS

You may often be called upon to create three-dimensional bricks for a wall. Here is a way of doing that with the sort of foam rubber that is used for sofa cushions. It is readily available at fabric stores. This foam product is made from latex and is very different from the polystyrene products mentioned in the chapter on working with foam. It is much more bendable. If you have a choice, be sure to select the densest foam available. It is more expensive, but it is much easier to work with. To make bricks, you should purchase foam that is about 2" thick, since this is about the height dimension of a standard brick. If you are making a stone wall, or some other specific texture, you may wish to select a size that is more appropriate to that project. You will eventually be slicing the foam into pieces that are only $1/8$" or so in thickness.

You can get an insight into making stage brick texture by looking at real brick walls. Notice that the bricks do not stick out very far past the mortar. In fact, most of the time they hardly stick out at all. On an older structure, the edges of the brick have been softened by time and indeed the entire brick may have small pieces flaked off and other imperfections. It can be difficult to reproduce these features using rigid materials. The foam rubber is really effective because it is so soft and pliable.

The difficult part of the process is slicing the foam into thin sections. If you do a lot of this work, you may wish to invest in special tools used by upholstery shops to cut and shape foam rubber. They use a blade that may well remind you of an electric carving knife, and indeed you can also use one of those to cut foam. However, they do not have the power or industrial strength of the real thing.

You can also use a bandsaw to do the cutting. The bandsaw will not make nearly so smooth a cut, but since the bricks look better with a slightly rough texture, that is not generally a problem. You must have a rip fence on the saw in order to make this work. If your saw does not have a rip fence, you can clamp two boards at an angle to the top of the table as a shop-built version. Any type of fence will work better if you wax the face so that it becomes really smooth and creates less drag on the foam. The foam itself is very compressible and difficult to cut on the saw. There is a tendency for the material to bunch up and get drawn through the table of the bandsaw. Don't even think about cutting foam rubber with any sort of circular saw. That will not work.

There are some other techniques that can help in cutting the foam, considering that you want to have very thin slices of the foam to work with. Set the bandsaw fence at about $1/8$" to a $1/4$" from the blade. This is somewhat variable. If the foam is really dense, you can get away with the thinner size. If the foam is very light, you will most likely not be able to run it that thin. You only need a very thin slice to create the texture of the brick, and thinner slices use less of the material and are easier to work with.

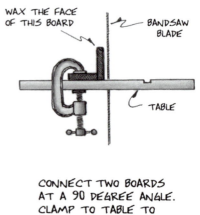

WAX THE FACE OF THIS BOARD

BANDSAW BLADE

TABLE

CONNECT TWO BOARDS AT A 90 DEGREE ANGLE. CLAMP TO TABLE TO MAKE A RIP FENCE.

It is important to pull the foam through the saw, rather than to try to push it through. If you push on the foam it will simply bunch up and jam the saw. Pulling will help to keep that from happening. Be sure to wax the guide or fence. Use a piece of wood as a guide to keep the foam pressed against the fence as you pull on it. That takes two people. You will need to practice a few runs to get the feel of what the best feed rate is and how much pressure to use in holding the foam against the fence. At some point, the piece of foam you are cutting from will become too small to work with and will bunch up around the blade no matter how careful you are. If that leftover is reasonably thin, you may still be able to use it. Put some tape over the throat plate that covers the hole where the blade dissapears into the table to make it smaller.

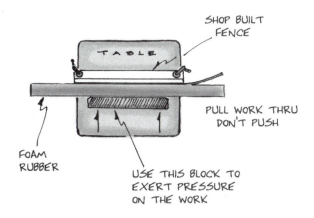

When the ripping/slicing work is done you will have lots of thin strips of foam. Some of them will be very clean, and some will have a more textural appearance. This is actually a good thing, because it will make for a more varied appearance to the wall. Use a pair of scissors to cut the strips to the proper length, which for most bricks will be about 8" or so. You will need some half bricks, and perhaps some that are odd shapes around windows and such. These are all easily cut with the scissors. Consult the plans or rendering to determine how the bricks are to be applied.

Use a chalk line to strike even lines across the surface so that you have reference points to work from. You may wish to use the more indelible red chalk for this project. If there are brick features like windows, or coins, or some other irregularly shaped areas, lay them out first.

Apply the foam using regular white or yellow glue. The yellow will set up faster, so pick the kind that is compatible with your working speed. Of course if the glue dries before you apply the foam, you can always just put more on. If you are working on a large flat surface, use a roller to apply the glue. Use a fairly thick coat of full-strength glue. Press the foam bricks down into the glue so that they are firmly attached. This process can move ahead fairly quickly on a flat wall. If you have pieces of varying thickness, try to get as random a pattern as possible There will be some pieces with torn holes, and/or extra blobs of foam on them. These are actually the ones that will make the project look really good when it is finished. Sometimes you can bend the pieces around a corner, but most of the time it makes more sense to use two separate sections. Especially since a corner normally reveals an 8" section of one side of a brick, and the 4" length of its end.

MISSHAPEN BRICKS ARE OFTEN THE BEST ONES. SPACE THEM OUT RANDOMLY.

Let the glue set up until it is really dry. Check the wall for parts that did not get stuck well, and reattach them with a small bottle of glue. You may need to use the scissors to do some last minute trimming of parts that stick out too much.

The foam needs some kind of sealer to look good. Actually, the more sealer you glop on, the better the brick will look. Used by itself, the foam will soak up too much paint and will have an odd, spongy appearance. The sealer will cover the seams between parts of bricks and make the mortar lines more realistic looking. There are actually several things that you can use for this process.

One is a type of scenic dope made from drywall mud and glue. Mix the two together with enough water to make it workable. Joint compound is very cheap and this material is very easy to apply. The only problem with it is that it is also somewhat brittle and tends to chip off. Also, it completely wipes out any compressiblity that may be gained from using foam rubber to make the original shapes. If you are fitting together various parts of a wall, the fact that the foam can be compressed as the parts fit together can be a big plus in acheiving a good fit. If these factors are not an issue, the scenic dope approach will work well.

Sculpt or Coat is a brand-name product available from theatrical suppliers. It will create a heavy, latex-like coat on the surface of the foam. It is very pliable, much like the foam rubber itself. This product is very viscous, and when slathered on in large amounts will do a great job of filling joints and creating a generally rounded over, well worn sort of appearance. It will not greatly affect the "compressibility" of the foam.

There are various generic brands of roofing material that are meant to be used in repairing leaky asphalt shingles. They can be found at home centers in the roofing material section. They too have a thick, highly viscous nature. It is very important to select a product that is water-based. If it is flammable, it is not a water-based product. Often you may find some versions that are thicker than others, and it is generally best to use the thickest version.

These coatings are very messy, and they are difficult to remove from adjacent surfaces. You should experiment, but it is generally best to use several coats for the best effect. Lay the scenery out so that the pieces are abutting one another to apply the coating to ensure a uniform appearance, but separate them before the material begins to harden. It may take quite a while for that to happen.

YOU CAN GET ROOF SEALERS
IN ONE, OR FIVE GALLON CANS.
THEY ARE RELATIVELY CHEAP.

INDEX